Empire of Dirt

WENDY FONAROW

✳

Empire of Dirt

THE AESTHETICS AND RITUALS

OF BRITISH INDIE MUSIC

✳

WESLEYAN UNIVERSITY PRESS

Middletown, Connecticut

Published by Wesleyan University Press, Middletown, CT 06459

www.wesleyan.edu/wespress

Printed in the United States of America

5 4 3 2 1

Library of Congress Cataloging-in-Publication Data

Fonarow, Wendy.
Empire of dirt : the aesthetics and rituals of British indie music /
Wendy Fonarow.
    p.   cm. — (Music/culture series)
Includes bibliographical references and index.
ISBN-13: 978-0-8195-6810-6 (cloth : alk. paper)
ISBN-10: 0-8195-6810-4 (cloth : alk. paper)
ISBN-13: 978-0-8195-6811-3 (pbk. : alk. paper)
ISBN-10: 0-8195-6811-2 (pbk. : alk. paper)
1. Alternative rock music—Great Britain—History and criticism.
2. Alternative rock music—Social aspects—Great Britain.
I. Title.
    ML3534.6.G7F66 2005
    781.660941—dc22   2006002876

For all of my ghosts

Contents

Acknowledgments

So if you're lonely, you know I'm here waiting for you . . .
Franz Ferdinand

This book has been a long journey. In some ways, it feels like an album that took ten years to create. I am very grateful to many people for their intellectual contributions and support during the research, writing, revision, and rethinking of this book. I would like to express my profound appreciation to my academic mentors: Alessandro Duranti, Jacques Maquet, Douglas Hollan, Janet Bergstrom, Donald Cosentino, and Stanley Walens. I would also like to express special thanks to Diane Drake Wilson, Ann Walters, the eloquent Lucy O'Brien, the gifted Derek Milne, and also Barry Shank for his brilliant comments on the earlier versions of this manuscript, which made such an impact and pointed me in the right directions. My thanks go to Alison McKee for her thoughtful copyediting, and to Sarah Thornton, Charles and Majorie Goodwin, Paul Kroskrity, Phillip Newman, Emanuel Shegloff, Elinor Ochs, Roger Bowerman, Ronnie Rivera, Steve White, Sharon Denner, Kit Crawford, Kim Yutani, Chris Giannotti and Jim, Allison Anders, Todd Silke, Terrylee and Eric, Tara Veneruso, Scott Scofield, Peyton Reed, Rick Bowman, Brian Almazan, Amy Nelsen, Rachel Walens, Peter Weingold, and the Museum of Jurassic Technology for their consistent support, advice, and constructive comments on this project. I would also like to thank the editors of the Music Culture series for including my work. Wesleyan University Press has been extraordinarily supportive and constructive throughout this process, and I thank Suzanna Tamminen, Poe Benji, Sarah Blachly, Ann Brash, Leslie Starr, Stephanie Elliott, and Alison Lerner. Special thanks to my family for driving me on: Barbara and Halei LaPearl, Gregg Fonarow, and Charles Fonarow. I would also like to thank my students, who were so passionate about what I did that they had me create the "indie list" and playfully introduced me as their professor at shows. For them, this publication was never soon enough.

There are many people involved with music in both Britain and North America who contributed immensely to this project by granting me access to their lives and work and sharing their experiences and perceptions of indie music and music performances. I would like to thank all of my interviewees for taking the time to discuss their passions, their experiences, and their thoughts on music. In the United States, I would like to thank Marc Geiger and Mark Newman for supporting me since the early days of this project, and Joe Janecek, Jo Lenardi, Michael Nance, Julia Kole, Zack and Barbara Horowitz, Ralph Cavallaro, Martin Devon, David Kucher, Candy Tobagen, Jason Pastori, Mark Neiter (whom I initially met behind the DJ deck at UCSD's radio station), Danny Benair, Piper Ferguson, Richie Williams, the brilliant Gina Davis, who laughed her way through the chapter on the music industry, George Couri, Steve Ferguson, Bill Ingot, Brian Bumbery, Brenda Hutinson, Liam O'Neil, Mark Sovel, Christine Biller, Andrea Canter, Melinda Mondrala, Alan and Wendy Sartirana from Filter, the amazing Mike McClain and Christine Karayan at the Troubadour, the gorgeous women of Goldenvoice, and the wonderful Blood Arm crew—Nathaniel Fregoso, Zackary Amos, Zebastian Carlisle, the silver-tongued Ben Lee Handler, and the remarkably observant and insightful Dyan Valdés.

There have been many people in the British music industry who have added immensely to this project by granting me remarkable access and privileges within the music community. Thanks to Mean Fiddler, Neil Penguilly for his brilliance in booking the Reading/Leeds festival, SJM, Barry Hogan and Helen Cottage at Foundation/All Tomorrow's Parties, Bob, Raye, and Paul at Metropolis, Dave Bedford, Bob Brimson, Colin Hardie, James Endeacott, Sonja Commentz, John Mulvey, Chrys Meula, Miranda Sawyer, Ian Watson, Neville Elder, Susie Babchick, Phil King, Alan McGee, Michelle Kerry, Noel Kilbride, Murray Chalmers, Colleen Mahoney, Leslie Felperin, Tim Jonze, Nick Shepherd, Sermon Management, Cerne Canning, Max Conwell, the Harding brothers, Fraser Lewry, Chris Bowers, Simon White, Shawn Conner, and everyone from the old Suede Management, including Charlie, Wendy and Eddie, Bernard, and Elisa. I offer special thanks to Janet Gordon at Mute, who found me counting people in the pouring rain outside the Garage in Islington and invited me into her life.

My research experience was indelibly enriched by my extended Domino family. I am especially grateful to Laurence Bell for asking me to work for the best independent company in the world, for embodying the very best that independent music represents, and for always making the distance between Los Angeles and London seem small. I still remember fondly all the mornings of storytelling over coffee with James in Domino's first "real" office. Thanks as well to all the other Domino people—Mitch, Harry, Hamish, Bart, Julie, Jackie, Gary, Kris, and Matthew Cooper, who also designed the cover of this book.

I want to thank all my friends from the Thames valley who were around long before this project began: those Oxford friends from the golden triangle of indie music, especially Jon and Rachel Burton, Nick Burton, Laurence Colbert, Mark Gardener, Giles, Neil Halstead for always being a shoulder to lean on, Ian McCutcheon and his wonderful parents, Terry and Linda McCutcheon, who have long awaited the fruits of my labors, and Rachel Goswell, my girlfriend abroad who always makes me feel as if no time has passed since we last spoke.

I would like to thank all of my friends from up north: all of the New Order crew, the extraordinary Peter Hook whose generosity is matched by his quick wit, Becks, Jack and Heather, Bernard, Sarah and the kids, Andy, Rebecca, Steve, Sarge, Roger, and Coatsy, and those people who made my time in Manchester interesting and eventful—the lovely Vicki Potts, Jay Beard, and the exuberant Jules. Thanks also go to my family in the north, the extraordinarily kind and welcoming Elizabeth and Marshall Cunningham, who always brought me special treats, tea, and newspapers, and Grandma Cunningham, who had an honest laugh and gave me bread to feed the sheep.

My friends from Glasgow contributed immensely to this project, not just with their words but by making my time there and abroad so filled with joy. Thanks go to Marc Percival, who bridges the world between academics and music with such grace and who always provided a warm place for me to lay my bags, to my favorite tricksters from Mogwai—Stewart Braithwaite and Grainne, who can make me laugh harder than anyone else, Dominic Aitchison for his appreciation of the merits of Sonic the Hedgehog even in a festival field, Martin Bulloch the pirate, John Cummings, and Barry Burns. I'd particularly like to thank those late heroes in the story: Alex Kapranos, Paul and Ester Thomson, Glen, Nick McCarthy, and Bob Hardy, who encouraged me, asked the right questions, and said the right things at the most crucial moment. When I was in mourning, they showed me everything beautiful in music—deus ex machina.

Thanks to all the bands that have helped me along the way: Ambulance Ltd., Arcade Fire, Belle and Sebastian, the Blood Arm, the Divine Comedy, Doves, Elbow, Flying Saucer Attack, Folk Implosion, Franz Ferdinand, the House of Love, Idlewild, the Jazz Butcher, the Kills, the Lemonheads, the

Libertines, Libido, Locust, Magnetic Fields, Mansun, Mogwai, Mojave 3/ Slowdive, New Order, Palace, the Pastels, Pulp, Quasi, the Railway Children, Ride, the Senseless Things, Elliott Smith, Smudge, the Stills, Suede, Swervedriver, Symposium, the Tindersticks, and the White Stripes.

I would like to express gratitude to my special friends, Marion Sparks and Russell Warby, for always being my home away from home and my beacon whenever I got myself into trouble, as you inevitably do when traversing foreign lands. I appreciate those times when you set my course to your door and made sure that I never felt I was a stranger in a strange land. Thanks to Lou Barlow, the most sensitive man in indie rock, and Kathleen Billus, who not only read and commented as I was writing this book but was my confidante. I owe thanks to Tanya Bernard as well, one of the kindest and most accepting human beings I have ever met.

To those who died during this project, I miss you all and I will never forget the people you were—our adventures and honesty, our looks of shared understanding in a room full of people. I dream for the Day of the Dead, when in some special ritual moment the dead return and we can be reunited again.

I would also like to thank everyone in the bands who have made the music I love for the sublime experience of their art and performances, and all the people who got me into shows when I was skint and the ones who got me in when I wasn't. And a final thanks goes to all those who have not left music behind.

Empire of Dirt

Introduction

As if you had a choice . . .
Snow Patrol

Beginnings

This project began in 1991 at a small, grotty underage club called Jabber-jaw, off Pico Boulevard in Los Angeles. I went to see Teenage Fanclub, a band from Glasgow, play one of its first West Coast dates. This club had only one entrance, located just behind the stage. To face the band, one needed to walk through the narrow corridor between the slightly raised stage and the coffee bar. On this particular spring evening, just like many nights at Jabberjaw, the place was packed to capacity. Equipped with nei-ther air conditioning nor ventilation, the venue was unbearable—a mael-strom of heat and sweat. When the band finished its set, the musicians jumped off the back of the stage and went through the only exit into the cool night air outside. I could see the door from the front of the stage where I was standing. Desperate to get outside and into fresh air, I began to file out like everyone else, around the stage and into the little corridor that led to the exit. However, one member of the audience who was stand-ing right behind me did something different. He stepped up onto the stage, walked across, and jumped off at the doorway just as the band had done. Why hadn't I taken the same route? There was nothing to prevent me from choosing the most direct path to the door to get much-needed re-lief. For some reason, I had perceived the stage as off limits. Even in my need to get outside, I could not imagine stepping up onto it and walking to the door. In that moment, I realized that I had internalized rules for being an audience member that stopped me from even entertaining the possibility of walking across the stage. While no one ever explicitly taught these rules to me, I had learned them through my participation in innu-merable events like this one.

I recognized the audience member who had crossed the stage. He was in the Los Angeles band Redd Kross. Although we were both members of the audience, our different experiences in going to gigs had produced different relationships to the space of the stage. This fellow audience member and professional performer saw the stage as accessible to him. I saw the stage as off limits to me. Did our different histories affect the way we viewed the event? How did my behavior as an audience member affect my experience of the performance? What cultural precepts were expressed by this distinction between performers and audience members? It was this moment that ultimately led me to Britain, to a study of audiences and to the international indie music community.

In an effort to answer these questions, what follows is an ethnography of audience members' behavior at the performances of a particular type of music—British indie music. Specifically, this is a study of multiple subjectivities and the spectacle of music performance in the independent music community. It is about what audience members do. It is also about how they think about what they do. This art form is a passionate concern to members of the community, who look to music not just as entertainment but as an expression of significant cultural sentiments and as a nexus of moral ideals of profound consequence.

In this book, I treat musical performance as a ritual.[1] Rituals address cultural conflicts and contradictions. Indie music performances and ideology are an expression of cultural values regarding the role of art, emotion, the body, asceticism, youth and the nature of creativity in modern Western industrial society. A part of the "youth" phenomenon, which is by definition a transitory category, indie music requires an understanding of the youth community, why people enter it, why people leave it, and what it means when it has been left behind.

Anthropologists have long noted the intersection of a culture's metaphysics and its aesthetic productions. Metaphysics is a culture's *a priori* philosophy of the nature of being based on its religious ideology. Metaphysics and aesthetics both address a culture's valued forms of creativity. The quintessential model of creativity is the divine creation of the world, and there is generally a resemblance between the concept of divine creation in a particular culture and what is considered valuable or important in aesthetic creations by that same culture. For example, in Islam, where divine creativity is manifested in the Word and there is a prohibition against the representation of human figures, artistic expression takes the forms of calligraphy and abstract visual designs. In West African societies, where divine creativity is seen in the unpredictable temporary manifestation of the gods on earth, there is a value placed on impromptu verbal skills. For the Pintupi, Aboriginals of

Australia, the aesthetic productions of value are depictions of hereditary stories of the Dreamtime, the period when the world was created by supernatural creatures. Conceptions of divine creativity intersect with the how, what, and why of art. The power of artistic performances and forms comes from their ability to display, and play with, cultural themes that are meaningful to culture members. In turn, religious notions shape our conceptions of human creativity. While this connection has been well examined in other societies, scholarship devoted to Western music and art seems mostly blind to how Western artistic productions express our own metaphysical themes. It is a Western conceit to think that only in other societies do religious notions pervade all domains of life. We consider our own secular spheres free of metaphysical concerns. Our notion of art is that it exists in a separate domain from religious philosophy. This book will challenge that notion and demonstrate how religious ideology shapes Western aesthetics and artistic practices, focusing on the British indie music scene in particular.

Theoretical Frame: From Observation to Communication

Contemporary anthropological theory has focused on intersecting themes in the rethinking of the ethnographic enterprise: a concern for communication, the rise of performance theory as a way of understanding culture, the reassertion of the importance of the body, and the constructed nature of subjectivity (Conquergood 1991). This reconceptualization has resulted in a major shift in the ethnographic endeavor from a subject/object dialectic to a subject/subject dialectic (Clifford 1988, Clifford and Marcus 1986, Geertz 1988, Rosaldo 1989). Ethnography is now thought of as a subjective interaction in which the once-privileged ideal of a detached observer neutrally describing culture has been replaced by a notion of ethnography as communication. There is no all-seeing perspective; rather, there is a multiplicity of perspectives. The anthropological viewpoint of culture has moved from a static one to one concerned with processes, from observation as monologic to interaction as dialogic, from an understanding that is abstract and atemporal to one that is concretely located in time and space (Bakhtin 1981, Jackson 1989, Rosaldo 1989, Theunissen 1984).

The focus on the dialogic nature of interaction has drawn renewed attention to performance theory as an idiom for studying culture. Victor Turner, whose groundbreaking work on ritual pervades performance theory, recognized performance as a process, one that is co-constructed in the relationships between performance, performers, and audience (Turner 1969, 1974, 1986, 1988). The incorporation of performance theory in anthropology has occurred, in large part, because it permits recognition of the agency of social actors (Geertz 1983); the performance paradigm "privileges particular, participatory, dynamic, intimate, precarious, embodied experience grounded in historical process, contingency, and ideology" (Conquergood 1991: 187). In short, a performance paradigm requires cultural productions from the grand and spectacular to the mundane and intimate to be examined in situ (Palmer and Jankowiak 1996). Here, performance theory links with practice theory, which locates culture in the concrete practices of individuals in real circumstances and actual settings (Bourdieu 1977). Both position culture not in abstractions but in situated, co-constructed activity.

Rethinking interaction as mutually constructed, Erving Goffman introduced the notion of a participant framework (Goffman 1974).[2] The notion of a participant structure was a way of thinking about speakers and hearers not as discrete, exclusive units but as mutual interlocutors in a co-constructed enterprise. A participant structure is the social recognition of an event and the expected behaviors within it. It provides a frame for the interpretation of activities, a context that allows participants to understand the behavior of other people. The participant structure is shared, and all parties are active in the unfolding of an event. Further, one's role in a participant structure compels a particular use of the body, whether one is controlled or wild, whether one speaks or is silent. However, this is not to say that a participant structure dictates interaction. Individuals have vested interests. They can and do break codes of conduct, and this can result in innovation and/or a reframing of expectations. However, these actions are interpreted by others according to their shared notions of an event (Auer and di Luzio 1992, Goodwin and Goodwin 1995, Philips 1983). These shared notions are learned over time through actions that embody them, and actions have consequences. Performance theory, practice theory, and the sociolinguistic interactive paradigm all emphasize the importance of examining culture as a set of active and situationally located processes.

Active Bodies

Dance, dance, dance, dance, dance to the radio . . .
Joy Division

Social scientists have recognized the need to address the body and incorporate the sensate dimensions of experience for the past two decades. History, sociology, ethnic studies, communication studies, film theory, and, in particular, feminist studies have all called for the "embodiment" of our understanding of human activities, a notion that incorporates the biological, the psychological, and the cultural. This can be seen clearly in the vast number of anthologies devoted to the topic of embodiment (Csordas 1994, Dunn et al. 1996, Welton 1998, Weiss and Haber 1999, and so on). Paying attention to the body is a way of approaching cultural practices and addressing phenomenology—the sensual, emotional, and physical aspects of experience (Turner 1986, Schechner 1988, Csordas 1993).[3] Some of the best work locating the body in practice has been done by linguistic and medical anthropologists. Linguistic anthropologists analyze language as it is actually used, focusing on the unfolding of interaction in time and space. This has necessitated looking at all modes of communication, including the use of the body as a physical instrument in the production of meaning (Hanks 1990). However, the internal, phenomenological, and sensate dimensions of activity are not as interesting to linguistic anthropologists as the interactive, external, and collaborative dimensions of activity. Medical anthropologists, whose research on healing requires an examination of the phenomenology and physiology of the body as well as performance, have produced some of the best material dealing with the cultural body (Csordas and Harwood 1994, Laderman 1995, Strathern 1996, Strathern and Stewart 1999).

Social actors are physical sensate interlocutors. What one does with one's body can concretely affect the experience of an activity and impact subjective perception (Crapanzano and Garrison 1977, Deren 1953, Greenbaum 1973, Kapferer 1983, LaBarre 1970, Locke and Edward 1985, Turner 1982a, Wasson 1971, Zuesse 2005). For example, in spirit possession rituals, repetitious physical movements accompanied by rhythmic drumming are used to induce altered states of consciousness (Rouget 1985). Such practices are central to our understanding of ritual, in which the body is deployed in specific ways in order to produce particular sentiments and sensations appropriate to the occasion. Not eating, eating "special" foods, dancing all night, not moving, or using pharmacological substances are just a few of the ways sensations are produced in ritual and associated with the cultural relationships that are enacted within ritual events.

Popular music studies are uniquely situated to address these concerns of embodiment because music performance and its communities of practice require an examination of sensate experience and aesthetic ideological systems (Shank 2003). The ethnography of musical performance that follows attends to the body, performance, and interaction in a detailed way. I examine how the body is used and read by participants in situated interaction (Hymes 1972, 1974b, 1975). I also follow Turner's phenomenological call for embodiment in performance studies by considering the potential psychosomatic consequences of the different uses of the body within the context of musical performance. This ethnography attends to the physical and communicative aspects of interaction with a concern for phenomenology—the sensation, the ideation, the *subjectivity* of participation in a situated event.

connect w/ embodiment?

The Audience and Subjectivity

Since the performance paradigm emphasizes the roles of all participants, it requires an examination of how the performance, performers, and audience influence one another. In the social sciences there has been a movement away from the creator, author, or artist as the preeminent analytic focus. Roland Barthes in "The Death of the Author" and Michel Foucault in "What Is an Author?" locate meaning not in the creator of a work but in the work itself in its receptive context (Barthes 1977, Foucault 1986):

Not social scientists!

> It has been understood that the task of criticism is not to reestablish the ties between an author and his work or to reconstitute an author's thought and experience through his works and further, that criticism should concern itself with the structures of a work, its architectonic forms, which are studied for their intrinsic and internal relationships. Yet, what of a context that questions the concept of a work? (Foucault 1986: 140)

Thus critical theorists have included the audience and context in their consideration of cultural productions such as reading (Derrida 1974), watching a film (Mulvey 1989), being inside a prison (Foucault 1979), or walking through a museum (Wilson 1994). Cultural studies, cognitive film theory, reader response criticism, and other contemporary theoretical movements have come to characterize all media spectators as active (Cho and Cho 1990, Fiske 1992, Iser 1980, Jenson 1992, Jones 1990). Thus, in the theoretical shift from looking to the author as the source of meaning to looking at a dialogic relationship between the work and its audience, receptive subjectivity has become a central concern in cultural studies.

The literature devoted to subjective reception has developed the notion of *spectatorship* as an analytic category. Spectatorship is a theoretical concept derived from a combination of psychoanalysis, linguistics, and film theory. Following Jacques Lacan's and Julia Kristeva's notions of subjectivity, the spectorial position has been characterized as "the inscription of a place for the reading or viewing subject within the signifying chain" (Doane 1987: 34). The subjective reading position creates a relationship between the viewer and the viewed. However, the enunciation of spectorial positionings is not necessarily explicit or obvious. The spectorial subject has been seen in point-of-view (Bellour 1979), voice-over (Metz 1986), and the use of the "generalized male third person singular" in writing

which one?

(Mulvey 1989). For, example, in an advertisement for an American sitcom, a male character is shown sitting behind a desk in a room looking down at some papers. A conventionally attractive woman wearing a trench coat enters the room. The camera focuses on the woman as she throws open the trench coat to reveal a sexy black dress. The camera cuts to the shocked and elated reaction of the male character and then returns to linger on the woman. In this short segment, we can see the articulation of the spectator position as male, viewing a female undressing. The male, shown first, is passive. However, the female enters and disrobes, becoming the object of not only the male character's active gaze but the audience's as well. That is, the two gazes blend in the camera's "look" at the female character. In the process, the audience has been placed in a similar viewing position as the male character who watches and reacts to a woman undressing. Thus, spectatorship refers not to the perspective of an individual in the audience but rather to a structural subjectivity articulated by a work in relation to its audience.

Research on spectatorship has demonstrated that this subjectivity can be inscribed by various social categories. As Donna Haraway notes in her introduction to *Primate Visions,* "The themes of race, sexuality, gender, nation, family, and class have been written into the body of nature in Western life sciences since the eighteenth century" (Haraway 1989: 1). Yet in the copious discussions of spectorial inscriptions across different disciplines, there is a major omission: metaphysic inscriptions have been left largely unexamined and unmarked. But to imagine that religious ideology would not also be inscribed in spectorial positions is almost inconceivable when so many of our tacitly held assumptions about the nature of the world and our place in it have their foundations in religious philosophy.[4] Perhaps this oversight is due to the fact that the religious foundations of Western thought are so ingrained that they are treated as utterly transparent by Western scholars. If anthropologists studying another culture ignored the religio-ideologic narratives that underlie social institutions, it would be considered a significant oversight. Yet in our own culture we are loathe to recognize or discuss them. The mind/body split that pervades Western scholarship is a fundamental dichotomy that emerges from a Western religious tradition. Franz Boas, Alfred Radcliffe-Brown, Talcott Parsons, and Edward Evans-Pritchard, key figures in the development of anthropological theory, have all discussed how metaphysic ideology pervades cultural institutions and practices. Yet critical theory and spectatorship studies remain decidedly averse to ascribing religious ideology to *Western* subjectivity. In large part, this book works to correct this omission and constitutes an examination of the metaphysics of spectorial embodiments.

One of the limitations of the scholarship devoted to spectatorship is that it examines a common receptive context and makes generalizations from this context. Spectatorship has generally been examined in settings of passive comportment, such as cinema. Western cinematic norms require audience members to maintain a controlled, contemplative bodily composure during the experience of the film. However, this is by no means essential to film viewing. The norms of the bodily comportment of film audiences vary between and within cultures. In India, audiences are much more proactive and kinetically involved. Audience members wander around, stand up and yell at the screen, or engage in public dialogue with fellow audience members.[5] This Western emphasis on contemplative and composed comportment extends to the experience of other artistic productions and settings, such as museums or symphonic concerts. It is far easier to ignore a still body in silent contemplation than it is to ignore a body engaged in vigorous physical and verbal activity. Thus, the majority of the examinations of spectatorship have been devoted to the intrinsic and internal relationships of film or literature as they inscribe subjectivity, rather than to what audience members actually do while interacting with these artistic productions. As Janice Radway has noted, these formulations have kept the media text, rather than the audience's use of it, as the primary object of inquiry (Radway 1984). By examining events and narratives in which the audience or viewer is physically passive, spectatorship studies have overlooked the significance of comportment and its role in the production of audience subjectivity.

Music as Activity

Spectatorship occurs and develops in activities such as storytelling, television watching, cinema going, and concert attending. Theories of spectatorship that attempt to explain the structure and content of a particular medium must take into account actual practice. This is a notion of "participatory" spectatorship. In his article "Professional Vision," Charles Goodwin shows how an individual becomes trained to apprehend and interpret events while engaging in professional activity (Goodwin 1994). For cinema studies, it is important to consider how the viewing subject is physically situated; for music performances, it is important to consider whether the viewing subject stands or sits, dances or is motionless, or is near to or far from his peers. Participant structure is a necessary component of spectatorship studies, because the experience of an event is constituted by the cultural production on display and its participant structure.

The idea that the experience of music is located in activity is central to Christopher Small's work, in which he considers music not only as sounds but as the setting, behaviors, and comportment of performers and audience members. Small reframes music from a noun into a verb, taking advantage of the useful term *musicking*. Musicking is the activity of music in a specific cultural context, from production to consumption in its particular social spaces. Small writes:

> To music is to take part in any capacity, in a musical performance, whether by performing, by listening, by rehearsing, or practicing, by providing material for performance (what is called composing), or by dancing. We might at times even extend its meaning to what the person is doing who takes the tickets at the door or the hefty men who shift the piano and the drums or the roadies who set up the instruments and carry out the sound checks or the cleaners who clean up after everyone else has gone. They too are all contributing to the nature of the event that is a musical performance. (Small 1998: 9)

Small sees the meaning of musicking as located in the relationships manifested in and articulated by the production of culturally meaningful sounds, in specific cultural settings, and in the relationships of participants in the ritual event of music performance:

> The act of musicking establishes in the place where it is happening a set of relationships, and it is in those relationships that the meaning of the act lies. They are to be found not only between those organized sounds which are conventionally thought of as being the stuff of musical meaning, but also between the people who are taking part, in whatever capacity, in the performance; and they model, or stand as metaphor for, ideal relationships as the participants in the performance imagine them to be: relationships between person and person, between individual and society, between humanity and the natural world and even perhaps the supernatural world. (Small 1998: 13)

Small's dissatisfaction with symphonic musical performance, as opposed to symphonic music, relates in part to the requirements for a high degree of body control and the limited physical responses allowed in the modern/postmodern symphonic concert participant structure. In his book *Music of the Common Tongue*, he contrasts the modern symphonic performance code to West African–influenced music forms, in which the line between performer and audience is often so blurred that the division appears arbitrary and irrelevant (Small 1987). Improvisational performances respond to the contingencies of the occasion—the particular individuals present, the artistic motifs introduced by the musicians, the dances of the dancers, and the verbal and sonic interjections of the "audience." This produces a musical experience where all present are active co-producers of an aesthetic experience. Small clearly recognizes the importance of participatory spectatorship, which significantly impacts subjective experience in musical performances.

Subjectivity in Action

The indie music performance offers a prime opportunity for examining participatory spectatorship. It is an explicitly receptive context, where the audience plays a conspicuous role in the construction of the event. Unlike cinema or symphonic audiences, indie music audiences have very different norms for bodily comportment. Indie audience behavior is often intensively active and dynamic. At indie music performances, the social space near the front of the stage is characterized by a high degree of direct contact between strangers and, at times, by spirited activity. Indeed, for a portion of the audience, the music performance is a physically taxing experience. However, not all audience members participate in vigorous activity. Some use a mode of comportment similar to that of cinematic audiences; that is, they are physically circumspect and interiorly oriented. For indie music performances, the situated use of the body by audience members entails the positioning of *different* spectatorships. Since bodily deployment is a constitutive part of spectatorship, it is essential to attend to the different behaviors and activities of audience members and to the relationships these different spectorial positionings have to one another.

Different spectorial modes have been a problem for film theory (Doane 1987). Since concrete practice was originally ignored in the development of spectorial theory, film theory often presented a monolithic model of subjective positionings in which all participants were seen to view the event (Mulvey 1989). When we introduce the notion of participatory spectatorship, a plethora of communicative modalities appear, far greater than the singular, conquering, all-seeing "eye/I" of cinematic spectorial articulations. In participation, subjective relationships can be articulated along other modalities. Participatory spectatorship does not replace or supersede the spectatorship of textual structures. It is just another code of communication. Spectatorship inscribed in the structure of spectacle is yet another. Embodied spectatorship requires an understanding of the intersection of the structural and narrative components of spectacle with the bodies of participants; in other words, the ways we organize and are organized by activity. Both discourse and practice need to be examined in order to understand the nature of subjectivity. Meaning does not come from a symbol itself, but from the interaction between symbol and social action, or the intersection of ideology and practice. To understand the social world, we must look at both internal narratives and practical actions for the consistencies and contradictions between them, and for the ways they can each reinforce or obviate the other.

Turn On the Bright Lights[6]

This ethnography is meant to add to the growing body of ethnographic and sociohistoric literature that addresses local music communities (Cohen 1991, Finnegan 1989, Shank 1994, Urquia 2004), music genres (Forman 2002, Grossberg 1992, Keil 1966, Negus 1999, Oliver 2001, Rose 1994, Walser 1993), the experience of music (Berger 1999, Grossberg 1997), and the meaning of music as cultural practice in other societies and transnationally (Basso 1985, Born and Hesmondhalgh 2000, Chernoff 1979, Emoff 2002, Feld 1982, Lipsitz 1994, Taylor 1997).[7] In popular music studies, the general trend has been to focus on the performance, the music performed, the artists, and the music's production and consumption. Several ethnographies include some examination of audience behavior. There is also literature examining the cultures of fans that seems to vacillate between abstraction and discussions based on interviews with subjects who were asked about their memories of their experiences. Some of the most interesting work in this area has come from those who examine the representations of fanship and fan behavior (Brooker and Jermyn 2002, Hills 2002, Lewis 1992). This ethnography is in a vein similar to the ethnographic writings of Small on classical music and Travis Jackson on jazz, both of whom write detailed examinations of audience practices and subjective responses (Jackson 2003, Small 1998).

Positing the music performance as the unit of analysis necessitates attending to the meaning-making activities of all participants—performers, crews, and audience members. A defining characteristic of the participant structure for indie gigs is that audience members get to choose where they locate themselves within the venue. Unlike traditional symphonic or arena rock concerts with assigned seating, indie gigs have relatively few seats.[8] This opens up a variety of organizational constructs. Concerts that occur in seated halls place participants in positions where they are equidistant from each other and generally discourage or limit physical contact between audience members. This setting fosters a contemplative and comfortable comportment. In contrast, at non-seated venues, audience members have the opportunity to be close or distant and active or passive. This difference in participant structure has a significant impact on how the event is experienced. While the music performance in the two different kinds of settings may be the same, the range of experiences of the audience in concert halls and gigs is quite varied.[9] This demonstrates why it is insufficient to merely examine the spectacle on stage. It is not just the spectacle that constitutes an event but a dynamic relationship among an audience, performers, and the performance.

Furthermore, the event space does not in and of itself determine participant structure. The same venue used for a gig one night may be used for ballroom dancing the next. Different music cultures have different notions of appropriate interaction between audience members and performers, and different genres of music frame expectations of appropriate activities in a performance space. For example, piggybacking or taking off one's shirt are extremely rare for indie shows but are frequent at metal or mainstream rock shows. At indie gigs, activity levels are segmented, highly marked, and disparate. For dance bands, there is a greater amount of movement shared over the entire venue space. In his discussion of southern medicine shows in the early part of the twentieth century, Paul Oliver notes that audience members were expected to interject and respond verbally during the performance, and the performer was expected to be responsive to these interjections (Oliver 1995). In indie, by contrast, verbal interjections are eschewed while music is being performed, and there is some expectation that performers will not respond at all to interjections from audience members.[10] Thus, different genres have different notions of what is appropriate and expected in the performance setting. Not paying attention to the norms of a particular community using a space is similar to not paying attention to cultural differences. It ignores the specific rules that different communities use to accomplish interaction. The physical space is the same, but the participant structure alters how the space is used.

The activities I observed in my ethnography of the British indie music scene were part of a specific community with a specific history. The term "indie" is a diminutive for "independent" rock and pop music. In a broad sense, it refers to the music on independently owned record labels. Indie music is considered to be more experimental, and it tends to appeal to a particular fan base or local community as opposed to a mass audience. Indie music fans are composed almost entirely of adolescents and young adults. Students comprise the majority of British indie music's fan base.

Indie fans come from a cross-section of classes, from unemployed youth on government relief to affluent private school students. However, much of the indie fan base comes from a middle-class background. In Britain, two-thirds of the indie community is male, one-third female.[11] Indie is also primarily a white phenomenon that has very little participation from Britain's other ethnic communities, which comprise on average only between 1 and 3 percent of an audience on any given night.[12]

Indie music is just one of the genres of music. Yet its members and its events transcend national boundaries. Indie music is played all over the world. The community's discourse can be found in the international music press and in online chat. Yet indie performances in different cultural settings have different participant structures. Bands report that Japanese fans behave very differently during shows than their European and American counterparts. The participant structure of British and American indie audiences, however, has much in common. Movements that originate in one country are soon found in the other.[13]

Several factors played in the decision to focus my study on independent music in Britain. The first is the comparatively greater cultural focus on music in Britain. In Britain, music and football (soccer) are national passions. However, while football is a passion that takes its fans from childhood to old age, an interest in music is considered to be a youthful pursuit (Frith 1981, Hornby 1992). In Britain, there is a great depth of musical knowledge among the general population. Musical performances are an important part of Britain's festival cycle. In summer, there are several large music festivals that fans travel from all over the country to attend (Reading, Glastonbury, Gathering of the Tribes, the V Festival, Finsbury Park, T in the Park). These festivals are held so dear that in 1991 the two major weekly music papers (*Melody Maker* and *New Musical Express*) listed the Reading festival as the event of the year, two places over the fall of the Berlin Wall. Music is also extensively covered in the British press. At the onset of my research, the aforementioned weekly magazines had a combined circulation of approximately 175,000.[14] Several glossy monthlies were devoted to music, and there was a substantial variety of televised music programming. During my research, I was consistently surprised by people's passion for music. When having a drink in a nondescript pub in my neighborhood of Islington (a borough of London), I found that the people who befriended me, sometimes fifteen years my senior and whom I would never have suspected of being music enthusiasts, were avid gig goers in their teens and twenties. People told of how they religiously watched *Top of the Pops* growing up, and of the excitement of listening to the BBC's weekly countdown of the Top 40. Musical landmarks were everywhere. It even turned out that my local pub, the Hope and Anchor, selected for its proximity to my flat and its particularly fine pinball machine, was one of the key sites for the embryology of the London punk and new wave movements.

This project required attending a considerable number of performances, and I wanted to select music for which I felt some affinity. Having been to hundreds of shows in America, I knew how important it was to choose music I found appealing. While indie bands come from the United States too, Britain is truly the cradle of indie music.[15] I therefore elected to study the music I already loved, the community for which I had a passion, and an event I knew to be centrally important to the experience of music—the British indie music scene.

Indie musical performances that occur in non-seated, indoor venues are called "gigs," and this is the term I will use.[16] Gigs are staged in all regions of Great Britain—rural, suburban, and urban. They take place in a variety of settings: indoor halls without seats, school gyms, or pubs. The number of participants at a single event can range from under ten to tens of thousands.

In the last few years, several exceedingly readable works have come out that document many aspects of British post-punk and indie music cultures. These books, which address the music's history, political implications, and connections to local communities' identities, have been written by scholarly journalists who have graduated from the British weekly music press—David Cavanagh on Creation Records (Cavanagh 2000), John Harris on Britpop (Harris 2003), and Dave Haslam on Manchester (Haslam 2000). As an enthusiast of the British weekly music press's style of writing about music—intellectually engaged, passionate, but with a playful disregard for formality and highbrow affectations—I find that their writing reflects the vitality of these contradictory impulses within the community. These books are excellent companions for those who are interested in independent music.

Methodology

I really, really wish I could be somewhere else . . .
Razorlight

Conceiving of spectatorship in terms of both empirically detectable signs and phenomenological components requires the application of more than one methodological approach. My methods included: (1) participant observation; (2) interviews (directed and conversational); and (3) text analysis using media produced by and representing the indie community.

The initial study comprised fourteen months of research in Great Britain from July 1993 to September 1994, when I observed and participated in more than one hundred gigs and five festivals.[17] These gigs and festivals varied in size—from small basement clubs to huge festival stadiums—in a variety of locations throughout the United Kingdom that ranged from small villages to urban sprawl.[18] I did not want my sample to reflect merely my own personal taste, so the majority of shows included in the study were bands currently being supported by the weekly music press. I went to shows regardless of how much I thought I would like or dislike them. A majority of the gigs were in London, because this is where I was based. At these gigs,

I documented setting features and participant interaction as well as the interactions between performers and audience members, and between audience members and other audience members, before, during, and after a performance. I also went on tours and documented audiences all over England, Scotland, and Wales on a regular basis. I continue to participate actively in the indie community, and this research includes material up to 2005.

I supplemented my participant observation with the video recording of data. Because I was using interaction as my primary text, it was imperative that this interaction be rigorously documented. Video data collection is a useful tool to make interactional strategies accessible. More than forty hours of audience behavior was taped from a location on the side of the stage or some other vantage point that would include both performers and audience members.

I further supplemented these observation techniques with interviews. While observation can give information about what is occurring, it cannot tell us what people think (Obeyesekere 1981). I conducted interviews with a broad range of indie community members from a variety of age groups and experience levels. I spoke to young fans who had just started to go to gigs, fans who followed bands on the road, fans who went to shows for a good night out, and fans who had been going to shows for years. I also interviewed people who had made indie music their lives and livelihoods: journalists, record label executives, booking agents, musicians, band managers, tour managers, road crew, distributors, promoters, and publicists. These interviews were conducted in private and audiotaped. But I also gleaned information from everyday conversations, such as listening to a journalist at a birthday party lament his age or overhearing a professional stammer an excuse for entering a club in the line for paying patrons rather than the line for guests. Their insights and perspectives are spread throughout this work. I have adhered to the anthropologist's convention of concealing informant identities by using initials. Since anthropologists ask people to reveal some of the most intimate and personal details of their lives, this convention was developed to provide some semblance of privacy and also to free informants to discuss personal topics. I have provided additional information such as age or professional position when it is relevant to the discussion.

My sources have also included the critical discourses and representations of music in popular media. Media and popular characterizations influence people's conceptions of their own participation. The media sources include documentary and cinematic representations of concerts in addition to British and international music press sources.

There is no single objective view of gigs because there is no neutral positioning. A person's placement, activities, and comportment are all read by other participants. Thus, a participant observer is not a neutral eye but an individual positioned in and engaged with an event. Those we try to understand actively try to understand us as well, and to locate us within their cultural landscape (Duranti 1994). In general, most communities do not feature the social scientist within the domain of their normal categories, and therefore she will be positioned by community members within a category they do have. It is imperative that the ethnographer know how she is understood within the community because this ultimately influences the type of data she acquires. My work in the United Kingdom was greatly facilitated by being an American and having an American accent. Britain is a deeply class-conscious society, and the various regional accents are generally associated with particular socioeconomic classes. A Briton speaking to another Briton with a native accent is immediately perceived as being part of a particular social class and having a particular local identity. My American status allowed me to talk to people from all over Britain and from a variety of social classes without the baggage or suspicion that is attached to specific socioeconomic brackets. At various times I was read as an American foreigner, journalist, female fan, tour manager, roadie, friend of the artists, band manager, record company employee, "scenester," or as a member of the very first category I was put in to—*plus one*.

Plus one is the amorphous category for the person who is a guest of someone who is on the guest list. The plus one is the companion of someone with status in the community. Plus ones gain all the privileges but bear none of the responsibilities. They get into the venue for free. They get the same privileged access as the person on the guest list without any risk to their status. The plus one's presence is not questioned and at times is even ignored, which is useful for observation. I spent the beginning of my fieldwork as a plus one. I was fortunate during my years of going to shows in Los Angeles to meet a large number of American and British music professionals. Upon my arrival in London, I was taken to shows as a guest. To most, I was seen as just another American indie music enthusiast who wanted to talk to everyone about music and had no sense of irony.

Before long my constant presence was questioned. The idea that I was a social scientist treating this entertainment form as something worthy of serious consideration was met with a variety of responses, ranging from joyous relief that someone concurred with their opinion of the significance of gigs to friendly chiding that someone would treat this frivolity so earnestly. There was even outright anger that I had somehow perpetuated a scam—shouldn't I be in a hut somewhere in Papua New Guinea? Wasn't anthropology something to do with people in third world countries? How could anything as enjoyable as going to shows have anything to do with science? Science should be sterile and unpleasant and have nothing to do with pleasure.

My desire to undermine these prejudices has been a consistent factor in my selection of subject matter. Anthropology is a comparative science. The stereotypical anthropologist studies a remote and small-scale community. However, our own culture should not be ignored or left to other fields. Without a comparative element, the tendency has been to generalize the case study to the ubiquitous. Additionally, the fact that a cultural spectacle is locally considered to be popular entertainment does not preclude its cultural relevance. If this were Balinese shadow theater, its anthropological value would be recognized immediately, but when we transfer these concerns to the institutions of our own society, which we otherwise tend not to question, the legitimacy of studying cultural forms that are characterized as low or popular is disputed.

What people presumed from my interest in music as a social scientist was that I would eventually be writing about it in some public forum; therefore, I was considered to be similar to a journalist. Many fans reacted positively, seeing a chance to talk with me as an opportunity to voice their opinions. My research also resulted in a change of attitude among some music professionals, who exhibited some caution in conversations with me. The British music industry is savvy regarding issues of journalistic and media representation. People wanted to know what my *angle* was.

About five months into my fieldwork, I was asked to help out at Domino Records, a then-fledgling independent. I felt that this was a chance to give back to the indie community, but working at Domino had many unforeseen consequences. Given the threadbare staff, I wore several professional hats, which gave me new perspectives on indie music. In the office, I participated in many of the challenges involved in running a record company, negotiating press coverage for artists, dealing with issues around musicians' royalties, and organizing guest lists. I took Domino's bands out on tour and experienced gigs as work, booking hotel rooms and making sure that bands were safely transported from one venue to another, and that equipment was set up on time. I experienced first hand the difficulties involved in putting on a live show. I quickly understood the cynicism that so many longtime crew members had about touring, and even the boredom that bands would speak of when they had to wait for six hours upon arriving in a new city with nothing to do until showtime.

Working at Domino had other unexpected consequences. It changed the way I was perceived by those in the community. It changed my role from one fraught with ambiguity to one that could be easily understood. I was no longer a vague plus one, or an anthropologist, whatever that meant. I was now seen as having vested interests rather than being a disinterested observer. I was still working as an anthropologist, but now I was "the American I talked to on the phone at Domino." The caution that I had observed while I was considered an unknown quantity disappeared. Now I was just another record industry person. I became affiliated with Domino's pedigree of staunch independence. I found out how a person is treated when she is perceived to have *credibility*, the cultural capital of the indie world. I saw people's faces light up when I said the name of an independent company rather than a major corporation. Suddenly, I was immersed in the large labyrinth of favors and indebtedness. At the Reading festival one year earlier, I was happily left alone to videotape audiences from the side of the stage. The next year, when I was working at Domino, it was "Can you get a ticket for my friend?" and "I'll just use your production pass for a minute to get into the photo area." I was now seen to be responsible for other people rather than someone that required caretaking.

When I returned to America to resume academic pursuits, my friends in the American music industry thought of me differently. My work at the British record company now meant that I was a potential colleague. The following summer I was hired by Reprise Records in Burbank and returned to London to work for the artists and repertoire (A&R) department. A year later I was working full time at MCA Records in Los Angeles as an A&R manager, and this went a long way toward funding my writing. Working for a major corporation in America, I saw that these industry professionals seemed more concerned with keeping their jobs than with getting the job done.

During the initial period of my research, the music movements of the new wave of new wave, Britpop, lo-fi, and trip-hop were lauded and bashed in the pages of the British weekly music press. Since indie music is led by a weekly press that constantly looks for new musical trends to fill its pages, these microscenes have been fast and furious—gothic, industrial, shoe-gazing, T-shirt bands, Madchester, crusty, Britpop, emo, or the early indie shambling scene, to name just a few of the most well known. During the period of my research, the British Phonographic Institute's rules for the formatting of singles have changed four times.[19] Writing about indie often seems like trying to hit a moving target: as soon as you hit one part, another part has already moved. I entered the field during the festival season of 1993 and returned home near the end of 1994. I continued to gather information on my many subsequent trips to the United Kingdom. I spend several more summers and autumns in London and Manchester. To date, several elements of indie have already changed. In 2005, indie is far more receptive to dance music, and there are far fewer prohibitions on synthetic technologies than was the case in the early to mid-1990s. The two weekly papers are now one. The gender ratio of females to males has begun to approach greater parity, though it is still strongly skewed toward males. Yet I still feel gleeful when I pick up a *New Musical Express* and find the same kinds of arguments from years ago, reframed in terms of a new band or the "new" trend of "miserabilism." My research hasn't ended. I continue my annual pilgrimages to the British music festivals, and my home in the United States is often co-opted by visiting friends, colleagues, or even friends of colleagues who have appeared in Los Angeles only to find that their hotels haven't been booked. In 2002, I finally made it to the Big Day Out tour, the premier independent festival of the Australian circuit, and I have an eye on going on tour in Japan.

Your Itinerary

Outsiders often represent contemporary rock music as a heathen, immoral, degenerate, hedonistic enterprise filled with idolatry for false idols (Cohen 1971, 1980, Denisoff and McCaghy 1973, Hall 1979, Martin and Segrave 1988, McRobbie and Thornton 1995, Rublowsky 1967, Young 1971). However, for those who participate in the indie community, music, music practices, and one's participation are meaningful cultural enterprises with ethical implications. Chapter 1 deals with the question of how to define the parameters of indie culture. I examine each of the contested, non-exclusive definitions of indie. Indie extols local/independent authority, the direct experience of music in a live setting, simplicity, the ordinary, asceticism in consumption, and a nostalgic gaze that looks back at a mythologized past of childhood innocence. Indie calls for a return to an imagined "golden age" of music prior to its debasement by the corpulent Leviathan music industry. Indie views its own aesthetic practices and the practices of others through a screen of ethics. It demonstrates at its core that aesthetics is a matter of morality. Indie, like cultural systems in general, has its share of contradictory impulses and practices. At a fundamental level, indie articulates the complementary and opposing principles of Puritanism, Romanticism, and pathos, which I review in detail in chapter 1.

Chapters 2 through 4 detail participatory spectatorship and the participant structure of indie gigs. Chapter 2, "The Zones of Participation," sets forth the basic outline of the participant structure of the indie gig and its three discrete zones of activity. For the audience members at an indie gig, there are different modes of participation, depending on where one locates oneself within the venue. At successful performances where there are abundant spectators, the area closest to the stage is usually characterized by vigorous movement and high density. Immediately behind is a less compact group of spectators standing relatively still, watching the performance, drinking, and/or smoking. In the back of the venue, in the areas around the bars, people mill about, chatting, ordering drinks, and paying attention to things other than what is occurring on the stage. Within the gig's participant structure, one's physical placement and comportment indicate a level of orientation to the performance, the types of activities one will engage in and expect others to engage in, and one's affiliation with the band performing.

While the first two audience zones are highly focused on the performance, the orientation in zone three is not toward the stage but toward the peripheries of performance. In chapter 3, "Zone Three and the Music Industry," I discuss the audience members who for various reasons—lack of interest, preference, or dissatisfaction—are not interested in watching the show. I also examine the professionals who comprise the music industry and whose attention often veers from the stage. The activities of the habitual denizens of zone three have enormous consequences for the transnational commerce of music. Gigs are where the status relationships among a professional coterie are established, articulated, and altered. At gigs, professionals portray themselves in opposition to fans by utilizing a system of freebies that includes guest passes and guest lists. This system is part of a general professional ideology of gaining gratis goods and services. A temporary status hierarchy is articulated in the gig setting, where access to privileged space and performers expresses the relative degree of status of a professional at this specific event. Within this context, the band functions as a valorized commodity, where access to performers is a marker of status in a hierarchical system of power and influence peddling.

In chapter 4, "The Participant Structure and the Metaphysics of Spectatorship," I consider the totality of participant structure and examine how the differing spectorial positions become meaningful in relationship to each other. As audience members age and gain experience, their mode of engagement changes. In the course of an individual's participation in gig culture, the audience member typically moves from a hot, physical engagement to a cool, composed spectorial mode. The meaning of comportment comes from its cultural and historic context. The gig, ostensibly about music and entertainment, reenacts the broader culture's ritual drama about metaphysic conversion. The movement from zone one to zone two that appears over time in the gig's participant structure represents a conversion narrative between the two primary metaphysical systems that combined to form rock music: West African and Western artistic and religious traditions. I argue that the active, bodily engaged comportment of zone one embodies a non-Western metaphysic in which the deployment of the body in danced ritual is essential for spiritual enlightenment. The circumscribed comportment of zone two embodies a Western European metaphysic of transcendence through the control and abnegation of the body and the amplification of contemplation. The understanding of these metaphysical systems and their relationship to each other is filtered through a Protestant perspective that ultimately views non-Western religions as inferior, immature, and heathen. Here, we find one of the primary narratives of Christianity, the conversion of the non-believing "other," acted out on the secular stage of musical performance, where audience members are to be transformed into adults who sublimate the pleasures of the flesh for the pleasures of the mind. Thus, gigs are both an expression of excess and the subjugation of it. This phenomenon is both religious and secular, artistic and commercial, inextricably intertwined.

Every ritual consists of a series of relationships—among audience members, between audience members and the performance, between the audience and the performers, and between the performers and the performance. My early chapters analyze audience members' relationships to each other. In chapters 5 and 6, I turn to the relationships between musicians and audience members. In chapter 5, "Performance, Authenticity, and Emotion," I deal with indie's performance conventions and the relationship between performers and audience members as a collective. Indie is an art form that is concerned with verisimilitude. Verisimilitude is often considered to have a visual connotation, but here I use it in the broader sense of the appearance or semblance of truth. Authenticity and credibility are connected to the notion of believability, the faith that audiences invest in the veracity of the musical performance. This chapter covers how credibility is conveyed in the indie genre by a lack of stress on virtuosity, an avoidance of the performance postures of other genres, and a valuing of innovation. In indie, emotions are considered to be the essential source of meaning. Indie music values verisimilitude and novelty within a circumscribed generic form. Within this system, emotions are initially valorized by the audience member's experience of the performance and then, ultimately, denigrated and devalued.

Chapter 6, "Sex and the Ritual Practitioners," is dedicated to indie's ritual specialists—musicians, professionals, crew, those audience members who do not opt out of the community, and those audience members who repeatedly seek intimate relations with performers. These participants continue to look to music for meaning long after their peers have left it behind; they believe in the value of music's emotional epiphanies and often devote their lives to the transitory rewards of participating in gigs. In refusing to leave music behind, ritual practitioners defy the Western Christian cosmology that values the mind over the body, reason over emotion, and capital commerce over nonproprietary experience. To understand the constellation of performer/audience/performance, I examine the relationship between performers and segments of the audience according to the distinctions made among spectorial modes within the indie community's spectacle and discourses. I discuss mainstream rock imagery and the moral distinctions made by indie audiences about issues of gender and sex. The stereotypes of the "groupie" and mainstream "musician" threaten how intimacy is displayed in the indie community, as well as indie's austere morality. There is a reciprocal relationship between music's ritual practitioners, between band members and sexual acolytes. I demonstrate that the gig is a sexual spectacle where male and female powers are symbolically joined onstage in performance and concretely enacted offstage in sexual communion.

I conclude with some final comments in the afterword. Because I come to explicit conclusions at the end of each chapter, the afterword is an overview and provides some final thoughts on indie music, spectatorship, performance, and the role of indie music fans transnationally and beyond.

Conclusion

Leave it all behind . . .
Ride

Subjectivity needs to be understood not just in terms of the internal structures of cultural productions but in embodied practice. In looking at social actors and their roles in a participant structure, we see in indie the articulation of a participatory spectatorship that is inscribed with religious ideology. Indie music performances enact a fundamental Western cultural dichotomy between sentient sensuality and a contemplative mode of sensual abrogation, between emotional expression and stoic internalization. In this economic and institutional sector that is considered to be wholly secular, one finds a community shaped by metaphysical concerns regarding authority, exploitation, and the nature of "authentic" experience.

Metaphysics is a theory of the manner in which one experiences the numinous, where essential meaning is found. Here, music stands in for an experience of divinity. Does one access the divine through bodily circumspection and mental contemplation, or does one access the divine through sacred dance and trance? Does meaning lie in the sacred text of the composer, an already existent meaning, which a conductor and musicians can enliven, or does meaning lie in the temporary improvisational interface between artist, sound, and audience, whereby the body is given over to sacred song and true apprehension is achieved? These are just two of the myriad metaphysical philosophies and possibilities. Indie finds itself wedged between these two, in the live performance of a pre-existing text where value is nevertheless found by momentarily capturing emotion and meaning in the temporary interface between audience, performer, and sound. The arguments regarding indie use a vocabulary of music that camouflages the metaphysical battle being waged. Indie produces the broader cultural narratives that arise from the West's own conflicts.

In rituals, contradictions can temporarily coexist—the extended family that must break down can be reconstructed, new and old identities can exist side by side. Indie inhabits a contradiction between Puritan asceticism and Romantic emotionalism, between Western and West African metaphysics, between commerce and art—all within a leisure pursuit viewed by the wider culture as frivolous, base, or even worthless. Rituals address cultural conflicts. Some rituals, like rites of passage, address resolvable conflicts. Others, like rites of intensification, address irresolvable conflicts and, therefore, need to be repeated ad infinitum. For most in the indie community, participation in gigs is a rite of passage. As a youth phenomenon, it is temporary; the majority of participants eventually decide to leave the community. The issues and meanings of "youth" addressed and reproduced by participation in this community are resolved by entering the adult world of family and work. The rejection of the community is accompanied by a rejection of its values—that music and emotion matter or that the body is a reliable vehicle for experiencing meaning. What was once meaningful to the insider is worthless to the outsider, which the insider has now become. This ritual event enacts over time an embrace of indie's values and then a subsequent thwarting of them. Members resolve the conflicts by leaving the community behind. However, nothing repressed is fully resolved, and this conflict will find expression in other ritual forms.

Not all members reject the community, however. For some, this rite of passage becomes a rite of intensification, presenting profound and irresolvable conflicts that only find temporary resolution in the liminal space of performance. For them, the liminal space of the gig is the only place that feels like home. These individuals have difficulty exiting the community and many become professionals—record industry personnel, musicians, or sexual acolytes—dedicating their lives to this art. These individuals represent a critique of society's cultural precepts. They persist in valuing emotions, revering art that is viewed by mainstream society as not art at all, and demonstrating that sex is not a commodity to be exchanged for material goods.

In the end, this book is essentially about how people make meaning in their lives in day-to-day activities. Meaning does not exist outside of culture but is created within it. Meaning is constructed in a multitude of ways, in mundane interactions, in cultural narratives, and in grand spectacles. These ways of making meaning may initially be imperceptible to the casual observer, but they are there, organizing and making appear ordered a meaningless and unpredictable world.

Here we go . . .
Jon Brion

CHAPTER I

What Is "Indie"?

This is the definition of my life . . .
The Beta Band

This chapter examines the definition of "indie." It describes the indie community, indie music, and indie's ideological foundations. Defining a collective within a complex social system is not just an exercise designating one's province of study; it also delineates how one conceives of cultural groups. However, attempts to characterize a category of music are fraught with difficulty. Defining a category like indie is not only problematic for scholars who seek to understand culture; it is also difficult for community members themselves (Frith 1981, Kruse 1993). Fans and members of the British music industry often struggle to come to terms with defining something they feel they can recognize intuitively. They cannot articulate general principles without excluding some music and performers they think should be included or including some they feel should not be.[1] For the indie aficionados, what comprises indie appears to be self-evident. For example, when asked to define indie music, one fan stated, "I don't know how to describe it, but I know it when I hear it" (M.K. age twenty-two). As with many cultural categories and practices, recognition in the absence of a clearly articulated definition is common among fans and professionals alike.

Why is there confusion in defining indie? In part, it is because indie is not a thing at all and is therefore not describable in the same manner as a stable object. Although indie has no exact definition, the discourse and practices around the multiple descriptions and definitions of indie detail a set of principles that reveal the values and issues at stake for the community. An attempt at self-definition is part of the process of forming a cultural grouping. To form a group, members need to create a set of boundaries between what constitutes and what excludes membership. Creating a boundary means creating an identity for oneself. Differentiation is at the heart of the process of definition.

Indie music has been considered by insiders to be: (1) a type of musical production affiliated with small independent record labels with a distinctive mode of independent distribution; (2) a genre of music that has a particular sound and stylistic conventions; (3) music that communicates a particular ethos; (4) a category of critical assessment; and (5) music that can be contrasted with other genres, such as mainstream pop, dance, blues, country, or classical. The indie community's arguments over membership deal with the nature of the ownership of musical recordings and their mode of distribution to a larger public, the nature of musical production practices and their relationship to musical forms, and the relationship between audience members and the music. I consider indie to be precisely this discourse, and the activities that produce and are produced by this discourse, as well as the artistic productions and community members who participate in and contribute to this discourse.

The strongest voice in indie is the British weekly music press. This press, which at various times has included *New Musical Express (NME)*, *Sounds*, and *Melody Maker*—the "inkies," as they were colloquially known—dominates and crystallizes the indie community.[2] Just as a magazine such as *Mix-Mag* is seen to cater to the dance community in Britain, or *Vibe* to the hip-hop community in the United States, *NME* speaks to the indie community.

The weekly press is powerful in shaping indie's discourse. It provides a forum for indie fans to debate issues in prominent letters pages and accompanying op-ed pieces, and it is read regularly by professionals and fans. As one reader characterized it in a letters page, "I read the *NME* avidly—it's what Wednesdays were made for" (*NME*, February 26, 1994).[3] For young fans, these papers are highly influential in shaping their opinions. Often, they directly paraphrase the weekly press reviews when giving their opinions about bands. For younger fans in their early teens, the music press is like a rare and exotic fruit, as well as a point of entry into a world they initially know very little about. Indie fans purchase music by bands they have not yet heard more frequently than any other British music consumer. They attribute their purchases to recommendations from the weekly press and from friends (IPC Music Press 1993, EMRIG Report 1993). The indie community has a rapid turnover of bands, in part because of the furious pace of a weekly press; there is a constant need for new bands and trends to fill copy. They are the de facto source for information about indie music.

The weekly press is not the only means of learning about indie music in the United Kingdom; there are radio programs, television, the internet, and local fanzines, the photocopied publications by fans. However, in many ways, when fans stop reading the weekly press they move out of the indie community and soon disconnect from the music scene. To see an unknown band appear on the cover of a monthly music magazine or to hear new singles air on the radio by a band that one has never heard of would be unacceptable for an active member of the indie community, which prides itself on knowing about the "music of tomorrow, today."[4] The indie community has a love/hate relationship with the weekly press, regarding it as a vital link to the indie music world but often furious at its distinctively vitriolic and opinionated journalistic style. When there were two inkies, many indie members, angry at the opinions of one paper, would profess allegiance to the other, a decision rendered ironic by the fact that both *NME* and *Melody Maker* were published by the same company, IPC Press, and operated on adjacent floors of Kings Reach Tower.[5] Indie is constituted by a distinct discourse, a discourse typified and consolidated by the British weekly music press.

Indie ... What's at Stake?

Some of the arguments of indie regarding production values, clothing, and musical style may seem trivial or hairsplitting to an outsider. It serves well to remember Jonathan Swift's two empires, Lilliput and Blefuscu, whose members fought to the death over which side of the egg to crack first. Swift parodied the differences between Protestantism and Catholicism, the arbitrariness of ritual, and the significance placed by members on ritual procedures. If the differences between indie style and practice and other musical genres were solely stylistic, indie's insistence on certain modes would be as absurd as the figures Swift satirized. However, indie's ideology reproduces a significant and unresolved ideological conflict in Western culture, one not unrelated to Swift's own satire.

The core issues of indie and its practices are in essence the arguments of a particular sect of Protestant reformers within the secular forum of music.[6] The goals of both Protestant and Catholic churches were essentially the same: to experience a true relationship with the divine. The various sects of Christianity in Europe at the time of the Reformation had a common goal in the fundamental notion of redemption through a moral and mystical experience. The primary difference was the means of reaching this goal. The debates between Protestants and Catholics dealt with the fundamental questions about the nature of *how* a congregation connects with the divine: where religious authority is located (individual/independent parishes vs. centralized papal authority); how the divine is accessed (directly vs. mediated); how ritual fosters an experience of the sacred (austere vs. baroque); and how one's elite status is measured (asceticism vs. aggrandizement). Which side of the egg does one crack first?

Within indie, we find similar arguments regarding the nature of experience, but in this case experiencing the divine is displaced onto the experience of "true" or "authentic" music. Should music be produced by a centralized authority (major labels) or by independent local operations (independent labels)? What form should music take to promote the experience of true music (the generic characteristics of indie vs. the generic characteristics of other genres)? How should listeners experience music to foster a true encounter with music (live vs. recorded)? How is one's authentic musical experience measured? Indie's arguments replace the experience of the true spirit of the divine with that of the true spirit of music. The common goal set forth for music listeners within indie cosmology is to have a communion with the sacred quintessence of music. Differences in musical practices are interpreted through a moral frame, producing an aesthetic system based on moral values.

Indie's core values promote and replicate the doctrine of a particular brand of Protestant religiosity: Puritanism. The central tenets of Puritanism are simplicity of worship, asceticism, a high regard for education, high standards of morality, and democratic political principles based on the autonomy of individual congregations (Knappen 2005: 7518). Puritans did not reject the liturgy but instead what they perceived as the Catholic Church's corruption of it. This corruption was seen in superfluous rites, intervention by a hierarchy of clergy, excessive adornment, outward pomp, and pandering to the worldliness of the body. The beliefs of Puritanism and its critique of perceived Catholic excesses are echoed in each of the defining aspects of indie music, a secular amusement that would have been banished, ironically, by the Puritans. Within indie, we find a Puritan distrust of authority, a preference for non-corporate, independently owned commercial operations, an avocation of simplicity in musical form, production, and style, a promotion of high moral standards regarding issues of sexuality and conduct, an emphasis on education, and an underlying theme of austerity and abstinence. Like the Protestants of the Reformation, indie fans continue the rebellious narrative first put forth by the punks, the paradigmatic British music reformers. They present a narrative of the deviation from true musical encounters through a hypertrophic growth of institutional machinery to benefit corrupt executives who exploit the faithful and debase music itself. As David Cavanagh writes of the "indie dream," indie "described a culture of independence that was almost a form of protest" (Cavanagh 2000: viii). This protest was against the church of mainstream music. Indie calls nostalgically for a return to and restoration of "original" musical practices and ideals.

In general, the indie ideology's appropriation of the theological arguments of Puritanism is not overtly recognized within the community. Rather, indie fans consider their participation to be wholly secular. There is some latent awareness of the Puritan foundation of indie ideology, particularly in the use of the terms "purist" and "puritanical" by indie fans and journalists regarding themselves. However, the notion that at the heart of indie lies what many feel to be a conservative and repressive religious ideology would be distasteful to those who embrace one of the fundamental and widespread folktales of youth culture, namely, that participating in a music scene constitutes a form of rebellion rather than a recapitulation of the dominant cultural ideology and narratives.[7]

Also within indie ideology is a parallel strand of Romanticism, with its characteristic cultivation of emotion, passion, and the spirit, its interest in artistic movements of the past, its preference for the natural, its acclaim for the exceptional man in the guise of the musical genius, its respect for local identities and the working class, and its distaste for middle-class society while being itself middle class. This Romantic manifestation is what Colin Campbell refers to as the "Other Protestant Ethic." In his remarkably insightful book *The Romantic Ethic and the Spirit of Modern Consumerism*, Campbell argues persuasively that the Puritan abnegation of sensual pleasure and the Romantic valorization of extreme emotion are interdependent: "The very practice of one kind of conduct creates the circumstance necessary for the performance, as well as the positive valuations of the other" (Campbell 1987: 221). In indie also is the dissonance of these two complementary theological strains. Indie ideology lives within these culturally produced complementary and conflicting impulses by finding the uneasy common ground between them.

It is the persistence of these metaphysical cultural narratives that creates such consistency in the indie community's discourse despite the changes in its personnel, the variations in its music, and the crossing of national borders. In the 2004 film *Our Time*, which looked at the American independent music scene of garage rock and the New York City music scene, issues and narratives are expressed by musicians and professionals that have consistently characterized indie music. The musicians claim that they are real and "organic," while other forms of music are artificial and disconnected to local interests. They discuss the importance of DIY ("do it yourself," a well-known phrase from the British punk movement) and how their experience is a return to the true excitement of the 1970s New York underground scene.[8] In an economic and institutional sector considered by participants to be free from religious ideology, one finds the recapitulation of religious drama and a community shaped by similar concerns regarding authority, exploitation, and the nature of "authentic" experience. Indie ideology is generated by the cultural principles of the wider society. Indie is a musical community centrally focused on how an audience can have the purest possible experience of music. In this endeavor, indie fans locate themselves as the anointed disciples of music who, through their own system of authenticity, recognize true value in music. Indie aficionados are not called "purists" without good reason.

Indie as a Mode of Distribution: An Industrial Definition

Play me a song to set me free
Nobody writes them like they used to,
So it may as well be me . . .
Belle and Sebastian

Indie, as a colloquial abbreviation of the term *independent,* reflects this community's historic association with the products of small, independently owned record companies. Independent music is a category that is widely recognized by the British recording industry. From the industry standpoint, records or artists are considered independent if their music releases can be included on the independent retail chart. The charts are a weekly ranking of singles and albums in order of sales from retail outlets throughout Britain. Records with independent distribution, despite the size or nature of the ownership of the record label, are eligible for inclusion on the independent chart. In other words, if the artist's record label utilizes a distribution network that is not owned by one of the four major transnational corporations, it appears on the independent chart.[9] Releases by independent distribution companies such as Vital, Southern (SRD), or Pinnacle are eligible for inclusion on the independent chart. Therefore, the music industry defines independent music by a specific set of practices regarding the nature of ownership of the mode of circulation to the public.

One needs to turn to the history of the British music charts to understand why distribution is the key feature in determining independence. The history of the independent chart is intertwined with the national chart and the role of charts as a tool for marketing bands to the public. Having a record appear in one of the national charts is seen both as a means to and a measure of success. In Britain, industry personnel discuss a band's success in terms of its highest chart placement and how many weeks it stayed there. In the United States, industry personnel evaluate a band's success primarily in terms of "units" sold. While both of these criteria are indications of success, neither is an accurate evaluation of the profitability of a release. The bottom line is the amount of income from records sold, less the company investment in the project. These two disparate assessment strategies are pervasive in everyday verbal interchange. In London, industry personnel will say, "We got that single to number two," whereas in the music capitals of Los Angeles and New York, industry personnel will say, "We're at one and a half million units," though they may have only sold 300,000, using shipping figures rather than sales figures in order to hype the success of a release to their colleagues. Thus, charting in Britain is the dominant dialogic gauge of a band's success.

Within the British music industry, having a single in the Top 40 is perceived to be an essential component of a band's success.[10] Historically, Britain had few media outlets for music and few radio stations that played contemporary music. Until the 1960s, there were only four national radio stations, supplemented by a meager number of stations broadcasting to local regions and a varying number of pirate broadcasters.[11] The BBC's Radio One was the chief national media outlet for contemporary popular music. Radio Two played music that was characterized as more "middle of the road" (Hunter 1977: 130). Radio Three played classical, and Radio Four featured news, current affairs, and dramas. Since Radio One's daytime playlist consisted primarily of songs that charted in the Top 40, this chart showing was deemed to be decisive for a band to gain national radio exposure.[12] This connection between chart position and media exposure was further augmented by the national television program *Top of the Pops,* a weekly show featuring artists with top-ranking singles performing live or lip-syncing their current hit. Thus, a single charting within the Top 40 would result in both national radio airplay and national television exposure, making the chart a key focal point for marketing strategies.

Getting a single to chart nationally is still seen as so crucial to a band's success that most major record companies plan to lose money on singles and treat the endeavor of releasing a single as part of the promotional expense for an album's release. Singles are sold to shops in bulk deals, "Buy one, get one free" or "Buy one, get four free," so that the new single will be on sale in retail outlets in an attempt to bolster a band's presence in the national charts.[13] Hence, it is far more likely that a new single will be on sale in retail outlets rather than older singles, which are not promoted to achieve chart placement. The fact that companies are willing to give away their product in order to get a single to rank in the national chart demonstrates the importance placed on a chart ranking in marketing a musical group.

Before the institutionalization of an independent chart, the national chart was the only chart that enabled one to get airplay and national exposure. The method of reckoning national chart placement played a significant role in the perceived need to establish a separate independent chart. In the mid-1970s, during the development of an independent chart, there were far fewer chart return shops and an inefficient system for accounting sales.[14] In 1977 there were 750 chart return shops in Britain, with 250 outlets recording their sales for the singles chart and 450 outlets recording their sales for the album chart. The UK charts were compiled from data on purchases made at selected outlets of major chain stores such as WHSmith and Woolworths, which also sell a broad variety of other goods, as well as from some of the megastores, such as Virgin, HMV, and Tower, which primarily sell music. Up until the mid-1970s, the weekly press was not yet specialized. Instead, it covered a broad range of music, with sections for various genres, such as blues, jazz, and folk. Music purchases made at small, independently owned specialty record shops such as Rough Trade and Rock On in London, Edinburgh's Avalanche, or Liverpool's Probe, were excluded from the chart altogether. These specialty record shops catered to a collector's market and carried older recordings and more obscure releases. Additionally, with so few retail outlets controlling the charts in an industry in which the names and locations of chart return shops were widely known, record hyping was rampant. Record hyping occurs when vested interests—a record company or a band's management—go to chart return shops and purchase a large number of an artist's single to bolster its position in the charts.[15] The combination of hyping and the lack of chart return coverage of the independent stores meant that the buying proclivities of specialized customers were excluded from participation in the national charts.

National charts were featured prominently in all of the music papers. In October 1975 *Sounds,* which was considered by many to be the most adventurous of the three weekly music papers, replaced their Capital Radio chart with an "Alternative" chart.[16] This chart was a straw poll listing the top-selling records at a selected independent retail shop. These chart lists were very informal and not necessarily accurate reports of sales. Often it was information made up on the spot by the owner or the clerk who answered the phone. The first week's Alternative chart was a reggae chart supplied by In-tone Records from Peckham, London. The Alternative chart would cycle through various genres, such as country, oldies, West African, and writers' picks. Ironically, it was the oldies chart, which came from stores with a large number of resale records, that featured some of the newest acts, such as the Stooges, who would become prominent in the burgeoning punk scene.

An "independent" chart debuted in the pages of *NME* in October 1979.[17] The weekly began to call selected independent retail outlets such as Flyover Records or Rough Trade to get a list of the top-selling releases at each record store.[18] Hence, the independent chart was designed to reflect the purchasing habits of those who patronized the independent specialty shop rather than the large chain establishments. Until June 1996 the independent chart listed in *Melody Maker* was still put together from a straw poll of a chain of independent specialty record shops called the Subterranean chain, affiliated with Southern Distribution. After June 1996 *Melody Maker* switched to the music industry's official independent chart using scanned data.

The industry followed suit with the magazine *Record Business*, establishing its own independent chart using the criteria of independent distribution. David Cavanagh attributes the impulse to create an official industry Independent chart to the owner of the independent label Cherry Red, Iain McNay (Cavanagh 2000). This official chart appeared in *Record Business* in January 1980. To understand why the industry selected distribution as the key factor in determining independence, one needs to look back to the development of the independent sector. Independent companies have been a constant since the inception of recording technologies. The history of independent labels is often traced back to the postwar years of the 1950s, when small independent labels proliferated in the patronage of rock and roll. However, the current crop of British independent labels have their strongest genealogical roots in the period of punk of the mid- to late 1970s, when small labels were set up under the auspices of punk's DIY manifesto.

During the punk period, many bands set up their own labels to record and release their material. Punk's rallying call of "do it yourself" was translated into the practices of these new labels: "do it simple," "do it quick," and "do it cheap." For example, the Chiswick label recorded and manufactured 2,500 copies of an EP for £700 in 1977 (Laing 1985: 10).[19] The band the Desperate Bicycles produced a single where the entire venture, including studio time, mastering, and pressing five hundred copies, came to £153.15 (*Melody Maker*, August 20, 1977). In the late 1970s key independent labels such as Fast Product, Rough Trade, Postcard, Zoo Records, Stiff, Factory, Mute, Beggars Banquet, Some Bizzare, Cherry Red, and Fiction were established in the musical wake of punk.

However, while recording could be done rather easily and cheaply, the biggest obstacle for nascent labels was securing a mode of distribution to get their records into shops for people to purchase. Some small labels obtained distribution deals with one of the major corporations. However, this had many drawbacks, including the loss of control over their release schedules. As often as not, it resulted in the label losing its separate identity and appearing to become a mere satellite for the larger corporate label. As Geoff Travis of Rough Trade said in an interview with David Hesmondhalgh in 1992: "The thing to do is to get your own distribution network, then you've got control, you've got power. You can decide with musicians what gets out to the country and give people alternate means of information" (Hesmondhalgh 1997: 265).[20] Distribution was seen as tantamount to control over access, and therefore control over expression. Since distribution seemed to be the major stumbling block for aspiring recording companies, it would in turn become the defining characteristic of "independence" in the British recording industry.[21]

Already in existence at the time of punk were two independent distributors, Pinnacle and Spartan, which distributed smaller specialty releases. However, it was Rough Trade's Geoff Travis, who opted to form a new distribution company independent of the majors, who would have the most significant impact for the independent community. Rough Trade formed its own label and distribution network, called the Cartel. The Cartel was a conglomerate of regional telesales teams that sold to retail outlets in each regional market. Each market had an independent specialty record store, including Revolver (Bristol), Red Rhino (York), Probe (Liverpool), 9 Mile (Leamington Spa), Fast Forward (Edinburgh), Backs (Norwich), and Rough Trade (London). (See map.) Each team would call orders into a main warehouse in London, where records would be packed for distribution to each region. The Cartel would sell the recordings of the Rough Trade label and other budding independent companies, as well as one-off projects by bands.[22] In the early days of Rough Trade distribution, records would be delivered on the backs of motorbikes and from the trunks of cars. However, Rough Trade soon became a viable option for those who wanted to put out their own recordings—provided that Rough Trade approved them. Though it was not the largest independent distributor, Rough Trade was felt to embody the values of independence and therefore was actively sought by new independent labels to distribute their releases.

Rough Trade was initially organized as a cooperative that stood in stark contrast to the structure of major corporations. Initially, all Rough Trade employees, from directors to those working in the warehouse, were paid the same. All company decisions were made at general assemblies, and all employees were allowed to have a voice in company decisions. If Rough Trade was distributing a record that someone did not like for political reasons, the employee could bring up the issue at a company-wide meeting and inform other workers of his or her concerns. Employees felt that they were involved in a historical undertaking designed to actively combat the organization of multinational media conglomerates and the values they represented. Rough Trade actively sought to circumvent the indulgences of those involved in the record industry. They would not send out promotional copies of records to radio stations or journalists, nor would they

Map of the United Kingdom with Rough Trade's Cartel.

have guest lists at their artists' shows. Several independent labels would flourish in the early 1980s, including Mute, Factory, and the label considered by many to typify the indie sound, Creation Records.

The independent distribution networks initially served the small independent labels. As Cavanagh put it, "The independent label dream . . . was that romantic notion of going it alone, pure and untainted by hype and multinational marketeers" (Cavanagh 2000: viii). Independent labels were seen to value unmediated artistic vision, facilitating rather than intervening in an artist's release to the public. Many of the themes of independent culture were associated with the independent label: a lack of concern for popularity, an interest in autonomy and local character, the rejection of the large corporations based in London, and an emphasis on direct artistic expression above all else. Many of the early labels represented the talent and flavor of their local principalities—Factory Records for Manchester, Zoo for Liverpool, and Postcard for Scotland. London, on the other hand, was the seat of centralized power. Going to London for a record deal was often viewed as selling out, a journey with hat in hand to beg for patronage from the power elite, who had no concern for local interests. For independent labels to persist, they needed a means to connect their art with an audience.

The independent distributors also favored independent retail outlets. Major chain retail establishments cut deals with distributors for exclusive releases or price discounts because of their large bulk purchases, enabling major chains to acquire records at lower prices. These deals put the independent retail outlet (or "mom and pops," as they are affectionately known) at a significant disadvantage in competing for customers. It was under the auspices of Rough Trade and the Cartel that the significant Chain With No Name was established.[23] The Chain With No Name, later affiliated with Rough Trade Distribution's progeny RTM-Disc, was an aggregate of independently owned record stores that was then large enough to secure deals, special formats, and exclusives on releases.[24] Rough Trade's development of the independent chain was an attempt to undercut the retail hierarchy and remove the advantage that the major corporations had over small specialty stores. As other distribution companies developed, each organized its own chain of independent stores to secure the advantages available to a large corporate chain: the Network for Pinnacle, Subterranean for SRD, Vital Stores for Vital, and Knowledge for 3MV.[25] However, an independent retail outlet can participate in more than one chain. Thus, a single specialty retailer, such as London's Sister Ray, Manchester's Piccadilly, or Nottingham's Selectadisc, can be a member of five or six chains, each affiliated with a different independent distributor.

By the late 1980s and early 1990s the situation became more complex for the independents. Heretofore, independent ownership and distribution had largely coincided in practice, but in this period the line between independents and major companies blurred. It was not uncommon for indie bands to have crossover success and to perform well on the mainstream charts. Megastores such as Virgin Records on London's Oxford Street, which had consistently stocked independent releases, now added special indie display sections highlighting the newest indie releases. Indie had developed a high profile from its coverage in the weekly press. As the independent chart became well established, it provided another way for a new band to chart, resulting in print coverage and airplay. Independent record labels became known for effectively breaking unknown bands. Professionals and fans alike turned to the independent charts to identify new talent.

Several independents were making a good return on a relatively small investment. Independent record companies traditionally gave smaller advances to the artists in exchange for a greater share of points (percentage of profits) on sales of recordings, resulting in a smaller initial outlay of funds. The ability of independents to return a profit, as well as their ability to sign and nurture new talent, made these companies acquisition targets for major media corporations. Consequently, many independent companies were bought by, incorporated into, or funded by major music corporations. Majors would sign acts after the initial legwork had been done by these smaller companies. Purchasing controlling shares of independents was a natural extension of the process. The pilfering of talent from independents extended to industry personnel, who often moved to the major music conglomerates for higher salaries.

The result of independents' transfer to major corporations was that bands, labels, and personnel that were considered independent were now part of a major's roster. For a significant period of post-punk and early indie, a band signing with a major label was seen as an immoral act. Cavanagh puts it this way:

The decision to take the independent route represented an emotional rejection, based on ethics and political beliefs, of everything the major labels stood for . . . major labels were greedy corporations staffed by uncool straights who maltreated and undermined their artists, and thought nothing of diluting the art itself to make it commercially viable . . . here was the righteous indie band making interesting music without compromise; and over there was the banally ambitious, morally capitulating group that had sold its soul to a major label for money. (Cavanagh 2000: 38–39)

Major labels would offer more money and greater exposure than independent labels, and the money they offered was seen as a pernicious temptation and corruptor that would undermine music as art for art's sake.[26]

For the broader community, independence was thought to refer only to the practices of small record labels. However, since a record's distribution network determines whether a record or an artist appears on the independent chart, corporate record companies exploited the loophole. Any major corporation could have an independent band by distributing the record through one of the independent distribution companies. Many of the acquired independents thus retained ties with their independent distributors. Creation Records sold shares to Sony in 1993 but maintained its independent distribution so that its albums could continue to be counted on the independent chart. Thus, many "independent" acts have the financial resources of a major corporation at their disposal but are still classified as independent.

Many corporations thought that developing a band as independent was an effective means of introducing it to the marketplace. Therefore they developed a number of "independent" labels (crypto-indies) that were fully funded by the major corporation but utilized one of the independent distribution networks. Thus a label like Dedicated, funded by BMG, had its records counted in the independent chart because its recordings were distributed by Vital.[27] For many bands, the opportunity to be on the independent chart was a large factor in choosing a label to sign with. However, a small, independently owned company run from one's bedroom, but using a major's distribution network would be excluded from the independent chart.[28] Thus, the industry use of a definition of independence based solely on distribution resulted in a chart that included artists signed to major labels.[29]

For the industry, membership in the independent community is constituted by the use of independent distribution, and the ideals and structures embodied within the system of independent distributors are essential. When RTM merged with Vital, Martin Mills, who owns a majority share of RTM, stated, "What is crucial is that both companies (RTM and Vital) have retained the philosophies which drove the Cartel" (*Music Week,* June 21, 1997). Through special arrangements offered exclusively to affiliated retail outlets, the independent distribution company consciously and overtly advocates independently owned specialty shops belonging to local entrepreneurs over chain establishments run by distant corporate executives. It privileges individual entrepreneurship over bureaucratic corporate structures and affiliated independent stores over retail cells that answer to a centralizing authority. Additionally, the decisions made by independent distributors are thought to be based on moral and aesthetic grounds, not just solely on commercial success. As Mills put it, "Being an independent distribution company, you kind of have a moral obligation." Thus, the practice of independent distribution in its ideal form is thought of as a moral, aesthetic, and egalitarian enterprise with authority vested in local members.

The industrial definition of independence echoes the Puritan value of individual congregations. Indie and Puritan reformists expressed a similar concern about the effect of hierarchy and bureaucracy on the relationship between patron and subject. One is a relationship between music fan and music, the other between congregant and the divine.

Indie's organizational principles parallel those advocated by the Puritans, who required a move away from papal authority toward individual parishes with their own elected pastors. Similarly, the Cartel was an affiliation of distinct local districts held together in a loose, Presbyterian structure. In addition, an independent distribution network provides the means for the independent record label to remain an independent entity, pure and untainted by the authoritarian organization of the "Industry." The model of Rough Trade's Cartel advances an anti-absolutist stance that values the local over the remote, egalitarianism over hierarchy, and theocratic over unprincipled capitalism. The philosophies of independent distribution are the organizational and infrastructural foundation of the Puritan stance of indie.

The Romantic ethic is also found in indie's infrastructural values: its revolt against established social and bureaucratically entrenched institutions, its perception of the power elite as corrupt and untrustworthy, its love of the local "folk," its values of freedom, individualism, and individual entrepreneurships. More than anything else, the independent community holds the romantic belief that self-expression is paramount.[30]

Indie as a Genre

pure and simple every time . . .
Lightning Seeds

Utilizing the nature of distribution as a mode of reckoning has meant not only that major labels can appear on the independent charts but that any type of music can be counted as independent as well. Various musical genres, particularly subgenres of dance such as techno, house, hardcore, and jungle as well as some mainstream pop, have been included in the official independent chart. Many indie enthusiasts, however, feel that indie does not reflect merely a mode of circulation but a particular genre of music as well, with a recognizable sound and collective conventions that distinguish it from dance, country, or R&B, for example. From this perspective, the boundaries of indie result from an adherence to specific musical conventions and specific practices in the production of music. In its generic characteristics, indie's issues of inclusion and exclusion center around concerns about musical form, musical production, and style. Permeating the indie tradition is an espousal of simplicity and austerity, a hypervaluation of childhood and childlike imagery, a nostalgic sensibility, a technophobia, and a fetishization of the guitar. As ex-*NME* journalist Simon Reynolds puts it, British indie "has itself settled into stifling orthodoxy: an insistence on short songs, lo-fi, minimalism, purism, and guitars, guitars, guitars" (Reynolds in Kruse 1993: 36). Adherence to indie's generic features allows bands that do not have an independent label or independent distribution to be considered by some to have membership within the indie community.

Indie music is generally played by slender young white males in their late teens to early thirties. Most indie bands are basic four-piece combos with electric guitar, bass, drums, and vocals. Although other instruments such as strings, keyboards, organs, or horns do appear, the four-piece combo is the primary structure for indie bands. In the mid- to late 1990s it became more common for acts to have more members, more elaborate instrumentation, and less technophobia. Yet bands like the Smiths, Travis, Bluetones, or Bloc Party are fairly typical examples of indie bands, and they all consisted of young, beat combos with guitar, bass, drums, and a penchant for vocal harmonies.

However, the indie community also welcomes female performers. The Pixies, an American band from Boston that was considered to be an important influence on indie music, featured Kim Deal on bass. New York's Sonic Youth, just as influential, had a female bassist, Kim Gordon. In Lush, an indie band from North London, women played guitars and sang. My Bloody Valentine had female musicians on bass and guitar. Elastica had a female singer-guitarist, bass player, and guitarist. The Primitives, Echobelly, Sleeper, the White Stripes, Quasi, Kaito, and Stereolab, among many others, have also had either female lead singers or female instrumentation or both. In many ways, indie has been a pioneer in the trend of the co-ed band.

A majority of the terms used to describe indie as a genre are gender-coded as feminine: "fey," "wimpy," "weak," or "effeminate." For example, in his book on Britpop, John Harris describes a series of key 1980s indie artists as "anti-macho shrinking violet," "terrifyingly fey," and having a "melancholic take on indiedom's bookish wimpiness" (Harris 2003: 386). In describing a fight between some indie band members, a fan was quoted as saying "Indie boys don't fight so much as have flirty, fumbly scraps" (*NME*, January 8, 2005). Indie is often associated with a more feminine stance than that which was evoked by the American term "Alternative." Particularly in the United States, indie music fans differentiate themselves from Alternative fans. Indie is defined as the more harmonic pop sounds of British bands, and Alternative designates the more abrasive and heavy sounds associated with nu-metal, grunge, and punk.[31] Within the British indie music scene, however, punk, grunge, and garage musical styles associated with laddish masculinity are included in indie despite the fact that indie is generally represented as feminine in most public discourse.

Indie is also a category characterized by a particular sound. Indie music is primarily guitar rock or pop combined with an art-school sensibility. The sound of indie is characterized as "fey jangly guitar pop" (L.P., age seventeen), "chiming melodic guitar pop" (Harris 2003: 17), "wan, sappy boys with guitars and vague poetry" (*NME*, May 12, 1992), or "anoraky Sarah bands" (R.G., age twenty-five). The anorak, also known as a parka, is a simple jacket considered to be synonymous with wimpiness (Thorne 1993: 124). Sarah was a record label based in Bristol that released one hundred singles, most of which were considered to be delicate, effeminate, sugary pop songs, often criticized for being cloying. Still another indie music fan described the genre as "badly played and poorly sung, because the emphasis is more on the overall sound rather than on musicianship" (M.C., age twenty-eight).

Some of the bands that are considered exemplary of the indie genre use feedback and effects pedals (equipment that modulates the sound of the electric guitars), such as Jesus and Mary Chain, Ride, My Bloody Valentine, Mogwai, and Sonic Youth. Indie also includes the melodic and intricate Smiths, Madchester's Stone Roses and Happy Mondays (guitar bands that used dance rhythms), and the stripped-down and intelligent Folk Implosion and Pavement.[32] Other notable bands are the melodic Teenage Fanclub and Belle and Sebastian, the zeitgeist-hopping Blur, and bands with falsetto vocalizations, such as Radiohead, Suede, Muse, and Coldplay. Bands influenced by the artists of the 1960s are also part of indie's heartland, such as the Boo Radleys, the La's, and Oasis, as are garage artists such as the White Stripes, the Strokes, and the Hives. Others include danceable art pop bands such as Franz Ferdinand or Artic Monkeys and pretty much anything that had been released on Creation Records.[33] Indie has been claimed to be typified by the C86 compilation tape put out by *NME* in 1986 that featured bands such as Primal Scream, the Pastels, the Wedding Present, Big Flame, the Soup Dragons, the Wolfhounds, the Shop Assistants, and the Weather Prophets.[34] Other C86 bands, such as the Servants and McCarthy, later mutated to become the successful indie bands the Auteurs and Stereolab. These bands, many of whom were Scottish, had short songs with an underproduced, introverted quality that was characterized as "shambolic."

Simplicity is a dominant motif permeating indie musical practices. The indie genre values little elaboration in technology and in presentation. Indie generally places a high premium on the guitar and a low premium on production values. Much of indie music has a raw, underproduced quality, and occasionally even established and popular performers release four-track or eight-track recordings as opposed to the industry standard of twenty-four tracks.[35] There is also a financial aspect to releasing eight-track recordings; some independents do not have the funds to finance extravagant high-end studio productions. However, that established artists with resources also choose a deliberately underproduced sound demonstrates that simplicity is a feature of indie style, not just a function of necessity. Of course, there are notable exceptions to this anti–lavish production bias: My Bloody Valentine spent several years and well over £100,000 making their second album, *Loveless*, which nearly bankrupted then-independently owned Creation Records.

This simplicity of production is extended to indie song structures, which are often basic verse-chorus alternations: verse, chorus, verse, chorus, middle-eight, bridge, and chorus.[36] Indie bands generally favor a traditional three-minute pop song format, at times even omitting middle-eights and bridges. While the guitar is the most highly valued instrument in indie, there is a pride in the avoidance of the guitar solo—or any solo, for that matter.* The guitar solo is strongly associated with other guitar genres, such as progressive rock and heavy metal. Indie's streamlined song structures are one of the ways that indie differentiates itself from other rock genres that utilize the same instruments and exhibit a proclivity for the guitar. The rejection of guitar solos is descended from punk's negative reaction to the use of guitar solos by mid-1970s rock bands. Punk's response to progressive rock's expansionism was to call for a return to the primal traditions and excitement of rock and roll—to be direct and short (some songs were just a minute long), with simple verse/chorus structures performed with speed and raw power. As characterized by Dave Laing, who took his book's title from an Adverts song, the punks became *One Chord Wonders* (Laing 1985). Indie bands could be characterized as three-chord wonders: in an end-of-the-year roundup, *Melody Maker* summarized 1994, which was dominated by Merseybeat fundamentalism and a call for return to "authentic" music, as "three chords on yer Rickenbacker, three stripes on yer shoulder, and clichéd sub-Lennon 'attitude'" (*Melody Maker*, December 23, 1995). The reference to the "three chords on yer Rickenbacker" suggests the prevalence of indie's three-chord song organization and guitar orientation. "Three stripes on yer shoulder" refers to the popular style of Adidas athletic clothing (the plain shirts with three white stripes on the shoulders that were worn by many indie bands and fans in 1994 and 1995). For indie, a raw, simple, underproduced quality to sound suggests closeness to the wellspring of musical authenticity. Though it certainly expands on punk's call for the most streamlined musical productions, indie continues the punk legacy of simplicity, directness, and avoidance of extravagance in musical forms.[37]

Simplicity also extends to indie's musicianship and performance. Many indie bands are considered lacking in technical proficiency, but this is viewed as a positive attribute within the indie community, because musicianship is

---

* The distaste that many feel about solos is expressed in a popular joke: A man travels to an exotic destination and notices constant drumming. He asks a native how long the drumming will go on. The native looks nervous and says, "Very bad when drumming stops." The man decides to travel to the source of the drumming, asking locals along the way when the drumming will stop. Each answer is the same: "Very bad when drumming stops." He finally arrives at the source of the drumming, hears the drumming stop, and then a man calls out, "Bass solo!"

viewed as formal training that distances a performer from the essence of music. As one writer characterized the indie sound, "The groups were spirited rather than skilled instrumentalists—indie records often sounded as though they came from a place beneath musical society—an austere underside to the affluent city life above" (Cavanagh 2000: viii). Formal musical training is seen as a form of mediation between musician and music. One of the most damning insults that can be leveled at a musician is to be called a "muso," implying a technically proficient musician without spirit or emotional attachment to the music he or she plays. Formal training, like priesthood, is thought to take the musician down the known pathways of the establishment, to stand between the artist and true creativity. For example, Peter Hook of Joy Division and New Order attributes his development of a totally unique bass style to the early days when the band had "crap" equipment. He would play his bass at the top end of the fret board so that he could hear himself. For indie, music of value is self-taught rather than learned in elite, sanctioned institutional settings. This distaste for formal codes is also a characteristic of Romanticism, where the creative spirit is more important than an adherence to traditional procedures.

According to indie values, live performance should be simple and straightforward also. Indie is often represented as lacking stylization, dramatics, or exaggeration in the presentation of the band during shows. This simplicity of style is often made fun of in the press and by members of the community themselves: "They look like an indie band—glamour-free four-piece with girl bassist seek gig in litter bin." (*NME*, September 25, 1993); or "Tonight, they play a gig that could be sent on video to a far-off star system as a definitive explanation of indie rock: three anonymous blokes and one mildly charismatic woman play songs with verses and choruses on guitars while bouncing up and down in front of a similarly bouncing crowd of people wearing T-shirts advertising the band or other bands like them and sweating a lot" (*Melody Maker*, February 2, 1995). While these reviewers are critical of the bands they cover, both point out the generic convention of austerity in indie's style. Showmanship is thought to reside in the aesthetics of the music and the attitude projected by performers, rather than in theatrics.

Indie's overall style can be characterized as dressing down with a particular ethic that favors conspicuous poverty for performers. It is extremely modest. Often performers do not look much different from their audiences, usually selecting T-shirts and jeans to perform in, with some bands even stating that it would be inappropriate to wear clothes onstage different from their everyday wear. As one musician put it, "People wear street clothes and let the music talk. Not all this pretense" (L.B.). The general staples of indie dress are items bought at charity shops, band T-shirts, tatty jeans, and a penchant for the color black (Polhemus 1994). Charity shop items and band T-shirts are often too large or quite tight. The look of the everyday is the characteristic style of indie. For example, the Wedding Present, a band once called "the Princes of Indie City," was described as follows: "They talk ordinary. They dress ordinary. They embody the proud discredited dream of indiedom, namely that in every no-hope English ghost town there lurks a poet laureate of disaffected adolescence" (*NME*, January 14, 1989). Even mildly dressing up is considered glamorous. For example, in 1994 indie fans and the press touted a resurgence of glamor among indie bands. This new fashion traded the oversized T-shirts for a tighter, form-fitting style, the inclusion of athletic clothing ("three stripes on yer shoulder"), and an increased number of people wearing moderately glittery clothing. When comparing indie's version of glamor to other musical movements such as glam, punk, and metal (all genres that included stylized make-up and highly altered clothing), indie appears very tame indeed.

The "shoe-gazer" musical movement of 1991 reflected paradigmatic indie style in many ways. The shoe-gazers wore plain clothes, relied heavily on guitars, and maintained the typical indie haircut, the "straggly-haired bob" reminiscent of a schoolboy (*Melody Maker*, October 9, 1993), worn unkempt and somewhat unwashed (although from an American perspective, unwashed could describe most British hairstyles).[38] In the shoe-gazing style, performers often stood in the same location during shows. Journalists claimed that the shoe-gazer band Slowdive actually looked down at lyric sheets rather than their effect pedals because they were so raw and unseasoned that they had not even memorized the words to their own songs. The downward look of the shoe-gazers also suggested the introverted and inward-looking quality often attributed to indie music.[39]

Indie's styles of dress embody its themes of childhood and nostalgia. As Simon Reynolds noted in a central work recognizing the conventions of the indie scene:

Mixed with these items are overtly childish things—dufflecoats, birthday-boy shirts with the top button done up, outsize pullovers; for girls—bows and ribbons and ponytails, plimsolls and dainty white ankle socks, floral or polka-dot frocks, hardly any make-up and no high heels; for boys—beardless and bare-eared and tousled fringes. One garment above all has come to represent the scene—the anorak. . . . Some hard-core activists on the scene will go all the way and sport a satchel or duffel-bag and then they'll really look like a Start-Rite kid. (Reynolds 1989: 251)[40]

As Stephen Pastel of the band the Pastels put it, "The anorak was a style statement. It was saying: everything else is fucked up and we've got to get back. Closer to the start of things. Being children" (Cavanagh 2000: 190). The change from oversized clothing (resembling hand-me-downs from older siblings) to undersized clothing in light colors (reminiscent of clothes one has grown out of) was a resurgence of the "cutie pie" style of the mid-1980s with its tatty babydoll dresses, a style that "concentrated on asexual, preadolescent garments and accessories in soft pastel shades" (Polhemus 1994: 122). The adoption of charity shop items continues this nostalgic principle of indie, in which different periods of resale clothing are renovated and reintroduced as stylish. Indie's sartorial style owes much more to the mod tradition than to punk with androgynous males and females, a childlike sexuality, prevalence of anoraks, and the so-called ordinariness of their look (Laing 1969). In fact, at fairly regular intervals indie has mod revivals. Segments of the indie community dress up in finely tailored 1960s suits similar to those sported by the Beatles in their early days. In the early 2000s, there was another resurgence of 1960s fashion. Performers dressed uniformly, in suits (the Hives) or striking red and white colors (the White Stripes). Indie's clothes typically do not fit—either the person or the time.

The childlike conventions of indie extend not only to clothing style but to modes of physicality as well. Simon Reynolds observes: "Against the mainstream image of a desirable body—vigorous, healthy, suntanned, muscled for men, curvaceous for women—the indie ideal is slender, slight, pale of skin, childishly androgynous" (Reynolds 1989: 251). Producing this wan look requires a particular type of bodily discipline: a renunciation of food, exercise, and outdoor activities. The standard dress and physical style of the thin, clean-shaven, pouty-lipped schoolboy and the slender, androgynous, shorthaired female evoke a childlike appearance in the young adult. Indie bands may wear tailored suits that recall the 1960s or uniform clothes, but these are not representations of contemporary adulthood. Essentially, indie is a return to the past, either the past of one's own childhood or the past of the early 1960s, which, as Simon Reynolds astutely notes, is seen by the indie community as "like pop's childhood, when the idea of youth was still young" (Reynolds 1989: 254).

The very name "indie" indicates a community aligning itself with childhood: the word itself is a diminutive, and diminutives suggest smallness, childhood, affection, and, at times, derision.[41] Diminutive names are the appellations of childhood: Billy, not William; Robbie, not Robert; Nicky, not Nicholas. Indie is the diminutive community of independence. The rebellious clarion call of punk's reformation is made diminutive and humbled in the name "indie." Each of the associations of diminutiveness pervades indie ideology, even its tendency to ridicule itself. The American Alternative is spelled with a capital "A," while indie is spelled in the small, modest lower case. Diminutive indie longs for a return to an imagined childhood.

Post punk!

more on this!

Indie's valuation of the past over the present and future is evidenced by its technophobia. The anti-technological stance that permeates many aspects of indie results in indie fans being called Luddites by outsiders as well as insiders.[42] For much of its history, computer-generated sounds were not welcome in the genre. Using a drum machine is still considered somewhat heretical, although there have been a few notable exceptions to this rule. As electronic music has persisted, it has presented less of a threat as the new, and more indie bands have begun to incorporate electronica in a lo-fi style.[43] The indie sound emerged after a period of great innovation in the use of new electronic instrumentation. At the time of their debut in 1983, the Smiths' musical approach and use of a traditionalist four-piece beat combo was considered a deliberate return to earlier, simpler forms, a "back to basics" (*Melody Maker,* July 20, 1983). They were cited as being in stark contrast to the other popular electropop bands of the new wave era, who used cutting-edge electronic technology to produce their sound (*NME,* May 14, 1983). Indie's aversion to synthetic sound is revealed in its criticism of dance music's use of samples and programmed drum beats, which I will address later.

However, indie does not shun all technology. The electric guitar is the most highly fetishized element of indie music, and effects pedals (which digitally modify the standard tone of the guitar) are used extensively. Within indie, the use of the electric guitar is not considered a use of technology. In fact, the electric guitar is the traditional instrument within the genre. One therefore needs to consider indie's technophobia in terms of a dialectic between the future and the perceived past, between new and old. Past technology is taken for granted as traditional. It is new technology, new synthetic forms, that indie eschews, and because the new eventually becomes the old, the bar regarding what is acceptable continually moves along.

Several of the most popular indie bands of the mid-1990s, such as Pulp, began to resuscitate synthetic sounds and synthetic clothing fabrics for the indie music community. However, contemporary indie artists use synthetic sounds in a nostalgic manner. When artificial sounds are employed, indie bands prefer the earliest versions, such as the early Casio machines, Hammond organs, or 1970s synthesizers—the sonic equivalent of polyester. Pulp's use of synthetic sounds revitalized an earlier sound form. Interestingly, a number of the early prototypical independent artists and labels were not technophobic but were innovators in the use of electronic synthesizers and electronic sound. Factory, with their maverick upstart New Order, employed digital technology to dazzling effect. Goth, a music rage after the demise of punk that was often featured on independent labels, was not adverse to using synthesizers. Depeche Mode, Erasure, and Yazoo were trailblazers in the use of new digital and synthetic technologies on the powerful independent label Mute. That so many technologically advanced bands are considered forerunners of a genre that, at its core, opposes digital simulation sound technology is a provocative contradiction.

The anti-technological stance of indie is pronounced in the community's reluctance to fully embrace CD technology. Indie fans' preference for vinyl records over CDs is a principal reason they are so often considered Luddites. Many indie fans are self-styled vinyl junkies. Vinyl—specifically the seven-inch vinyl single format—formed part of the identity for the indie community in much the same way that the twelve-inch single was associated with dance music and deejaying. However, it must be noted that while indie fans are most likely to buy the seven-inch format, most indie fans have huge CD collections as well. Nevertheless, the indie community both nurtures and supports the continuance of vinyl; as I noted earlier, indie labels often put out limited-edition vinyl recordings. There were even singles clubs like Sub Pop or Creation that released singles exclusively in the seven-inch format. Whereas most majors release singles in three formats—CD1, CD2, and MC (cassette)—labels that cater to the indie audience release a vinyl format in lieu of one of the others.[44] For example, Domino Records in South London releases recordings primarily in two formats: CD and vinyl, as do City Slang, Big Cat, and Duophonic. Record labels that consider themselves part of the indie music community make a point to release on vinyl whenever possible.

For the indie community, CD exemplifies technology and vinyl represents its antithesis. This distinction is related, in part, to the nature of each medium. CDs are digital and vinyl is analog. Many indie fans feel that analog sound is superior to digital sound. I was often told by members of the indie community that CDs sounded either "metallic" or "too clean" and that vinyl sounded "warm." However, even this difference in sound is complicated, because most recordings are mastered digitally and then reconverted to analog to put on vinyl. Many indie fans find that even the addition of scratches and minor skips are an enjoyable part of listening to a vinyl music recording.[45] A skip on a CD results in a high-pitched, repetitive pulse that makes the track unlistenable; by contrast, minor augmentations to sound on vinyl recordings were likened to the "aging of a fine wine" (C.W., age twenty-five).

The physical appearance of CDs is also criticized within the indie community. The shiny metallic discs look high-tech compared with the matte-black surface of standard vinyl. For many indie fans, there is a certain amount of fetishism in the enjoyment of the purchase of a vinyl recording. Many fans discussed the smell and other sensual qualities of vinyl, its inner sleeve, its cover. Vinyl junkies inspect their records carefully before playing them. I was told, "Vinyl gives more information about the recordings. On vinyl, you can look at your record and you can see how long the songs are. You can see changes in music, and how much music there is on the record, by looking at the grooves" (R.G., age twenty-six). CDs have surfaces that are uniform to the naked eye and that impart only a fraction of the information that vinyl does. To the indie fan, CDs look anonymous, slick, and undifferentiated.[46]

The anti-CD position advocated by indie enthusiasts is evident in the discourse of bands. In an interview, the members of Flying Saucer Attack, a band on the independent record label Domino who had slogans such as "CDs destroy music" and "Buy Vinyl" printed on their CD-format releases, summarize their antipathy for the CD format:

> "I hated that Eighties rock sound, and it's sort of spilled over into an irrational hatred of digital," says Dave. "I don't even own a CD player. I just can't relate to CDs. It's not so much the way they sound as the things themselves, those horrible plastic boxes." "A piece of vinyl is a physical object—you can see the songs," concurs Rachel. "With a CD, it's like a satellite's beaming the music into your room." Continues Dave: "I am a very miserable person, right. Records are your friends. You can look at the song you're hearing; it's physically there in the spirally groove." (*Melody Maker*, October 14, 1995.)

Flying Saucer Attack differentiates between the two mass-produced, technological objects, emphasizing a semiotic dichotomy that identifies the CD as plastic and inorganic and the vinyl as organic. While both vinyl and CD are composed of plastic, CDs, composed of aluminum acetate, are generally packaged in a clear plastic jewel case while vinyl is generally in packaged in the more organic paper or cardboard. Flying Saucer Attack also contends that the vinyl recording brings the listener into intimate contact with the recording, while the CD is unrelated to the music produced from it ("beamed in from a satellite").

The desire to hold on to vinyl is not merely due to the technophobic stance of indie: there is a nostalgic element in maintaining the format of cultural artifacts associated with one's introduction into a field of interest. Flying Saucer Attack's comment that CDs are associated with the music of the 1980s indicates that, for them, vinyl harkens back to the era prior to that technological boom. Vinyl is thought of as the original form of musical recordings, and though it is a technologically mass-produced object, it has become traditional when contrasted with the newer CDs. For indie, as for many cultures, most individuals believe tradition is what one did in one's own childhood. While indie fans wax lyrical about seven-inch singles (the format in which most of the indie fans during the tenure of this project had bought their first records), indie fans do not romanticize 78s or other early forms of recording technology. Thus, as indie ages and the community becomes composed of younger individuals with little experience of vinyl, there is a great likelihood that the seven-inch will disappear. One indie label boss commented to me that "there is a romance to vinyl that CDs don't have." Allied with the associations of tradition, analog, and nostalgia and contrasted with the metallic, synthetic, digital, modern CD, plastic vinyl has been transformed by the indie community into an organic, originary art form.

Indie's eschewing of the technological is not confined to sound and format. Indie possesses an overall ethic of technological nonproliferation. Live performance is championed over prerecorded music. This is a continuation of a punk ethic that privileged live music as direct and immediate over musical recordings as constructed and removed (Laing 1985: 53). Bands are considered "proper" if they perform convincingly live.[47] Bands that cannot deliver onstage even when they have fine albums become objects of speculation and commentary: though occasionally excusable, this inability typically indicates that the band is a sham. The use of synthetic sound under the guise of being a live ensemble is regarded as a form of moral turpitude.

One thing about Jesus Jones that sticks in the throat is how little has been made of their dubious image as a band. In some puritanical corner of my mind, this carefully nurtured rock and roll fallacy indicates some kind of moral corruption. The fact that multi-instrumentalist Mike Edwards works in solitude, flanked by banks of technology as opposed to his hired hands (which is all, in effect, the rest of the band are) seems a bit of a con, really. Big deal, say you. This is 1993, Mr. Indie Saddo, not a world of residencies at the Reeperbahn and paying your dues. (*NME,* January 23, 1993)

The reference to the Reeperbahn, the district in Germany where the Beatles had a residency prior to their success, points to the idea that a "real" band is generated by performing in front of live audiences. The performance of music in a live setting is a measure of a band's authenticity within the genre.

While many of its traditional generic components represent a longing for, a connection with, and an appreciation of preceding eras and musical antecedents, indie does not advocate the wholesale restoration of previous musical trends and eras. While it is nostalgic, indie is not revivalist. The reintroduction of previous styles is to be met with a contemporary sensibility—the present longing for the past is not the same thing as the past itself. Although indie has a playful, youthful quality, it is constantly undercut with melancholy: "Although the cutie look was essentially fun and playful, underlying its childlike innocence was a deep-rooted sense of gloom and doom" (Polhemus 1994: 122). The indie fan wears black on the outside because black is how he feels on the inside. Indie aspires to a return to a childlike state of innocence for those who are on the brink of adulthood. This unappeased longing is the wellspring of a melancholic lyrical focus: loss of love, loss of innocence, loss of the 1960s. Although traditionalist and nostalgic, the indie community nevertheless emphatically believes that it is a domain of artistic innovation and originality while still calling upon the values and tools of the past.

Puritan tenets permeate the generic conventions of indie. For Puritans, lavish ritual, stately dress, and non-essential embellishment created distance between the individual and the divine. Puritans removed ornaments from houses of worship, substituted ordinary dress for clerical vestments, and held simplified services. Similarly, indie bands perform in everyday wear. Indie advocates simplicity in songs, modesty in adornment, modesty in consumption, and a particular type of physical discipline to acquire a look that suggests an aversion to worldly pleasures. Even the use of the lower case "i" in indie suggests modesty. Indie advances a program for music that is basically simple, in structure, in production, in accoutrements, and in style, in order to foster a pure, unmediated experience of music. In indie's generic characteristics, we find again the underpinnings of Puritan ideological practice.

Romantic tendencies also sit in an uneasy reconciliation within indie's Puritan conventions. In indie, we find none of Romanticism's fanciful exaggerations, opulence, or imaginative posturings. Yet a Romantic strain does exist in indie's tendency to value the natural or organic, in its introspection, and in its preference for ordinary people. The untrained artist combines the simplicity of Puritanism with the Romantic notion of the untrained artistic genius whose intuition, instinct, and spirit govern his artistic creations.

Indie promotes a return to basics: the simple, the ordinary, and the untrained. All superfluous elements should be stripped away to purify music. The Puritans, too, called for a return to basics, a restoration of the moral ideals of Christianity, a purification of the Church of corrupting excess and a return to a true, unmediated relationship between the divine and the congregant. A desire for a return to the past informs the beliefs, styles, customs, and practices of indie. Indie's childlike style is a longing for a vanished past. At its core, indie's generic features correspond with Puritan metaphysics—it is anti-technological, anti-futuristic, and longs for the presumed purity of the past.

Indie as an Ethos

Complete control, even over this song . . .
The Clash

In the broad strokes I have used to paint indie as a specific sound with generic conventions, I have not yet discussed the very real elements of diversity that exist within the indie category. For each of the general principles there have been bands that defy the conventions and are still considered indie. There are indie bands that top the mainstream charts, indie bands on major labels, indie bands with major distribution, indie bands that utilize complex studio-produced sounds that cannot be played live, and indie bands that make eight-minute songs. There are even a few indie bands that do not use a guitar. If indie is a genre of music recognizable by a sound or mode of distribution, then how are bands that defy these conventions incorporated into the category? The Tindersticks are a fine example. They were signed to This Way Up, which was owned and distributed by a major company. Numerous members played a variety of instruments, including strings. The band did not have a typical indie sound but instead featured music that suggested a combination of soul and crooning, rarely written in 4/4 timing. The members wear subdued suits. Since a band like the Tindersticks can defy indie's generic conventions yet still be considered part of the indie world, it is clear that there is more involved in the constitution of indie as a genre than a distinctive sound, fashion, mode of production, and performance style. Indie is an ethos, an attitude. Indie, much like hip-hop, is a way of life.

For many, indie is the spirit of *independence,* being free from control, dependence, or interference. Self-reliance, not depending on the authority of others, has been the guiding value of indie music, as has the autonomy of the artist. For indie, its paradigmatic models are the "independent" record shop, the "independent" distribution company, the "independent" record label arising from individual entrepreneurship, and the indie band appearing on the roster of an independent label, at least in its formative stage.[48] Independence in music means actively eschewing a centralized corporate hierarchy where decisions are made by distant executive bodies. As Tony Wilson, one of the heads of Manchester's Factory Records, put it, "The theory of independence was discovered in the act of putting out your own records, doing very well, being friends with your artists, and not ripping them off. And by 1981 we were all doing it" (Harris 2003: 8). Independence, the notion of self-expression and self-control, pervades all aspects of the indie community.

Artists' control over their music has been a central element in the notion of independence: "The propelling idea, at least since 1976, can be summed up in the one simple phrase: 'release your own records'" (*NME*, February 8, 1986).[49] On one's own independent label, musicians have total control over the recording, artwork, and whatever else went into the particular production, with no intervention by establishment professionals. Therefore, the record that appeared in stores would be the unmediated musical vision of the artist.

While it has become less common for indie bands to set up one-off labels to release their own records, the independent record label is considered to continue the fight for the performers' artistic control. As one label boss remarked, "Indie is an attitude and dance labels are the indie ones now. Where someone will put out a record from their bedroom and it will sell something like 3,000 copies. This is what indie has been" (*NME*, July 18, 1992). This comment points to individual entrepreneurial spirit in a nonconventional setting and smallness as both being constitutional elements of indie. Indie is the commitment to individual artistic expression. The individual is able to envision an idea, produce it, and then distribute it to the public without intervention. The independent label is seen to have the same agenda as the artist, delivering unmediated music to the public. One of the reasons bands sign to independent labels is the expectation of artistic control and limited intervention by the independent record company.[50]

There are other general characteristics about indie's ethos. Indie is generally a middle-class phenomenon, yet it idealizes the working class with its supposed "authentic" experience. Bands, in particular, are criticized if they are perceived as coming from a background of affluence. Those from the upper class or upper middle class often obscure their backgrounds. The indie fan is usually educated and paradigmatically is a university student. In Britain, most fans range in age from about fifteen to twenty-nine, with 80 percent under the age of twenty-five.[51] In a general way, the discourse of indie is politically liberal, reflecting the middle-class value of empathy; there is little tolerance for racism, sexism, or homophobia. The letters pages of the indie press and magazines are constantly filled with diatribes against racism, the BNP (British Nationalism Party), and the rise of neo-Nazism, despite the fact that very few members of the indie audience are ethnic minorities. *NME* and *Melody Maker* were regularly characterized as having a middle-class, white male, liberal agenda. These positions are fairly characteristic of student populations in England, as well as other youth music communities, and are not particularly unique to indie. However, a unique component of the indie ethos is the representation of indie as miserable and pathetic.

Indie as Pathetic

*Regarding, then, Beauty as my province, my next question referred to the tone of its
highest manifestation—and all experience has shown that this tone is one of sadness.
Beauty of whatever kind, in its supreme development, invariably excites the sensitive soul to tears. Melancholy is thus the most legitimate of all poetic tones. . . .*
Edgar Allan Poe

wishing for a time that never was. . . .
Doves

Indie is strongly associated with the mien of pathos. Indie fans are often
represented as being depressed, obsessive loners. Invoking the image of the
anorak, as one indie fan did in his definition of indie, not only aligns indie
with childhood but also associates it with trainspotting. In Britain, the
trainspotter is an emblematic image of pathetic obsession. Trainspotters
can be seen in anoraks at the end of rail platforms, waiting to glimpse trains
and record their sightings in ledgers. While it is important to the trainspotters, the meaningfulness of this obsession eludes outsiders. For many, indie
connotes a similar compulsive obsession with esoterica.

Many indie fans have comprehensive collections of their favorite artists
and/or favorite label releases. Indie and dance both have audiences that
purchase recordings by label without knowing the particular artist or song.
For many indie fans, a comprehensive collection includes not merely a copy
of every track, but every track on every format in which it was released.
Record companies have been able to exploit the purchasing habits of obsessive British fans. The general recognition that some fans want to have complete collections resulted in rampant multi-formatting, in which recordings
are released with different tracks and versions of songs for each format.[52]
Since the collector fan often purchases a copy of each format, releasing a
single in several formats can bolster a single's position on the charts. This
process was later curtailed by limiting the number of formats that would be
eligible for inclusion in the charts.[53] The practice of comprehensive collecting of what appears to the outsider to be obscure and irrelevant materials
generates the comparison with the trainspotter.

The indie community parodies its own proclivities and outsiders' criticism of them, demonstrating a community enmeshed in self-referentiality.
Indie fans will at times call themselves dull or boring because of their obsession with the small details of their records or record collections. The press
as well as indie fans use the term "saddo" when referring to themselves; a
saddo is a sad and lamentable person. The term "indie" itself is, at times,
applied in general conversation to indicate a shortcoming or something
small and not particularly well done. The image of indie as pathetic is so

prevalent that an international conference held in Dublin in 1995 on the topic of "the pathetic" suggested indie music in its call for papers.

Indie ideology is indeed characterized by pathos. The word "pathos" is the hybrid of the Greek roots *path* (feeling), *pathia* (suffering), and *patheikos* (sensitivity). Pathos represents being prone to suffering and the quality of evoking a feeling of pity or compassion. The most common characterization of indie fans and artists is that they are prone to extreme suffering because of their sensitive, introspective natures. Dele Fadele of *NME* characterized indie as an "inward-gaze" (*NME,* December 12, 1992). This quality of intro-spective sensitivity has Puritan resonance: the internal and passionate experi-ence of the numinous was essential in Puritan philosophy. As Ed Ward points out, "In Puritan religious thought there was originally a dynamic equipoise between two opposite thrusts, and tension between an inward, mystical personal experience of God's grace and the demands for an out-ward, sober, socially responsible ethic, the tension between faith and works, between the essence of religion and its outward show" (Campbell 1987: 219). Thus, the inward experience of profound personal sensitivity is part and par-cel of indie's Puritan metaphysics.

There are certain topics that recur as themes and tropes within indie song lyrics and reflect the motif of pathos in the indie community. Indie songs are often brooding and contemplative and address the issue of not belonging:

What the hell am I doing here? / I don't belong here—("Creep" by Radiohead)

I'll be the corpse in your bathtub / Useless—("Newborn" by Elbow)

I sit all alone / Alone is all I'll ever be—("Season" by Ash)

i can show you sadder poetry / than you ever dreamed there could be / i know all the saddest people / most of them are dead now—("Save a Secret for the Moon" by the Magnetic Fields)

I think I'm drowning / asphyxiating . . . —("Time Is Running Out" by Muse)

So you go, and you stand on your own / and you leave on your own / and you go home and you cry / and you want to die—("How Soon Is Now" by the Smiths)

These are a mere sampling of the vast compendium of depressed, despon-dent, and disconsolate lyrics that characterize indie's core. Many indie song titles also convey a sense of despairing paralysis: "Isn't Anything," "Noth-ing Much to Lose" (My Bloody Valentine); "Nowhere," "Decay," "Para-lyzed" (Ride); "She Is Suffering" (Manic Street Preachers). More aggres-sive or angry lyrics reflect angst, an introspective mode of aggression (see the *Guardian,* July 7, 1995). This second mode is best summed up by the band Nirvana's often-quoted title "I Hate Myself and Want to Die."

Indie's introspective pathos and obsession is reflected in its playful self-mockery. Nowhere does this acknowledgment and ironic self-criticism manifest itself with more regularity than in the weekly press:

Readers, let me tell you about my life. I'm called David, and I am an Indie guy. Every day, I play my Indie Records and put on my "Captain America" T-shirt, just like the one Kurt Cobain used to wear. I like to be called Dave, but the neighbors call me sad. Nobody understands me, but I am a fun person. When I am not hanging outside the Camden Falcon hoping to get a glimpse of Steve Lamazq [sic], I spend time advertising in the music papers for pen pals to go to gigs with. . . . The lyrics are pretty profound too. . . . Do you think if I carry their record around it'll help me get a girlfriend? (*Melody Maker,* January 29, 1994)

Stereolab are now just about the perfect indie art rock band. That's not necessarily a compliment. It means they don't sell millions of records, you can't dance or mosh very well to it, and shagging to it is a bit of a tall order. But they are so many of the things wet dreams are made of for wannabe art-pseudish young people with skin problems. (*NME,* September 25, 1993)

Instead of sharpening their wits on illicit sex, drugs and joy-riding, they chose to stay in their bedrooms, wank and listen to their Poppies, Neds, and Megas records. (*NME,* March 20, 1993)[54]

Here, being a member of the indie community is presented as highly unattractive. The last passage in particular speaks directly to the image of the pathetic indie fan, isolated in the private space of the bedroom, with music as his only sexual outlet.[55] The bands that are referenced—Pop Will Eat Itself (Poppies), Ned's Atomic Dustbin (Neds), and Mega City Four (Megas) were all known as "T-shirt bands," thus characterized because of the bold slogans on their T-shirts and their fans' habit of sporting them. T-shirt bands were described as outgoing, effusive, and fun. However, the *NME* passage above demonstrates that even though there are some lively and exuberant movements in indie, in postscript they too are represented in terms of the "pathetic" indie fan isolated in his bedroom. Both serious and comical, indie's self-parodies play with a negative caricature of its own identity. Indie accuses itself of being "elitist and insular" (*NME,* February 5, 1994), "pitiful, tedious, hyper-elitist indie saddos" (letters page of *Melody Maker,* November 6, 1993), or, most comprehensively: "Congratulations, you win a year's subscription to Luddite Muso Indie Saddo Magazine" (*NME,* January 2, 1993).

Clearly this introversion and valorization of pathos and melancholy are expressions of the Romantic thread in indie music. In indie, one finds the exaltation of emotion and sensitivity, the sorrows and sufferings of young Werther, the privileging of creative spirit over an adherence to formal rules, and an interest in specific cultural/local identities.[56] Colin Campbell accounts for the development of Romanticism in terms of a cultivation of emotional sensitivity and responsiveness as "a further evolution of that essentially pietistic current of feeling" traceable to Puritanism (Campbell 1987: 179). This sensitivity luxuriates in the pleasure of emotional experience, and the more acute the emotions are, the more profound and morally validating the experience is:

The later Romantics . . . widen[ed] the range of emotions from which pleasure could be obtained. . . . In this respect, the Romantics came to emphasize that algolagnic sensibility, or "agony," which Praz considered unique to them; a delight in the "Medusean" beauty or the pleasure that comes with pain. . . . Disillusionment, melancholy, and an intense longing for the perfect pleasure that will not die, thus become characteristic attitudes of the dedicated romantic pleasure-seeker. (Campbell 1987: 192)

In indie, this Romantic thread meets with the Puritan thread of asceticism, nostalgia, and intense moral rigor and helps us to partially understand indie's pleasure in pathos. Indie fans love their music. They get an inordinate amount of pleasure from listening to it and talking about it. They see depth and value in the examination of personal suffering. The Romantic/Puritan duality manifests itself in the elevation of pathos and melancholia as the highest forms of experience. Indie does have songs about happiness, enjoyment, and playful youthful pursuits, but these are far less valued than the songs of pathos. When I asked informants for examples of sad or melancholic songs, they could all tell me lyrics right off the top of their heads, but when I asked for examples of happy or upbeat songs, I was invariably told that they would have to get back to me (which they seldom did). The Puritan distrust of sensual pleasures and valuing of the profound internal emotional experience of the divine finds its common ground with the Romantic in emotional melancholy. While Romanticism exalts the experience of all of the senses, indie fetishizes sensitivity and suffering. Unrequited longing is held as superior to physical satisfaction. Emotional Puritanism and Romanticism overlap, producing pathos as the most elevated form of emotional experience.

Indie's ethos can be summed up by two major spirits—*independence* and *pathetic melancholia*. The Puritans and Romantics were nonconformists, born of rejection. This spirit of nonconforming independence suffuses the infrastructural and generic characteristics of indie. Within indie, independence conveys rejection of the status quo and an embrace of the spirit of rebellion. However, indie's relationship to melancholy is even more interesting. Pathos and melancholia function as badges of worthiness indicating that one is a genuine disciple. For indie, suffering is the sign of elect status—it demonstrates sensitivity and depth of character. Because of their contemplative melancholia, indie fans view themselves as the elect who can recognize *the truth in music*.

Indie as a Mode of Aesthetic Judgement

Can you feel the sadness in our love?
It's the only kind we're worthy of . . .
The Divine Comedy

While indie fans prefer indie music, other styles of music are at times embraced by the independent community. To understand how and why indie includes the music that defies its own conventions, one must understand that one of indie's motivating principles is its assessment of value in recordings and performers. Indie conceives of itself as discriminating; community members maintain that they possess the ability to assess the true value of music. Viewed from this perspective, indie is a mode of evaluation that assesses the relative value of various types of music and bestows critical acclaim on what it believes is the best. Indie fans' preference in music is not thought to be due to their own personal tastes but arises from their belief that there are objective criteria to support their claims. It is not that they believe indie is the only music of value; rather, indie members consider themselves anointed music disciples whose acute sensitivity allows them to recognize any music of value. It just happens to be that most of the music that they consider valuable is the music of their own community. As an *NME* journalist put it in an article discussing the meaning of indie, "At its best, 'indie' is this strange industry that flourished and is still flourishing in the aftermath of punk, and has made half or two thirds of all the most interesting music in the world . . . mountains of good music" (*NME,* July 18, 1992). Indie is not merely a sound with generic conventions but a discursive practice of critical judgment as well. Indie divides the world into a musical hierarchy in which indie aficionados identify themselves as those who can recognize quality in music. Hence, their music of standard preference, indie, must be the music of the highest quality. As one of my informants put it: "I know what indie is: if it's good and I like it, it's indie" (L.F., age twenty-eight).

At times, other clearly different styles of music are embraced and incorporated into the indie aesthetic canon. Strikingly, American hip-hop and rap bands often come to Britain and find themselves with an indie audience. Public Enemy, Kayne West, and Gangstarr have appeared high on the bill at the Reading festival, the annual and preeminent indie music festival since 1989.[57] Bands such as OutKast and Cypress Hill have a large indie following in the United Kingdom in contrast to their hip-hop fan base in the United States. Rap's perceived "realness" and radical form attract indie critics and fans alike. The music of other genres accepted into the indie canon generally conforms in either its production or attitude to one or more of indie's values.

Other forms of music are covered by the indie music press, but in general only as a token sampling to justify to the community that the press really has surveyed all forms of music and to assert indie as the arbiters of artistic value. As a reader wrote to the letters page, "I think the *Melody Maker* has given music of all types a fair hearing and I hope it continues" (*Melody Maker*, March 12, 1994). This version of a fair hearing means that on occasion one finds a review of the re-release of a John Coltrane album or a feature piece on a jungle artist. Only one or two of the fifty-two covers a year of the weekly press are devoted to black or Asian artists that specialize in other genres of music. As one letter writer eloquently put it, "While your coverage of indie, dance, and U.S. rock is as good as anyone could reasonably expect, I do think that any claims you make to a diversity of coverage will always carry with them a hollow ring until you finally deal with that big bad booga [*sic*] man that is black music" (*NME*, October 9, 1993). Interestingly, it was during the time of the punk reformation of the mid-1970s that the weekly press began to specialize. Previously, the weekly press had large sections devoted to jazz, folk, blues, country, and rock.

Publications nurturing indie music articulate a discourse of quality, not genre. Perhaps the nature of indie's critical discourse of aesthetic assessment is best examined by looking at *NME's* list of the one hundred greatest albums of all time (see appendix 1). In justifying its list, as well as preparing for the inevitable onslaught of outraged letters regarding oversights, the introduction stated that "the results show that the *NME* is still a remarkable broad church, happy to welcome Coltrane, Sinatra, Marvin, Beefheart, and Dusty as well as the many illustrious guitar abusers that have defined this paper's heartland" (*NME*, October 2, 1993). In this move, the *NME* journalists position themselves as evaluators of a broad range of music who can then use their expertise to judge the relative merit of all artists' productions. It is more accurate, however, to call the list *indie's* most influential records. The top ten on this list strongly favor bands that are most often named as influences on indie musicians. Nevertheless, the list also includes a perfunctory and superficial sampling of other genres. Here, the legendary indie band the Stone Roses is located at number five, while the only recording of Michael Jackson on the list, *Off the Wall*, is at ninety-three. This rhetorical strategy crystallizes most visibly when reviewing albums of the 1980s, the decade during which indie emerged as a distinct category of music (see appendix 2). More than 50 percent of their top fifty albums of the 1980s were indie, and Manchester's Stone Roses was given top billing for this decade.

Since indie's discourse of aesthetic evaluation privileges indie as the very embodiment of quality, indie fans often balk when other genres of music get significant airtime on the radio or television. Thus, when both fifty- to eighty-page weeklies simultaneously introduced four-page sections devoted to dance and clubs, an avalanche of protest letters arrived from outraged readers suggesting bandwagon jumping or abandonment of indie music. A journalist's response: "We'll continue to cover the *best* music from both fields. We're no more likely to give house room to an uninspired, formulaic club cut than to a bunch of talentless guitar droners. We crave excellence, whatever the genre" (*Melody Maker,* February 26, 1994). When an occasional letter writer points out the discrepancy between this assertion and the quantitative content of the paper, the token sampling of indie's broad church is hauled out and recited in litany.

The privileging of the indie community's ability to recognize value in music is starkly illustrated by *NME's* campaign that "the BRITs" should be "the BRATs." The BRITs is the name of the annual awards ceremonies of the British Phonographic Institute (BPI). Here, critical recognition is bestowed upon musical artists in a British equivalent of the American Grammys. As in the United States, there is often a great disparity between what music critics think is worthy and what the BPI thinks is worthy. *NME* decided to create its own set of awards, called the BRATs, insisting that their nominations were the truly deserving award recipients.[58] A reader criticized this move in the typical exuberant inkie letter-writing style: "You miserable losers. Just because none of your sad, derivative, outdated indie bands received BRIT awards, you deem them to be a failure and a music industry marketing fix" (*Melody Maker,* March 5, 1994).[59] The quality of the acts that had won BRITs was critiqued by a *Melody Maker* writer: "Whether this was because record companies find it easier to flog recognized (and crap) brand names, or because most people have inherently bad taste, is still to be determined" (*Melody Maker,* March 12, 1994). For the indie fan, a preference for popular music outside the indie canon is synonymous with poor aesthetic judgment, while appreciating indie constitutes enlightened taste.

Ironically, the BRAT awards soon appeared superfluous, because a year after their inception, the BRITs and the BRATs overlapped for the winners in many categories. Several bands that had been championed in the weeklies had crossed over to mainstream chart success with the explosion of Britpop. This resulted in several of the inkies' favorite indie bands winning BRITs. Additionally, the music industry had inaugurated the annual Mercury Prize for best album of the year, the musical equivalent to the Booker Prize in literature. The Mercury Prize habitually goes to bands championed in the indie music weeklies. This award was won by Primal Scream (1992), one of the C86 bands; Suede (1993), a band dubbed "the Best Band in Britain" on

John this is clear. Harris better!

the front page of *Melody Maker* before even a single had been released; M-People (1994), a dance band that had consistently received good reviews in the weeklies and had close connections to the independent music scene in Manchester; Portishead (1995), a trip-hop band, another favorite of the inkies that was initially supported by the indie fan base; and indie stalwarts Pulp (1996).[60]

Indie is often privileged in the broader media as the genre where music and art overlap. A discriminating art-school mentality permeates much of indie. Indie has often been associated with aesthetic movements in the fine arts, where music is combined with an intellectual perspective. Many indie bands form during musicians' tenures at art institutions, and the education that performers receive in those settings is considered to influence their musical productions. Indie music often issues from the same wellspring of ideas that generates other aesthetic movements, and this connection can be seen in the intellectual and artistic reference points scattered across indie lyrics—surrealist films, underground books, existential philosophers, modern art, performance theory, Romantic poets, and Shakespearean plays. Indie music's points of reference are other elite forms of artistic expression that share the same belief that artistic expression takes precedence over commercial concerns. Independent labels and bands often self-consciously apply intellectual, philosophical, and semiotic concepts. At the same time, their love of the working class means that these serious highbrow pretensions are met with a playful dismissiveness. This combination of high art and no-nonsense disregard of traditional values echoes punk's combination of situationalist art and vulgarity (Hebdige 1979, Marcus 1990).

Indie's modes of assessment of artistic merit closely parallel the academic and commercial art establishments' discourse on value in artistic production. Indie's criteria are often applied to rock and pop in general. The result is that the music that indie enthusiasts prefer is then regarded by much of the general media as having the privileged position of art, and a small specialist community secures an extremely strong voice in the public discourse about music. While there may be just as many (or more) dance fans or mainstream chart fans, their aesthetic value systems do not dominate the public discourse on music. The indie community has been very effective in asserting the legitimacy of its critical valuation system, garnering a great deal of coverage in print, on radio, and on a significant number of television programs to boot. The extent of indie's print coverage is quite impressive. The weekly press is devoted to indie. *Select, Q,* and *Vox* give premium coverage to indie bands.[61] Additionally, the weeklies are an important training ground for music journalists and public personalities. Many journalists, radio disc jockeys, literary music writers, and television presenters who cover music have been writers for *NME* or *Melody* some point in their careers.[62] It is little wonder, then, that the system of the indie community is often conflated with the aesthetic sical discourse in Britain in general.

The weekly press plays a commanding role in establishing the d_____ around any artist within British music criticism, often taking the first critical stand. For example, when Primal Scream released the album *Give Out But Don't Give Up,* the follow-up to their wildly successful and critically acclaimed dance album *Screamadelica,* a journalist in one of weeklies called the band "dance traitors." This description was reformulated as a question ("Are Primal Scream dance traitors?") and discussed in subsequent reviews in monthlies and in broadsheet papers. The stance taken in the weeklies is often the defining position to which other journalists respond in their commentary on a particular artist, in part because journalists read other journalists. Moreover, press officers compile press coverage and then send an artist's previous press clipping to different journalists to prepare for a new article or review. Thus, there is an insular recycling of commentary on early press coverage. A small incident related by a band in an early article or review can snowball and dominate a band's interviews for years. The weekly press's publishing timetable produces the earliest articles read by subsequent journalists.

The voice of indie is also strong internationally. Music industry personnel and music fans in other countries read the British weekly music press. *NME* is available in Europe, the United States, and Japan. Most American record companies have an *NME* sitting on a desk somewhere. Press packs are sent to journalists in all markets. An example of weeklies setting the tone of international discourse is the characterization of the Boston band Sebadoh in *Spin.* Lou Barlow, a member of the band, was described in *Spin* as "the most sensitive man in indie music"—a moniker bestowed on him by the weeklies after a particularly stupendous display of sensitivity at the Reading festival in England.[63] What becomes apparent is that the specialist indie music community has a huge influence in the transnational discourse on popular music.

It is important to understand that this discussion of critical assessment is not just about music journalism; rather, it is a discursive practice of the indie community itself. At a fundamental level, indie music fans consider *themselves* to be music critics. The letters pages of the indie press are filled with correspondences from indie aficionados who are outraged by reviews that contradict their own opinions. These are often followed by cogent (although most journalists might beg to differ) arguments in support of their claims. Critical analysis of music is also rampant in fanzines. British indie fanzines parallel the weeklies' format style. Fanzine writers evaluate music, performances, and artists and assert that their own assessments have more validity than the judgments of professional journalists.

The discourse of artistic assessment that includes the music of other traditions within the indie canon is the result of the indie members' desire to position themselves as the true scholars of music. In the domain of artistic assessment, indie asserts to the world that its members are the true disciples of music, with their ability to ascertain true music as opposed to false idolatry, to identify the authentic and eschew the counterfeit, to embrace quality and reject worthlessness. Hence, in their discourse of aesthetic value, indie fans designate themselves as the anointed ones who can recognize, through their own system of authenticity, the truth in music.

Perhaps nowhere else does indie's underlying theology manifest itself more than in its self-positioning as the arbiter of taste; in this way, members designate themselves as the spiritually elect. The ability to recognize beauty and value serves as an indicator of virtue. Once again Colin Campbell's discussion of the development of Purito-Romanticism is particularly apt as he traces the development of "taste" and ethics in the form of *sensibility* as a crucial moral quality. In Romantic theocracy "taste" becomes the essential indicator of spiritual merit: "The key attribute of taste became transformed into a capacity for seeing into the nature of sacred truth, relabeled 'imagination,' and used to link the aesthetic with the spiritual rather than the ethical. In consequence, the perception of beauty became linked to gaining of privileged insights" (Campbell 1987: 182). Later, he continues: "The middle classes, by contrast, true to their religious heritage, regarded taste as a sign of moral and spiritual worth, with an ability to take pleasure in the beautiful and to respond with tears to the pitiable, equally indicative of a man (or woman) of virtue" (Campbell 1987: 205). Correct aesthetic judgments are direct evidence of virtue. Thus "good taste" demonstrates one's elect status. Indie has been effective in that much of the community's musical taste has attained the privileged position of "art" in the broader cultural arena, as its successes with the Mercury Prize have shown. In defining themselves as arbiters of artistic merit, indie fans effectively portray themselves to both their own community and, less efficaciously but still influentially, to the transnational congress of musical producers and consumers, as true visionaries able to recognize music of real value.

The Mainstream Is a Centralized Hierarchy

An identity is often forged in opposition to the contrived images of others. To demonstrate what indie is, proponents advance images of others to show what indie is not; indie creates a representation of others to conjure an image of itself. The two categories that indie invokes most frequently are the over-generalized and under-examined category of "the mainstream" and the wildly diverse category of "dance." Indie's representations of dance and the mainstream are not necessarily accurate, but they are a means by which indie constructs an image of itself. The characterizations I describe below are indie's own, not ethnographic descriptions of dance or mainstream audiences or cultures.

From its very inception, indie music was considered to have an antithetical approach to the mainstream production of music. Here, "mainstream" designates the majority of music that appears in national charts and appeals to a broad cross-section of the public. The need to differentiate indie from the mainstream, particularly mainstream rock, is crucial, since many of the stylistic elements that define the indie genre could be used to describe rock generally (four-piece combos, the emphasis on the electric guitar, etc.). It is in the nuances in the application of standard instrumentation that indie differentiates itself from the mainstream. This difference is particularly evident in indie's production style. The DIY ethic of punk stood in stark contrast to the lavishly produced studio bands of the 1970s, the contemporaries of the punks, who would often take months to record an album and utilize all forms of technical wizardry during production.[64] Punk's bias against elaborate production was inherited and embraced by the indie community. Indie opposed mainstream's many stylistic flourishes, such as studio overdubbing or pre-programmed dance rhythms, hence indie's persistent lo-fi production style.

A key element that distinguishes indie from mainstream music is its "size." Indie connotes small, personal, and immediate, while mainstream evokes all that is enormous, distant, and unspecialized. Indie bands are seen to use grassroots campaigns and fanzine promotions, while mainstream music uses multimedia campaigns to achieve market saturation. Smallness for indie is a trope in its performance spaces, budgets, and popularity. The mainstream is stadium music, while diminutive indie is the music of small, intimate venues. The majority of successful indie bands play at venues that hold five hundred to two thousand people. However, festivals such as the Carling Leeds/Reading Weekend, Glastonbury, the V Festival, or T in the Park, where multiple bands perform, are exempt from this size prohibition. Indie fans oppose traditional large-scale arenas. Indie bands that become popular know that if they play a large stadium, many indie fans will see this as a conversion to the mainstream and will no longer patronize the band. Thus, the most popular indie bands attempt to circumvent this prohibition by playing their large shows in non-traditional locations that suggest a festival atmosphere or a one-off event. Blur, after it achieved massive success, arranged a stadium-sized show with multiple acts at Mile End, a non-traditional stadium often used for football matches, rather than at Wembley, where mainstream acts often perform. At the height of their popularity, the Stone Roses arranged a performance on Spike Island, another non-traditional large-scale performance space. In 2002, Pulp played a series of gigs in national forests.

Indie gigs are about being near to performers. Indie bands often mingle in the crowd before and after shows, and artists are easy to meet in these settings. Audience members regularly approach band members at shows. Several fans said having direct contact with performers was one of their favorite aspects of indie music. Indie also attempts to maintain an equal relationship between musician and audience member—hence the everyman trope and the similarity of dress between audience and performer. A major reason for indie's denigration of stadium shows is the distance created between the performer and the audience member, which is seen as an impediment to the direct experience of music.

This size distinction between indie and mainstream is not confined to the size of a venue but also extends to the relative success and popularity of a band. As one *NME* journalist put it, "Ever since the advent of 'Independence' as both a musical and business proposition, massive success has always been frown [*sic*] upon. The logic goes that if you reach millions of homes, you must have tailored your music for that very purpose, sold out to the corporate ogre and diluted any sparks of real life you once had" (*NME,* February 5, 1994). Indie's distaste for arenas such as Wembley is largely due to their size, although it has also to do with the community's occasional, but by no means consistent, distrust of popularity. As John Harris notes, "The most hard-bitten indie disciples seem to view mass market success as a pollutant of artistic purity" (Harris 2003: xv). In a particular segment of the indie community, once a member personally discovers a great band, he feels a certain proprietary right to the band. He will try to get other friends to like the band, but at the same time he feels that the band is "his." When the band becomes successful, his ownership feels diluted, as if some personal control over the artist has been lost. He will stop counting the band in his personal repertoire or will remind people that he liked it before anyone else did. It is common for people to brag that they saw some wildly successful band years earlier in a venue holding only one hundred people. Other indie gig goers continue to like a band after it has become successful but will refrain from seeing it at large venues, because they miss the intimacy of the small club setting. An indie band that becomes successful and plays stadiums instead of clubs may be transforming devotion into a mass production and is necessarily suspect. Turning away from a band merely on the grounds that it has achieved popular success is not a uniform reaction among indie fans. However, successful bands are scrutinized to make sure that they have remained true to their roots and have not been transformed by their success. The community looks to see if a band has been polluted by its exposure to the corrupting influences of the mainstream. Thus, indie sees popularity as an ethical issue, a perspective that includes a belief that a band is "morally superior because they are not successful" (Cavanagh 2000: 177).

Indie's proponents view indie as a rebellion against the mainstream and its morally bankrupt value system. Indie cultivates an image of rebelliousness as an alternative to corporate consumerism. Indie is not the only music genre that celebrates the image of the rebellion, however; because indie is a subcategory of rock, one would expect some of the same images to prevail in both.[65] This connection between rebelliousness and postwar musical productions that come under the rubric of rock and roll has resulted in a certain consistency in musical iconography. The leather jacket was popularized by Marlon Brando in the film *The Wild One* (1953). The use of working-class imagery within the film produced a sense of iconoclasm and seductive danger that remains a potent image associated with rebellion. Similar connotations are evoked by the Doc Martens boots associated with punk, some phases of indie, and American grunge. Despite being a primarily middle-class phenomenon, indie considers itself to be "down with" the working class, perceived as a wellspring of authenticity that is denied to the bourgeois class. Therefore, the behaviors and stylistic tropes of the working class are fetishized by the comfortable classes (a phenomenon common in academic settings as well). Manchester, home of several of the most important indie movements, is viewed as working class, and therefore bands with Mancunian dialects are valued for their "authentic" voices.

Indie's ideological stance contrasts with its own image of the mainstream as bloated, safe, clichéd, and banal. In this view, the mainstream is seen to produce "products" that are overprocessed and slick. Indie invokes the mainstream as a bogeyman full of avaricious Frankensteins, large corporations with their legions of men in suits, manipulating the gullible public by pandering to their worst instincts. As one *Melody Maker* journalist put it in a viewpoint piece, it is "music made with anaesthetized suburban housewives in mind—the same people their friends sell washing-up liquid to, with an equal amount of aesthetic concern" (*Melody Maker*, March 12, 1994). Indie, in contrast, creates an image of itself as taking the intellectual high ground, privileging aesthetic concerns over commercial interest. Often bands pride themselves on giving the audience not what they want but rather what the band thinks they need: My Bloody Valentine's 1992 tour show featured twenty minutes of modulated guitar feedback that sent many fans into venue lobbies. Indie finds the music of the mainstream hollow; in the words of a Smiths song, it "says nothing to me about my life." Indie, on the other hand, is meaningful. Indie music is filled with specific literary and political references, while the mainstream uses bland, repetitive clichés peppered with absolutes such as "never," "always," and "forever." Within indie's aesthetic discourse of evaluation, indie music reproduces the high art/low art dichotomy that marginalizes the study of popular music in the first place.

These contrasts do not occur in a vacuum but are part of an ideological drama played out within a moral universe. Thus, indie views mainstream's use of lavish production style, and its popularity, as corpulent, unoriginal, impersonal, and unspecialized. Indie sees its own lack of elaboration and its love of live performance as lean, personal, immediate, raw, and human. Each of the contrasts in musical practices between the different communities is submitted to subjective evaluation as an ethical concern. Thus, these contrasts in definition are reinterpreted by a community in value-laden terms that usually privilege the community doing the defining.

What emerges from this portrait of indie contrasted with the mainstream is an ideological system with implied moral stances in musical practices. These contrasts can be mapped out in Lévi-Straussian fashion:

INDIE	MAINSTREAM
independent labels	major corporations
gigs	stadiums
independent	centralized authority
local	global
intimate	distant
personal	impersonal
simple production	elaborate production
no guitar solos	guitar solos
modest	self-indulgent
live	prefabricated
self-made	other-made
authentic	phony
original	generic
specific	general
lean	fat
transit vans	tour buses
unprofessional	muso

raw	slick
austere	lavish
intelligent	insipid
substantive	empty
art	commerce

Indie positions itself in relation to the mainstream as an oppositional force combating the dominant hegemony of modern urban life. Any band that is seen as "chipping away at the facade of corporate pop homogeny" (*Melody Maker,* April 1995) is a positive addition to the indie fellowship.

One telling difference between indie and mainstream rock can be glimpsed in the importance that indie bands place on the avoidance of the guitar solo, which I discussed earlier. Some fans joke that indie bands can't do guitar solos because they can't play their instruments well enough, noting the contrast in the professional abilities of rock performers and young indie upstarts. However, eschewing guitar solos is regarded by most as a moral issue. Guitar solos are seen as self-indulgent, pretentious, narcissistic displays often likened to masturbation. The avoidance of guitar solos places indie as modest and unpretentious.[66] In general, indie inhabits a position of leanness and sexual austerity, though the latter waxes and wanes within indie. The "Madchester" scene of 1986 combined features of indie with dance's openness to drugs and sexual expression. Being tight, taut, and lean are positive attributes when noted by reviewers in their discussions of indie bands, and most bands manifest this notion of thinness physically as well.[67] In this sense, the emphasis on slender performers is a simulacrum of the ideological stance of indie in contrast to the mainstream. Indie views the mainstream as slovenly, bloated, corpulent, clichéd, excessive, sexually promiscuous, overripe, and rotting from decadence. Contrasts in genre function in the community as barometers of virtue.

The mode and manner of indie's debate with the mainstream is not new in British history. While the topic is different, indie's stance about appropriate music practices is analogous to arguments over the nature of appropriate worship set forth during the Reformation. Indie and the mainstream play roles in an ancient and continuing religious drama between Protestants and Catholics, Swift's Lilliputians and Blefuscudians. Indie fans are the Puritan reformers against the established Roman Catholic Church of the mainstream music industry. In its ideological endeavor, indie paints the mainstream in a manner similar to the Reformation's portrait of the Roman Catholic Church. The mainstream, like the Catholic Church, is depicted as a corrupt bureaucracy of clergy who are susceptible to bribery and appointed by higher authorities who are unrelated to local interests. It creates a caste of businessmen who exploit the masses for their own personal advantage. It is tantamount to a church that has deviated from the original purity of the musical experience. Indie views the mainstream as filled with empty rituals, featuring excessive flourishes and ridiculous costumes. The mainstream and majors are represented as a Catholic church filled with unscrupulous, dissolute men in suits who exploit the faithful and encourage indulgences. The mainstream is held to be a force that desecrates music by turning it into a commercial enterprise devoid of its sacred character.

Indie traces its heredity to the inception of protest in the music industry: the punk movement. The moment of punk itself was a reenactment of the philosophy and religious warfare of the Reformation, the moment when the corrupt autocratic and hierarchical "church" of the music industry was assailed by local organizations wishing to establish their own independent congregations who were able to (s)elect their own ministers. Punk assailed the existing church of music and demanded reform in both the production and the consumption of musical forms. Both indie and punk demand the purification of the existing liturgical order by stripping away the excessive accoutrements of the dominant system and replacing them with the lean and austere music, production, performance, and style, to become the "purest incarnation of the spirit of music" (Laing 1985: 23).

NME journalist Stuart Bailey once asked in a column soliciting views on indie, "Why are indie kids so tight-assed and elitist about their music?" (*NME*, July 18, 1992), but he may as well have asked why Puritans are so puritanical. Being "tight-assed and elitist" are fundamental tenets of the ideological system that produces the specific form of music and ritual practices he was attempting to define. The Puritans believed that they had purified their form of worship from all traces of Catholic and pagan influences. Indie is also a drive for purification. Indie attempts to free itself from anything that debases, pollutes, or contaminates music. The language of indie's musical discourse is peppered with religious overtones. Indie fans are called the "indie faithful" or "disciples." Various marketing reports characterize indie fans as "musical evangelists" who attempt to convert others to this style of music (IPC Music Press 1993). Indie fans are characterized as "purists" in their own discourse, as well as in marketing reports (EMIRG UK 1993). Indie's purists take up the Puritan gauntlet and continue the battle of reformation and transformation through the act of reform in the milieu of music.

Dance Is Not the Way the Future Is Meant to Feel

a happy day and then you pay . . .
Elliott Smith

Indie opposes itself to other musical sects. Just as the Reformation brought about a number of new religious sects, indie is not the only alternative to the mainstream church. Dance music is a vibrant youth phenomenon and a contesting UK musical community vying for the attention of the kingdom's youth. At times, indie grants a grudging respect to some of the sub-genres of dance, such as techno or trance, as fellow youth (and therefore protest) movements. But primarily indie views dance as another type of music to oppose.

Indie's technophobic stance obviously clashes with dance's apparent technophilia. Dance, a category that actually subsumes many musical styles, typically embraces the use of drum machines and synthetic sounds. Many dance bands use programmed drumming to achieve beats per minute or BPMs that are impossible to produce on manual drums. Programmed drums are just one of a plethora of dance music studio techniques employing synthetic, pre-programmed sounds and samples. Hence, indie sees dance as technologically produced, while indie is composed on conventional instruments. For indie, there is a high premium placed on creating one's own compositions. Bands are expected to write their own material, while much dance music is perceived by indie as written by someone other than its performer.[68] Dance producers are thought of as technological Svengalis who manipulate various sounds, including voices, as they see fit. Also, dance music often uses samples of other people's music. Dance acts use prerecorded material during performances if the artists perform live at all (and many do not).[69] For many, the use of prerecorded material invokes an association with lip-syncing, an indicator of inauthentic live performance. Dance's use of programmed sounds interpreted through indie's ideological frame is mechanistic, cold, and impersonal, while indie's use of live musicians is physical, immediate, and human.

DJ sets are artistic compositions arising from the combination of a variety of musics that are usually not created by the DJ. The DJ is a mixer who uses the sonic fragments to produce a new musical creation. The DJ set is an elaborate interplay between the artists, the mix, and the energetic response of club attendees.[70] The primary dance location is a club, whereas indie's is a venue. As its title suggests, dance music is for dancing; in contrast, indie music is for contemplation. Indie sees itself taking the intellectual high road, reproducing the Western dichotomy between mind and body and privileging the former over dance's embrace of the latter. However, this division is hardly clear in practice. Most major cities have indie dance nights at clubs, and some dance bands perform as live ensembles.

Indie and dance part ways on the value and use of the guitar as well. Indie is associated with its use and dance is associated with its absence. Using the guitar as a point of opposition may not be unique to indie's self-definition, either: in his *Vibes* review of the dance band Underworld, Ben Turner reports that a club goer at a dance show asked, "But how can they be any good? There's a bloody guitar on the stage! Can you believe it? A guitar!" (*NME,* March 12, 1995).

Indie publications often represent dance as anti-personality. Indie is represented as advocating "artists" and dance as "faceless." Facelessness refers to an ideology that is antithetical to the valorization of performers' personalities or individual charisma.[71] Facelessness is an issue in the dance community as well. Club DJs at times advertise nights as "no faces," meaning that acts that have become well known as personalities will not be played. Facelessness is also read into dance's practice of playing "white label" pre-releases on which no information is printed. In dance, this is seen as judging the music by its merits alone, but for indie it means anonymity. Several club acts, such as Transglobal Underground or KLF, used masks to cover their faces during shows. The quintessential image of dance music is found in the fluorescent yellow happy face. As Dave Haslam points out, "the exclusivity of the punk sneer was replaced by the embrace of the smiley face" (Haslam 2000: 133).

A key ideological divide between indie and dance focuses on the issue of pleasure, particularly physical pleasure. As stated by *The Face,* a pro-dance publication, indie philosophy "dictates that you achieve insight and fulfillment through your painful alienation from society and, in extreme cases, from pleasure itself" (*The Face,* August 1995). Dance espouses an indulgence in physical pleasure as the means by which one receives fulfillment and insight, which indie sees as Dionysian—orgiastic, frenzied, and undisciplined. Dance embraces all forms of pleasure: sex, dancing, and drugs (ecstasy in particular). Hence, dance and indie propose two different ways of achieving musical communion: dance, through the gratification of physical desires, and indie, through physical denial. Dance is "celebratory," while indie is "earnest and self-denying" (Harris 2003: 11). The dance community sees the indie fan as "the weirdo for whom sex and drugs holds no appeal" (*The Face,* August 1995), while one indie fan described the dance fan as "a mindless kinetic freak" (K.B.).

Dance and indie are not always opposing cults. There was a short period in 1988, the second British Summer of Love, where indie and dance came together for a short time. Throughout the United Kingdom, with its leading light at the Haçienda Club in Manchester, there was a period of great cross-pollination of indie and dance music. Most famously, the Stone Roses and Happy Mondays produced songs inspired by the dance floor. While indie's usual drug of choice is alcohol, during the Summer of Love many indie fans experimented with dance club drugs: ecstasy for the experience of euphoric physical pleasure and speed for dancing until daybreak. In indie, the use of drugs is usually encouraged solely in performers and at the annual summer festivals (which are, admittedly, indie bacchanalias). However, indie soon reasserted its position that dance is empty, meaningless, and eventually detrimental. In 1995 Pulp, the indie superstars, wrote "Sorted for E's and Wizz" about the period of indie's dalliance with dance:[72]

Oh is this the way they say the future's meant to feel? Or just 20,000 people standing in a field. And I don't quite understand just what this feeling is, but that's okay 'cause we're all sorted out for E's and wizz. And tell me when the spaceship lands 'cause all this has just got to mean something . . . Everybody asks your name, they say we're all the same and it's "nice one," "geezer" but that's as far as the conversation went. I lost my friends, I dance alone, it's 6 o'clock, I wanna go home. But it's "no way," "not today," makes you wonder what it meant. And this hollow feeling grows and grows and grows and grows.

Pulp critiques dance as a pseudo-pleasure in which the sense of bonding experienced by participants is merely surface, actually hinders genuine communication, and ultimately produces greater isolation. The drug excesses do not produce enlightenment but rather complacency ("that's okay cause we're all sorted out for E's and wizz").[73] While acknowledging that dance may appear to produce closeness and communion, indie ultimately asserts that the hedonism of dance is hollow and meaningless. It intensifies isolation in the midst of twenty thousand people. Pulp's criticism of the dance scene reiterates a persistent theme in indie regarding skepticism towards the dancehall. Central indie protagonists the Smiths wrote a song denigrating dance music: "Burn down the disco / Hang the blessed DJ. / Because the music that they constantly play / It says nothing to me about my life" ("Panic," the Smiths, 1986). Such attitudes of self-identification through opposition to the practices and conventions of dance have been consistent in indie discourse over a period of ten years.

The differences between dance and indie can also be mapped out as a system of binary oppositions. It is important to restate once again that this is indie's dichotomy and not an accurate depiction of the dance community. As a successful DJ friend of mine browsed through this list sitting open on my laptop computer, he said that from his dance perspective, he would invert most of the associations, "except for the guitar, of course" (M.V.):[74]

DANCE	INDIE
clubs	gigs
impersonal	personal
faceless	charismatic artists
electronic drums	electric guitar
technophilia	technophobia
synthetic	organic
instrumentals	lyrics
extroverted	introverted
for body	for mind
prerecorded	live
undifferentiated	original
mindless	intelligent
empty	substantive
pleasure	pathos
hedonistic	austere
sexual excess	sexual austerity
ecstasy	alcohol
entertainment	art
future oriented	past oriented

Within this ideological scheme, indie reproduces many existent cultural dichotomies, positing art and commerce, mind and body, as antithetical.

Dance's advocation of facelessness places it on the opposite side from indie in a battle over the role of the individual in the contemporary era. Dance music clubbers, with their happy-face T-shirts, appear to embrace technology and the modern era with hippy-dippy abandon, reveling in mechanized and impersonal experiences. To the indie fans, dance fans appear to accept the death of the individual and amplify it with the genre's lack of musical personalities, its generic white label records, and its masking of faces. Dance looks to the future with a generic smile painted over its face.

Within indie discourse, the theme that other genres of music are empty facades is repeated in various guises—mainstream as a generic, watered-down form of expression, an opiate to the masses; dance as "faceless techno bollocks" (*Melody Maker*, April 20, 1993; see image 1.1).* The unspecialized mainstream, considered to aim at the lowest common denominator, is also an affront to indie's values of individualism and local identity. Indie sees itself

---

*   Jazz is also given short shrift as "the last refuge of the untalented. Jazz musicians enjoy themselves more than anyone listening to them. Like theater, it's what you do when you can't get a gig." This is a quote from the film 24 *Hour Party People*, which rather humorously portrays the low regard indie enthusiasts have for modern jazz.

IMAGE I.I. T-shirt rack at Virgin Megastore. *Photo by author.*

as continuing the Romantic image of the artist as a natural, self-actuated genius borne of emotional pathos, self-referential introspection, and internal
longings—the eternal outsider. Indie is a call for the persistence of the value
of personal experience in an era when people are just numbers and audience
members are mere faces in a crowd. Here we can understand indie's continuation of the rock tradition of the rebel, a positive model of individualism in
the postwar years. Indie sees itself as intimate, personal, urgent, and, most of
all, meaningfully human in an age of faceless transnational corporations and
synthetic sounds. The ethic of live performance is a puritanical stance in the
age of mechanical reproduction. Indie views itself as a painting to the
mainstream's and dance's disposable postcards.[75]

However, the most important difference between indie and dance is the relationship to temporality. Indie views dance as millinarianistic, embracing the future. As Pulp asked in their "Sorted for E's and Wizz"—"Is this the way they say the *future's* meant to feel?" [emphasis mine]. Dance is the embodiment of futurism. Its technophilia is seen as part of its love of the future. While the names of indie clubs and labels express wistful nostalgic threads of the past, dance clubs and artists have names that reference the future or new technologies. Much has been made of the significance of punk names that were meant to assault, shock, and subvert— Rough Trade, a pseudonym for indelicate gay sex; Stiff, for what one wanted a record not to do (not sell). Indie's names are retro and wistfully childish. Creation was named after a 1960s band. Domino was named for a line in a Roy Orbison song, and it reminded the founder of Chess, the classic jazz label. Other important indie labels founded in indie's heyday were Sarah, Too Pure, One Little Indian, Fierce Panda, Heavenly, and Tea Time, the names evoking a sweet, precious quality. In contrast, dance labels have names such as XL Recordings, Neo, Triple XXX, Astralwerks, Automatic, Deconstruction, Electrolux, LCD Records, Mo'Wax, Millennium, NRK Sound Division, and Future Groove (a Mute label dance imprint). Alternative spellings are rife in dance labels and band names. The extensive use of X and the use of K are of particular interest. X is used in product branding to suggest science and cutting-edge advancements.[76] X is also the nickname of ecstasy, the drug associated with the world of dance. The embrace of technology and futurism is extended to its graphic style of computer-generated imagery and virtual worlds. This is contrasted with the handwritten graphics of indie, which are also populated with images of the past and of childhood (see images 1.2 and 1.3).[77] Blur sums up indie's take on the future (and, by extension, dance's embrace of it) with the title of their second album, *Modern Life Is Rubbish*.

Indie, on the other hand, is a call to the past, a restoration. Indie's ideology is Luddite at its core, professing skepticism at technological advancements, demanding face-to-face performative experiences, finding originary value in mechanically reproduced objects, while casting a nostalgic and longing gaze at the past. It is only when looking at indie as a whole that one can understand Flying Saucer Attack band member Dave's comments about his antipathy towards CDs: "I am a very miserable person." Fetishizing vinyl locates one as being a member of the indie community and embracing its ethos of nostalgia and miserable longing. It is as if in saying "I like vinyl and I don't like CDs," one is at the same time saying, "I'm miserable; I'm indie."

IMAGE 1.2 Dance album cover using computer-generated graphics. *Copyright Moonshine Music.*

Indie's nostalgic miserablism is potent in the lyrics of the Radiohead song "The Bends": "My baby's got the bends. We don't have any real friends. Just lying in a bar with my drip feed on talking to my girlfriend waiting for something to happen and I wish it was the 60s. I wish we could be happy. I wish, I wish, I wish that something would happen" ("The Bends," Radiohead, 1995). The protagonist of this song is alienated and bored, turns to alcohol for relief, and yearns for the 1960s, which is imagined as a golden age. His "I wish, I wish, I wish that something would happen" is an indistinct longing for something elusive. Indie is filled with longing for something lost or perhaps wishing for something that never was. It longs for the authenticity it associates with the working class, which is in turn another longing for something that is other than

IMAGE 1.3. Sebadoh album cover with image of child and handwritten title. *Copyright Lou Barlow.*

oneself, a history that is not one's own. The adolescents and young adults wear ill-fitting T-shirts two sizes too large or small pastel shirts worn so tight as to almost burst the seams. Indie kids no longer fit into the clothes of childhood and long for a return to an imagined innocence. The consistent melancholic demeanor expressed in the black clothing worn by indie protagonists invokes their loss. It is only through the Puritan process of purification, austerity, and renunciation of pleasures of the flesh that the indie fan can hope to enact an impossible return. Indie is melancholic because it is in mourning; it longs for some indistinct something lost somewhere in the past. Yet, in the wish for this return, there is joy and hope; in the playing of the music, there is pleasure and faith. The indie community goes forward, beating "against the current, borne back ceaselessly into the past" (Fitzgerald 1925: 189).

Indie: What Is It?

How do we understand these contradictory modes of defining what indie is? Is it a means of distribution, a genre, an ethos, a style, or an aesthetic? There are many indie fans who listen to dance music, who are not technophobic, who don't have any particular proclivities for the seven-inch format, and who like some mainstream chart acts, even as they say they think they ought not to. There is an indie ideology, but defining membership in a community by adherence to its associated ideological framework results in the inclusion of only the most fully dedicated members. However, people are far more complicated than strict definitions permit, and they participate in more than one community. Indie is located ultimately in its discourse about its boundaries, in discussions about what it is and is not, because what it is constantly changes.

What we find when looking at indie's discourse is an articulation of unresolved conflicts regarding the ritual means of accessing the numinous. Ideological concerns about the nature of how one experiences the world are not confined to the domain of the sacred. Indie's non-exclusive series of definitions affirms a particular world view about how to establish an appropriate relationship between music fan and music. Indie's support of independent ownership of the means of production and distribution, its assertions regarding the debasing influence of centralized authority, its valuing of a direct (rather than mediated) experience of music, its tropes of asceticism, introversion, autonomy, piety, simplicity, and the everyday, and its call for a return to the purity of a previous era articulate a Puritan ideology suffused with Romantic emotionalism and sensitivity. Are we to believe that this convergence of concerns and details regarding practices is merely random happenstance? In cultures all over the world, the ideas of religious ideology pervade narratives, practices, and aesthetic productions regardless of their "secular" or "sacred" origins. In the economic and institutional sector of indie, we find the recapitulation of religious ideology regarding the means of accessing genuine and meaningful experience. These ideological impulses have generative consequences. The concerns of the punks regarding the appropriateness of contemporary musical practices resulted in concrete changes in the infrastructure of the British music industry. Independent distributors linked independent retail establishments into a "cartel" to compete with corporately owned retail chains. Ideology can impact structure.

To indie fans, it makes a difference whether or not there are guitar solos, elaborate or simple song structures, lyrics about fun or pain, or costumes instead of ordinary clothes. These differences are not seen as personal tastes but as signs of moral convictions. The combination of sensitivity, discipline, intellectualism, irony, and austere modes of production expresses the pain of isolation and the belief that there was once a time when things were different. There was a time when one's sense of self was felt in an intimate fashion, when one felt connected to someone and some place. It also speaks of the hope that it can be that way again. We find those fleeting moments of togetherness in the event that is the focus of indie's face-to-face interactions: the live musical performance, the indie gig.

CHAPTER 2

The Zones of Participation

✳

When examining the specific practices of indie, we find a complex system that locates its members within a ritual structure. Since indie is not merely ideology, it needs to be examined in habitus: participation in the indie music scene is a process. Definitions focus on the boundaries between insiders and outsiders, making the heterogeneity of membership in a community less apparent. In the next three chapters, I discuss factors that produce and affect audience behavior and audience subjectivity at indie gigs. There are varying degrees of affiliation to the music community and to particular bands, contrasting modes of participation, and diverse statuses of audience members; and there is a range of spectatorship correlated with spatial domains and age sets. The egalitarianism of indie's ideology belies a system of hierarchies and difference. The indie audience's participation in gigs is as much about making and marking distinctions among members of the indie community as it is about making and marking distinctions between different musical communities.

The gig is indie's preeminent participatory event. The gig converts the indie community from one of discourse to one of interaction. Since indie is not a geographical enclave, members find others by participating in the activities that designate one as a member of the community: going to specialty music stores, buying the specialist music press, participating in internet chat rooms devoted to indie music and labels, wearing band T-shirts, and attending gigs and festivals. The gig, occurring regularly and bringing together large numbers of indie fans, is the key event for face-to-face interaction.

As I discussed in the last chapter, privileging the live experience of music is one of the platforms of indie purism. Live performance is the essential domain where a band can reveal itself as the conduit of "true" music, thereby demonstrating its own authenticity. Often a scholar's first impulse is to analyze the show onstage. There is a logical reason for this. In many cases, audience members do very little at events—their bodies are composed; they are silent. And, after all, a spectacle is a spectacle—it is what everyone else is paying attention to. It is easy to neglect audience comportment as a facet of performance. However, meaning is built interactionally across modalities; it is made cognitively, verbally, spatially, temporally, and through bodily deployment. The actions of audience members at shows are a part of how meaning is constructed and social relationships are articulated. Where a participant locates himself in space is read by other participants as communicative (Duranti 1992a). Space is culturally organized, and therefore the use of the body in space is a meaning-making process. These culturally relevant distinctions in space and activity are empirically present both in indie's taxonomies and in the unspoken but visually detectable distribution and activity patterns that characterize face-to-face interactions. For indie gigs, the venue space is not neutral but socially, historically, and semiotically produced. To understand audience behavior in the gig setting, we need to understand the participant structure.

We are all fluent in hundreds of participant structures: classrooms, movie theaters, sports events, family dinners. Within the specific participant structure for gigs, differences among members are established that articulate the values and tensions involved in participating in the indie music scene. For the audience at a gig, there are different kinds of participation, depending upon location. Activities that are appropriate in one area are entirely inappropriate in another and could even result in ejection from the event. Some areas are marked by intense physical interaction, often in ways that are rarely seen in other cultural settings. Other areas are characterized by physical distance and inactivity.

The distinctions in performance setting are relevant to indie fans' classification of musical performances. When an indie band performs at a venue with seating (generally referred to as a "concert"), many gig goers complain that the setting makes it difficult to enjoy the show. So essential is the non-seated venue to indie that fans often regard a change in venue type (i.e., from non-seated to seated) as a sign that a band is no longer acting as a member of the indie community and is catering to a mainstream clientele.[1] Indie members make a distinction between their first gig and their first concert. Most gig goers I spoke to had been to one or two concerts in seated venues as preteens or as children, years before becoming members of the indie scene. The concert was usually by some Top 40 band not favored within the indie community; most indie fans refer to this first experience of live music with some embarrassment and will generally discuss their first club date as their first gig.[2] Thus, gig goers make a distinction in the participant structures of music performances. Concerts are those seated events that you went to with your mum or your brother or your uncle. Gigs are active events where you meet fellow youth.

Participant structures are not fixed; they change through time while retaining continuities with the genre's earlier organizational principles. Rather than a static set of parameters, these structures express how cultural expectations shape the production of events. At the same time, the ongoing introduction of new events shapes indie culture too.

The Event

What follows is a brief description of indie gigs and some of the basic parameters of the gig experience. Indie events occur in a number of different settings, from small pubs without stages to huge open fields such as the Reading festival with its large stages, security personnel, and gap of some twenty feet between the performers and the audience. Gigs are predicated on a rudimentary distinction between the space of the performers and the space of the audience. In the typical gig setting, the performers occupy an elevated stage and perform facing the audience, although many small indie shows take place in venues without stages.[3] In general, the stage is an exclusive space for performers, and the audience is denied access to it. In a small venue without security and with only a piece of tape to designate the "stage" space, audience members voluntarily recognize this as a privileged space that is reserved only for performers and crew. On occasion, the boundary between performers and audience is breached: someone in the audience gets up on the stage to have contact with a performer, or a performer reaches out to touch or jump into the audience.

Most gigs occur at night and feature anywhere from one to several bands. In general, the last band that plays is considered the headliner, the most prestigious position on the bill. Bands usually perform for between twenty and ninety minutes. Between musical sets, audience distribution alters moderately and approaches the distribution patterns that are common in non-spectorial social functions. As in clubs or at parties where people stand in small circles, visual orientation is not focused on a single location and there is no uniformity of involvement in activities.

The visual components of the gig, as in many spectorial events, include a lit stage; the rest of the venue, except for the bar areas and foyers, is usually dark.[4] The performance itself consists of watching the musicians perform. At times, there are light shows, slides, videos, or a fog machine, but in general the audience at an indie gig watches and listens to musicians sing and play electric instruments at high decibel levels. The energy of performers' activities varies. Many indie bands rarely move while they perform, while other bands use frenetic or stylized movements. Even when a band is wildly energetic, however, their movements are somewhat circumscribed because of the limitations of playing their instruments. Singers are customarily the most animated of the performers. At gigs, the audiences are often as active and lively as the performers onstage, if not more so.

For the purposes of analysis, I have classified the space occupied by the audience as three zones based on the distinct types of activities exhibited in these areas (see figure 1). This description of zones is based on the spatial organization of a gig that is well attended, with at least two hundred participants. Gigs range from a performance in a venue where only the club or pub employees attend to a show before approximately five thousand audience members. However, the number of people who engage in this participant structure can be much greater; for example, the distribution of audience members at indie festivals like Reading, attended by between 38,000 and 50,000 people, functions like a big gig. For shows that are well attended, the three zones almost always appear. The first, the area closest to the stage, is the most complicated in terms of physical activity. The second zone generally begins a quarter of the way back into the venue and reaches to the rear of the dance floor area. It is far less dense than the first zone and the most static of the three. The third, the area in the back of the venue, features the most varied activities and has the most far-reaching effects on the transnational community of music production and consumption.

Zone One

Zone one, the area closest to the stage, is composed of the front rows of the audience (an area referred to as the "pit") and the people in the front sides and immediately behind the pit (see figure 2). The space and the participant structure at the anterior of an indie gig present rather unique kinesic and somatic conditions for social interaction. Within the zone closest to the stage, density is very high. Often horizontal pressure is such that a person might be lifted off the ground from the sheer force of other bodies pressing against him or her. There is often a high degree of movement in most of zone one—dancing, jumping up and down, and head shaking. In addition, zone one presents the opportunity for having intimate bodily contact with strangers. The density of human bodies in the front allows for distinctive activities such as stage diving and crowd surfing, the latter an activity in which an individual is hoisted above the crowd and, supported by other members of the audience, rolls about on top of them (see images 2.1, 2.2, and 2.3).

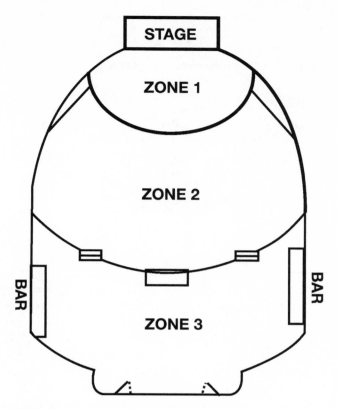

FIGURE I. Model of zones based on the London Forum.

Crowd surfing developed in the late 1980s and became ubiquitous in the early 1990s. By 2000 or so, however, this practice had become more infrequent and passé. Tracking the development of crowd surfing reveals the transnational character of music participation. Indie has also influenced and been informed by music audiences far beyond the scope of Britain, particularly those in the United States, France, Japan, Germany, Canada, and Thailand (that is, the biggest international markets for indie music). The evolution of crowd surfing has several crossings of the Atlantic and a typically vociferous indie debate regarding its appropriateness.

The evolution of crowd surfing is rooted firmly in the punk era, the generative period of indie ideology. British punk audience interaction at gigs was characterized by vigorous and, at times, violent activity directed at other audience members as well as at the performers onstage.[5] In Britain, punk inaugurated the development of pogoing as a style of audience dance. Pogoing is a form of dancing in which audience members would jump up

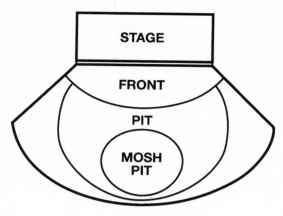

FIGURE 2. Zone one (detail).

and down, often into other pogoing audience members.[6] Taken up in the United States, pogoing soon evolved into slam-dancing or moshing. This was a style of dance where punks would run about, pushing, elbowing, and slamming into each other. The area where this dancing took place often resembled a mêlée, and this is how the "mosh pit" took its name. Because of the aggressive nature of the interaction, it was not uncommon for actual fights to break out, because there was a fine line between the boisterous aggression of slam-dancing and that of actual transgressive offense.

When British punk came to the United States, American punk fans added new elements.[7] American punk shows saw the advent of stage diving, the immediate precursor to the contemporary indie activity of crowd surfing. In stage diving, a member of the audience would get up onto the stage and dive back into the audience where, for the most part, he would be caught and then dropped into the crowd. Most stage divers would immediately jump back into the crowd; more experienced divers would flip back. However, it was not uncommon for an audience member to interact with performers by grabbing a microphone, putting an arm around a musician, or even physically assaulting the performers on the stage. During the period of punk acceptance in American circles, the slam-dancing in the mosh pit became a highly stylized mode of dancing, in which moshers would move in a circle, flapping their elbows in a fashion reminiscent of an angry chicken.[8]

By the time the audience practice of stage diving was introduced to Britain, punk had come and gone. It was in turn associated with two new subgenres of music, gothic and psychobilly, both popular post-punk styles. Stage diving was a mainstay of audience interactional style in Britain until the early 1990s. During the period of its institutionalization, divers would

IMAGE 2.1. Two audience members crowd surfing. *From author's videotape.*

not be immediately dropped into the crowd but were rolled to the back to be let down, allowing the diver to spend more time on top of audience members. Crowd surfing grew out of this prolonged period on top of the audience: stage divers would land on audience members and be held up and moved over a sea of human bodies. Even the term "crowd surfing" is an extension of the aquatic metaphor of stage diving. However, while stage diving was popular, it was not always possible. Many venues placed security barriers between performers and audience to preclude audience access to the stage and any possibility of stage diving. Crowd surfing, on the other hand, did not require stage access and could be performed despite security barriers. Crowd surfing had a stronger embryology in the United States, where promoters took more precautions to prevent stage diving than they did in Britain.

During the early 1990s, stage diving fell out of favor and crowd surfing took precedence. One reason was that stage diving became the source of controversy due to its impact on female gig goers' participation (*Melody Maker*, May 18, 1992). Stage divers and moshers were mostly males. Some females claimed that they avoided the front to steer clear of being jumped on. Several female gig goers claimed that the free participation in stage diving for men meant a circumscribed participation in gigs for women. The argument that

IMAGE 2.2. Two audience members crowd surfing. *From author's videotape.*

stage diving was anti-feminist was a particularly powerful one for indie, because it prides itself on its egalitarianism. Stage diving was felt to have become an egotistic activity, like a guitar solo, and therefore a distasteful practice. Punk viewed stage divers' access to the performance space as obliterating the differences between performer and audience, an undermining of the stage as a privileged space and therefore challenging elitist hierarchies. However, over time it became viewed as self-elevation by the audience member. Stage divers would often hold their arms aloft in a victorious and self-aggrandizing pose prior to throwing themselves back into the audience. Thus, stage diving became somewhat associated with vanity and a desire to show off to other audience members. By the end of 1992, the period immediately following this debate, stage diving had become much more infrequent and crowd surfing took over as the normative activity that characterized the first zone of gigs. Interestingly, crowd surfing, while initially seen as more female-friendly, would be criticized later on the same anti-female grounds.

The Pit

The pit is the most active area in the venue. Within the main pit area there sometimes develops a specialized section, the "mosh pit." During

IMAGE 2.3. One audience member crowd surfing, legs akimbo. *From author's videotape.*

the mid-1990s, mosh pits passed out of favor for British audiences while becoming popular among American audiences. Mosh pits are mainstays that have shown remarkable consistency for bands perceived as punk. In the early 2000s in the United States, as indie music took hold as an alternative to "Alternative" music, mosh pits became less of an element of gig participation. While crowd surfing occurred at most indie shows, the mosh pit appeared only sporadically, generally at larger shows by bands that played a more frenetic style of music. At big events and festivals, popular bands may have more than one mosh pit form simultaneously, while no mosh pit develops whatsoever for the quieter and slower-tempoed indie bands. When mosh pits do form, they appear yards behind the main front section, so that there is generally a buffer of people between the front and those in a mosh pit. If a mosh pit has large pockets of space, crowd surfers cannot traverse this area. The stylized chicken dance went out of favor, but a mosh pit is still characterized by circular movement and pushing and running into others. If one stands around the pit area adjacent to the mosh pit, one is sure to spend a good portion of the performance being jostled and run into. The mosh pit is mostly composed of males; if a female goes into the pit, it is an occasion for comment.

IMAGE 2.4. Audience member getting up on top of crowd. Fan is lifted by male underneath. *From author's videotape.*

Crowd surfing is focused in the main pit and the central front portion of zone one. Rather than chaotic, participation in crowd surfing is extremely collaborative. In this way, crowd surfing stands in stark contrast to stage diving. In stage diving, a person makes the decision himself to get up on the stage to dive off. Audience members choose either to catch the individual or move out of the way (although the latter is not always an option). The stage diver takes the risk, and crowd members may or may not respond by catching him. In crowd surfing, getting on top of the crowd, maintaining oneself on top of the crowd, and getting down again involve the assistance of other audience members. Crowd surfers need at least one other person to enable them to climb on top of the crowd. In general, a person who is being hoisted up uses two other people—one to lift and one to push (see images 2.4, 2.5, and 2.6).

The crowd surfer's social space is composed of human bodies. Most move across the audience on their backs, the majority of their momentum coming from being pushed by the people below. They usually remain on top of the crowd for between one and four minutes, depending on a number of factors, such as the rules for the security personnel, the number of other people rolling on top of the crowd, the size of the crowd itself, the

IMAGE 2.5. Fan is lifted by male behind and male underneath. *From author's videotape.*

style and tempo of the music, and the crowd's willingness.[9] Additionally, when a song ends, audience members let crowd surfers down. The activities of zone one are done in coordination with the music: between songs, activity levels drop dramatically. If an individual gets up on top of the crowd as a song ends, he is immediately dropped back down. While not as starkly vulnerable as stage diving, crowd surfing is also a risky venture. Getting up is fairly easy to coordinate with one or two other people, but there is less certainty as to how one will get down. For the most part, crowd surfers move either toward the front row, where they will be pulled off by concert security workers standing behind a barricade, or toward the periphery of zone one where there is insufficient density to stay on top of the crowd. Then they slip down—ideally, feet first.

The majority of people that compose the crowd surfer's social space need to comply with the exercise of crowd surfing for it to occur. Those in the main pit area are the most active crowd surfers. Audience members in the front or on the peripheries of zone one rarely initiate and engage in surfing, but they will help those who do. While people in the area closest to the stage are often not very happy about spending a large portion of a show with people rolling over them, it is considered one of the hazards of being

IMAGE 2.6. Fan is pushed on top of the crowd. *From author's videotape.*

close to the band. If the audience members in zone one do not collaborate, crowd surfing is simply not possible. For example, when the Lemonheads played at Norwich UEA in spring 1994, there was only a small number of audience members who wanted to crowd surf. During the set, the same seven young men tried repeatedly to get up onto the audience. Each attempt was rebuffed by audience members who, instead of passing them forward, pushed them back until they dropped to the ground. By the end of the headliner's set, not one individual had succeeded in staying on top of the crowd for more than twenty seconds.[10]

Audience members also do not collaborate with individuals who violate norms of conduct while crowd surfing. Violations include not keeping one's feet up, kicking people, concentrating one's body weight in a single location rather than distributing it horizontally, or staying in one location rather than moving across the space. If an individual rolls improperly, this person is dropped immediately.

The norms of conduct for zone one extend beyond appropriate behaviors for crowd surfers. They also include the specific behavioral comportment of those standing in the crowd. While there is a great deal of physical intimacy between audience members, sexual overtures in this context are seen as severe violations. Most experienced female gig goers have been groped by a male fan at a show at some point, but it is the exception rather than the rule. Groping women is considered to be an extreme abuse of the trust involved in going to gigs and is frowned upon by both males and females.

While there are several mechanisms for monitoring behaviors, violations are uncommon. In general, people in zone one are very careful to make sure that no one gets seriously hurt during the proceedings. When one engages in these socially constructed activities, there is a risk that the diver or crowd surfer will not be caught. There are times when, despite the efforts of others, a crowd surfer will fall in the middle of the crowd or slip down from the top of the crowd headfirst. This is a dangerous moment, for there is a real risk of being smothered or trampled. If a person falls through a pocket in the crowd in any way other than feet-first, those around him will grab hold of anything they can to prevent the surfer from hitting the ground. If a person does fall, the people in the area around him will stop jumping and dancing and help him get up. At festivals, this is a far more complicated and dangerous project. Many can fall simultaneously because of the great number of people in the back and at the sides who exert a constant pressure as they move forward and toward the center. This pressure often causes huge horizontal waves that result in whole audience sections collapsing. Helping everyone up can take a significant amount of time (images 2.7–2.8). Because of the shared risks, audience members are aware of a responsibility involved in being a member of zone one: "There's an etiquette in the mosh pit. When people dive, you expect them not to kick you in the head or to be violent. If someone falls over, you expect people to pick them up. As for girls being groped up, there are unwritten laws. When you go to a gig you expect people to have a good time and get along" (letters page, *Melody Maker,* May 18, 1992). Initially the frenetic activity of zone one can appear wild and uncontrolled, and it is often presented that way in the media. However, when one observes the microlevel of interaction, one realizes that the activities of zone one are regulated by participants, and there are numerous mechanisms that allow the crowd to monitor itself.

In many ways, crowd surfing fits the liberal ethos of indie more so than did stage diving. Crowd surfing corresponds with more females taking residence near the stage. Although it is still rather uncommon, far more females participate in crowd surfing than stage diving. Crowd surfing does not require access to the stage and is therefore considered more modest, more communal, less dangerous, and more difficult for security to preclude.

IMAGE 2.7. A section of the crowd collapsed. *From author's videotape.*

The Front

The front is highly focused on the band. The people in the crush in the front of zone one are devoted fans who want to be as close to the performers as possible. Many of these fans have location preferences that extend beyond being near the stage to include their placement near a particular band member whom they want to watch. Avid fans learn to examine the gear onstage prior to the band's set and select the location that will place them in front of their favorite performer's instrument. There is not a lot of turnover in positions in the highly dense area closest to the stage. Generally, those packed in the very front are the first ones in the venue, who go immediately to stand in the front for the duration of the show, including all support acts as well as the headlining band.

The very front is where the most committed fans can use the performance as an opportunity to demonstrate their status. Although they can see the set lists displayed on the stage and know that the songs for that night's performance are already decided, they will often shout out some of the most obscure and least well-known songs of the artist performing.[11] The most obscure songs are generally not the band's best songs, but these requests are not really a communicative act designed to get the song performed. Rather, they convey to the band and to fellow audience members that this individual knows the band's entire oeuvre.[12] For these particular

IMAGE 2.8. Standing audience members help those in the crowd get up. Note fallen audience member's hand reaching toward standing audience member, and adjacent audience member crouched down and lifting up another audience member. *From author's videotape.*

fans, the gig is an exercise in a different form of intimacy, one that brings the specific individual into his own personal relationship with the band and differentiates him from everyone else in the audience.

Within the front area of zone one, the density is the highest of any place in the venue (image 2.9). The pressure in the front can become so great that even breathing is difficult. Simon Parks, the owner of the Brixton Academy, a large venue that holds 4,921, told me that the television program *Tomorrow's World* (April 8, 1992) set up pressure-sensitive pads on the front security barriers during a performance of the popular indie band Ride. During the majority of the set, the pads reached and remained in the red zone, designating critical pressure to the human body.

Some fans in the very front who want to concentrate on the performers find all crowd surfing a painful distraction, but it is a sacrifice that they are willing to make in order to be close to the band. Fans who want to be in the front and near the stage but do not want to have to have people rolling over them select the regions on the sides of the stage. Since crowd surfers are pushed front and center, these areas are generally free of flailing bodies. These peripheries of the stage have the highest density of females.[13] Within

IMAGE 2.9. Highly packed audience members near the front of the stage. *From author's videotape.*

zone one, females generally stand in the highly dense area of the front few rows, the less dense periphery of the front, or the back. There are some female fans who willfully oppose the pit as a male domain and thus purposefully enter it as a matter of principle, feeling that not doing so would reconfirm stereotypes of passive femininity.

Females also eschew the main pit area in order to avoid being groped, which is more likely to occur in the pit. A groping incident usually causes a female to rethink where she places herself in the venue. Groping is a possibility in the front because bodies are pressed against each other, but since the front of zone one is also more stable, the likelihood of catching and confronting a groper is great. The pit area has much more movement, and therefore it is more difficult to monitor personal violations there. In the other two zones there are greater proxemic distinctions between bodies that make the possibility of groping and personal violation highly unlikely. However, it is important to remember that most fans, including male fans, find groping reprehensible and come to the aid of someone who is being molested. For example, on one occasion I watched a girl confront a young man for groping her. Three other males standing nearby dragged him violently away from the front.

In the front, one is often surrounded by and in pronounced propinquity to friends as well as strangers. For many, zone one—and the front in particular—presents a unique context for interaction. Most individuals in zone one come to the venue with friends; therefore, most know some people near them. One habitual participant discussed how she disliked physical contact with strangers but loved going up to the front at gigs: "I've always been a bit phobic of strangers and sometimes even friends touching me, but I often say to people that gigs are the only place I can deal with crowds and actually enjoy it. For me, I feel that I don't need to be on guard at a gig and it lets me enjoy being next to people rather than being anxious. I even like being squashed up next to everyone" (D.H., age twenty). In many ways the intimate physical contact, in conjunction with highly regulated norms of behavior, allows people more comfort. Being in close proximity with other audience members accompanies the choice of one's placement in the front.

For the people who habituate zone one, the other areas in the venue are boring and lack "atmosphere." As one informant told me, "If you aren't going to come up to the front and get into it, you might as well just listen to the record at home with earphones" (R.R., age seventeen). The people who inhabit zone one regard this area as the best in the venue. They say it is the most exciting area and they are "closest" to the band, literally and figuratively. Value judgments are thus made about the types of behavior found in the gig setting.

Zone One Spectatorship: The Initiates

I gave my soul to a new religion . . .
B.R.M.C.

Zone one is primarily composed of the youngest members of the audience, ages approximately fourteen to twenty-one. Most people in the front come to gigs in fairly large groups (four to eight people is the norm). Because they are the youngest, the individuals in zone one initially have little experience with gig going. Nevertheless, most have well-defined expectations of what to do at a gig even before attending one. Many have been reading the weekly press for some time prior to their first gig, and they form clear expectations of what people do at gigs from reviews, photos, and videos. One young fan mentioned that he had read about stage diving and had seen it in a music video, so the very first time he and his friends went to a gig, they were the first to stage dive.

Members of zone one are ardently enthusiastic and invest a lot of energy and anticipation into going to a show. For the youngest audience members, money is frequently an issue, and they are very selective regarding the shows they attend, usually only going to see their favorite bands. Often they will look forward to a gig for weeks in advance and spend a great deal of time getting excited about a particular show.

The process of gig attendance by the young fans of zone one lasts longer than it does for those in the other two zones. These audience members will show up at the venue hours before the doors open. The people who plan to stand in front are the first ones in line, so they are the first non-professionals in the venue. This stands in stark contrast to the industry personnel of zone three, who will often call promoters or the venue to find out what time the headlining band is going on in order to get there only minutes before the headliner's performance.

While they are outside waiting to enter the venue, young fans talk excitedly about the band, and many will go get alcohol while a "mate" keeps their place in line. Alcohol is by far the drug of choice of indie fans at gigs, even though many in this community use illicit substances in other settings; the use of illegal drugs by audience members at or before gigs is relatively infrequent.[14] Those in zone one drink before the gig begins for several reasons: to entertain themselves while they wait in line, to avoid leaving the front during the band's set to drink, and to buy alcohol more cheaply than they can inside. During the show, some zone one participants are inebriated during their manic displays of physicality.

It is in line that zone one fans get their first sense of what a particular gig will be like. Many times, fans commented that they could tell from the excitement and energy level in line how good the gig was going to be. For many people in the front, the focus is not on how well the band performs that evening, but on how much excitement there is for the band in general.

The habitués of zone one who enter the venue first run directly to the front to select their favorite location.[15] As a female fan put it: "When you go, you have to go right to the front, even if you don't like the support acts. The goal is to get into the pit and stay there as long as possible, no matter how sweaty you get. Then afterwards, you have to try and get the set list. It's just what you do at gigs" (S.S., age sixteen). Not only are the fans of zone one likely to be the first to get to the venue, they are also the ones who will wait outside the venue afterward to try to meet the band. For example, at a Suede show at Blackpool in February 1994, the band remained inside the venue for over an hour after the show. When they left the venue to board their tour bus, there were about twenty fans that had been waiting in the seaside winter night air to say hello and get autographs. These were the same fans who had been waiting in line out front for several hours before the show and had been in zone one during the show. The fans who try to make personal contact with their idols meet other similar fans at gigs, sometimes making friends, sometimes playing a game of one-upmanship. They will brag about getting the set lists or other materials that come directly from the band, or the times they have seen band members or spoken to them personally. These fans from the front are most likely to follow a band on its tour. They generally focus on one or two specific bands at a time and research them heavily. They find out where they live, what places they frequent, or other bands they like. These fans often stake out these places, waiting for the opportunity to run into their favorite artist "by chance."[16] They may save their money and then try to attend every show on a tour, traveling around the country for a couple of weeks. With limited resources, one's entire social life may be geared to only one or two particular bands. Most older fans and professionals I interviewed had followed a band on multiple dates on a British tour at one time or another.

For many of the young fans in the front, this introduction to gigs marks their embarkation on an essential part of their social life for many years to come. Going to gigs opens up a new youth lifestyle. Fans start going to gigs with friends they already know who come from the same background, but as time goes on fans make friends with other fans while waiting in line or being squashed next to someone during a gig. Many of these new acquaintances are from outside a fan's original social network and from different socioeconomic backgrounds. A major social goal expressed by indie fans was the desire to meet like-minded people at shows. As one informant put it, "I feel if other people like the same music than they must feel the same as I do" (J.C., age nineteen). Indie fans translate liking the same music into feeling the same (a sentiment echoed in Blur's lyric "We wear the same clothes coz we feel the same"). Thus, gigs provide the opportunity to cross class ties in favor of aesthetic and ideological ones. This is a period in which friendship is based more on taste than on social class, and it points to a liminal component to gig participation. It is a time of antistructure, when the structured social roles that keep people apart are temporarily redrawn based on the organizational principles of the ritual event.

For the young indie fans, gig going marks the time when music becomes the most important thing in their lives: "When I was 15, I began reading *Melody Maker* and music became the most important thing in my life" (letters page, *Melody Maker*, February 24, 1996); "I live for music. There is nothing more important to me" (J.S., age seventeen); "I feel close to people who like indie. It's probably the biggest thing that I look for in my friendships. I mean isn't music supposed to be the most important thing in the world to you when you are a teenager? I take my music very seriously" (E.B., age twenty-two). Because music is the emotional focus of many indie fans' lives, we can understand the vociferous passion of the ideological debates about the nuances of music practices and the ardent fervor associated with indie. Ideological positions on music are often the defining factor in fans' friendships and a constant topic of conversation. Reading the indie press is a weekly highlight and a daily pleasure online. Young fans would spend nights listening to presenters such as the late John Peel, Steve Lamacq, Jo Whiley, or Zane Lowe playing the newest independent records, or they scour the internet for information and post opinions on fan message boards.

The Psychosomatics of Zone One

somehow the vital connection is made . . .
Elastica

A picture of zone one has emerged as a place where you are extremely close to other people, where people pick you up if you fall, where people will put their arms around you and press against you. The physical intimacy we see in zone one is akin to that seen in sport and sport spectatorship in British or American society. It provides the opportunity to have intense and intimate physical contact with others in a highly structured form.[17]

Ritual organizes bodies into specific activities in order to produce particular psychological states in the participants. All participant structures, to some extent, organize bodies in activity, from shaking hands to standing in silence. Rituals have their own participant structures to produce certain sensations and emotions in order to associate those emotional states with the cultural issues that the ritual event addresses. Rituals have rules about using the body that range from eating specific foods to loosening the rules associated with one's social position to very specific acts such as sleep deprivation, flagellation, kneeling, circumcision, or the inhalation of caustic substances. For example, the exhaustion and pain experienced by coming-of-age initiates in some societies are associated with the profundity and responsibility of becoming an adult and produce emotional bonds between initiates. The hazing of the Masai bride by the women of her new village dramatizes her dependence on and vulnerability to these women, with whom she will spend the rest of her life (*Masai Women,* 1975). On Valentine's Day, the idea of romantic love is to be associated with the sweet taste of chocolate and obscures the ideas regarding the commercial exchanges involved in courtship. Rituals are supposed to produce these sentiments, but they are not foolproof.[18] The special rules of rituals are about trying to produce particular sensations in the individual.

The participant structure of indie's zone one creates a scenario in which there are certain physiological stresses to which the body is submitted during the course of a gig. These physical stresses are conducive to certain sensations that, when they are matched with interpretive guidelines, have psychosomatic consequences. The participant structure of the gig promotes the use of the body in specific ways that have material effects. Therefore the participant structure of the gig *promotes* certain psychosomatic consequences in audience members. The activities in zone one utilize a bodily form of engagement to produce sentiment.

Gig goers in zone one voluntarily submit themselves to great physiological stress. Maintaining oneself in the front of a gig is often very arduous. Often people in this zone leave the venue with clothes in tatters, bruises, shoes lost, black eyes, and even broken bones. Damage incurred in the front is often referred to as "battle scars," and indie fans take pride in recounting how they incurred their injuries. No one who had attended gigs for more than a few years and spent time in zone one lacked a story about some minor or major injury they had sustained—getting kicked in the head, cut, pressed against the security barrier so long they had marks on their stomachs, smashed by people in the mosh pit, or nearly fainting from a lack of oxygen.

One key physiological stress in the front is heat. Zone one is the hottest region in the venue. Between the intense activity and the high density of people, the audience members of zone one usually leave the venue dripping in sweat. For example, when indie band Supergrass played at Glasgow's T in the Park in July 1995 the interior temperature of the tent in which they performed became so elevated that sweat from audience members condensed on the canvas ceiling and literally rained down on them. Standing outside a venue after a show, it is fairly easy to distinguish between those who were in zone one and those who were standing in other parts of the venue. Those in zone one leave the venue with their clothes disheveled, their hair soaked in perspiration, chatting enthusiastically about the performance. Those from the other zones do not appear terribly different from when they entered. The heat and density of people makes breathing difficult as well. Those in the front submit themselves to the physiological stresses of somatic pressure, intense heat, oxygen depravation, and physical exertion, often in conjunction with the use of alcohol.

One of the potential material effects of the use of the body in zone one is the production of a mildly altered state of consciousness. An altered state of consciousness (ASC) is a mental state that is characterized by enhanced attention and sensation. Individuals in an altered state of consciousness often experience altered thinking, a disturbed notion of time, the loss of physiological control, a change in emotional expression or in the perception of the signification of events, or feelings of rejuvenation, suggestibility, and perceptual modification (Fischer 1975). The emotional and psychological dimensions of ASCs are often present for audience members in zone one. Many find being in the front simultaneously frightening and exhilarating. Many gig goers discuss the singular sensation and energy there is at the front of a gig:

There is nothing else like being in the front of a gig. It is totally overwhelming. You're in the front and the music is so intense. It overcomes you and robs you of your ability to stand on your own. You can't control yourself. You are at the mercy of the people around you. It is like being drunk or high without drinking or doing drugs. (J.G., age twenty-two)

The rush of being at the front is mammoth. It is like you aren't even there. You lose yourself into what is going on. (S.L., age twenty-one)

When I'm at a gig, I can't help feeling that this is the most important band in the world. I mean I only go up front for bands I really love, so it's not like I feel that way with just any band. But when you're up front for one of your favorite bands, it is like you are inside the music; the music is your body. (P.M., age sixteen)

It's a different feeling than anything else, than just getting drunk. Everyone is just jumping around and you are just going with them. You don't care what you do. (K.B., age nineteen)

Each of these audience members reports some experience of an altered state of consciousness: loss of control, loss of self-consciousness, feeling elated, increased signification. In addition to the emotional components of ASCs, some audience members also experience a temporal disjunction: "I remember, once, at Loop, we were really having a good time and it really seemed the gig was over in a couple minutes because we were so into it. It seemed they had played for only a few minutes. It turns out they had played for over an hour" (M.C., age twenty-eight). Thus, in zone one, audience members often experience characteristics that appear to be those of a mildly altered state of consciousness.

This is hardly surprising, because the somatic conditions at the front of gigs share many of the characteristics used for the induction of ASCs cross-culturally.[19] ASC induction techniques often have both kinesthetic and auditory components. Modes for producing ASCs include the repeated use of patterned drum beats (Needham 1979), the use of narcotic substances (LaBarre 1970, Locke and Kelly 1985, Wasson 1971), ecstatic dancing (Cosentino 1995, Deren 1953, Greenbaum 1973), or a combination of the above in conjunction with the use of other sensual materials, such as incense (Bascom 1969, Crapanzano and Garrison 1977, Kapferer 1983). Percussive instruments are a particularly conspicuous element of ASC induction technologies (Ludwig 1969, Needham 1979). At gigs there are the patterned use of rhythms, the use of intoxicating substances, and spirited dancing—all key elements in the production of an altered state of consciousness in other cultures' ritual settings. The music played by indie bands, like the majority of music in the family of rock, is arranged around rhythmic patterns. At shows, this music is played at a loud volume, so that the experience of that rhythm is often a somatic experience in and of itself.

It is important to point out that the event of an altered state of consciousness is a combination of both a psychobiological state of arousal as it is interpreted by the experiencer and the social context in which that arousal occurs. While these feelings are discussed by those who experience them as significantly different from "ordinary" experience, they are rarely referred to as a categorically different state of consciousness. Participants often say that the experience of being in the front is difficult or impossible to describe, implying in some way that they don't quite have the language to do the experience justice. The most frequently used analogies are being on drugs or having a religious experience. There is an expectation of qualitative difference if pharmacological substances are taken, but the indie fan does not expect to feel qualitatively different merely by the deployment of his body. That chemicals can materially affect the mind is generally accepted, but the idea that the body alone can generate a similar emotional alteration is somehow foreign. This disjunction between expectation, interpretive frame, and phenomenology makes the experience difficult for participants to explain.

Many of zone one's audience members report that their participation results in intense feelings of connection and bonding with other audience members, particularly after experiencing some of the more dramatic aspects of the front. As I discussed earlier, zone one is an area that can be fraught with danger. Falling in this setting is very frightening, and a fan can be seriously hurt. Being caught or picked up by a stranger or friend is an exhilarating and bonding experience.

Listen, let me tell you what it is like at the front. You are totally packed with other people where it is so tight that it seems like you can't breathe. You can't control what you are doing, because there are all these people everywhere pressed up against you. Imagine what it is like when you fall down, either alone because you were surfing or in a large group because your whole section has fallen over; all you can see is people's bodies. You just think, I'm gonna die here and then someone you don't even know picks you up. It is the most incredible feeling—the fear mixed with the joy and gratitude . . . the endorphins in your brain just explode. Like at my first Reading, I had gone up to the front with this girl I had just met and when the band started the whole crowd went berserk and she and I were being pulled apart. I was petrified and I felt totally overwhelmed. Then she just put her arms around me so I wouldn't fall and so we wouldn't be separated. I became incredibly elated like I was on drugs or something, but I wasn't. It was the most intense experience I have ever had and I still feel comfortable saying that to this day. I felt this incredible closeness, not just with her but with everyone around me. I mean years later I still have never felt anything like it in any other place except at other gigs. (S.C., age twenty-six)

Once at the Senseless Things, I went down and I couldn't get up because the mosh was so tight. Eventually some blokes came round and helped to pick me up. It was pretty scary though. I couldn't breath and there are people almost trampling you. I didn't think I could get back up. But then that bloke came and helped me and I was so happy . . . I really remember the way my head was spinning and the excitement. It was just one of those experiences that you never forget. I'd seen other people do it. They had all been caught. None of them had fallen down; there was always someone there to catch you. (I.A., age seventeen)

You get an adrenaline rush at the front. You don't know where you are going to go next. There is so much danger involved and that's where the fun comes from. The people who want the rush are down there. Everyone in the pit is a bit high and everyone down there is out of it. It's not from alcohol or drugs. It's the atmosphere down there. Everyone's enthusiasm feeds everyone else's and you need to rely on them. It's like a form of hysteria where everyone is the same. (E.F., age twenty-five)

Participants in zone one report euphoria, volatility, vitality, and a feeling of ecstatic bonding with those around them.

It is through participation in the activities of zone one that these strong emotional feelings of connection with others are produced. While members of other zones report elation at times, intense feelings of euphoria and *bonding* characterize the participation of those audience members in zone one. The sense of euphoria and connection with others at a gig is a particularly good example of what has been called "communitas." For Victor Turner, communitas is the "sentiment of humanity" (Turner 1974: 274); "a recognition of an essential and generic human bond" (Turner 1969: 97). Communitas is the emotional sense of community and unity that is produced from shared experience, especially shared suffering during ritual events (Turner 1969). The experience of communitas has been well documented in initiation rites (Herdt 1982). The strength of these sentiments toward co-initiates is born of the experience of shared suffering, and it is the reason that grueling tasks are so often a component of entering warriorhood or the army. In her ethnographic study of Liverpudlian bands, Sara Cohen found that the experience of communitas at gigs was common for both performers and audience members, a feeling of a sense of unity with others during the shared experience of live music (Cohen 1991). Many in zone one feel that they are part of a community of sentiment during the performance.

However, it is important to remember that not everyone experiences communitas. Simply deploying the body in particular ways will not automatically result in certain psychosomatic effects. When the body experiences a sensation, individuals read and understand the sensations through their cultural and personal ideational systems. Different individuals have distinctive responses to the same physiological conditions. If the individual does not identify what he is experiencing as part of what other people are experiencing, other emotions may result instead of communitas. Some audience members can feel frustrated, angry, or alienated by their participation in the front. This may occur when other audience members violate interactive norms or merely when the front becomes too taxing for a particular individual. This difference between feeling the way you are supposed to in a ritual event and feeling differently determines whether the event seems meaningful or not. When a gig is working for others, but not for an individual, that audience member feels alienated from the present community rather than part of it. Pulp's criticism of dance music could be applied to what it feels like to be in the front of a gig when it is not working for the participant: "Is this the way [the gig]'s meant to feel? Or just 20,000 people standing in a field?" For a gig, occupants of zone one ideally feel euphoric, imbued with a sense of something greater than oneself. When it does not work, it seems to be exactly what it is at face value, just people on a dance floor or in a field, moving and listening to sound and nothing more. Indie gigs are structured so that the participants of zone one ought to feel passionate, exuberant, and emotionally united with their fellow participants in the state of communitas. When a gig does not produce these emotions, individuals will either opt out of zone one and move into another area of the venue or leave the gig altogether.

Communitas is produced in part from the participant structure that breaks down the boundaries ordinarily in place between non-intimates: "You feel like you can do anything. Nobody really cares. Everyone is there to have a good time. It's like if you bump into someone, you just start talking to them. The atmosphere at gigs is so good. You just go up to someone and touch, start talking to them" (I.A., age seventeen). Comments such as this convey how different being in the front of a gig is from everyday experience. Barriers between people seem to disappear ("you can just go up to someone and touch, start talking").

The feelings of joy, connection, and freedom also work to deny the sexual undercurrents to being in zone one. The girl who was afraid to be physically close yet enjoyed being pressed against people at the front of a gig later told me that it was due to her fear that physical intimacy could be construed as sexual. At gigs, the overt context of the physical intimacy of zone one is not sexual. It is a context where one is free to be as physical and intimate as one wants without fear that the intimacy will be interpreted as sexual. This may provide a window on zone one participation, allowing the pleasure of physical intimacy with the sexual context and anxiety removed. Remember the gender ratio of gigs—65 percent male, with a higher concentration of males in zone one. In the front of zone one, males have full bodily contact with other males. Physical interactions between males in British society, as in many Western societies, are highly regulated because of anxiety over same-sex contact. Yet this does not mean heterosexual males do not have the desire to be close to one another. At gigs, as with sport, males can be close and physical with one another without the threat that their male-to-male contact will be interpreted by themselves or others as sexual (image 2.10). Here, we find the dual nature of the sexuality of the front: the gratification of physical intimacy with the sexual context removed. We can now easily understand why males would object to groping of females, since it sexualizes the context of the front. Groping transforms the non-sexual into the potentially sexual and introduces the threat of homoeroticism for males and sexual threat to females. Sexualizing the context of the front is as threatening to males as it is to females, albeit for different reasons.

In the embodied practices of zone one fans there emerges a metaphysic of physicality, the body as a means to perception. Zone one entails the hypertrophic exertion of the body to drummed rhythms by participants as an expression of one's connection with the music; bodily movement is the conduit to musical appreciation. The activities of zone one, with the presence of ASCs, the utilization of ASC induction techniques, the intense physicality, the ecstatic use of the body, and the use of patterned drumming, produce a form of spectatorship that overtly uses the body as a means to producing sentiment and meaning. In zone one, there exists a participant structure that sets out particular and rather uncommon dimensions for bodily comportment. This includes the hyper-density of the front, crowd surfing, stage diving, moshing, dance, and physical intimacy with strangers. Participant placement within zone one constitutes a specific spectorial position. A particular segment of indie fans places itself in zone one: the youngest, least experienced, and most conspicuously expressive people venture there. The audience members of zone one experience a joyous sense of connection with their fellow audience members and a reduction in their personal boundaries in which contact with strangers and friends is welcomed, not feared.

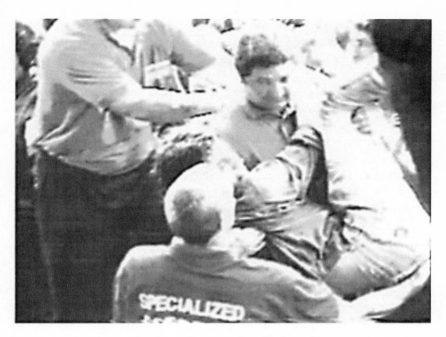

IMAGE 2.10. Security guard pulling audience member off of crowd. *From author's videotape.*

Zone Two

baby britain feels best floating over a sea of vodka . . .
Elliott Smith

In zone two audience members enter into a very different kind of spectorial comportment. Rather than exhibiting the wild and physically exuberant displays of zone one, zone two audience members are physically circumspect and deeply focused on the performance. The different mode of comportment in zone two also has concrete phenomenological consequences; the experience of the gig has to do with contemplative focus rather than physical engagement. The comportment and contemplative register of zone two correspond to traditional Western comportment modes in their passive bodily demeanor and mental focus. This change in physical register from zone one to zone two is also a transformation in the audience members' subjectivity.

Zone two begins immediately behind zone one and extends toward the back of the venue. The line between the two zones is generally well-defined and abrupt. Audience members in zone one move about a great deal during a performance, while audience members in zone two do not.[20] As David

Cavanagh observed, "Only the youngest fans actually danced to music, while those who regarded themselves as mature preferred to watch, nod or, as the songwriter Robyn Hitchcock memorably put it, 'vibrate internally'" (Cavanagh 2000: 303).

In general, zone two is the largest segment of the audience.[21] While the line between zone one and zone two is quite distinct, it is far more difficult to identify the boundary between zone two and zone three, in part because the audience members in the rear of zone two often flow back and forth between the second and third zones. Zone two's posterior limits can vary according to the architecture of a venue, the number of people in the venue, the audience's composition, and the musical style. For example, at the Powerhaus in Islington, a relatively small venue, the limit of zone two was marked by an architectural feature.[22] Within this venue, zone two reached back to the carpeting that separated the bar from the floor. This carpet, which paralleled the perimeter of the bar, was used as a line to separate the activities of the bar from those of the people attending to the performance, designating the bar as zone three. For the Sheffield Leadmill, zone two often reaches to the very back wall of the main performance area. Since the Leadmill has an exterior room with a bar, those not interested in watching the performance can stand in this separate room. Audience composition and music style also factor in to the relative parameters of zone two. When a band has older fans or a more sedate style of music, fewer individuals participate in the activities of zone one, thereby expanding the relative proportions of zone two.

The Mode of Comportment of Zone Two

Zone two has clearly recognizable features for its participant activities. In some sense, it can be characterized as "just standing there." Participants are visibly and physically oriented toward the band and stand facing the stage. There is a modest amount of physical response—rocking back and forth, a gentle movement of the head, tapping feet in rhythm to the music. Between songs, audience members of zone two show their appreciation with applause, although they are often less vigorous in their applause than those in zone one. Those farther back in zone two are less likely to applaud to solicit a band for encores.[23]

The association of specific spatial domains with particular behaviors designates a particular participant structure. If someone in zone two wants to be more physically active, they do not just start dancing in this area; rather, they will move up front. If a person does become physically active in this area, those around him will respond negatively: they will stare, laugh, or make negative comments. Additionally, if a person does the activities associated with the front (bumping into other people, jumping on them), that audience member can be ousted from the venue. In the entirety of my fieldwork, there was only one occasion where I observed audience members actively dancing in any location other than the front of the venue. These people were told by the bar staff to return to the dance floor or risk ejection.

The primary orientation to the performance by those in zone two is an intensive focus on the band. This is the area where one observes the performance with the least amount of distraction. While zone one audience members are engaged in a number of activities that can distract from visual focus on the band, those in zone two stand in visual contemplation of the band for the duration of the band's set.[24] Thus, while members of zone two are muted in terms of their physical response to the music, their concentration on the musicians and the music throughout the performance is pronounced. Members of zone two watch the band or close their eyes. Informants have mentioned that if other audience members catch them looking around, they feel embarrassed, as if the authenticity of their spectatorship had been brought into question. As one fan put it: "If you are looking around and catch someone noticing you are not looking at the band, you feel like they are thinking, why are you there? As if you aren't really there to see the band" (P.W., age twenty-three). In contrast, in zone three there is no self-consciousness regarding looking around, and participants are quite unabashed about rarely watching the performance at all. For zone two, however, giving the band one's undivided mental, auditory, and visual focus is the norm constituting appropriate fan behavior.

Within zone two, participants engage in some activities that are not necessarily connected with the performance onstage. While zone two is primarily the zone of standing and watching the stage, it is also the area for drinking and smoking. The audience density in the front makes it prohibitively difficult to drink in that area, and smoking in the front is often equally onerous. At times, someone in zone one who wants to have a cigarette or a drink will stand in zone two prior to reentering zone one. However, it is far more likely for individuals who are drinking and smoking to remain in zone two.

Comportment Features That Vary over Space

There are several features that vary gradually within zone two: the amount of conversation, the density, and the age of audience members.

These factors extend over the three zones of participation, making each of them key features in the overall participant structure of the gig. Speaking is one of several features graded across zone two, with more speaking toward the back and very limited speaking toward the front. In zone one, fans rarely speak to companions during songs. In zone two there is limited conversation during the performance. In contrast, the habitués of zone three generally spend the majority of the performance conversing with associates, moving into the back of zone two when they want to watch some portion of the performance. These zone three individuals hold conversations throughout the performance, often to the chagrin of those who want to hear the band play. Those toward the back of zone two who are annoyed by talking will try occasionally to exert social pressure by turning around and staring at the offender to make him stop. However, most audience members are aware that if they wish to hear the music without distraction, they need to move into the heart of zone two to do so. It is far easier to stop someone in the front from talking than it is in zone two as limited conversation is acceptable. The area closest to the stage is the loudest, and therefore conversations are more difficult, making the back the logical location in the venue for speaking.

The entire audience space is graded in density. The highest area of body density is the front of zone one, and this decreases as one moves toward the exits. Those in the front of zone two are still in fairly close proximity to each other, though not the body-to-body crush that is associated with zone one. Zone two is where one first sees proxemic distinctions between strangers and those who know each other. Individuals who know each other stand in clusters, and there are greater distances between strangers. The farther back into the venue one goes, the greater is the increase in these distances. Near the back, there is almost no physical contact between strangers, while in zone one the limit of one's personal space ends with one's own body.

The social organization of space is also gradated in terms of age. Participants generally distribute themselves in space by age, with the youngest participants in the front, where there is the most physical activity, and the older ones in the back. Nevertheless, younger people can be found throughout the venue at times, getting drinks or waiting for a different band to perform. However, it is rare for older individuals to be in the front. Within the space of zone two, younger members (that is, early twenties or so) are found toward the front, and ages increase as one moves back. Zone two continues several general participant trends of grading in terms of bodily proximity, talking, and age.

Gigs as Social Life

Most of the people in zone two are zone one fans who have moved back as they have become more experienced. In general, the audience members in zone two range in age from their early to late twenties. For the most part, this area includes people who have been attending shows for years, but it also includes a small number of those who come only on occasion, primarily as companions of those who attend habitually. In other words, zone two contains both highly experienced indie fans and those who would not consider themselves members of the indie community.

It is during the period of their late teens to early twenties that indie participants begin to attend gigs regularly. For those in zone one, the gig is an occasion, a big event. For the majority of fans of indie music, music is an all-consuming passion of their adolescence, and by their early twenties it has become the core of their social life. It is not uncommon for many zone two fans to go through periods where they will go to one to three gigs a week in large cities and a few times a month in regions with fewer venues. Because many of the smaller cities, especially those without student unions, have corresponding smaller youth communities, it is quite difficult to attend gigs as frequently there as one can in cities such as London, Liverpool, Manchester, or Glasgow.

Getting to a city with lots of gigs is often a factor in deciding which university or college to attend or where to live:

I had to go to University in London to see the gigs I wanted to see. I had to be close to where it was happening. I wanted to meet other people who wanted to talk about the same sort of music. Trainspotting, I guess. You have to get to where the gigs are coz that's where you'll meet the same sort of people. I mean coming from a village, you are always reading about these shows you can't go to. When you go to university you want to go to a city that has the shows. You want to go to a place that has *lots* of shows. (E.T., age twenty-nine)

I moved to Manchester in part because of the music scene. It had a history of good music coming out of there—you know, Joy Division and Factory Records—but then again, any big town in England has good music coming out of it. (R.G., age twenty-five)

For many, moving away from home and into a city with gigs means being able to feel that one has finally become a full-fledged member of the indie community. For young fans, there is a certain elusive quality to the indie scene. There always seem to be limits on their ability to participate: not enough money to go to shows, not enough money to buy CDs, no permission to go out enough, or the gigs are too far away. Younger fans are very selective about gigs, largely due to their financial circumstances. Going to one band's performance often means missing others. But when fans come of age, they move to a city with more shows if possible. Older fans tend to have more money, be it from college moneys, personal income, or public subsidies, and suddenly they can attend gigs with much greater frequency. This is a very exciting period of participation in the indie community:

There was excitement all the time—the people I was reading about in the press for all that time, they are real in person, right in front of you. You can connect what you are reading about with something that you see in person. You don't feel excluded anymore. (E.T., age twenty-nine)

I just went to gigs perpetually. As many as I could. It's all I would think about. Planning shows and making new friends who were into the same music I was into. After that point everyone I knew was a really big indie music enthusiast. (M.S., age twenty-three)

I try to go to gigs as much as possible. I'd go to one every night if I could. Most of my friends now are people I've met at gigs or old friends who are into indie. (S.H., age twenty)

It is during this period of constant gigging that the importance of the gig as an event and the social life it confers achieve parity with each other.

Since gigging has become a huge part of their social life, indie fans eventually become more lax in terms of selecting what bands to see. As mentioned earlier, indie is one of the few genres of music where fans make their record purchases without having previously heard the music, and this holds true for gig attendance as well. Many indie gig goers will attend gigs merely upon the recommendations of friends or a good review in the weekly press. It is not uncommon for those in zone two to accompany friends to see bands that they do not even like. Fans in zone two are highly motivated about gig-going in general but perhaps less so about the particular gig they attend. During this time, they develop a great knowledge of the genre and its history and experience the changes in micro-trends firsthand. They develop a connoisseurship, an expertise in indie music.

The Process of Change from Zone One to Zone Two

Since the majority of fans in zone two were once members of zone one, it is important to understand their decision to leave zone one. This move implicates changes in their lives, and in their expectations and desires for participation in the indie scene. The process of change is usually gradual. Most people cannot remember when they began to stand further back. However, there are two experiential processes related to the decision to move back: (1) a seemingly temporary decision related to a lesser affiliation to the band performing on the specific occasion; (2) a rejection of the activities and the physical conditions of the front for a preference toward a less distracted experience of performance. As fans age, they move out of zone one. On the rare occasions when someone who is significantly older moves into the main area of zone one for a prolonged period, they are subtly ostracized and given a wider berth. They are not supported in activities such as crowd surfing and are generally treated as if they are violating codes of conduct.

For many, the process of moving back initially appeared to be temporary and therefore did not seem notable when it occurred: "I gradually moved back, it didn't happen one day. I would wedge myself in the front with the odd going into the mosh pit. Then I moved to the edge of the mosh pit. Then I just moved back" (M.C., age twenty-seven). Initially, this act of moving back does not seem to represent a fundamental change in participation but rather an innocuous part of the selection process of locating oneself in the venue. For experienced fans, though, the mere novelty of going to a gig eventually passes. Opting to remain in zone one requires audience members to be highly motivated, because it involves great effort. The fans of zone two are not nearly as selective regarding the gigs they attend, but they do become selective about their location within the venue.

As fans go to more shows, they end up at shows they do not like as much. Since many of those in zone two follow the recommendations of journalists or friends, they sometimes see bands that have a style they do not like, or they see relatively new bands whose performances are not particularly polished. With greater experience, fans expect more of a band's performance. Bands can be disappointing. Experienced fans learn that there is the distinct possibility that they may not wish to remain in the front for the duration of the performance. When they do not like a performance, they no longer have the motivation to suffer the hazards of zone one and consequently move back. Fans transitioning into zone two will initially place themselves in zone one and then move back if the show does not please them.

After a time, experienced fans need to feel moved before they are willing to go into the physically taxing front. Individuals who have been disappointed with bands in the past begin to place themselves in zone two initially, to determine how much they like the band, before moving into zone one. It is out of their repeated exposure to and experience of gigs that fans' location preference changes. More experienced fans begin to initially locate in zone two and then occasionally foray into zone one. In contrast, the young fans of zone one initially locate in zone one and move out of the region if they do not like the performance:

You get more selective. For every three gigs you go to, there is one that you want to go up front for. (S.P., age twenty-one)

When you first go to gigs every show is really exciting, but after you've been going for a long time you see that even your favorite band has good nights and bad nights. You just aren't as easy to please. The band has to draw you forward. (J.G., age twenty-six)

It is an assessment of a particular performance and not just fan enthusiasm that is a determining factor in the perceived quality of the event. The band must win over the fan with its performance in order for a fan in zone two to move closer to the stage. However, when zone two fans do move up, they spend less time in front. They are generally there for a few songs rather than the entire set. The friends they come with may not wish to go up front, so often the fan who moves forward during the set does so alone.[25] Most fans come with friends who have a similar level of experience with the music scene, and the individual often coordinates location selection with the people he or she comes with. For young fans, it is taken as the de facto state of affairs that they all wish to stand in the front. However, there are more differences of opinion among the experienced fans of zone two. The increased experience of gig going results in many fans having higher performance standards and an increased frequency of dissatisfaction. They have become connoisseurs.

The older fans now enter the venue a bit later than their younger counterparts, because they do not need to be early to ensure that they are at the front at the beginning of the performance. The closer one moves to the stage, the more likely it is that the audience member has arrived at the venue earlier in the evening. Many in zone two choose to arrive after one or two opening acts have played. In time, audience members become habitual members of zone two, rarely moving up at all.

One reason given for moving back is openly discussed by gig goers. Many participants move back because they no longer like the activities of the front. Thus, the movement from zone one to zone two involves not only the factor of increased experience and stricter criteria regarding successful performance but a rejection of the nature of fan expression in the front. Fans cite the difficulty involved in remaining in the front.[26] Even with careful monitoring of the crowd, it is not uncommon for a person to get kicked in the face or for a crowd surfer to land on someone's head. Many of those who moved into zone two are tired of the physical activities that are associated with zone one:

I was tired of spending the whole gig just trying to stay standing up. (M.C., male, age twenty-seven)

I was sick of it. I just didn't think there was any reason that I should suffer to see a band I like. It was just easier to stand further back. I don't know. I was older and I didn't want all these people squashed up next to me. (S.C., female, age twenty-five)

I had enough of sweaty bodies all pressed next to me. I've had enough of being sweaty. Now I like to see bands from the balcony. I don't know, I'm just getting too old for the pit. (S.T., male, age twenty-three)

I didn't want to get kicked in the face anymore and besides you always end up looking better when you stand further back. You don't have the sweat of fifty strangers making you look like a drowned rat. (J.G., female, age twenty-six)

Who likes to take a bath with yer clothes on? (I.M., male, age twenty-four)

The physical intimacy that was once an exhilarating and novel experience becomes something that is actively eschewed by older fans. They reject the activities of zone one based on a preference for greater comfort and decreased exertion and hardship.

This is not merely a rejection of a previous mode of engagement but also a selection *for* a different style of comportment. Members of zone two claim that the activities of zone one make it difficult to concentrate on the performance. To stand in zone one means vigorous dancing and a relaxation of consciousness, of mental focus. In zone two, the goal is a heightened perception, an intense engrossment in the nuances of the live performance of music, a total immersion in the aural elements of the event. It is the comportment of the aficionado. The rest of the world recedes from mind—the music is all there is. During this intense focus, every bump or extraneous sound is an intrusion, an interruption in focus. The bliss of zone two is the total mental involvement in the music, in the savoring of musical subtlety, in the relishing of the shifting consonances and dissonances. Indie is an art form with its own distinct language and conventions. In zone two mental reverie, one can hear in detail the harmonic and melodic interrelations in the composition. It is a total absorption in the music.

Many suggest that zone two is a superior location because of the sound quality. Many participants in zone two claim that it is the best location in the venue for sound and that they are able to experience the music better there. The sound deck is usually in zone two and it is where the music is mixed by the sound engineer. However, the same distribution pattern emerges even at venues where the sound deck is located elsewhere.

Audience members of zone two express fanship in a qualitatively different fashion than those in zone one. Rather than being physically wild and boisterous, the audience members of zone two are calm and reticent. In addition, there is a change in subjectivity that speaks to how one embodies and expresses spectatorship during a gig—the bodily oriented expression of appreciation in the front and the contemplative expression of appreciation in zone two. The change that results in habitually placing oneself in zone two is a barely perceptible process. At some point, the participants simply realize that they do not stand in the front anymore and they wonder how this happened.

The Heterogeneous Audience

When individuals select a position, they locate themselves within a set of distinctions in comportment. When someone decides to stand in zone two, they also are deciding against zone one or three. Audience members in each of the different zones privilege their own spectatorship over the spectatorship of others. The distinctions made by audience members are not merely in terms of preferring different activities; they are also value judgments about the relative merits of these different activities. These value judgments address how a good or "authentic" fan comports himself and what is important during a performance.

Those in zone one criticize other participants, particularly those in zone two, for being undemonstrative and boring. In addition, zone one audience members privilege themselves over zone two because of their own physical proximity to the performers and the sacrifices they are willing to make to exhibit their fanship. Those in zone two claim that the people in zone one are not really interested in the band and are more interested in the activities associated with gigs, such as crowd surfing and stage diving. Habitués of zone two describe zone one activities as distracting, irritating, or something one has to live with. However, their main criticism of the behaviors of those in zone one is that those fans do not pay sufficient attention to the music. The members of zone two posit that full concentration on the performance makes them better fans and that focused attention is what constitutes "authentic" fanship. They also criticize the enthusiasm of fans in zone one as undiscerning. Zone two members are much more vocal in their criticism because they need to look over the heads of those in zone one and are constantly confronted by its different mode of spectatorship. For many, the selection of the new comportment of zone two means a rejection of one's prior participation strategy. Fans in zone two remember how they loved all gigs—even gigs by bands they now believe to be poor artists. They recognize their own lack of discretion then and criticize members of zone one for the same thing. They understand their own participation in zone two in the context of their previous participation in zone one. Thus, most zone two participants privilege their spectatorship as a form of aural discernment.

However, both zones do agree on something. They both condemn the industry talkers and those not paying attention to the show. For gigs, the axis of distinction falls along a line of variable participation. The distinctions in spectatorship are based on making assessments in both positive and negative ways about the quality of spectatorship in other areas. Each mode of comportment is seen by the members who engage in it to produce the true authentic relationship with music; conversely, the other modes of comportment are viewed as producing inauthentic relationships with music and performance.

There are fundamental distinctions in the modes of participation between the first and second zones. For the majority of zone one (the exception being the very front rows) participatory spectatorship is embodied in demonstrative physicality coordinated with the music and in following the proper etiquette associated with being near the stage.[27] For zone two, participatory spectatorship is embodied in mental concentration on the music and a prolonged visual focus on performers onstage. Participation in zone two is a significantly different somatic experience from zone one. Participants in zone two rarely exert themselves physically, except for the effort involved in standing for several hours. Without the vigorous activity or density of zone one, the temperature in zone two is quite moderate. Only at very crowded venues will the temperature of zone two rise. Within zone two, music is at a lower decibel level because of the increased distance from the speaker stacks onstage. Additionally, the many bodies between zone two and the speaker stacks absorb a portion of the sound. Thus, music while still somatic experience becomes a more aural and cognitive one.

The phenomenological consequence of inhabiting each of these zones is likewise different. Habitués of zone two do not report experiencing a sense of connection to fellow audience members. In zone two, audience members suggest a sense of connection only with the music and the performers. Zone two does have elements that can produce a qualitative shift in consciousness, such as the experience of patterned rhythms and, more significantly, a prolonged visual and mental focus on the space of the stage, both of which produce qualitative changes in consciousness (Fischer 1975, Hughes and Melville 1990).

Rather than through the shared exertion and suffering of those in the front, the positive or euphoric feelings one has in zone two result from the mental and visual immersion in the rhythmic performance itself:

I find at shows, especially a show that I'm really excited to go and see, I'm usually really jittery when I first get there. Once the show gets going, I get fixed on listening to the music and then I just relax and get into it—like there is nothing else but the music. It is one of the things I like best about being at a show. I get really still and I have this really strong sense of well-being. I used to like standing at the front, but this is different—it seems more to be a shifting down rather than getting worked up. It really bothers me if people are talking too much because I can't really focus and then the whole thing isn't as good. (L.J., age twenty-five)

When I'm standing at a gig, it really works for me when I go into a sort of mental reverie. I'm listening to the music and I sort of relax and the music fills my mind instead. It's like I'm not aware of being there, but thinking the music rather than thinking of it. (C.N., age twenty-two)

It's weird going to thousands of concerts because all you do is just stand there and watch. My rave friends always say that gigs are a bore, because all you do is stand there. But that is the point, to stand there and just be really focused on the band and music. (M.C., age twenty-seven)[28]

Members of zone two experience pleasure in the total mental absorption in the music. They savor the nuances of performance and the textures and intimate qualities of the music, the rattle of the snare drum, the harmony of voice blended with instrument, or to see fingers make the chord that creates a sound. In this context, other elements such as talking or new visual stimuli are interruptions in focus and therefore hinder a concentrated emotional state. The different participation by those in zone two also creates a qualitative shift in signification, but it is produced by different means than by the rigors of the body. In zone two an event that once represented physical and emotional connection becomes instead one of increased physical distance and mental contemplation, a pleasure in the experience of the nuances of sound and performance. Just as the physical activities of zone one impinge on the subjective experience of being an audience member at the gig, the change in activity between zone one and zone two constitutes a change in participatory spectorial orientation. The two are produced within a field of possibilities.

A Move toward the Exit

It was so good we got bored . . .
The Divine Comedy

For most fans there are several years during which their participation in zone two is very satisfying, enjoyable, and consistent. However, the process of moving back in the gig space does not end there. The gradated distribution of fans according to age within zone two generally corresponds to the experience of the participant. Those who situate themselves at the front of zone two are usually those who most recently stopped participating in zone one. The back area of zone two has those who have attended many more shows and have not participated in the activities of zone one for a very long time. There are also some (though not many) late bloomers to gig going who started in their twenties and never went up front.

The excitement that initially characterized going to shows and that drives constant attendance at gigs does not last. After years of seeing bands play, fans in zone two find gig going part of their routine, like going to the pub; something that you do to meet up with friends and have a good night out. During my research, I encountered many in zone two who had been to gigs spanning the various subgenres of the British independent music scene for twenty years. Many fans in the back of zone two have attended literally thousands of gigs.

With the excessive repetition of the highly structured gig, the older, more experienced audience members of zone two become very blasé. Performances are often less satisfying. Older fans become so well-acquainted with the conventions of their genre that it takes something really extraordinary to excite them. In many new songs they recognize songs of the past, thus finding them derivative rather than inventive. They can easily map out where new bands fit within the indie cosmos and immediately recognize an artist's influences.

With an extensive background in indie shows, seasoned veterans' relationships to gigs alter over time. They often find that going to gigs involves a new type of discomfort:

I sometimes think going to concerts is a form of masochism. I find about half the time I'm bored out of my skull and thinking how much longer is this band going to last. I mean even with bands I really like . . . I find myself bored and wanting it to be over. Even at your favorite band, I go "God, this is boring." I was never bored at a Smiths show, but that was at the peak of my adoration of a band. I saw the Smiths like nine times. I would follow them. I wasn't bored at shows when I was younger, cause I spent half the show just trying to stay standing up . . . It never occurs to me to leave. I'm just bored. I'm going to wait for this to be over to see if something happens. (M.C., age twenty-seven)

There was a period, I went to three or four gigs a week and my tolerance went down, even for bands I liked. My threshold for gigs that makes me happy is two gigs a week, but when I went more, I started to lose my appreciation of going to gigs from over-saturation. I had this curiosity that trailed off when I went all the time. (S.C., age twenty-seven)

I swear sometimes I can't believe how bored I am at a gig. I mean sometimes I think it is really fascist to be so loud and expect everyone to pay attention to you and only you for like an hour and a half. My endurance level is only like forty-five minutes. After that I'm just thinking when will this be over. (K.E., age twenty-eight)

Older fans complain that their legs get sore from standing relatively still for one to four hours. Their newfound dislike for standing makes going to musical performances that have other participant structures (such as concerts

with seats) more appealing. Often older individuals find themselves waiting—waiting for the gig to be over, waiting for something to happen—
rather than enjoying the performance itself.

For the connoisseur, the stakes of a gig are raised—the experience of live
performance in itself is no longer enough. The more the connoisseur
knows of indie shows, the more he recognizes the ritual of live performance—and the more it seems conventionalized, non-spontaneous, and
formulaic. Knowledge of conventions means knowledge of the conventionality of a particular performance. The first time you go to a performance, you are involved in the unfolding of the event. The novice does not
know what comes next and is therefore immersed in the narrative progress.
The music connoisseur is like the cineaste seeing his favorite film for the
hundredth time. He knows what comes next. When a song by a new band
sounds like a song by a band ten years before, the illusion of innovation is
removed. The connoisseur's life history intrudes into his experience of the
performance. He is not merely present but past-and-present. This critical
knowledge formed by his experience of the genre over time is an intellectual pleasure that draws the fan away from emotional immersion. He com-
pares this gig to other gigs. The greater his awareness of the codes, the less
artistic the music that confines itself to the genre's boundaries seems.
Knowledge can make a show seem clinical rather than passionate, a routine
rather than a spontaneous creation. For the experienced member of the
indie community, an encore is no longer a band responding to the enthusiasm of the audience; it is merely part of the performance formula. The
fan needs to overcome the resistance produced by his own overexposure.
The connoisseur needs to forget the conventions temporarily to make the
event work and just hear the music.[29] Connoisseurship increases emotional
distance from the performance and makes it more difficult to attain reverie.

For many in the back of zone two, the opportunity to be social commonly takes precedence over the experience of the music. Most individuals
in zone two come to gigs in smaller groups of two to four people. Many
males express the hope of going to a gig to meet girls, but with a two-to-
one ratio skewed in favor of males it is not the most statistically likely place
to do so. Interestingly, since there is not the same degree of physical intimacy in zone two as in zone one, it is more difficult to meet new people in
zone two. Additionally, because zone two participants come to the gig
later, they no longer meet other people in line. An event that once seemed
to present great opportunities for new relationships instead appears to be
an exercise in frustration. Gigs in general, rather than any one gig in particular, begin to fail. In many ways, some of these older fans continue to attend gigs as if they were on some kind of social autopilot until they settle

into some stable form of adulthood or find another interest. Many older fans who no longer enjoy gigs with the gusto of their previous years observed that they just don't know what else to do and that if they stopped attending gigs, it would leave a void in their lives.[30]

The experienced fans' disillusionment with indie music is not confined to a sense of emptiness and boredom at gigs but encompasses the community itself. At this point, fans are extraordinarily confident in their own assessments of bands. After years of intense focus on the music scene, many gig goers are very skeptical about the weekly press and the conventional rhythms of trends. The indie press is famous for the "build them up, knock them down" style of music journalism that many fans eventually find frustrating and capricious.[31] For older fans who have read these papers for years, the weeklies' discourse of highly polarized assessments becomes offensive and dictatorial. Angry letters written to suggest a boycott of the papers are regularly printed: "*NME*, I'm utterly sick of you. Every week I go down to the newsagents to buy your driveling and I can't stand it anymore" (letters page, *NME*, June 12, 1992); "Wave goodbye to another reader" (letters page, *NME*, December 2, 1993). The older fan, rather than looking to the weekly press for leadership, vigorously contests its assessments of bands. Older fans buy the press irregularly and, in some cases, not at all. When they do, they become less apt to read the features and concentrate on news, new releases, and upcoming shows. Without reading the weekly press, it is difficult to maintain ties to the indie community.

While their interest in gigging and their involvement in the music scene is languishing, the oldest people in zone two still privilege their fanship over others', even those who claim to be bored out of their skulls. They say that they are better fans because of their ability to assess merit. They attribute their boredom to the lack of quality of the band or the performance, or to the fact that bands aren't as good as they used to be.

When participants begin to find gigs boring and less satisfying, they attend gigs less often and move toward the back of the venue.[32] At this point, usually in one's mid- to late twenties, many gig goers begin to make the transition away from being a member of the indie music community. For them, the gig has stopped being a meaningful event. This can also occur when there have been changes in the audience member's lifestyle that make gigs seem less important. It is common for fans to lose interest in gigs if they have a child or if they get married, or if other life changes make them feel that music is no longer the most important thing in the world.

When gig going becomes infrequent and audience members stop paying attention to the weekly press, their musical tastes usually freeze. It is more difficult for them to see the smaller, less-established bands. Older audience members are likely to see only the bands with whom they are already familiar. However, bands will often break up, because indie bands generally do not have long life spans, unless they have a degree of mainstream success. Gig attendance becomes infrequent, and when the older fans do attend performances, these often feature established bands that perform in seated venues. Their engagement in indie public discourse ceases, and the music becomes a footnote, an aside done occasionally. For all intents and purposes, they no longer consider themselves active members of the indie community.

Conclusion

It's such a shame for us to part . . .
Coldplay

There is a relationship between the specific activities found in each zone and subjective experience. Thus far, within the participant structure, there are two embodied participant modes—the bodily engagement and physicality of zone one and the mental interiority of zone two. In zone one audience members' physicality and somatic circumstances can induce an altered state of consciousness and/or the state of communitas. For these people, the gig is a physically involved and emotional experience. In zone two we find little movement or physical activity and an emphasis on contemplative focus. Audience members visually orient toward the stage or close their eyes in an internal reverie that is tuned to the music and the performance.

That audience members move into zone two as they age is an inherent part of the participant structure of the gig. Zone two audience members have developed a great deal of knowledge of the genre and the conventions of indie performance. Over time, they become connoisseurs of indie, capable of distinguishing the textures of the genre. It is in the selection of location, with its corresponding norms regarding bodily comportment, that a transformation in subjectivity is enacted in members of the indie music community. The reasons that audience members give for changing their position in the venue—a nonchalance that comes from greater exposure, a desire for greater comfort, and a sense that they no longer need to submit themselves to physical suffering in order to express their affiliation with the band—are rather mundane and express, in part, their preference for physical tranquility. Yet this move is a transformation from one mode of spectorial comportment to another. Examined synchronically, the distinctions in participation are apparent, but those distinctions appear to be merely the results of individual preferences on a particular occasion. However, if one considers the changes in the individual's participation over time, or diachronically, the differences in participatory spectatorship are revealed as sequential and therefore in a narrative relationship to one another. The consequences of this transformation in subjectivity have great significance. The privileging of one zone's participation over another is the privileging of one type of epistemological system over another.

In the examination of the spectorial positioning of the zones, there emerges from participation a spectorial lens not of the inscribed cognitive "eye/I" of the structural relationships of the performance onstage, but rather a spectatorship of comportment, and a heterogeneous one at that. The gig audience articulates contrasting models of how to experience music. Here, we find one of the first ways that practice and the requirements of a participant structure can produce participatory spectatorships.

CHAPTER 3

Zone Three and the Music Industry

✳

In the previous chapter, I examined audience behaviors in zones one and two in terms of different modes of orientation in spectatorship. The interactions of those audience members are geared to the ongoing performance onstage, and both spectorial modes focus on an aesthetic experience of the musical performance. In zone three, however, there is a significant change in orientation away from the spectacle onstage; individuals are more concerned with fellow audience members than with the performance. Yet a specific segment of people in zone three, those individuals who are ostensibly paying little heed to the performance, are often crucial to the band, and to the music industry generally.

Zone three is primarily composed of three distinct segments of the audience: those who are indifferent to the particular performance or band, those who are temporarily engaged in other tasks, such as going to the restroom, getting a drink, or buying band merchandise, and those who are music industry professionals. In this chapter, I discuss briefly the behavior of those who temporarily place themselves in zone three and discuss in detail those who habitually locate themselves in zone three, the industry professionals.

Professionals at gigs want to highlight their professional status and their status among peers, what Erving Goffman would characterize as "face work" (Goffman 1959, 1967). The face work of industry professionals is performed in the interactions that occur before, during, and after the performance. These interactions take precedence over paying attention to the performance onstage. The spectorial orientation of professionals at gigs is therefore essentially vocational. In general, industry professionals have invested a great deal of energy in music, even when they do not pay much attention to a specific performance. In many ways, the interactions of professionals in the gig context are not very different from the interactions of professionals in other fields. It is just that for British music industry professionals, this colleague-to-colleague face work often occurs in the context of music performances. Music industry professionals use the performance event and its status markers to articulate their membership within a professional coterie and to advance their own agendas.

The activities and behaviors of these professionals have far-reaching consequences for the production and dissemination of indie music. Shows that take place in industry meccas such as London and Manchester or any of the summer festivals present an opportunity for music professionals to meet, interact, cement and augment professional ties, and display and potentially alter their status within the community. For industry personnel, the gig has a detailed and complex system of status markers based on access to gigs and artists and one's ability to acquire goods and services for free. Degree of access enhances or diminishes the status of a music industry professional. For professionals, gaining entry to an event by getting on the guest list is an important display of prestige that differentiates the professional from the ordinary fan. There is an elaborate system of guest passes with various degree of access. Greater access confers greater status within the particular event, and an industry insider who consistently obtains high access at musical performances increases his status within the professional coterie.

Complimentary merchandise and services facilitate the establishment and maintenance of relationships among professionals, and they are the currency of the British music industry. Additionally, professionals display their own unique mode of "cool" comportment in order to differentiate themselves from the fan and position themselves among their colleagues at gigs. While many professionals at gigs display relatively little interest in the ongoing performances, important machinations related to the running of the music industry are nevertheless taking place.

The Activities of Zone Three

There is no clear line of demarcation between zone two and zone three. In the nether regions of zone two, some individuals display zone three behaviors, such as talking and not paying attention to the band, or standing next to others who are quietly attending to the performance onstage. Therefore, the distinction between zone two and zone three is not articulated in terms of space, but in terms of orientation and comportment. The size of zone three usually depends on the size of the venue. In larger venues, this zone may extend to a separate room. Smaller venues are often composed of a single room with a small entry space. In these venues, zone three is usually the area farthest from the stage, in the vicinity of the bar.

Zone three's activities and focal points are relatively diverse and lack the degree of specificity and regularity of activities of the other zones. Individuals in this area purchase drinks, smoke cigarettes, converse, flirt, or simply sit and watch others. Visual orientation toward the stage is lax. The gaze of the participants in zone three is generally not focused on the band, but their physical orientation is still primarily toward the stage; even in this area, a participant is loathe to turn his or her back on the performers. Those in zone three are disengaged from the performance onstage. They generally do not respond physically to the performance and rarely, if ever, applaud between songs or at the end of a band's set. Rather than being focused on the stage, their attention is devoted to interacting with others in zone three or watching other people within the venue.

The density in this zone is the lowest within the venue, and there is an expectation that no one will come into contact with one's body except in the region closest to the bar, where people cluster closely together while trying to purchase drinks. The crush at the bar is much greater in the United Kingdom, where drinking is a much more fundamental part of social activities, than it is in the United States. The bar area of zone three is most active between band sets, moderately active during supporting acts, and relatively quiet during the main performance. However, if there is a large number of music industry professionals present, the bar area will remain rather active during the headlining band's set as well.

Within zone three there is a great deal of conversation, and the more people there are, the louder the conversation level will be. However, because zone three is farthest from the speaker stacks, it is also easier to talk there. If people in the front wish to talk, they move back into zone three to do so, just as those who want to be more active move forward into zone one. When an audience member does not like the band but also does not wish to leave the venue, he moves into zone three. Hence, this area includes those who have come to watch the performance but have found it unsatisfying. Most of these individuals do not habitually locate themselves in the back. These disaligners initially locate themselves closer to the stage and move into the back of the venue to disengage from the performance. There they will join the people who choose zone three in the first place: the music industry professionals.[1]

The Liggers

You'll get the pass
So you can tell your friends how you made it back . . .
No Doubt's

Zone three is routinely populated by journalists, booking agents, promoters, press agents, managers, crew, record company staff, distribution company employees, retail record buyers, and musicians. These professionals' goals are to obtain privileged access to the band, to attend the aftershow party, to expand their network of colleagues, to access the backstage area, to engage in activities that will enable them to gain access at future events, and, like most audience members, to have a good time. Access to privileged areas such as the guest area, backstage, and aftershow party are highly coveted markers of prestige. Additionally, by providing the opportunity to interact with performers, privileged access is extremely pleasurable for fans and professionals alike.

Significantly, the contrast between zone three and the rest of the audience is the primary emic distinction of spectatorship that members of the British indie scene make. The local taxonomy distinguishes between zone three participants, or "liggers," and the rest of audience members, or "punters."[2] A punter is a paying customer, and the term does not refer solely to audiences at music performances but to any paying customer.[3] Liggers refer to the people who attend events, parties, clubs, or gigs for free. At gigs, they are primarily people who get into events because their names appear on one of the complimentary guest lists, but the term may also apply to individuals who habitually finagle their way into festivities without paying or being placed on the guest list.[4] The parties that occur after the performance are often called "ligs," particularly when there is complimentary alcohol present. Hence, liggers are individuals who get things for free, not necessarily rightfully, and a lig is an event where free items are present.[5] Nearly all professionals are considered liggers by the general music fan, and liggers also include a specialized group of fans who have learned how to gain access to bands. Many of these "professional" fans will later become professionals themselves. In their desire to increase their contact with band members, they make allegiances with professionals and can often parlay those relationships into career opportunities. Hence, contrary to the widespread belief that journalists and music industry professionals are failed musicians, it is more accurate to think of them as highly successful fans who have parlayed their interest in contact with musicians into successful careers for themselves.

Liggers spend most of a performance talking to colleagues or meeting new professionals, including artists. For these individuals, it is the socializing and the party that are the highlight of the night. The general fan base criticizes those who stand in the back of the venue and appear to them to be indifferent to the performance. For them, the term "ligger" implies a parasitic relationship with the band, a person who is less interested in music and more interested in privileged access and personal advancement. In the United States, where such terminology does not exist, the attitude of fans toward professionals is still nearly identical.

The distribution pattern between professionals and punters applies to gigs throughout the country. At gigs, a certain number of professionals are present, whether it be the manager, tour manager, local promoter, employees of the local indie record store, record executives, or journalists who traveled from other areas to attend the show. It is hard to imagine attending a gig in England, Scotland, or Wales where there are not members of the industry present. However, the existence of a professional status hierarchy is most conspicuous in London.

As with many other groups and societies, the music industry possesses a system to express the individual's placement within the hierarchy of the music industry. Gigs and performances present the opportunity to display prestige, extend one's network of business opportunities, or enter into the music industry itself. Vital work relating to the functioning and maintenance of industry ties is done at music performances. Professionals discuss business, hear about new unsigned bands, and make arrangements for meetings. Shows provide intensive networking opportunities and can function as professional conferences, allowing one to meet new colleagues face-to-face and extend or reinforce existing ties.[6]

There are many music performances on any given night, so the first work of a professional is to determine which shows are important to attend. Going to a show where other key colleagues are not present does not augment status, unless, of course, the professional discovers some unknown talent. Gigs become "events" when there is a "buzz" about a band. In other words, a band has received some press coverage, has attained a favorable critical consensus, has recently acquired management, or has signed with someone who is well connected in the music industry. These "events" are most common in London, where most British music personnel are located, and to a lesser extent, the other major music centers of Glasgow, Manchester, and Liverpool. All the major summer festivals are events as well.

The prestige of any gig among industry personnel varies according to a complex range of factors. An unsigned band's gig can become an "event" for lower-level industry personnel. For signed prestigious bands, or an unsigned band in the midst of a bidding war, more established members of the industry will attend.[7] At most shows, individuals who work with the band are expected to attend. However, for "events," a broad cross-section of industry personnel will attend regardless of any professional connection to the band performing. For example, when Black Grape played London for the first time in summer 1995, it was a major industry "event." This show was a veritable who's-who of the British recording industry. Most industry personnel in attendance were not directly affiliated with Black Grape but rather with some other professional who worked in some capacity for one of the organizations affiliated with the band. At shows that are major events, personnel from all areas of the music industry try to attend.

Individuals who are just starting out in the music business (the "junior squad," as they are familiarly called by more established industry professionals) attend the gigs of unsigned bands. At these small gigs, junior squad members—the lowest A&R people for labels and publishing companies, new booking agents, and new journalists—begin the longstanding associations that will take them through their music careers. Junior squad members spend most of their working hours attempting to do two things: (1) making sure that they are not missing out on a new band by calling other junior squad members and finding out what bands they are seeing; (2) attempting to get on guest lists or acquire other professional privileges. There are extensive phone networks among junior squad members, and if several people report that they plan to attend a particular show, the other junior squad members will attend the same show. For unsigned bands and their management, it is their goal to get a junior squad member to commit to attending a performance, because if they are successful, the other junior squad members will follow, clustering together at the gig to exchange cryptic and noncommittal assessments of the band's merit.

On average, junior squad members will go to between one and four venues a night, between four and six nights a week, to total approximately four hundred gigs in their first year. As they travel around London, they see the same set of bands that the other junior squad members see, and the same set of people at all of the locales, and they rarely pay to see any of these performances. While they do not support the promoters of gigs financially, the junior squad nevertheless do wonders for the London taxi industry.

As members of the junior squad rise through the ranks of their respective companies or move into higher positions at other companies, their cohorts do the same. These people become their stable network of colleagues with ties that cut across company lines. Therefore, a person at a major label will also have strong ties to writers at the weeklies and monthlies, booking agents, publicists, and individuals at other labels. As a member of the British music industry, it is a disadvantage not to have been a member of the

London junior squad. The gigs that the junior squad members attend are almost exclusively indie, or occasionally dance. Since the shows attended almost perfectly mirror the demographic musical interests of the weekly press, the British record industry is strongly composed of individuals who have experience primarily with one genre of music. This goes a long way towards explaining the lack of popular media coverage for other music forms. As members of the junior squad move up in the industry, they begin to attend full shows at a single venue rather than seeing single sets by bands at various venues all over town. While the number of shows they attend decreases for the average member of the music industry, that person's life is still almost fully consumed by attending gigs.

As industry people rise in rank, it is less necessary for them to display prestige, because it will be evident in their day-to-day interactions. They do not have the same need to extend their network of colleagues as when they were younger. Senior industry personnel who have gained a great deal of power and stability do not regularly attend shows. When they do appear, however, they can add prestige to an event. Senior personnel are likely to attend only the performances of well-known, established acts.[8] Still, after seven years in the industry, the average music industry person in London will have attended well over two thousand band performances at gigs and festivals.[9] It thus becomes more understandable that, having attended so many music performances, many industry insiders prefer to remain in the back of venues, socializing with colleagues.

The Guest List

The culture of freebies is dominant within the music industry and pervades most social and professional ties. Obtaining goods and services for free is an important goal for British music industry professionals, and they brag profusely about their successes in acquiring freebies. A large number of individuals feel they are underpaid for their jobs, particularly in relation to their American counterparts, and they like to supplement their incomes with professional gratuities. The ability to acquire goods and services for free is a sign of a professional's power and status as a member of the music industry.

The British record industry uses guest lists extensively. For example, at a Pulp performance at the Forum in May 1994, one quarter of the audience consisted of people on the guest list—a full five hundred people. There were eleven separate guest lists, with five different types of passes handed out at the door. When Oasis played at the London Astoria in September 1994, by 8:30 P.M. there were more people in the guest list line than in the paid ticket line. Although the show was scheduled to end at 11:00 P.M., at 10:30 the guest list line still reached back more than thirty feet.

As a rule, individuals in the industry will not go to a show that they have to pay to see. As one journalist put it, "I won't go to something that is not free. It's been so long since I paid retail price" (C.E.). When asked why he didn't attend a particular show, the professional's answer is commonly "I couldn't get in," despite the fact that tickets were still available for purchase. "I couldn't get in" does not describe the individual's inability to attend but rather his inability to get on the guest list. If attending these shows is so important, why not just buy a ticket? This would guarantee entrance. Instead, industry personnel invest significant time and effort in order to avoid paying admission for performances that often cost only a few pounds.

The reason for this is complex. While many find it preferable not to spend money, most members of the industry have access to far more funds than ordinary audience members. Rather, industry personnel resent going to an event where they have to pay, after having spent so much time getting into gigs for free and having privileged access. As a couple of professionals put it:

There are so many freebies. You can travel around and friends or the friends of friends will get you in. There is a big pool of freebies, bigger than you as a punter ever imagined. It really does divide it into the consumers, the cattle who queue up to get the short end of the stick, and the liggers who are part of the in-crowd and get in on the list. (S.R., age twenty-six)

I've been on guest lists for so long; I'd feel like a second-class citizen if I had to pay. (N.D., age twenty-four)

These two comments point to the perceived status of being on the list. If one doesn't get in on the list, one is a second-class citizen, not part of the in crowd. Procuring a position on the guest list is a display of one's power in the industry.

The ability to make the list demonstrates that the individual is directly involved with other members of the profession. For many if not most events, industry personnel attend shows where they do not have a direct relationship to the artist. Therefore, they need to request a favor from someone in order to get on the list. Procuring a position on the guest list requires the institution of some form of balanced reciprocity between parties (Mauss 1967). Once a successful exchange has taken place, this link is considered one that can easily be called on again for future exchanges, including placement on future guest lists, free CDs, and/or free promotional items.[10] Material objects obtained in these exchanges are called "swag," a term invoking piracy or inappropriate means to ownership. One day while I was sitting in a record company office, the product manager wanted a CD from a major label where he did not have a reciprocity partner. He called an acquaintance of one of his friends and asked for the CD, and the record executive agreed. He then added that the record executive should let him know if he wanted any of his company's merchandise or lists. After the call, the product manager turned to me and said, "Great, now I can get anything I want at [*record label*]." I asked why and he replied, "Well, now I've got [*record executive*] to give me that, I can call him next time I want something. See, he'll call me when he wants to get on one of our lists or something." Rather than being a singular transaction, an exchange implies an ongoing relationship of indebtedness upon which both parties may call. Therefore, being indebted to someone else in the music industry is as beneficial as someone being indebted to you.

The more difficult it is to get on the list, the higher the presumed status is for gaining entrance. Getting on a guest list may mean many hours of work on the phone or at the door, but it has become a fundamental marker of status. To pay to get into a gig is a sign of impotence. At the Stereolab and Flying Saucer Attack gig at Camden's Electric Ballroom in June 1994, a woman in the guest list line flagged down a male colleague entering the venue through the paying line. Before she could speak, he stammered that he "hadn't even tried to get in on the list." He said he thought it would be a hassle because he knew that it would be a "tight" list.[11] His embarrassment at being seen walking into a club as a paying customer seemed to far outweigh the woman's initial obliviousness to his predicament. Not attending a performance is generally preferable to attending a performance by buying a ticket, because colleagues may become aware that the professional was not successful in networking a way in. If one does not attend an event, it could be for any number of reasons and not necessarily due to an inability to acquire a ticket.

Industry personnel will spend a great deal of company time trying to get onto guest lists and acquiring swag.[12] Although most people try to arrange a guest list position a few days before the event, people will begin making calls and inquiries weeks in advance for some gigs. For the junior squad, the amount of time spent on this pursuit may grow to ludicrous proportions (for a few people it can take up to 50 percent of their in-office work time). However, given the significance that attending gigs has for a professional's career advancement, this is hardly surprising.

Lig culture is based on two premises—obtaining privileged access not granted to punters and getting items for free. A good lig should essentially have something beyond free entry—alcohol, T-shirts, or CDs. The music artists are the valorized objects that make an event more than just a crowd of record industry personnel getting drunk. Next to having access to an array of prestigious performers, the most valued freebie is complementary alcohol. Alcohol is an important ingredient in British public social relations, and doubly so within the music community. Within the record industry, access to complimentary liquor is a significant indicator of the quality of a lig, and professionals will brag frequently about drinking large quantities of free liquor. For the industry, like most social functions in England, a party ends when alcohol becomes unavailable.*

"No booze" farce spoils bash. The Smash Hits party ended in farce when the staff refused to serve any more alcohol after 11 P.M. Hundreds of cases of free XD lager, donated by sponsors, were left untouched after a licensing cock-up by party organizers forced the bash to end two hours early. As word spread that the only refreshments available were soft drinks at £1.50 a shot, guests scurried for the exit like lemmings heading for the cliffs. (*The Sun,* December 7, 1993)

The lig culture is based on free liquor, free swag, free entrance, and an emphasis on privileged access to the ultimate status markers, the performers themselves.

It is very important to professionals to make sure that once they attempt to get in on the guest list, they succeed at getting inside. With a guest list line swollen with industry personnel, an individual whose name is not on the list has to walk past a gauntlet of his peers in order to leave. As one scenester said outside the London Astoria, "When your name is not there, it's humiliating. Everyone thinks that you are just trying to get in and that you don't belong" (M.K.). Since mistakes do occur, it is not uncommon for names to be left off a list accidentally, especially given the multiple lists coming to the door in the hours before the venue opens. The guest list thus becomes a double-edged sword. On one hand it confers the benefit of getting into the performance for free and indicates privileged status. On the other hand, every time an individual comes to the list door, there is the chance that he or she will not get in and will consequently lose face among his or her peers.

People will use a number of strategies to gain admission if a problem arises and their names do not appear on one of the door lists. These verbal strategies are called "blagging" (a term derived from the French word

---

* In England, alcohol consumption is usually limited by either licensing hours or limitations in funds. Individuals rarely stop drinking because they feel they have imbibed enough. It is not uncommon for individuals to drink until they become paralytic. I have viewed individuals passed out with a drink in hand, only to awaken, have another gulp of ale, and pass out again, somehow never spilling their drink. Thus, beware of industry events that have an unlimited open free bar. Invariably, these events end in abject shambles and tears.

blague, meaning playful deception or a practical joke). Most people attempt to blag their way into gigs when their name is supposed to be on the list but is not. Yet it is not uncommon for a person to show up at a gig knowing his name is not on the list and blag his way in anyway. Hence, blagging is considered to be rooted in deception.

It is industry personnel and scenesters, the members of zone three, rather than ordinary fans, who are most likely to blag their way into an establishment successfully. Guest list positions generally include a "plus one" to allow a member with status to bring his or her own guest. However, just as often, the guest does not have a plus one. A common blag is for the person on the list to assert that his name was supposed to include "plus one" or "plus two" to get extra people into the gig. Because the blagger has already demonstrated a rightful position on the list and because the extra person is right there, this is fairly effective.

Successful blagging entails a display of insider knowledge that begins with one's first utterance to the door person. The insider knows that he or she needs to display knowledge of the functioning of guest lists by asking for a particular guest list. A person's name may be on the house list, the promoter's list, the booking agent's list, the record label's list, the publishing company's list, the publicist's list, the management company's list, or the band's list. Merely saying "I'm on the list" demonstrates a lack of knowledge and may undermine later claims if one's name is not found. Because no person knows for sure that his name will appear, the first moments of interaction with the door person are often suffused with some anxiety, a moment to assert in linguistic and metalinguistic ways one's professional status and right to gain entry. Some individuals use a professional code of succinct nonchalance that suggests that the individual is both unimpressed and has other matters to attend to. Others use a personable and friendly code that is geared to solicit the goodwill of the door person.

Routine 1: Example of Professional Strategy

Guest list line in the foyer of a venue. One woman (W) is in line behind two other individuals. There are two men running the list. One doorman (D1) works for the promoter, the second (D2) works for the venue.

1.　　((*Woman looks away until the people in front have cleared the way.*))
2.　W: Savage and Best guest list Emma F——.
　　　(*spoken quickly in a monotone without pause*)
3.　D1: Sorry?

4. W: Savage and Best guest list . . . Emma F——.
    (*utterance slightly slower, still in monotone*)
5.   *Four-second pause. ((Woman looks over at envelopes with tickets.))*
6. W: It should be over there. Yeah.
7. D2: Here you go.
8. W: Cheers. ((*walks away*))

By looking away prior to walking up to the door, the woman avoids making eye contact with any of the doormen inside the booth, creating a clear boundary for the start of the interaction. She then demonstrates her professional status in several ways. Her first utterance (line 2) asserts in both content and delivery her position as an industry insider. By stating "Savage and Best" rather than "I'm on the list" or even "I'm on the publicist's list," she gives the specific name of the band's publicity company. With this statement she acknowledges her awareness of the existence of a number of lists at the door as well as the doorman's need to know the specific list where her name appears. Her professional status is also indicated by her monotone and the continuous delivery of the guest list name and her own name, which suggest confidence and a certain urgency. Both urgency and a blasé tone imply professional status, because the code of music industry personnel is to display a need to be present in conjunction with a certain coolness and indifference.[13] The woman's interaction with the doormen is minimal. As soon as she is given her ticket and pass, she enters the venue. The interaction contains few superfluous elements and conveys to the doorman that the woman is an experienced professional.[14]

The second strategy used at the door is much more casual, one that attempts to engage the door person in a friendly exchange while the transaction of the guest list takes place:

Routine 2: Example of Personable Strategy

Two women (W1 and W2) approach the guest list booth in the foyer of the same venue. There is one doorman (D1) in the booth with the guest lists.

1. W1: Hey there.
2. W1: Um, we're on Pulp's guest list. I think. ((*W2 flips through a magazine.*))
3.   ((*W1 does a mild eyebrow flash.*))
4. D1: What was that look? (*laughs*)
5.   ((*W1 smiles.*))
6. W1: Ross I——plus one. (*One-second pause*)

7. W1: It's Pulp or Island's.
8. D1: Who put you on?
9. W1: Um, either Georgina or / ((*W1 grimaces.*))
10. D1:   /Found it.
11. W1: Ah, here we are. ((*smiles broadly.*))
12. D1: Do you want some party passes?
13. W1: (*laughs*)
14.   ((*D1 flips two passes at her playfully.*))
15. W1: Lovely, thank you.
16. D1: Bye Ross.

In this interaction, a very different strategy is employed. Rather than expressing confidence or bravado in her interactive strategy, the woman seems uncertain of the potential success of the interaction until her name is actually found. Her quizzical raising of the eyebrows; her modification of her assertion of being on the list with "I think (line 2)," and the "um" preambles all suggest uncertainty. However, she demonstrates insider knowledge by suggesting which list she may appear on and the name of a person involved with the band who may have called in the guest list. This is an effective alternative strategy to the professional style used by the woman in routine 1. This woman opts instead to engage the doorman in a friendly exchange that she hopes will result in goodwill on his part should problems arise. Her initial utterance, "Hey there" (line 1), engages the doorman in an informal exchange rather than a mere business transaction. "Hey there" is a very casual greeting, as opposed to a more formal "Hello," or the even more formal avoidance of salutation, as was exhibited by the woman in routine 1. This informal demeanor is shared by the doorman, who jokes with her about her facial expression, offers her guest passes, playfully tosses her the passes, and even says goodbye to her by name at the end of the transaction. The use of an informal and friendly demeanor has enabled the woman to solicit the goodwill of the doorman. If there is a problem, a person who uses the informal code can generally cajole the door person into letting her into the venue or finding a person who can. Both the professional register and the friendly register are strategies that offer support if a problem arises at the door and the professional's name does not appear on the appropriate guest list.

Often professionals code switch from professional to friendly style during the course of a single interaction.[15] Code switching from the more professional code to the personable code occurs after the professional is given some evidence that the interaction is running smoothly. Usually a code switch occurs when the door person demonstrates his recognition of the individual, or immediately after it is established that the professional's name does indeed appear on the list.

Routine 3: Code Switch from Professional to Personable

Two individuals, a male (P) and a female (S), approach the booth, where one (D) of two doormen interacts with them.

1. P: ((Pointing to top list)) Hi, I should be on that list (*monotone*)
2. P: Paul R—— (*pause*) Sasha G—— (*pause*) (*Same monotone*)
3. D: Well, you might as well tick yourself off then. (*Laughingly*)
4. P: (*Smiles*) Thanks very much. (*smiles broadly*)
5. P: I might do it for you then.
6. D: Yeah, why not, you know.
7.   ((*Looks at list for four seconds*))
8. S: Oh yeah (*quietly*)
9. P: (*Addressed to S*) Did I put myself on?
10.   ((*S points to name*))
11. P: Yeah, that'll do
12. P: (*Laughs*) ((*looks up*))
13. P: How *are* you? ((*while walking away*)) ((*S walks off*))
14. D: I'm ve-ry well.
15. P: Good. Do I need, uh (*pause*), a thing?
16. D: / Yeah yeah yeah.
17. P: I was just about to walk off. I don't know why I was about to walk off.
18. P: ((*takes passes from Doorman*))
19.   ((*P starts to walk away*))
20. D: There you go.
21.   ((*P turns back*))
22.   ((*P purses lips to begin utterance, then walks away*))
23. D: ((*Addressed to man in line*)) Big Bad Bernie G——, his time's up.

This interaction begins with the guest initiating the interaction. He uses the formal monotone and expresses insider knowledge that he should appear on the specific list to which he points. He continues in the formal mode, stating his and his associate's name. It is not until the doorman recognizes his status in line 3 that he changes to the informal demeanor. After the doorman shows the guest that he knows who he is, P smiles, laughs, stumbles over words, and initiates casual conversation (line 13: "how *are* you?"). Once the guest is given evidence that the transaction will go well, those using the professional demeanor frequently code-switch to the informal.[16]

A seasoned doorman is often a promoter who knows a large number of people in the industry and initiates the interaction in a friendly manner. He may call the individual by name, or ask a question that shows his recognition of the professional, or start the interaction by making a joke. This is precisely what occurs at the end of routine 3, when in line 23, the doorman calls the next person in line by name, "Big Bad Bernie G——, his time's up." An interaction initiated by the doorman in the personable code, by friendly solicitation rather than the formal "next," will not code-switch back into the professional code but will continue in the congenial style. Many of the professionals that the doorman recognizes and calls by name are allowed to enter the venue and given passes without the doorman even checking to see if their names appear on the list.

The fact that code switching occurs after the professional has evidence that the interaction at the door will go smoothly suggests that there is some anxiety involved in the guest list transaction. The professional code asserts the individual's right to be on the guest list and can be a potential aid in resolving problems at the door. Once it is established that the interaction is going to run smoothly, however, there is no need to use the more controlled interactive strategy. Often there seems to be pleasure in the switch from professional to informal, with solemnity involved in the formal code and laughter and relaxation of tension occurring during the switch to the informal code. The professional's pleasure in the code switch seems to express some relief that the transaction has been successful.

Since essential face work goes into this interaction on the part of the professional, the individual who is plus one does a number of things to distance himself from the negotiation of the guest list. Most plus ones stand aside, turn their backs to the guest list area, and look away. They generally do not speak, unless on a topic totally unrelated to the door transaction, or unless the doorman initiates conversation with them.

If his name does not appear on the guest list, the professional will attempt to gain entry by rhetoric.* The ligger attempts to assert his or her right to gain entry by communicating insider knowledge: the name of the person who should have put the name on the list, the name of the band's

---

* Musicians are an interesting exception to this rule. Most performers feel uncomfortable asserting their status as a band member in order to receive privileges. Most performers will not argue when their name is not on the list. Generally, they will stand outside until some other professional inquires about their situation. The professional will then go and blag the musician in. Aside from being embarrassed, musicians learn to not attempt to solve problems at shows. Most successful performers are infantilized at gigs from their experiences of being on tour, where all matters are dealt with by tour manager and crew. Most musicians have the expectation that if they just stand there and do nothing, their problem will be solved by other industry professionals—and it usually is.

manager, the name of someone at the record label, or other names with whom most lay people would be unfamiliar. Because professionals are the most versed in techniques to gain entry to events verbally, when mistakes are made it is the nonprofessional friends of the band, people the performers most want to attend the show, that are most likely to be denied entry. Many nonprofessionals do not perform well at this transaction point, because they do not know the proper answers to questions that insiders take for granted. They do not know how to respond to queries such as "What list are you on?" or "Who put your name on the list?" Many bands complain that their own friends are prevented from getting in or getting passes through mixups, while the professional liggers always make it into the gig and aftershow party. As one musician put it, "I show up at the after party, expecting to see my friends, only to find out there was a problem at the door and they were sent home. It really upsets me that my own friends can't get in to see me, but all these people who I don't know are always there" (B. B.).

Many professionals will refuse to take no for an answer at the door and become indignant if they are not allowed to enter the venue. Seasoned professionals rarely leave the door area without successfully gaining entry by one means or another. At times, blaggers can gain entry from sheer persistence; eventually the door person finds it easier to let the ligger in than to deal with his consistent and tenacious demands. Professionals whose names do not appear on the list stand outside the venue or next to the guest list area until someone is found to help them gain entry. For example, Oasis and Whiteout played the 100 Club in London in April 1994. Oasis had been tipped by both of the weeklies as a top new band and had been booked into a tour of small non-standard venues. When an event is at a non-standard venue, the lines to procure entrance are narrowed, increasing the prestige for those who do gain entry. While the 100 Club had hosted gigs for bands on independent labels and some notable punk gigs in the 1970s and 1980s, it became primarily a venue for jazz in the 1990s. This venue presented a particular challenge for entrance because the club staff would not recognize indie professionals. Several professionals stood outside for the duration of the set, trying to blag entry rather than admit defeat and leave.

The influential role of guest lists means that those who consistently control guest lists—promoters, booking agents, and venues—have a great deal of power and influence over other industry professionals. Industry personnel need to cultivate goodwill within these relationships in order to secure guest list positions regularly, particularly on the most difficult and therefore most prestigious lists. The guest list system thoroughly serves the music industry, irrespective of the needs and desires of artists.

Passes

I heard that it was a really big deal
then I found out it was just nothing at all . . .
Razorlight

The importance of attending a performance by getting on the guest list is demonstrated not only at the guest list transaction point but also inside the venue for shows that feature guest passes. A guest pass, usually a sticker, confers some specific access to the recipient. In the United Kingdom, most passes are distributed at the door. Getting on a list does not necessarily ensure a guest pass, but it is the customary way of obtaining one. Therefore, if one pays to get into a venue, he or she will need to find other means to get hold of a pass. One can receive a pass directly from the band, crew, record label, or promoter, or from another professional who chooses not to use his, or by surreptitiously exchanging passes with someone who has received one at the door. Once inside a venue, there is a great deal of pass manipulation among professionals.

For industry personnel, the gig has a detailed system of markers of a status hierarchy based on access. At a small gig such as one at the Garage in Islington, there is only one kind of guest pass, but for a show promoted by Metropolis, Mean Fiddler, or SJM Concerts at large to mid-size venues, there are usually different classes of passes. There may be as many as five levels of guest passes—Guest, Aftershow, Photo, All Access, and laminate—each one a different color and indicating a different level of access and prestige (image 3.1). The Guest pass allows the individual to go backstage after the show and to remain within the venue after the show is over. The Aftershow pass allows a person to remain in the venue after punters are forced to leave. The Photo pass is for photographers and allows someone to enter the cordoned-off area at the front of the stage.[17] Both the All Access and laminate passes allow access to all areas in the venue, including stage, backstage, dressing room, and guest area, at all times. The laminate, a pass that has a plastic coating, comes from the band or band management. Band members themselves use laminates, which are the rarest form of pass and have the highest status. At particularly large gigs there may also be table passes. Since most gig venues have very limited seating, the few tables in the venue are reserved and can be accessed only with a table pass.

People regularly put their passes in particular locations on their clothing, and this placement also suggests a particular status. Conspicuous pass placement is a sign of the novice. First-time or occasional pass obtainers place their passes somewhere on the outside of their clothing in some

IMAGE 3.1. Various passes and levels of access. *From author's videotape*

highly visible location—the outside of the jacket, on the upper arm, on the center of a dress between the breasts, on the shirt directly over the breast (image 3.2). Professionals, on the other hand, customarily place their passes discreetly. This is part of the professionals' overall ethic of a composed and unimpressed demeanor at shows. The experienced ligger wears his pass in some location that is not readily visible, most commonly on the inside of a jacket. Individuals not wearing jackets will use any number of non-overt display strategies, such as placing the pass in a pocket, or putting it on the underside of a shirt or the inside of a skirt (images 3.3 and 3.4). The individual will lift the portion of clothing to display the pass to security when he or she wants to enter access points. Clearly this method is not the most efficient means to get inside or outside areas; it underscores the lengths to which industry personnel will go to use a specific mode of placement to distinguish themselves from a novice. At times, security personnel try to get all pass-holders to wear their passes overtly; it makes their job easier and provides less opportunity for individuals to transfer passes between friends. When a door or security person hands over a pass, it is not uncommon for him to insist that the pass holder stick the pass on immediately, or the person will place the pass on the guest in a prominent position. As soon as he or she is out of sight, the experienced ligger will remove the pass and put it in a covert position.

IMAGE 3.2. Overt pass display. Pass placed prominently on chest. *Photo courtesy of Neville Elder.*

The removal and repositioning of passes by experienced liggers demonstrates that pass placement is not unconscious. Participants are aware of the different readings and the significance of their pass placement. Experienced liggers will make fun of individuals who use overt pass placement, though there are certain circumstances in which even experienced pass wearers will choose to use overt placement.

Within the indie community, pass placement functions as a code of communication. Pass placement, a communicative act regarding access and prestige, depends not only on *what* one wants to say but more importantly to *whom* one wants to say it. Placing a pass overtly makes the utterance of access available to the general audience. Hence, overt placement is an act that has its object of address as the punter. Covert pass placement makes the utterance of access available only to those who are also within areas of privileged access; both have made it to the inner sanctum. Thus, covert pass placement is a mode of address that is directed toward others with passes; the liggers make this utterance available only to the desired recipients, one's

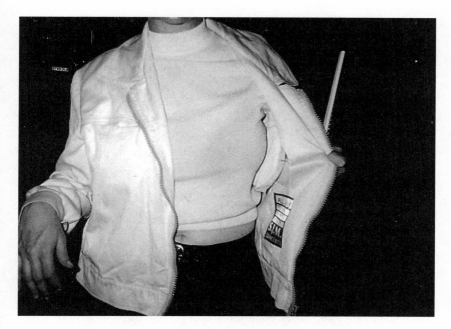

IMAGE 3.3. Covert pass display. Pass placed on interior of jacket. *Photo by author.*

colleagues. Covert placement provides the opportunity to display one's status to one's peers while excluding the larger portion of the audience.

A visible pass, the announcement to the entire crowd of privileged access, is regarded as unprofessional for several reasons. Overt placement is seen to impute a valuation of the pass by the wearer that is antithetical to the appropriate demeanor of being blasé and unimpressed. It is very important that the professional *appear* unconcerned with guest passes, because this is part of the general trend of coolness, an attitude representing unflappability, equanimity, and a distant demeanor. Public pass placement is seen as a kind of braggadocio that implies that having a pass is either a novel experience or that the wearer is himself as impressed as a fan might be. The suggestion of an affinity with fans is problematic for professionals, because this is the group from which professionals want to differentiate themselves. Covert placement is seen as modest. Finally, overt pass placement demonstrates a lack of knowledge of the norms of the profession.

Nevertheless, professionals do value their passes; many maintain pass collections, and they all expend great effort to obtain them. Most professionals' homes are filled with used guest passes (image 3.5).[18] Nonetheless, any public acknowledgment of the valuation of passes is embarrassing. Although the norms of professional conduct include their covert

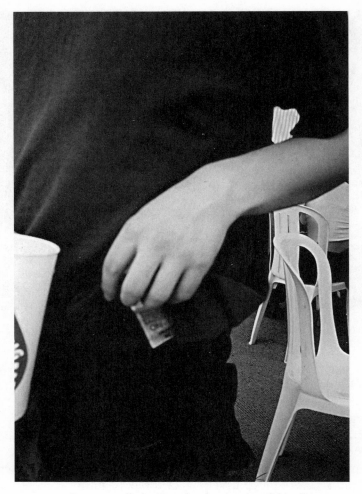

IMAGE 3.4. Covert pass display. Pass placed on interior of shirt. Pass holder needs to lift up and display underside of shirt for security personnel at access points. *Photo by author.*

placement and the ethic of coolness and indifference, industry personnel are concerned with displaying their status to both punters and colleagues. Often industry people will find ingenious ways to show off a pass while seemingly indicating its insignificance to themselves. One professional related the story of placing an All Access pass on his rear end as a means of expressing his supposed disregard of the pass while simultaneously displaying it to the crowd and colleagues. Later, his girlfriend told me that on that same evening, he couldn't find his pass and panicked, claiming it had been

IMAGE 3.5. Guest pass collection on bedroom door. *Photo by author.*

IMAGE 3.6. An example of an artfully placed guest pass, half visible and half obscured by jacket. *Photo by author.*

stolen. When he got home, he found it on the bottom of his shoe. A professional may make a pass visible if he has received a higher-prestige pass. For example, a journalist at a gig in London with an All Access pass chose to place this pass not on the inside of his jacket, as he had done at all of the other shows he had recently attended, but he meticulously placed the pass directly on his shirt, half visible and half obscured by his jacket (image 3.6). This placement allowed the professional to display his greater access to colleagues in such a way that the conspicuousness of the display appeared inadvertent. Professionals are likely to alter their standard pass placement when attending shows outside of the industry enclaves of London, Manchester, and Glasgow. Being away from industry centers gives the professional license to address a different audience. In most other cities, there are far fewer professionals in attendance. Therefore, with an insufficient audience of professionals to share status with, it may be more satisfying to address the audience of punters.

Laminates are a special class of passes and have their own particular norms of display. Laminates have a lanyard so that the pass can be worn around the neck or on a clip that can be attached to clothing (image 3.7). Laminates are the highest-prestige passes because they assert a direct connection with the band that is playing rather than a generalized status conferred by the industry. Record company professionals who do not regularly

IMAGE 3.7. Festival laminate pass on clip. *Photo courtesy of Neville Elder.*

IMAGE 3.8. Covert display of laminate. Band manager with laminate on lanyard with pass tucked into front pocket. *Photo courtesy of Neville Elder.*

have access to laminates will generally wear them in some visible position to alert their colleagues, most of whom do not have laminates, to their increased access. Band managers who regularly have laminates generally keep their passes in pockets, so that, as one band manager put it, "I don't look like some fucking record company guy who's showing off" (image 3.8). The more success that professionals have in obtaining laminates, the more likely it is that they will revert to covert pass placement, even of laminates.[19]

Performing band members are given laminates but rarely remember to bring them to the venue. They rely instead on being recognized. Saying you are in the band is the most effective of all blags, but one that is rarely used. Saying you are with the band might get you in, but saying you are *in* the band means you *will* get in. Performers are reticent about wearing passes, and even when they bring them to the venue they often leave them in the dressing room. Band members, like their managers, do not like being viewed as showing off their status. However, when a musician is at a show where he or she is not performing, he or she uses the same mode of pass placement as other professionals.

Laminates are used quite differently by crew members. Crew members are employees of the band who set up equipment and perform as technicians during the show. Going in and out of access areas often carrying gear makes discreet placement prohibitively difficult. Crew members keep laminates on the lanyards, which they wear around their necks or attached to their belt loops. Some crew members wear more than the single laminate they have received for the current tour; sometimes they wear nearly all of the laminates for all of the tours they have worked. This practice was very common in the early 1990s but fell out of fashion and became "uncool" in the 2000s. It is now seen as lame, and often one's current band will make fun of the other bands that the crew member has worked with. However, the old-style laminate stack showed the tour experience of a crew member and would function as a portable resume. When non-working crew people came to shows, they would flip through working crew members' laminates to determine what colleagues they shared in common.

Laminates are not used solely for access. At times, crew members will wander conspicuously around the venue among the crowd with their passes prominently displayed to attract attention from female fans by demonstrating their band access. This activity is called "trolling," suggesting that the crew member is fishing for females. The indie scene disparages trolling and views it as unethical by most band and crew members. This is in accordance with the general indie attitude against immodest sexual promiscuity, braggadocio, or the misuse of power.[20]

The prestige of the access accorded to various passes is especially pronounced at the large summer festivals, where thousands of industry professionals converge. The institution of the summer festivals (Reading/Leeds, T in the Park, the V Festival) as important industry events has meant that access has become easier for industry personnel. Since no one in the industry would be caught dead at a festival such as Reading without some form of backstage pass, the Mean Fiddler organization, which promotes the event, began selling guest passes in 1994 so that they would get income from the thousands of industry personnel who demanded them. As a result, the basic guest pass is much more available and therefore less valuable. At times, the backstage area rivals the density of the regular venue areas. Production passes allow holders into the area immediately behind the stages, where the bands' dressing rooms are. The stage passes allow access to both the production area and a cordoned-off section that allows one to watch the performance from the side of the stage. The difficult-to-obtain production and stage passes confer the prestige originally accorded to guest passes: "Figured that, if nothing else, I might be able to blag a few bottles of whiskey from bands' dressing-rooms with my access-all-areas 'Everett True' pass. Yep! That'd annoy a few of my 'cooler' contemporaries. I can get there, they can't! Nyah, nyah, nyah-nyah, nyah!" (*Melody Maker*, September 3, 1994, in reference to the Reading festival). This quote from journalist provocateur Everett True correctly identifies the production area as the true locus of status and the main guest area as a prestigeless domain. It allows Everett True to flaunt his own status (a trademark of *Melody Maker*–style journalism) while simultaneously denigrating the "cool" and covert displays of his contemporaries.

There is a variation in display strategies for passes at festivals as well. Most individuals with guest passes are given wristbands that they are compelled by staff to put on immediately or are manually placed on the guest's wrist by a staff member (image 3.9). Guests with greater access are further designated by stickers or specially colored wristbands. Because most people do not wear jackets at summer festivals or remove them at some point, professionals place their passes differently at festivals. Again, to differentiate themselves from the novice or fan, experienced liggers select a position that suggests covert display. At festivals, music industry professionals place passes on the hip, a less conspicuous position that fits in with the ideology of discretion (image 3.10).

Because an individual may have different degrees of access at different events, the high status conferred by a high-access pass is an ephemeral one, one that applies to one event only. The experienced scenester knows that a pass extends only temporary and immaterial status and often fears that someone will take it away. Several professionals said they used covert display to keep their pass from being stolen. However, no one could produce a story of a pass actually being stolen, only of times when they mistakenly thought so. On the other hand, the punter, with no experience of the backstage, has the idea that the backstage area contains a coherent group of people that can recognize each other and that someone who does not belong will be easily identified. Therefore, punters do not usually view passes as transferable. Anxiety about a pass getting stolen does not seem to be based on actual threat but rather on the overall transient status that the pass confers.

IMAGE 3.9. Festival goer with guest area wristband. Note: another Aftershow pass from a previous event is located on the interior of her jacket, showing the standard covert pass strategy used by most professionals and scenesters at gigs. *Photo courtesy of Neville Elder.*

IMAGE 3.10. Alternate festival style of guest pass display. Pass is located on hip or thigh, which is less conspicuous than upper-body placement. *Photo courtesy of Neville Elder.*

Privileged Spectatorship

Take me to the backstage . . .
Beck

Just as members of zones one and two privilege their spectatorship and location within the venue, so do the professionals in zone three. Professionals often joke that the back is where the bar is and that it is far more important to be near alcohol than it is to be near the band. Within this community, a great deal is made of drinking to excess, so that a valuation of alcohol is a humorous way of validating one's participation in the back of the venue.

Professionals use the gig as an opportunity to portray themselves to other professionals not as ordinary audience members but rather as members of a special class of music elite. They define themselves as "non-fan." Fans inhabit an asymmetrical relationship to performers, exhibiting submissive postures and submissive interactive strategies. Revealing that one is impressed by contact with a band presents the individual as a "fan" with an inferior relationship to the artists. Professionals need not only to express a positive affinity with a band but also to refrain from exhibiting fan behavior, which would set up a relationship that gives power to the musicians and negatively impacts the professional's position in working relationships. Interestingly, in the early days of a band's career the professionals are seen by band members as high-status individuals with whom the musicians want to develop peer relationships. A professional needs to demonstrate an appreciation of the band but create a distinction between himself and fans. The standardized comportment of coolness—covert pass placement, lack of attention to the performance, casual demeanor—is how professionals display their non-fan relationship vis-à-vis performers. Professionals point to their access to the band and to the fact that they are effectively "guests" of the band rather than fans. They also emphasize the fact that they interact with the artists regularly in other settings.

Although those in the back of the venue privilege their spectorial position, professionals also feel some need to justify it. Their view of the performance includes a view of what other audience members closer to the stage do. Their view of zones one and two are images of their own histories at gigs. Professionals readily admit that they had more fun at shows when they were younger and went all the way up front with no thought of meeting the band afterward. However, while wistfully remembering their younger participation in the front, most professionals either are not sufficiently motivated to return there or feel that they cannot because of their age and temperament. One label employee put it this way: "I sometimes think, wouldn't it be fun to run up front again and jump about? But then I think I wouldn't really enjoy being bashed about and all sweaty. I'm just too old for all that" (A.B.). Another added, "I would never allow a band to see me that way again" (G.P.).

Once exposed to the comforts of the backstage life, most professionals find it too seductive to return to less privileged forms of participation. Their activities at shows are increasingly focused on career advancement, obtaining swag, and collegial contact with musicians and other professionals, and they are less and less about experiencing live music. Many find themselves waiting impatiently for the set to end or are bored unless they are engaged in conversations with others. If they do wish to watch a band, they stand in the very back of zone two, often chatting throughout the performance to the chagrin of those older fans who just want to watch the show. At big prestige events such as the summer festivals, a significant number of professionals will rarely leave the backstage area and actually see very little, if any, of the bands performing. It is as if when one becomes a participant in the world of the professionals, the behind-the-scenes workings of the music world, it becomes more and more unfeasible to locate oneself as a fan again.[21]

Conclusion

Zone three, the area in the back of the venue, has a significantly different orientation than the other two audience regions. Those in zone three do not respond to the performance. They do not applaud between songs. Zone three is where paying audience members go when they wish to disengage from the performance, and it is habitually selected by professionals. While the other zones have embodied forms of spectatorship regarding the experience of music, zone three is different. At gigs, professionals strive to represent themselves to fellow professionals as non-fans. By getting on the guest list, the professional is separated from the punter, the paying customer. The guest list cuts two ways, however: while it can confirm one's power in the industry, it can also result in the loss of face when the transaction does not result in entry. In this setting, guest passes are signs in a hierarchy of access to exclusive space and performers. They confer a temporary and ephemeral status. Guest passes function as a form of address, one that marks to whom an audience member's orientation is geared. The goals and activities of zone three may at times make the performance seem superfluous; however, it is precisely the activities of these specialists that make gigs possible.

The ties among professionals, established and reinforced in the gig setting, have repercussions far beyond the limits of the gig itself. Not only is a large portion of company time invested in obtaining access to these events, but at gigs information is distributed among colleagues that impinges upon future business transactions, such as the assessments of new talent or the hiring of personnel.

The gig oils the machinations of the music industry; it serves as an opportunity for professionals to display themselves as active, networked members of a professional class. The band functions as a fetishized commodity within a hierarchical system of power and influence peddling. The tools of the industry at shows—the passes and the guest lists—are used by industry members to display status and articulate the dominant comportment mode of the industry: being cool and nonchalant. In addition, they express a dominant ethos regarding the procurement of freebies, which differentiates the professionals from the fans, the liggers from the punters, the powerful from the impotent.

CHAPTER 4

The Participant Structure and the
Metaphysics of Spectatorship

✳

In my previous chapters, I described the modes of participation at gigs of segments of indie audiences in ethnographic detail. Each of the gig zones has distinct modalities of comportment. Zone one spectatorship is embodied in active physical engagement and close proximity, and zone one is inhabited by the youngest and most demonstrative fans. Zone two spectatorship is characterized by a contemplative focus and more controlled passive bodily comportment, and zone two is composed of older, more experienced fans as well as individuals who are not particularly involved with indie music. Zone three is composed primarily of those who find the performance unsatisfying, as well as professionals in the act of networking and distinguishing themselves from ordinary fans.

In this chapter, I show how different spectorial modes and locations assume meaning within the totality of a participant structure. By examining the participant structure both synchronically and diachronically, it becomes apparent that indie gigs are events that articulate youth as a time of physical engagement and adulthood as a time of composed demeanor and mental contemplation. Additionally, the relationship among spectorial modes over time articulates the pervasive cultural narrative of the transformation from out-of-control, unconverted youth into Protestant adulthood; from youthful Romanticism into stoic utilitarianism.

Spatial relations among individuals in face-to-face interaction communicate about their relationships. Raymond Firth, in his discussion of a traditional hierarchical society, points out, "With the Tikopia, as with most if not all other communities, space relations in personal contacts are translated into status relations" (Firth 1978: 91). Firth goes on to discuss how focus of orientation, proximity, and relative verticality are used to express status relationships. These features articulate an audience member's relationship with performers, their music, and, by extension, other audience members. They also articulate issues of critical concern involved with gig going: (1) affiliation; (2) the status of performers; (3) consensus-building; (4) age and the category of youth; and (5) contesting modalities of spectatorship.

Proximity, Affiliation, and Consensus Building

Orienting with body and gaze toward the performers onstage is one way of demonstrating alignment with the band. In the gig setting, orientation to the band designates the band's high status in the event and the audience members' recognition of that status. However, as research by cultural and linguistic anthropologists on interactive modalities has demonstrated, orientation and direct gaze toward a person do not necessarily correspond to an articulation of high status. It is a fairly common cultural strategy to have eye-gaze aversion between low-status individuals and high-status individuals, as is found in India and among several Native American groups (Appadurai 1990; Basso 1979). However, in the gig setting the orientation toward performers *is* an acknowledgment of the performers' valued status.[1] Let us turn to an example where an audience member quite visibly refused to orient toward the performers onstage.

On a single occasion at a small venue in Brixton, a drunken and belligerent audience member positioned himself in such a way as to disengage with the band that was performing. This small pub venue had a stage raised only a foot above the floor. The audience member stood directly in front of the band with his back to the performers, arms crossed, defying both the band and other audience members who were enjoying the show. Later, this man sat on the stage, ignoring the gig convention that identifies the stage as space reserved for performers. He eventually left the venue before the performance ended.[2] By turning his back to the performers and accessing their privileged space, he attempted to physically deny the performers' status and their value as a band.

Individuals do not visually orient toward the performers in zone three and thereby undermine the assumption that the band has a high status. Most punters consider industry professionals to be the antithesis of fans, in large part because of this lack of orientation to the performance. Thus, the insider's distinction between punters and liggers parallels a relationship between those who interactively assert a high status for performers during the show and those who do not.

To understand the meanings of spatial distribution at gigs, it is important to remember that location selection at gigs is voluntary and intentional. Location is seen by audience members as a deliberate act rather than an arbitrary or financial one. As such, location has developed in the gig setting as one of the chief means of expressing affiliation with the band performing. Additionally, this participant structure allows individuals to move in response to their ongoing assessment of the band and the event at hand during the course of a gig.

This relationship between closeness and the public statement of positive assessment is evident when comparing a well-attended show to one that isn't. Our discussion of distribution up to this point has covered gigs with full audiences. However, since indie shows are often in small venues with bands that are not established, many gigs are sparsely attended. Interactive norms are most clearly evident when they are breached (Goffman 1959). An event with meager attendance can demonstrate the underlying norms of participation and illustrate several very significant components of audience behavior.

At a show of a band with poor attendance, the distribution density of the audience is generally inverted. Few, if any, audience members stand in the front; the majority of audience members in the venue stand in zone two and zone three. The back is the most densely occupied part of the venue. At some shows, such as professional showcases, the distribution density of the back may rival what is ordinarily seen in the front at a well-attended gig.[3] Additionally, one does not find the intense physical dynamics characteristic of larger performances. For example, at a show at the Harlsden Mean Fiddler, distribution density was inverted. Here, the audience members closest to the stage stood approximately twelve feet back. At sparsely attended shows, distribution is usually organized around some architectural feature within the venue. Often, this distinguishing feature between zone one and zone two is where the stage lights fall on the dance floor. At this particular show, however, the closest audience members stood just outside of this light, and most of the people in the venue stood in the bar region in the back and side periphery areas. No one danced, jumped on top of other people, or engaged in any of the activities associated with zone one. At poorly attended gigs, zone one is often a no-man's land.

How can we understand the inversion of distribution found at shows that are not well attended? Obviously, standing in the front is not merely the result of an a priori assumption that the front is the best place to be or that age is an all-defining determinant of location. If the former were the case, the front would consistently be the most densely occupied location, despite the relative size of the audience. If the latter were the case, distribution would be strictly correlated to age demographics. Neither is true. At

gigs, selection of location is a visible index of an assessment to other participants, including the band. Audience members stand in the front, close to
the stage, when they wish to communicate their own identities as loyal fans
to the band. The more distant one's position, the more distant the fanship
articulated. Placement in the back indicates a lack of commitment or a non-
fan relationship with the band. The understanding that proximity represents one's degree of public statement of affiliation comes from audience
members' shared experiences of the indie participant structure, moving
forward and back in relationship to one's assessment of the band. The
meanings assigned to the different geographic regions of the floor—close
equals strong fanship; distance equals reserved fanship; the back equals
non-fanship—arise from experience with gigs

It happened at the Afghan Whigs show. I got this urge, I have to go forward. The
show was really amazing and you have this revelation to go forward; it was just this
urgent thing. You get drawn forward at a really good show. Up there, it is more
connected—to the audience, the band, the whole show. I only move up when the
band is that good. (J.G., age twenty-six)

There was a massive stampede for them and we just stayed in the back coz we don't
like them. We only go to the front for our favorite bands. (R.C., age twenty)

For popular bands, audience members will wait in line for hours to be in
the front. For unknown bands without fans, the gig becomes in part a place
to entice people to move closer and inhabit the space of fans.

Most indie bands' early experiences of performance take the shape of
the inverted distribution of audience density, with a large gap between the
stage and the audience members. Bands want to close this gap. Many un-
successful bands or bands just starting out will try to get friends to come
and stand in the front to avoid having this open space and to lure other audience members to stand there, too. Performers will try, at times, to cajole
audience members into moving forward, or they will berate audience
members for standing back. Asking audience members to move forward
may result in a few individuals shuffling a couple feet forward. However,
this request often makes audience members uncomfortable. I was told:
"When you are at a small gig and hardly anyone is there, you feel sorry for
the band and it makes you feel really awkward. It's even worse if they ask
you to move up. I always go to get a drink if that happens." (J.B., age
twenty-eight). If we understand location selection as speaking to the fan
relationship between audience member and performer, then asking audience members to move forward is, in effect, asking the audience to have a
different relationship to the band, asking them to behave as though they
like the band more.

However, merely inhabiting the front is not necessarily enough to communicate positive enthusiasm. The audience members also need to participate appropriately. A violation of interactive norms can undermine proximity as an indicator of affiliation.[4] It also speaks to the individual's relationship to other audience members. Persons comporting themselves in comparable or opposing manners correspondingly comment on whether they have a similar or different spectorial relationship to other audience members. The Brixton man to whom I referred earlier not only opposed himself to the band but also to the other audience members who in turn refuted his position by continuing to participate appreciatively.

At an indie gig, where one places oneself is a physical enactment of a statement of assessment. Physical proximity, physical activities such as movement corresponding to the music's rhythm, and visual concentration on the performers are socially constructed markers of alignment. Physical distance and attention to other activities are acts of disalignment, noncommitment, and/or status differentials. Thus, while there may be many reasons to stand in a particular location within the venue, here it is read as a statement about one's relationship to the band onstage.

Nevertheless, this does not answer the question of why sparsely attended shows are characterized by a no-man's land between the stage and the majority of audience members. Surely, someone who has paid to attend the show considers himself a fan. To fully understand inverted distribution, we need to consider what audience members want from their participation at a gig. If it were merely an experience of the music or a desire to be close to the performers, the number of attendees would not matter. If this were the case, one would expect the effects of small crowds to be random.

The regularity of inverted distribution is based in part on audience members' wish for a group experience (Whiteley 1997). The reason I have taken pains to stress that location is a statement rather than a simple correspondence to the audience member's actual feelings toward the performers is that there may be a disjunction between actual and displayed affiliation. It is important not to conflate the public display with the affect itself. Since one cannot actually enter the minds of fellow participants, it is difficult to impute emotional states from the mere display of communicative features. Within the ongoing event, audience members merely have the displayed behaviors of other participants from which to take meaning. This is particularly true at gigs, where talking is often difficult. Audience members rely on displayed behaviors to monitor fellow audience members. This distinction between sentiment and display is particularly important in the gig setting, because fans often select positions in the venue in relationship to where other fans locate themselves. An individual may wish to be more enthusiastic and active but may not act on these desires because others have not located themselves in the same area. Most experienced audience members relate similar tales of the uncomfortable experience of selecting a location in the front without first monitoring other audience members.

I got to the show with two of my friends early, and they went to the bar to get some drinks, and so I just went right up front the way I always used to do. Then, you know, the band started up and I realized I was the only one standing up front. I just felt really embarrassed and uncomfortable, and I knew that all those people watching the stage could see me. I felt like I couldn't move, but I didn't want to stand there anymore. I don't really know why. After like five minutes, I went to the bathroom even though I didn't need to and after I went to go to stand with my two friends at the bar. (S.R., age twenty-one)

We walked up front and then the band started and no one else was there. It's kind of embarrassing. You feel the band is just looking at you and you feel intimidated by the other people in the venue. Once you picked the position, you feel obliged to stand there. You feel that if you walk away you are kind of giving in. (M.C., age twenty-seven)

These individuals located themselves in zone one only to find themselves alone. Each felt uncomfortable and conspicuously on display. If we understand the selection of position in the venue as a means of taking a public stand, we can understand each individual's reluctance to move. In some sense, it would be backing down from the stand he had taken. However, remaining in the front is equally uncomfortable. Not only is the fan aware that no one else has taken a similar stand, but he knows that everyone else in the venue can see him; his spectatorship is conspicuously apparent.

In the embarrassment and reticence to stand alone in zone one, we can see one of the underlying components of the successful gig experience: the desire to be part of a consensus. To be a member of a group allows the audience member to feel unselfconscious. Studies on crowd behavior have shown that individuals feel diminished responsibility and a lack of awareness regarding the consequences of their actions when they are participating in large crowds (Hughes 1972, King 1991, Moscovici 1985). When the audience member is alone, he is aware of his spectorial position and its visibility to others. In place of the lack of selfconsciousness of the crowd that contributes to giving oneself to the narrative unfolding of the event, the individual becomes hyperconscious of his own role in that event.

Gigs can change the isolated experience of music in private contexts into a community of sentiment. Indie songs speak emotions—isolation, melancholy, longing, the joy of connection. When audience members recognize their feelings in lyrics or music, they feel they are not alone; someone else feels the same. When this music is played in public—on the radio or at a live performance—this emotional consensus can expand to include other listeners and other audience members. The gig presents the opportunity to be intimate with others, physically and emotionally. When an audience member stands alone in the front, he is publicly isolated in his stance rather than part of a community of sentiment. Consensus building and producing shared sentiment are integral elements to an audience member's ability to participate in the event.[5] It is when the audience member is isolated that he must confront the visibility of his audience status. He feels part of the spectacle itself rather than the recipient of it. This creates a bind for the audience member: he does not want to be seen to be altering his stance due to peer pressure, but at the same time he is painfully aware that everyone in the venue can see him as clearly as the performers. The gig is an event about temporarily overcoming distance, about finding closeness and connectedness with other audience members, the performers onstage, and the music itself.

Verticality and Asymmetry

The movement through the venue also marks changes in the symmetry of the relationship between band and audience. The closer one is to the stage, the more that relationship is asymmetrical, with the artist being treated deferentially and devotionally by the fan. Further back, audience members exhibit far fewer conventionalized fan behaviors until zone three, where professionals ostensibly treat performers as peers. This change in relationship symmetry is mirrored in the relative verticality of perspective from different regions of the venue.

The young fans of zone one exhibit the often stereotypical and asymmetrical fan behavior associated with interactions between performers and their fans. Zone one fans become rather nervous and deferential around performers, particularly offstage. Zone one fans exhibit a series of submissive postures. Young fans generally approach performers with their heads downcast. The head is tilted downward and sideways so that the fan can look up at the performer while talking to him/her. Fans often clasp their hands behind their backs, lower their shoulders, visually orient toward the performer, and give performers wider berth than they do in interactions between peers. Because professionals wish to assert a peer relationship, they consciously avoid displaying behaviors that suggest an asymmetrical relationship in face-to-face interaction. Fans direct all speech to the performer, and when several people are present they position themselves directly opposite the artist rather than standing at their side as the artist's friends and peers do. At moments of assessment in conversation, these fans will wait for the response of the performer before they offer an opinion on a subject in order to make sure that they do not express an opinion that may be contrary. It is the fans in the front who persistently exhibit submissive and deferential conduct to performers, mirroring the lower position of their visual perspective during the show.

The more experienced fans exhibit far fewer stereotypical fan behaviors. Only a small portion of zone two fans attempts to interact with performers on a personal level. Industry personnel in zone three perform as professionals by opposing themselves to the behaviors of fans. Those in zone three who do not like the performance have opted out of being in any affiliatory relationship with the band whatsoever. They may even express hostility.

This change in symmetry of relations matches the alteration of the perspectives set forth by moving through space. The majority of stages are elevated, and therefore the closer one stands to the stage, the more one literally looks up to the performer. As one moves back in the venue, the perspective changes and the audience member looks directly at the performer. The Western convention is that occupying a higher space designates a correspondingly higher status (Firth 1978).[6] Within the English language, "looking up" indicates admiration or respect, conveyed in terms of a spatial metaphor. In the gig setting that metaphor is literally and physically enacted. As one moves back, both the metaphoric and the literal activity of looking up to performers declines.

Physical space as a mirror of social relationships is also seen in the careers of bands. The unpopular bands often play in venues without stages or with stages with only a slightly raised platform, suggesting more parity between band and audience. Successful bands perform in venues with stages elevated several feet above the main floor. Thus, as a band increases in popularity, there are more individuals who both literally and metaphorically look up to it.

Contesting Spectorial Positions: Closeness and Distance

Audience members do not have a homogenous relationship with performers. Each zone privileges its mode of participatory spectatorship over the others. The habitual denizens of each zone, while possessing different modes of comportment, utilize different metaphors of closeness as an indication of their elevated spectorial positions over other audience members—either physical closeness to the performers onstage, closeness to the music itself, or personal closeness to the artists offstage.[7]

As mentioned earlier, the individuals who habituate each area give reasons why their own location in space is best and denigrate participation in other zones. People who inhabit zone one claim that it is the most exciting and the physically "closest" to the band. Members of zone two claim their spectorial position as closest to the music. Both zone one and zone two members criticize the professionals of zone three for not being fans. They describe liggers with a litany of abuse fed by the lore of professional exploitation and manipulation that is rife in music mythology: "record company scum," "a bunch of tossers," or "wankers." This distaste for professionals is matched by the professionals' denigration of punters: "I feel I have some power, power because I don't see myself as a consumer. I think consumers are dupes." (S.C. label employee); "I can't stand punters—the great unwashed masses." (P.L, journalist). Zone three members privilege their spectatorship in terms of their access to artists and the role they play behind the scenes. They often assume that other audience members are jealous of their privileged access. The professionals consider themselves so personally close to performers offstage that they do not need to be close to or involved with them when they perform. As one professional said to me, "I don't need to watch them play. I can see them backstage afterwards" (J.O., publicist). Within this participation structure, the performers in the band function as valorized objects, and audience members distinguish themselves from each other in terms of their access to and association with these fetishized personae.

While similarities and differences are mapped in terms of relative degrees of closeness, they are also contested on the grounds of different modes of engagement. Zone one can be a violent maelstrom of activity or an area of quiet intimacy, but the front is consistently the domain where there is the most physical contact among participants and the greatest physical response to the music. Zone one participants select physical engagement with the music as the superior mode of comportment at a gig. Zone two, on the other hand, is relatively stable and introverted, with audience members exhibiting a muted physical response to the music. These individuals privilege a mode of comportment that represents a growing intellectual and cognitive intimacy with the music. The professionals in zone three, while not paying a great deal of attention to the ongoing performance, do attend to the intricacies of the music industry. The professionals see themselves as sharing a co-creator role in the gig event.

The audience at the gig embodies contesting spectorial modes. Within the event, the processes of making distinctions between participants are as integral to the gig experience as is the process of making positive associations. Members of the indie community are intensely concerned with distinctions among members and who has preferential access to the band and the music. Furthermore, the contrasting and contesting spectorial positions found in the actual interactions of audience members at gigs contradict the representation of "youth" cultures as a utopian ideal where young people come to revolt against the hegemony of culture. Instead, the gig appears to reproduce a set of hierarchical distinctions all its own.

Age

now that I'm older,
my heart's colder,
and I can see that it's a lie . . .
Arcade Fire

As I suggested in earlier chapters, age is a critical issue for the indie music community. The participants in indie music are predominately late adolescents and young adults. The social organization of the space at the gig is age graded with the youngest participants in the front. As older fans put it:

As you get older you stand further back. I mean five years ago, I'd stand right up front, but then you move back and you think, shit, I'd never stand up there. I mean you'd never see a young kid who is really into it standing in the back. (J.B., age thirty-one)

The first time, I went with a few friends and we went down in the front and were jumping around and I thought this is great and I had a really good time. This is really good, I'll do this again. . . . Gradually over the years I've got further and further back. Now as a professional, my attention span is so short, I get bored. I start at the back and then go to the upstairs bar. (S.C., age twenty-eight)

It just doesn't seem right when you have all these kids around you. You just feel old, like you don't belong up there. (M.K., age twenty-eight)

Age is revealed to be a key component in the cultural organization of space at the indie gig. As individuals age they move back through space, until they are aged out of the venue altogether.[8]

Age is not merely an element in the participant structure of indie music gigs; it is also a topic of great concern and attention in the indie community. Regularly, bands are positively assessed by the fact that they appeal to a teen fanbase or are themselves teenagers: "They were and still are great songs to be a teenager to" (*Melody Maker,* December 23, 1995); or "Hail Menswear! They're young! They're crazy! They don't want to be told what to do by men in suits" (*Melody Maker,* April 1, 1991). Moreover, aging is seen to marginalize one's ability to participate, and being called old is an insult of the highest order.

So high on her horse that she can't get near the level of the kids the Indie Day was meant for? Maybe she should stick to reporting on the Over-25s Disco . . . (letters page, *Melody Maker,* June 25, 1994)

Please tell your older hacks that The Clash and Generation X are *dead*. Manic Street Preachers are very much now. You should write about them, that's why

I'm one of your newest readers and that's why you're called *New Musical Express* and not *Necrophiliac Mortuary Echo!* Youth—You love us! (letters page, *NME,* June 8, 1991)

Segal also seems to think they're too young to be in a band, even though they are over 21 (old enough to be Northern Uproar's granddads). Maybe you should have sent her to review Phil Collins or Dire Straits. (letters page, *Melody Maker,* June 1, 1996)

The It Girl is an amazing album crammed with emotive indie-pop catchy tunes for the kids. Or maybe you are just past it. (*NME,* June 1, 1996)

Still you are all over 18 at the *NME.* And you will soon transform into Burchills and Parsons and Sweetings and all the other "grown ups" who have betrayed their childhoods . . . (letters page, *NME,* July 5, 1994)

This last comment, an attack on the *NME* itself rather than a specific journalist, received the following response: "Burchill left *NME* at 19, adamant that pop is for young people. Parsons, last seen writing about a hot new singer called Diana Ross, was never a kid—he was always just crap. And not everyone at *NME* is over 18. For the record, myself, Bidisha Bandyopadhyay and Emma Morgan are so young we haven't even heard of the Clash" (*NME,* July 5, 1994). These comments demonstrate that to be young is to have an authentic voice and position in the indie community; to be old is to be out of touch.

Age is not just an issue in public discourse; it is also a private anxiety. Many individuals speculate about how old they can be and still effectively participate in the indie scene. Most older fans remember when they were young, going to shows and criticizing the older people in the back as being over the hill. One journalist commented as he turned twenty-six: "I don't know why I'm so worried about getting old; I'm one of the youngest at the paper" (J.M.). But worry they do. Fans still in their teens lament the fact they feel they are getting old. This fear of aging is also regularly expressed in the indie press: "I feel old and jaded, and I only turned 17 this month" (letters page, *Melody Maker,* February 24, 1996); "It's shredding your ears, it's piercing your reserve, it's reminding you of your (premature) age" (*Melody Maker,* December 23, 1995). The parentheses in this latter review seem in many ways to capture the anxiety about aging in indie discourse. While the journalist is expressing fear of aging, he also distances himself with the claim of "premature," asserting that while he feels old, he is not actually old, because this would be a reason to dismiss his opinion. The issue of age and aging is apparent everywhere in indie, in its public and private discourse, in the mode of assessing the value of bands, in the clinical examinations of prospective talent by record executives, and in the participant structure of the gig itself.

Indie music is imagined as a youth phenomenon. This attention and concern regarding age points to the role gigs play as an age-set activity. As Lisa Lewis notes in her article on the representations of fans in cinema: "Fandom is overwhelmingly associated with adolescence and childhood, that is, with a state of arrested development or youth-oriented nostalgia, not mature adulthood" (Lewis 1992: 157). Gig going and an interest in popular music are activities that mark one as being a "youth," a transitional status between childhood and adulthood. In the gig's social organization of space, we see the progress through this liminal "youth" category. Individuals stop going to shows because they are no longer satisfying; this generally coincides with both a sense of disillusionment and the rising importance of other things, such as committed relationships, family, work obligations— basically, an adult life.

The movement across zones is also a movement across different spectorial comportments. The front embodies a particular way of being in the world—passionate and physically expressive, leaving an event drenched with sweat, physically exhausted. Moving through space, one finds the embodiment of a different engagement, cool rather than hot in both demeanor and body temperature. Those standing distant from the stage are physically composed. The professional is also part of this continuum. The undemonstrativeness of the pass placement of the professional is part of a way of being that values being "cool" and composed. Coolness here is a state of being in control—not passionless, but in control of one's passion. Each of the zones invokes a different form of spectatorship, with the most actively passionate in the front and the more reserved and remote in the back.

This movement from hot to cool, from active and demonstrative to inactive and undemonstrative, is a marker of aging. In this social organization, one can see the gig with its accompanying participation structure as an event that marks one's course through youth. When older people stop going to gigs, they do not stop attending music performances. They attend concerts, which are performed in venues with seats, a move that compels even more reserved and passive bodily comportment. They no longer need to exert themselves even to stand. The gig is an event that communicates about the expected behaviors associated with aging: youth as the time of physical and emotional expressiveness and adulthood as a time of reserved, composed demeanor and sedentary lifestyle. The young fan in the front is ardently expressive. Moving further from the stage, age and distance increase to the perhaps equally ardent but diminutively expressive older fan in the back.

The Metaphysics of Participation

The movement from zone one into zone two represents a significant change in metaphysical spectorial modes. Activities found in the zones are related to subjective experience. The different comportments represent different embodied modes of apprehension. The participant framework sets out particular activities that have compelling potential physical and emotional responses. In the examination of the spectorial positioning of different zones, a participatory spectatorship emerges that is inscribed not in terms of gender or specific ethnicity but rather in terms of metaphysic cosmology.

Zone one has its own singular spectorial positioning, one that is distinct from the spectatorships of the other zones. Zone one's pro-body physicality, which often results in ASCs or communitas, embodies a metaphysic associated with a sentient bodily apprehension and experience of knowledge. For those in zone one the gig is a physically involved and bonding experience. Zone two begins an initiation into a different metaphysic, embodying a different mode of comportment characterized by visual focus and intense contemplation, passive bodily posture, a mentalist means to knowledge. Zone three, the zone of disengagement, no longer looks for metaphysical meaning within the confines of performance; instead, status relationships within a professional domain become the focus of one's experience.

These different modes used in the production of meaning need to be understood in terms of broader cultural principles and historically bound culture systems. To understand the meaning of these different comportment modes, one needs to consider rock music's historical antecedents in West African religion, European music, and Western ideas about the role of the body and sensuality in metaphysical thought. First, we will consider the historic origins of African American music genres in West African religion and the role of music in West African metaphysics. It is a painful reality that one cannot consider any form of modern rock and roll without addressing in some way its origin in West African slavery and the contemporary submersion and obfuscation of race relations that lie beneath the surface of this pleasurable spectacle.

As Paul Friedlander states in his book *Rock and Roll as Social History*, "Rock and Roll was primarily African American music" (Friedlander 1996: 16). The association between rock and roll and African American cultural and musical styles was so strong that rock was originally called "race music." Rock and roll grew out of rhythm and blues, the blues (rural and urban), gospel, jump band jazz, folk, and country (Friedlander 1996).[9] Each of these was in turn shaped by previous music forms, such as antebellum spirituals, slave work songs, minstrel songs, Irish folk ballads, and so on. These different forms of music are a synthesis of African and European elements, the product of an African American sensibility in the context of slavery (Murray 1989). Rock, R&B, jazz, blues, and gospel—each of these styles is widely recognized as having emanated from the cultural practices of slave populations. These musics blended styles, instruments, and traditions from West Africa, Europe, and a variety of other cultures (Borneman 1975, Courlander 2002, DeCurtis 1992, Gillett 1970, Herskovits 1941, Murray 1989, Oliver 1970). The history of the drum set is a useful example of these influences, blending as it does the percussion instruments of the European military band, the West African drum families, Chinese and African toms, the Latin cowbell, and Turkish cymbals (Nicholls 1997). Ted Gioia (as well as other scholars) notes that "gospel, spirituals, soul, rap, minstrel songs, ragtime, jazz, blues, R&B, rock, samba, reggae, salsa, cumbia, calypso" all bear the imprint of West African influence (Gioia 1997:6). As for rock, its influences are primarily African and European in origin.

Its [rock's] musical ancestry can be traced back many centuries to the musical traditions of both Africa and Europe. We hear, in the same music, the call-and-response patterns from an African village mixed with classical music harmonies of eighteenth-century Europe. It is these and many other elements that contribute to the African-American styles of blues, gospel, jazz (and subsequently rhythm and blues), and elements from folk and country music that form the foundation of rock and roll. (Friedlander 1996: 17)

Blues is also strongly influenced by African musical traditions:

The simple musical form used to create the blues incorporated three practices that were fundamental to African American folk music, all having their antecedents in West African musical traditions. Cross-rhythms, the centerpiece of African American music, were used extensively in the blues. In essence these were simple polyrhythms which have always been the foundation of West African drumming. The second major innovation with roots in African music was the melodic tendency to express rising emotions with falling pitch . . . This tendency, which was also practiced by the Akan people of Ghana, produced what is now known as blue notes. Finally, blues musicians used a variety of vocal techniques, from coarse guttural tones and slur to falsetto. . . . All these techniques had counterparts in West African vocal styles. (Barlow 1989: 4)

The underlying dance-beat disposition is obviously West African in origin and so are the definitive stylistic elements that give the incantation and percussion—which is to say, blues music—its special idiomatic character. (Murray 1989: 65)

The influence of West African cultural traditions and aesthetics on these music styles is enormous.[10] The major aspect attributed to a West African origin in these music forms has been described as "the dominance of percussion" (Waterman 1952: 212). Christopher Small writes that "rhythm is to the African musician what harmony is to the European—the central organizing principle of the art" (Small 1987: 25).

It is important to point out that there is some unfortunate scholarly slip-page in the usage of "West Africa" and "Africa" when discussing musical in-fluences.[11] Africa is an immensely diverse continent ethnically, linguisti-cally, aesthetically, and socially. It has historically been home to foragers, pastoralists, horticulturalists, and agriculturalists. Its populations include sedentary, nomadic, and semi-nomadic peoples. As one scholar character-ized it, treating Africa as a whole is akin to thinking of the cultures of the Inuit and the Pennsylvania Dutch as identical (Borneman 1975). West Africa was the region exploited in the antebellum slave trade, and therefore this area influenced the African American and African European music gen-res.[12] West Africa itself is diverse, containing about six hundred ethnic groups, of which approximately 90 percent are sedentary agriculturalists with primarily polytheistic traditions couched within a notion of a monotheistic whole (Zahan 1987).

However, central to the genealogical connection between modern rock music and the traditions of West Africa is that musical practices are part and parcel of West African religious phenomena. Scholars have pointed out the politics, economics, history, kinship, and moral codes involved in West African music, as well as its essential role in ritual life (Borneman 1975, Chernoff 1979, Small 1987).[13] These are overlapping phenomena in a reli-gious philosophy that values renown in life as the means of becoming an ancestor rather than "to wander the bush alone" (Zahan 1987: 374), which is essentially a dissipation of the spirit. The Yoruba orishas who line the path to heaven are human ancestors who led extraordinary lives of emi-nence. Shango, the passionate god of fire and thunder, was a legendary king of Oyo. The veneration and mediation by ancestors in Fon religion is also the focal point of social organization (Herskovits 1938). The Western tendency to view religion, the state, social life, and aesthetic expression as discrete spheres is truly misleading.[14]

The West African groups most exploited by the slave trade (the Yoruba, Fon, Ewe, Ibo, Akans, Mbundu, BaKongo, Wolof, Fulbe, and others) had religious rituals centered around spirit possession and veneration. The quintessential and principal ritual of this religious constellation is the pos-session trance (Bascom 1969, Maquet 1972). In the intersection between the divine and the living, certain supreme beings can intervene or advise on human affairs. For many of the societies of West Africa, such as the Yoruba (Bascom 1969), the Fon peoples of Dahomey (Herskovits 1938), and the Kongo (Rouget 1985), drumming and dance are used to induce the gods to manifest themselves in the bodies of religious initiates by creating a tempo-rary fissure between worlds.[15] The deployment of the body in dance is an essential component of spiritual experience. Possession is induced by deploying particular styles of dance in conjunction with specific rhythms. John Chernoff notes that, for West African groups, to know the music is to know the dance (Chernoff 1979).[16] Bodily manifestation and the cultural understanding of sound are one and the same. Drumming, rhythm, and physical engagement are essential for the production of a spiritual state, as both Albert Raboteau and Harold Courlander point out:

Dancing, drumming, and singing play a constant and integral part in the worship of the gods. (Raboteau 1978: 15)

In most of Africa, ritual dance, like singing and drumming, is an integral part of supplication. Not all religious rites in West Africa include dancing, but most of them do; certainly at some stage of supplication dancing plays an essential role. Among West Africans, dancing in combination with other elements is regarded as a form of appeal to supernatural forces. (Courlander 2002: 366)

The connection between drums, percussion, dance, and ritual action is so strong that in some West African languages one word covers them all (Turner 1968). Robert Farris Thompson went so far as to characterize West African religions as "danced faiths" (Thompson 1983: 85). Drums themselves are considered sacred, and in several cultures the origins of drums and drumming are key elements in creation myths. In several West African groups, drums are baptized to confer spiritual power in order to be effective in invoking the gods for spirit possession (Rouget 1985). In the possession rites of West Africa, as well as the syncretic religions of the New World shaped by slavery such as Haitian Vodou, Brazilian Candomblé, and Cuban Santería, the production of an altered state of consciousness through the physical engagement of dance is essential for ritual experience. The sacred domain is experienced through the use of the body.

In his discussion of West African religions in Mircea Eliade's *Encyclopedia of Religion*, Dominique Zahan characterizes the rituals from this region in the following manner:

Initiation rites engender an internal disposition that guarantees a way of life different from ordinary existence. This disposition is acquired through the development of spiritual techniques that train the body and promote a sense of abolition of finitude. . . . Here the initiates attract the divinity to themselves and the meeting between the divine and human results in possession or trance. The physical tests that neophytes undergo during their initiation have a specific goal, even though the initiates may not be aware of it. It involves a spiritualization of the senses, particularly vision, hearing, and taste. . . . Hence, adherents to West African religions find recourse to initiatory techniques that view the body as the starting point of religion and mystical feelings. The body becomes the authentic symbol of the elevation of the human being to the peak of spirituality. Mystical life in religion does not detach humanity from the earth. (Zahan 1987: 376–377)

The specific metaphysical philosophy that Zahan describes views the body as a fundamental part of the production of spiritual experience. It does not conceive of the mind and body as separate domains, and it certainly does not predicate spiritual transcendence on transcending the body.[17] This philosophy does not split mind from body, rationality from sensuality. The ritual of spirit possession is about overcoming the distance between the embodied consciousness of humans and divinity. This is what Zahan means by the "abolition of finitude." The metaphysic of possession is a form of spiritual worship that is constituted by an indivisible bodily and mental manifestation.

Most importantly for my discussion here is that the musical lineage of rock preserves this West African metaphysic, so that the performance of rock music continues a legacy not only of musical traditions but of religious traditions. This connection between religious and musical practices has been noted by a number of scholars, who have discussed the performance of different African American musics in terms of their ritual significance (Floyd 1995, Jackson 2003, Levine 1978, Small 1987, Szwed 1978):

Rock preserves qualities of that African metaphysic so strongly that it unconsciously generates the same dances, acts as a major antidote to the mind-body split, and uses a derivation of Voodoo's techniques of possession as a source, for performers and audiences alike, of tremendous personal energy. (Ventura 1985: 156)

African survivals exist not merely in the sense that African-American music has the same characteristics of its African counterparts, but also that the musical tendencies, the mythological beliefs, assumptions, and interpretive strategies of African-Americans are the same as those that underlie the music of the African homeland. (Samuel Floyd, quoted in Jackson 2003: 136)

The similarity of the jazz improvisation event to the African dance-possession event is too striking and provocative to dismiss. (Jackson 2003: 141)

Each of these writers suggests that African American musical forms express a philosophy and metaphysic directly connected to possession rites and the West African ritual context, rites in which the body is part of the path to spiritual enlightenment.

This metaphysic is present not only in music practices but also in religious denominations informed by the West African Diaspora. Harvey Cox notes that the roots of jazz and Pentecostalism are found in possession rituals, where "music is not an incidental part of worship but provides its substance" (Cox 2001: 146). Melville Herskovits notes that at a service of Spiritual Baptists, the ritual performed in its original context would result in spirit possession (Herskovits 1938). This connection between music and religious ritual has been documented extensively:

Afro-American preaching is more similar to the transplanted African religious rites found throughout the Caribbean and in Brazil. Ultimately these performance styles have their origin in West African possession rites, such as can be found among the Yoruba and the Akan. . . . The priests were assisted by musician drummers and other helpers who along with the audience all took an active part in the proceeding. (Gumperz 1982: 189)

While singing these songs the singers and the entire congregation kept time to the music by the swaying of their bodies or by the patting of the foot or hand. Practically all of their songs were accompanied by a motion of some kind . . . the weird and mysterious music of the religious ceremonies moved old and young alike in a frenzy of religious fervor. (Robert Anderson, quoted in Raboteau 1978: 66)

Blacks had Africanized the psalms to such an extent that many observers described black lining hymns as mysterious African music. (Lomax 1993: 81)[18]

There runs a cultural thread of African origin which left its mark on the behavior pattern of the entire Protestant south. From snake worship, through trance and spirit possession, to the song and dance patterns of white spirituals. (Borneman 1975: 9)

West African religious philosophy infused Christian traditions with movement and music, part of the invocation of a spiritual state in congregants. In places of Catholic colonial rule such as Latin America, the Caribbean, or New Orleans, there formed unmistakably syncretic religions that maintain the ideal of possession trance by supernatural deities. In areas of Protestant rule, this philosophy was translated into a more conventional Christian framework, where if possession is found, it is possession by the Holy Spirit. In Protestant religious traditions of the American south, one finds the other music/religious performance styles of lining, call and response, and the integration of rhythm and percussion into religious ceremony.[19] As Christopher Johnson characterizes it, "Black Americans found a multitude of ways in which to reassign or redistribute the function of the drum in music and dance" in religious practices (Johnson 1999: 98).

Within indie music culture, specifically in the activities of zone one at an indie gig, there is a clear connection to the metaphysic of the body as a vehicle of perception. The activities at the front require an intense use of the body, dancing in accordance with patterned rhythms, and at times induce an altered state of consciousness. The boisterous activity of zone one is an expression of a metaphysic where the sentient body is an essential conduit of musical appreciation. Thus, the activities of zone one all clearly inscribe the metaphysic of spiritual communication through the body, mind, spirit, and soul.

Zone two embodies a different metaphysic, yet one that still retains some features of zone one. In zone two the experience of music is based on visual engagement and mental concentration. The eyes and ears are the primary means of experiencing music, rather than the movement of the body in dance. However, zone two still experiences an event that is dominated by percussion. There are still clearly visceral elements to the experience of music, but the focus on how to appreciate it has been altered. The focus on mental reverie is a movement toward the Western metaphysical tradition that values apprehension by the mind alone. Many have noted that Western thought is based on an assumed dichotomy between emotion and reason, mind and body (Shweder 1984). Some have traced this to the Enlightenment ideal of rationality. Reason is associated with the objective apprehension of reality, while emotion is associated with the subjective, the imaginative, and the irrational (Jenson 1992). Others have identified Christianity as the source for the mind/body, reason/emotion dichotomy:

In contrast, most academic disciplines following Augustine and the Church Fathers have constructed a Mind/Body hierarchy of knowledge corresponding to the Spirit/Flesh opposition so that mental abstractions and rational thought are taken as both epistemologically and morally superior to sensual experience, bodily sensations, and the passions. Indeed, the body and the flesh are linked to the irrational, unruly, and dangerous—certainly an inferior realm of experience to be controlled by the higher powers of reason and logic. (Conquergood 1991: 180)

Thus, the West has produced a mind/body hierarchy in its construction of apprehension for spiritual enlightenment.

Christianity, predicated on a mind/body dichotomy, has produced a love/hate relationship with the body (Hanna 1987). One of the basic tenets of European Christianity is a denigration of the body as a means of knowledge or spirituality. From Thomas Aquinas onward, there is a persistent idea that one gets to God through thought. Spirituality in Christianity is developed by overcoming the body and pleasures of the flesh. The body is thought of as the source of temptation and, in some cases, the source of original sin. For Jewish/Christian/Islamic systems, the origin of the human body is dirt. Its spiritual animation comes from the breath of God. It is a consistent trope of Christian and Islamic liturgical traditions to produce rituals of mental focus in order to elevate the spirit from the material and fleshly concerns of the earth. For the West, enlightenment is produced by the contemplative mind, not the body. Indeed, the body (mis)leads downward, toward the fall, toward sensuous pleasures. The mind leads upward, toward purity, selflessness, and truth.

In the Western spectatorship of elite music, high art, and religion, the goal of the audience member/congregant is to become pure mind. Christianity's apotheosis is gained by overcoming the body. Hence, it is a consistent trope of Christian liturgical traditions to limit bodily activity (as expressed in the telling title of a nineteenth-century religious pamphlet, *Methodist Error, or Friendly Christian Advice to Those Methodists Who Indulge in Extravagant*

Religious Emotions and Bodily Exercises [John Watson, quoted in Small 1987]). John Chernoff's comments in contrasting Western and African performance codes are particularly illuminating.

As Westerners, we habitually look at art as something specific and removed from the everyday world, something to appreciate or contemplate, something to which we pay attention in a concert hall, a museum, a theater, a quiet room. Learning to appreciate an "artwork" usually involves developing an awareness of its place within a tradition of influence and innovation among other artworks. In other words, we isolate the work of art from the social situation in which it was produced in order to concentrate on our main aesthetic concern . . . we might say that someone who talks or moves around during a musical performance is not "really listening". . . . But if you begin clapping your hands in time with a symphony, people will tell you that you are disturbing them. The effectiveness of music, for Westerners, is its power to express or communicate directly to individuals, and we would defend our right to a personal aesthetic judgment independent of the tastes of everyone else. (Chernoff 1979: 31–32)

What Chernoff suggests is that Western conceptions of ideal spectatorship are based on complete mental engagement predicated on abnegation of the body or audience co-participation. The idea is that people who are engaged bodily are not "really listening," not experiencing the music in a legitimate fashion.[20] Ironically, these exact sentiments are expressed by those indie fans firmly entrenched in zone two regarding those in zone one. Christopher Small's examination of the symphonic concert discusses the focus on undistracted hearing in both architectural design and the participant framework:

Care is taken so that listeners will not be disturbed by the presence of others as they listen. For this purpose the auditorium floor is raked to give uninterrupted sightlines, the audience is fixed in the seats and knows it is to keep still and quiet; the program booklet politely asks us to suppress our coughing, and nobody enters or leaves during the performance. The very form of the auditorium tells us that performance is aimed not at a community of interacting people, but at a collection of individuals. (Small 1998: 26)

Both scholars acknowledge that the Western convention of elite art (in this case music) is framed outside the context of social interaction. Social life exists separately from the art object. In addition, the idea that music is to communicate directly to the individual suggests that the aesthetic of symphonic appreciation is to create an unmediated experience of the sublime, echoing that Protestant notion of a direct relationship between man and divinity.[21] The isolation of the listener is "not felt as a deprivation, but as the necessary condition for full enjoyment and understanding of the musical works being played" (Small 1998: 42). The West's institutions of enlightenment require contemplative and passive bodily comportment. Western museums, symphonic concert halls, and sites of religious worship are places for musing, not dancing.[22]

Once again a consideration of drums and rhythm is informative in understanding the Western attitudes toward the body and the physical pleasures of dance. Drums and rhythmic instruments are conspicuously lacking in Christian liturgical traditions (Ellingson 1987).[23] In the West, drums were used primarily in state or secular milieus such as warfare (Hart 1991). Western ecumenical associations with drums are persistently negative.* Christian imagery of hell includes sinners imprisoned in drums. Anxiety regarding drums is based in part on the West's own culture-specific associations of drums with dance and sexual abandon. Moreover, the invocation to movement that one finds in the use of drums is seen as a moral threat. Missionaries, particularly of the Protestant faiths, would destroy the sacred drums of the peoples they forcibly converted.

In zone two of the indie gig we find a movement into a metaphysic that reflects this European legacy, a mode of engagement in which response during performance is internalized rather than outwardly expressed. The experience of music in a traditional Western group setting is not about bonding with other participants but rather one's individual discovery of the sublime in music. It is a mode in which the body is controlled so one can overcome its distractions and focus all of one's thoughts on the musical art. The focus of mental apprehension within ritual is introduced in zone two. It would be perhaps more accurate to say "reintroduced," however, because Western Protestant metaphysics is the religious foundation for the majority of members of the indie community in England. However, the music's form, the somatic experience of its volume and percussion, and the act of standing with some physical responsiveness to the music still retain ties to a physically engaged spectatorship. Thus, zone two participants are not fully integrated into this traditional Western metaphysic of spiritual enlightenment via pure mind transcending the body. They stand betwixt and between African and Western metaphysical modalities. Zone two is a liminal spectatorship in a liminal ritual drama.

---

* Interestingly, there is a carry-over of this negative attitude toward drums in various genres of modern music. In the symphonic context, "there is a distinct social hierarchy, with the string players accorded the highest status . . . the brass and percussion, on the other hand, a distinct blue collar image, being generally regarded as jolly fellows, not oversensitive, and given to the consumption of large quantities of beer" (Small 1998: 69). There is an elaborate joke cycle for drummers, in which they are portrayed as stupid and illegitimate. For example, a joke attributed to a well-known band leader in the 1930s was, "I have sixteen musicians, and a drummer." It has been claimed that this was because drummers, unlike "real" musicians, could not read sheet music. (What is the best way to confuse a drummer? Put sheet music in front of him; How do you really confuse him? Put notes on it.) In the rock era, most musicians cannot read sheet music, but the traditional of debasing drummers continues (Why do drummers have pea-sized brains? Alcohol makes the brain swell; Why does the drummer keep his drumsticks on the dashboard? So he can park in the handicapped spot). Even dance music has jokes to insult drummers (What's the difference between a drummer and a drum machine? With a drum machine you only need to punch the information in once.)

African Expression in a Protestant World[24]

I'm watching my body and mind divide . . .
Folk Implosion

At gigs, the strains of two different metaphysic embodiments exist to different degrees, each tied to the two primary cultural traditions that inform rock music.[25] As we have seen, the individual participant experiences these metaphysics sequentially, moving from West African–informed metaphysic toward European-informed metaphysic. This change is only fully completed when audience members leave gigs behind. This transformation creates a ritual narrative over the course of the individual's participation in the music community.

To understand the meaning of this difference and chronology, one needs to examine how the West views the differences between these two metaphysic systems. It is important not to conflate the representations of non-Western traditions with the traditions themselves. Cultures tend to present other societies' philosophies and practices in terms of their own conflicts. As Edward Said showed in his critique of Orientalism, the West constructs a representation of the alien "other" through its own set of assumptions, so that the other is seen as inferior and therefore deserving of subjugation (Said 1994). Western colonial representations reduce varied and complex social and religious traditions around the world into one-dimensional facsimiles. The creation of an "other" allows us to express the conflicts within our own society as a contrast between Western and non-Western cultural modes. The discourse we find on the interplay and blending of Western and non-Western music forms is framed in terms of our own culturally produced dichotomies—mind and body, emotional expressiveness and sober rationality. Our own cultural issues are projected into our representations of African-influenced music practices. The West African religions brought by force to the United States and the countries where the abomination of slavery was also practiced are understood according to a European system of representation rather than within their own cultural contexts. European representations of West Africa are not West Africa.[26]

The privileging of one's participation in a particular cultural practice over another is also a privileging of one epistemological system over another. Using the body as a vehicle for spiritual enlightenment is viewed in the West through its own metaphysical framework, which finds the body to be a dangerous temptation to spiritual corruption. For West African religions, the body is a legitimate conduit for spirituality; "this premise means that the body and even at times the erotic is seen as part of the experience of divinity" (Ellingson 1987: 495). Within this premise, the body is not separate from the mind but inextricably bound together with it. However, the West's demonizing of the body and sensuality interprets this religious philosophy as exalting the body only and then reproduces it within a system of a mind/body split, a split the West views as transparently natural. This split is then used by the West to produce a Western/African dichotomy. In the West's eyes, the West African embrace of the body and mind is seen as a valorization of the body alone, in service to the West's construction of the African "other."

African-Western music forms have been repeatedly associated with and criticized for their African origins, physical engagement in dance, sensuality, paganism, and devil worship by Western critics, often in egregiously racist terms:

It is deplorable. It is tribal. And it is from America. It follows rag-time, blues, Dixie, jazz, hot cha-cha and the boogie-woogie, which surely originated in the jungle. We sometimes wonder whether this is the Negro's revenge. (*Daily Mail*, September 4, 1956, quoted in Blecha 2004: 15)

Smash the records you possess which present a pagan culture and a pagan concept of life . . . Phone or write a disk jockey who is pushing a lousy song. Switch your radio dial when you hear a suggestive song. (Shaw 1974: 235)

It's the jungle strain that gets 'em all worked up. (Martin and Segrave 1988: 30)

While the wild chanting, the rhythmic movement of hands and feet, the barbarous dance, and the fiery incantations were at their height, it was difficult to believe that we were in a civilized city of an enlightened republic. Nothing indecent occurred in word or gesture, but it was so wild and bizarre that one might easily imagine he was in Africa or in hell. (Charles Warner quoted in Johnson 1999: 26)

The music would turn people into devil worshippers, to stimulate self-expression through sex, to provoke lawlessness and impair nervous stability. (Martin and Segrave 1988: 49)

Either it [the music] actually stirs them to orgies of sex and violence (as its model did for the savages themselves), or they use it as an excuse for the removal of all inhibitions and the complete disregard of the conventions of decency. (Martin and Segrave 1988: 53)

The audience's physical reaction to the music was seen as the quintessence of the threat, a fear that this physical contact would lead to sex and moral decay. West African–influenced music forms are regularly seen as an incitement to immorality that would heat the blood.

Rock and roll gives young hoodlums an excuse to get together. It inflames teenagers and is obscenely suggestive. (Denisoff 1975: 22)

Rock and roll, often known now as rock, roll and riot is sexy music. It can make the blood race. It has something of the African tom-tom and voodoo dance. (*Daily Mail*, September 5, 1956, in Peterson 1990: 99)

The . . . objection went beyond the realm of musical taste or propriety into that of morality in the framework of the Puritan fathers. More than the music, the dance, given its physical nature, was subjected to attack. (Denisoff 1975: 18)

The prevailing idea is that by the very nature of its rhythmic beats, music incited and excited, made one hot rather than cool, prodded one to activity. This transposition is particularly interesting, as John Chernoff has pointed out that coolness is a moral principle behind West African drumming (Chernoff 1979). The readings of rock and roll as both jungle and devil's music construct it as foreign in its moral and religious significance.[27] Here, the attacks on West African–influenced musical forms are thinly veiled attacks on blacks and their indigenous religious philosophy. This "foreign" music has at various times been characterized as a threat to society as a whole, but eventually the criticism focused on what was perceived to be a vulnerable section of the population, the "youth" age set.

"Youth" plays the role of a corrupted "other" in an ongoing cultural-religious drama. Rock music has been portrayed as something that was African, religiously demoralizing, and filled with false idolatry. As described by Dena Epstein, these accounts tell us "that Africans dance in a manner that was considered heathenish" (Epstein 1977: 39). The American Heritage Dictionary defines a heathen as "a person who does not acknowledge your god. *The unconverted*. One regarded as irreligious, uncivilized, or unenlightened" (emphasis mine). From the perspective of the West, rock music and other West African–informed music styles manifest a form of expression that contravenes Western moral codes, a form favored by those not *yet* converted to Christianity.

The spectacle of youth culture enacts one of the primary narratives of Christianity, namely the conversion of "innocent heathens," under the sway of false ideology, to Western morality. In contemporary Western culture, the adolescent continues to play the role performed in earlier times by the whole wide heathen world, which the West saw as in need of "civilizing" and conversion to the Protestant order. The desire to convert was an integral tenet and justification of the colonialist enterprise and the subjugation of foreign populations.[28] This narrative has been played out for generations between Western and non-Western societies. The Christian missionary imperative was to spread the gospel and rescue the heathen "other" from paganism. This was the "white man's burden," the obligation Christian countries felt to save the foreign others from the corrupting influences of their own religious practices.

Youth plays the role of fallen innocents in the ongoing narrative of proselytizing and conversion. This religious narrative drive toward conversion is manifested in the cultural positioning of various segments of society that are constructed as in need of salvation. "Youth," with its aberrant music tastes and leisure pursuits that excite the body, is positioned as a heathen "other" who needs to be saved from music's pagan polytheism; young people need to learn how to sublimate hedonistic impulses for deferred gratification. In both Britain and the United States, youth is created as a discrete category whose members perform the role of an ideological other within a broadly Protestant cultural system, an other that needs to be returned and restored to Western ideals. Youth is literally the "heathen other" in our midst. In the cultural manifestation of youth, one finds the continued expression of the conversion narrative translated into an individual's life cycle.

At the heart of this association between adolescents and immorality is their affiliation with rock and roll's various music genres (Denisoff 1975). Since the introduction of rock and roll many, if not most, of rock's numerous musical scions have been met by a moral panic experienced by those outside the music community. They view rock as a threat to the moral order and the morals of those involved. Moral panics are often directed at new technologies, specific ethnic communities, or sexual practices (Hall 1979, Turner and Surace 1956, Watney 1987). Music's moral panics have focused particular concern on sexual mores and the use of the body.[29] In the post–World War II era, the youth age-set moral panic has been a persistent motif.

In a key article addressing the literature on moral panics, Angela McRobbie and Sarah Thornton demonstrate the internalization of deviance and threat to the moral order as an agenda within youth culture (McRobbie and Thornton 1995). Acting in a way that produces a moral panic is part of the youth culture ethos: "Moral panic can therefore be seen as a culmination and fulfillment of youth's cultural agenda in so far as negative news coverage baptizes transgression. What better way to transform difference into defiance, lifestyle into social upheaval, leisure into revolt" (McRobbie and Thornton 1995: 572). For those who participate in youth culture, the moral panic is a desired outcome. This stands in stark contrast to the moral panics associated with homosexuality or ethnic groups, in which members bristle and are quite reasonably threatened by being labeled deviant and by attacks on their practices. In contrast, the youth culture's agenda is to participate in subversive activity, validating the potency of their movement. As opposed to "alienating everyone, [the moral panic] will be attractive to a contingent of consumers who see themselves as alternative, avant-garde, radical, rebellious or simply young" (ibid: 565). In the case of youth culture, the moral panic is the result of an agenda of both youth (whose members revel in the status accorded by rebellion) and the general culture (who revel in reviling the moral laxity of youth). In sum, the moral panic associated with music can be seen as part of a larger cultural agenda, adhered to by both the youth groups and the wider community. Adolescents are presented as succumbing to and being corrupted by the nefarious influence that rock music has—the incitement to sexual license, the physicality and sexual expressiveness of dance, and the threat embodied by West African religious forms. Moral panics are met with calls for the moral regeneration of society, a return to the ideals of work and the subjugation of hedonistic impulses, which are met in turn with new threats, and so the cycle continues.

The Nature of the Moral Threat

I spent the summer wasting
The time was passed so easily . . .
Belle and Sebastian

The leisure amusement of rock is seen by critics in the general culture to induce moral laxity in youth. Youth cultures and music are characterized as assailing Protestant ethics at every turn.[30] For example, the hippie ethos of "overt expressivity in behaviors and clothes, hedonism, and a disdain for work" was contrasted to values of deferred gratification, sobriety, and respectability (Young 1971: 78). As Stanley Cohen put it, "the dangers of youth culture are thought to be premature affluence, aggression, permissiveness, challenging the ethics of sobriety and hard work" (Cohen 1980: 198).

The corrupting influence of affluence is perhaps one of the most telling of the traits applied to youth groups, and affluence is applied to youth groups regardless of their actual wealth. Geoffrey Pearson, discussing hooliganism, points out that calling working-class teddy boys the children of affluent society was an absurd pretense.[31] They were not blessed with affluence or anything like it. Pearson also notes that affluence was considered one of the causes of the original working-class "hooligan," despite the fact that these hooligans lived in slums. The Adolescent British Medical Association in 1961 noted that "not poverty, but unaccustomed riches, seems an equally dangerous inducement to wild behavior, even crime" (Pearson 1983: 6).

As Max Weber demonstrated in *The Protestant Ethic and the Spirit of Capitalism*, the Protestant imperative required work but not indulgence in the fruits of labor (Weber 1958).[32] Success and the accumulation of wealth were signs of one's elect status. However, using wealth for pleasure was a sign of moral dissolution. According to this religious paradigm, surplus wealth could be legitimately deployed only into investment. Amusements in all forms were considered demoralizing, since they promoted leisure rather than work, and gratification during one's life rather than in the afterlife. Affluence, not poverty, was seen as a pernicious temptation toward pleasure, leisure, and criminality. A government commission explained that "crime is caused by dissipation, not by want" (Pearson 1983: 168). Because poverty does not provide temptation for dissolution, those impoverished people who lived in squalor demonstrated that their conditions resulted from spiritual lack.[33] Affluence's perceived potential for producing moral rot demonstrates the Protestant context for the moral panics directed toward youth. Within the Protestant framework, it is through austerity that one demonstrates one's elect status and connection to the moral order.

The outstanding moral negligence of the "teenager" identified by mainstream culture was rooted in the fact that, whatever their actual degree of affluence, teenagers spent what money they did have on themselves, and therefore they must have had too much. Money spent on oneself meant that the suffering of labor was not for the glorification of God but rather of self. That many teen cultures attribute their behavior to boredom (mentioned in nearly all of the ethnographies of youth musical communities and made into a rallying cry by punks) only serves to lend credence to the stereotype of affluent youth with too much time on their hands: because they do not need to work for their suppers, they delight in idle gratification. This representation of teenagers spending their money on frivolous fashions to be a ted or a mod or a rocker or a club goer or a gig goer was to present them in perfidy with the tenets of the Protestant work ethic. Rock music presented the lure of crime, deviance, drugs, lewd behavior, miscegenation, and sexual promiscuity.

Youth, ruled by foreign corrupting impulses, constitutes a cultural segment that is an internal and corrupted other. The moral panic is "the outcome of complex chains of social interaction rather than the product of young people with a predisposition, individually or environmental, toward crime or rule-breaking behavior" (McRobbie and Thornton 1995: 561). In his discussion of the moral panic around mods and rockers in the early 1960s, Stanley Cohen also notes the irrationality of such a panic stemming from relatively mild events. It was the spectacle of threat, rather than actual events, that threatened. In this case, youth culture becomes a cultural spectacle. Adolescents are portrayed as internal enemies assailing the existent social order.[34] This display is one engendered by societal factors that position a cultural segment as "other," different and separate from the main cultural body and lacking in moral values.

The need to convert rather than expel youth is expressed in the characterization of youth as merely led astray rather than inherently corrupt. Rock music is presented as threatening to the individual participants, something from which they need to be protected. Those involved with youth culture are seen as innocents who have strayed from the fold under a foreign influence and that need to be returned to it. As Jock Young characterizes it, "The stereotype is of contrast, along the lines of corrupter and the corrupted, that is the pusher and the buyer" (Young 1971: 41). In other words, the truly evil are not the adolescents themselves, who have merely been led astray, but rather those who lead them. The members of the industry, the men in suits and the musical performers, are regularly portrayed as dissolute pushers who force this unseemly music into the ears of innocent youth: "The editors of *Melody Maker* . . . issued their own call to arms to stop 'Pop Rot.' They were of the opinion that the public really didn't want rock music and even those who produced the music all privately deplored it. They urged the profession, the industry, and the public to 'rebel against the handful of men who are responsible for this lowering of musical standards, such as agents, managers, and disk jockeys'" (*Melody Maker*, November 8, 1958, in Martin and Segrave 1988: 54). According to this view, the music industry creates an artificial market by forcing rock music upon unsuspecting and impressionable youths. The payola scandal associated with Alan Freed in New York provided ample evidence to support the suspicion that rock music needed to be manipulated into the marketplace.[35] Positioned within this context, the adolescent is a sheep who has been led into vice by the false, deceitful, and corrupt members of the music industry.

Scholars' view of youth cultures as subcultures is problematic because it does not examine the role that youth phenomena such as indie play in the larger cultural milieu. Mainstream culture obscures the internal nuances of transformation that inform indie's musical practices, and indie is represented as part of a larger constellation of youth activities that are out of control and under nefarious foreign influences. According to this perspective, gigs are simply part of an overall representation of youth as a transitional category of foreign hedonistic excess.

The role youth plays in a broader cultural narrative goes some way toward answering one of the questions I had regarding music participation in the West. Activities such as the vigorous dancing associated with rock and pop music are seen as age-specific in the West but not elsewhere. In West Africa, possession is not an exclusive province of the young. Young and old participate in possession trance, and in some cases older participants are more valued for their experience. As Chernoff reports his drum master telling him, "The old men have knowledge and they have experience, so it means their minds are clear . . . the experience makes the difference between old men and the young men, and these make every dance to be nice" (Chernoff 1979: 105). In the West, these physically expressive behaviors are understood as the province of youth. It is taken for granted that these activities are of interest to youth precisely because they are young. However, when one considers the Western attitude toward the body as something to overcome, we can see the association of youth with sensuality and physical expression as part of a larger ritual drama of the subjugation of these experiences.

A Ritual of Transformation

I tried to explain exactly what I lost . . .
Razorlight

In analyzing gigs as part of the general phenomenon of youth culture, one can see that the narrative of the conversion of physically and emotionally exuberant youth to Protestant adulthood is recapitulated in the indie participant structure. In zone one, we find a display of physical behaviors, ecstatic dance, and frenetic activity embodying the metaphysics of West Africa. In zone two, we find the beginnings of the circumscription of the body and the contemplative focus of Western metaphysics that locates rational thought as the most highly valorized means of perception. Zone two exists between the West African and Western forms of metaphysical expression. As we have seen, these zones of spectorial comportment and subjectivities are phases in the developmental experience of participation within the music community. That these are different modes that participants move through during their participation in the indie community indicates that we are observing *transformation*. The long-term indie participant moves from a West African, bodily-infused metaphysic to a Christian, contemplative metaphysic, one that gradually removes focus from the sensate aspects of bodily experience. This movement recapitulates the metanarrative of religious conversion from one system into another. In indie's participant structure, seemingly wild, bodily-oriented audience members are transformed into adults who sublimate the desires of the flesh for the pleasures of the mind. This transition is completed when the participant leaves the community altogether. Thus, gigs are an expression of both the sentient body and its subjugation. In the postmodern age, youth dramatically comes to stand in the popular imagination as the exotic other in a state of heathen disgrace prior to conversion to the Protestant moral order.[36] The West's engagement of "otherness" is understood in terms of our cultural history by linking the pantheism of other cultures to the West's experience of pre-Christian pantheism. The West renders them both illegitimate under the rubric of paganism. However, these behaviors can only be considered pagan within the context of a Western dialectic.

This Western contrivance of a polarity between Western and West African metaphysics is the representation of internal conflicts within Protestantism. The two complementary Protestant incarnations—living at one with nature and given over to irrational emotionality and sensuality; living in bourgeois society and governed by self-control and sober rationality—parallel our chronological metaphysical modalities. That is, Western representations of Africa constitute projections of the ideological conflicts within Protestantism. As discussed earlier, Colin Campbell in his *Romantic Ethic and the Spirit of Modern Consumerism* meticulously argues that the production of the man of reason who is dedicated to work simultaneously produces the man of feeling and of luxuriant sensuality (Campbell 1987: 223). He suggests that a "purito-romantic" personality system is produced in the West by the raising of children with the values of emotional restraint and deferred gratification—which, in turn, produces the Romantic tendencies toward sentimentalism and imagination. He finds that culture's solution to this conflict of mutually produced sense and sensibility is manifested sociologically as phases in the middle-class life cycle, which corresponds to the conversion model between West African and Western subjectivities I have outlined above.

It is certainly necessary to recognize that a cultural contradiction can easily be a sociological compatibility. That is to say, attitudes and beliefs which directly contrast will nevertheless not lead people to experience tension or conflict if their expression is successfully separated in time and place; something which is generally true of the way puritan-utilitarian and romantic sentimental values are institutionalized in contemporary middle-class society. Perhaps the most pertinent illustration of this is the way in which the middle-class life cycle is divided into Bohemian youth followed by a bourgeois middle-age, thus leading to a serial form of integration. (Campbell 1987: 223)

Romantic and rational-utilitarian values are serially institutionalized in the life-cycle of bourgeois man, one which asserts that the romanticism of youth is but the culmination of an entire childhood of exposure to such values. (Campbell 1987: 224)

Western culture's youth is performed as the Romantic hedonist, reveling in physical pleasures and given to idealism, only to transform into the adult, the sober rationalist submitting himself to the Protestant work ethic. This argument has great resonance for the individual participant in the indie community.[37] Campbell suggests that these contradictions are not experienced as conflicts but rather as life phases. However, indie's ideology expresses these contradictory values simultaneously at every turn, demonstrating Romantic Bohemian youth still deeply embedded in a Puritan aesthetic moral system. The Romantic mode may dominate during youth, but it is still experienced as in conflict with Protestant values; similarly, while Protestant values prevail in adulthood, they are still experienced as in conflict with Romantic and emotional needs. These conflicts are expressed in our representation of non-Western cultures and our understanding of childhood and adulthood as oppositional states bridged by a liminal period of youth. Yet these conflicts find an uneasy coexistence in our arts and liminal ritual moments.

This structural organization of a narrative of conversion raises an interesting question for participants in the indie music community whose religious heritage is not Protestant. The modern Western world is filled with "others" with different metaphysical systems that do not conform to Protestant dictates. How do these "others" fit into this world? The pressure of converting to the dominant order is constantly exerted on these minority groups. Leaving the music community does not resolve their conflicts unless they truly assimilate their world views to the majority culture's metaphysical system. In the context of our discussion, this is not merely a question for those ethnic minorities that form such a small percentage of the indie world, but for those religious minorities as well, which would include Catholics, Jews, Eastern Orthodox Christians, Muslims, and Hindis, to name just a few. For "others," be they religious, ethnic, or sexual, the ability to find a place that fits within the dominant culture is a constant struggle.

The liminal space of the gig's participant structure is a compromise between cultural worlds, a space where inherent contradictions can coexist. The resolution of leaving the community for a Protestant conformity is not as easy or appealing for those whose identities are torn between the dominant order and their minority community. While within the community, there is still a compromise between emotionality and rationality, between physical exertion and passive comportment, between polytheistic pluralism and monotheistic conformity. For many, the intended outcome of this ritual drama is unsatisfying. Leaving the community only limits these individuals' ability to find a space where their multiple identities can coexist.

Conclusion

I want to see my family
My wife and child waiting for me . . .
New Order

The discrete participatory activities of different zones in indie culture can only be fully understood in relationship to each other as part of an overall structure and narrative of participation. Within the gig's participant structure, the selection of location is a communicative act, one that designates comportment, status, and one's relationship to the band and its music, in terms of closeness and distance, symmetry and asymmetry. Audience members go to a gig not just to experience music but also to be part of a community of sentiment within a culturally constituted ritual.

Participatory spectatorship is inscribed in physically embodied participatory modes. For indie music gigs, this physically embodied spectorial mode is inscribed with religious ideology, in which different metaphysical subjectivities are experienced at different moments in the individual's chronological participation in the event. Zone one enacts a metaphysic of the sentient body as the conduit to musical communion, whereas zone two begins the transformation into a metaphysic where the body is forsaken and mental contemplation is the conduit to musical communion. They are experienced in developmental relationship to one another. The indie gig enacts a transformation from the effusive and physically expressive fans of the front to circumscribed, interior-oriented spectators who progressively distance themselves until they leave the community altogether.

The sequential organization of these subjectivities suggests a conversion narrative. Youth is consistently presented as immoral, hedonist, devilish, and savage. Youth's association with West African–influenced music is part of the way this cultural image is constructed. These musical forms were clearly something that was not Christian that stole the nation's youth. The music encourages the joys of the flesh and leads one down the path of moral decay. Youth is positioned as the protagonist in an ongoing Christian narrative of the exotic other in a state of pagan disgrace. In their worship of false secular prophets they need transformation into the Protestant moral order. The conversion narrative is echoed within the indie participant structure. Indie's pluralistic idolatry of musicians is to be left behind, the golden calves of misspent youth. The gig is about inserting a foreign metaphysic into a broadly Christian society and about youth leaving this metaphysic behind to become full-fledged adult members of society.[38] The transformation of spectatorship and the rejection of the indie community is the successful articulation of a conversion to Protestant values. In this transformation, we find the specter of the pervasive cultural narrative of the return, restoration, and conversion to Protestant ideals.

Gigs are not the only cultural ritual that marks one's transition from childhood to adulthood. They are just one form of the West's narrative of the fallen innocent child (to liminal idealistic adolescent) who believes that art is more important than money, that leisure is more important than work. It is just one part of a larger cultural phenomenon of socializing "youth" into "adult." Gigs become what adults used to do. Music is no longer the most important thing in their lives, and it is hard for them to understand why they ever thought it was.

This conversion and rejection of the metaphysics of a sentient body should not suggest a clear and unabridged resolution. As specific, culturally constituted conflicts are inherent in every society, leaving the music community of the hybridic body/soul/mind/emotion is merely an initial vanquishing of this other metaphysic. However, the suppressed still exerts a need for expression. Thus, there will always be new battles to fight and different rituals to address this culturally produced conflict between emotional expressiveness and rational asceticism.

CHAPTER 5

Performance, Authenticity, and Emotion

Be Here Now . . .
Oasis

LOS ANGELES TIMES: *"The business aspects of the movies are becoming bigger and bigger news. Every director has a story about how their grandmother in Poughkeepsie knows the grosses the day the film opens. Is this a good thing or a bad thing?"*

Harvey Weinstein: "I think it's a terrible thing. When you see that the Wizard of Oz is just a traveling salesman from Kansas, it spoils the illusion. The best story I can tell about that is a bad story to tell on myself, but I'll tell it anyhow. When I owned a theater in Buffalo and was producing concerts, I had Doug Henning the magician for two nights. And when he comes to town everybody has to sign a confidentiality agreement, promising you won't go backstage and won't reveal anything. I saw his show the first night and I loved it. I thought it was amazing, he made me a two-year-old again. And at 4 o'clock in the morning I woke up, got into my car and drove down to the theater . . . So I walked in and looked at every one of the tricks, saw how he did it. And because I know how it works, I cannot go to a magic show again. I ruined it for myself. So all that proliferation of be-hind-the-scenes stories . . . to me it spoils the wonderful illusion of walking into a dark room and waiting for the magic to begin" (Los Angeles Times, *December 29, 1997*).

It may seem odd to start a chapter on musical performance with a quote about magicians, cinema, and the Wizard of Oz, but in order to understand the nature of musical performance, we must understand the concert as an event on a par with other artistic spectacles. As discussed in chapter 2, indie is a genre that values authenticity over artifice. In this chapter, I discuss verisimilitude, credibility, and authenticity—how credibility is conveyed in the indie genre, how indie posits emotional presence as the apogee of experience, and how the individual's experience of the event over time ultimately obviates and undermines those very assertions.

Going behind the scenes changes one's perception of an event. There is a mantra among music journalists and professionals, "Never meet your idols," that is born of experience. Most professionals have been disillusioned at one time or another. They meet the creator of music they felt revealed some esoteric truth, only to find that the performer is a barely coherent drunk. When a fan or audience member sees a performer as himself or herself rather than as the character he or she envisioned, it is difficult to go back to believing in the character. When you see how the trick is performed, you can't believe in the trick anymore. This chapter is about the trick of indie music. Ritual, performance, and art deal with the play between the real and illusion, truth and artifice, the trick and seeing the trick, wanting to be tricked and how it feels to be tricked. The trick of indie is to appear as if the barriers between audience, performer, music, and emotion are temporarily effaced and that music conveys something of value about your life.

Indie's Version of Authenticity

all the names and places I have taken from real life . . .
The Postal Service

To understand the gig, we must first understand it as performance. Gigs deal with the same issues as all other artistic productions. The indie community has an elaborate discourse concerning what constitutes "authentic" music. As previously noted, indie's notions of authenticity include performing one's own material and valuing a working-class identity despite a primarily middle-class audience. For indie, "authentic" music is personal, live, youthful, organic, self-made, original, and motivated by concerns of artistic expression rather than commercial acquisition. This aesthetic morality is one of the ways indie asserts its music as more valuable than other genres. For indie, it is art over dross, or as put by the band the Divine Comedy, "Elegance against ignorance, difference against indifference, wit against shit."

Authenticity addresses a difference between what is read as real versus artifice or sincerity versus deception. The relationship between the real and artifice has been a central concern of art, art criticism, and cultural studies.

In *The Truth in Painting,* Jacques Derrida devotes an entire book to the issues within the boundaries of this phrase (Derrida 1987). "The truth in painting" is the conundrum of attempting to convey truth within a medium of artifice. Derrida states it thus: "The painting of the true can be adequate to its model, in representing it, but it does not manifest it *itself,* in presenting it" (Derrida 1987: 5). The production can represent a truth but cannot be the thing it represents. This of course begs the question of how a representation that is not the thing itself can be true. When the artistic endeavor is to express truth, how can it be done in a medium that is patently not the thing itself?

This places the endeavor of authenticity in the domain of Bateson's double bind, the act that contradicts itself, and Plato's tabula rasa, the tablet for writing that cannot be written upon, the effaceable space. Verisimilitude in musical performance is a trick. The performance that strives for authenticity will always be a traveling salesman from Kansas. It will have something to hide, because it is not the thing itself. *Never meet your idols.* Why? Because they are not who you think they are. The idol is a performer. If you meet the performer, how can you go on believing the performance is real and the actor is the part he plays?

Herein lies the trick of the trickster. The musician needs to make the audience (and perhaps himself) believe that what they are seeing, hearing, or experiencing is real. Temporarily, he needs to make the audience see the salesman as a powerful wizard, when he is really just an ordinary person with a few tricks up his sleeve, a bass slung at her waist, or a pair of sticks in his hands.

Authenticity's sister concept in the world of music is credibility. Credibility, or "cred," is the cultural capital of the music world. Credibility is not how much money one has or how many records one has sold but the respect and honorific status one is accorded in the community. Like status, credibility is something members have in incremental amounts. Much has been written about credibility and authenticity in music (Frith 1981, Frith 1987, Frith 1990a; Gilroy 1993; Thornton 1995). Here, I am concerned with the source of the term "credibility." Credibility is a matter of believability. Can the performance be believed to be true? A credibility gap is the disparity between what is said and the actual facts, the difference between the performance of an utterance and its verifiability in the world beyond, between (what one perceives to be) truth and deceit. Thus, credibility and authenticity, the paramount terms of assessment in indie music and the status of individuals within the community, bring us right back to "the truth in painting," the degree to which what is displayed by the magician/musician can be believed and relied upon to be true.

Credibility is secured differently for different segments of the indie community. For musicians, credibility is something one possesses based on one's music, one's lifestyle, one's social class, one's persona, and one's performance. For indie audience members, credibility is manifested in liking credible bands. It demonstrates the audience member's ability to make distinctions of aesthetic value. Yet fans must express some unique personal taste or they are seen to be followers who cannot determine the difference between merit and dross, the real and the phony, the true artists and the poseurs. Thus, the indie fan, in articulating bands he or she likes and dislikes, needs to conform to the accepted indie canon but not entirely, as wholesale adherence suggests indiscriminate devotion rather than discernment. The professional demonstrates his or her credibility by working with credible bands and artists, or working at a credible independent label or a credible company. For all members, credibility is an association with credible artists, and therefore a band's honorific status and believability is a central concern for all.

Credibility and authenticity as cultural capital and believability are regularly discussed in the popular press. During my fieldwork, the issue of authenticity and credibility for indie music was expressed in the phrase "4 Real." This term originated in a conversation between a journalist and the band Manic Street Preachers before a gig. The journalist had asked the band, who spouted punk manifestos inspired by Greil Marcus's *Lipstick Traces*, if they were "for real." During the performance, one of the members, Richey Edwards, carved "4 Real" in his arm with a razor, sparking a great debate about whether this gesture was real (deriving from authentic feelings) or a ploy (to gain media attention).* The phrase became the indie shorthand for authenticity—the truth in music and musical performance:

Just what kind of credentials would satisfy you that NIN are "4 Real"? A sworn affidavit? Admission to a mental institution? Suicide? Look, there are a whole load of more palatable and commercially secure ways to package your personal problems than NIN's. (*Melody Maker*, June 4, 1994)[1]

Perhaps the most telling song, however, is the calm confessional of "I Am A Cinematographer," which not only matches what we know of Will's muddled life story, but resolves our 4 Real conundrum. Like a master film maker, Oldham instills the *spirit* of his experiences into his creations rather than the actual details, using a hard-earned understanding of the human condition to animate

* Richey Edwards, more popularly known as Richey Manic, went missing on February 1, 1995, after several well-publicized bouts of depression. His car was found by the Severn Bridge, and many assumed that he had killed himself. However, his body has never been found and there has long been speculation that he staged his own disappearance. He never escaped from the "4 Real" query.

and enhance the mumblings of his imagination. There is no real need to be personal: distinct scenarios would only obscure the far-reaching impact of his hazy, nocturnal magic. Your life is what's important here. (*Melody Maker,* July 1, 1995)

Indie's authenticity demands a consistency between personal experience and what is represented in performance.[2] Indie wants the musical persona onstage to be consistent with the performer's experience and persona offstage, to have the actor be the part he plays. This is a genre in which the performers are to play themselves: "Methinks Jarvis Cocker is faking it. Maybe that's just his stage name" (*Vox,* May 1994). Indie requires the performance be imbued with the authentic spirit of the artist's experience. In looking for the real, the authentic, the credible in a performance onstage, the audience and critics want the musician to *be* rather than to act. They want to believe that the musician is being himself, that the performance onstage has some truthful relationship to the world beyond.

This requirement that musicians perform themselves very much extends to live gigs. The audience wants to believe that the musicians experience the music during a show. When I asked fans, performers, and professionals what the difference is between a good show and a bad show, the answer was almost invariably "When the band are into it" (J.R.). When I asked them to explain, they would comment:

When musicians aren't just going through the motions. When they are really feeling the music. (P.T.)

When the band engage the audience with the purity of their musical vision. (L.B.)

For me a good show is if the band is musically putting it over. I'm not taken in by big performance and theatrics. At a good show, I'm going to get something different and better than the record. I want some evidence that the band made some real effort to put across an idea, but not in a labored way. When it is emotionally absolutely beautiful—when I could feel myself crying, this is what I want. The music needs to be deeply engaging at an emotional level and it needs to be of a very personal nature. (A.D.)

There can be something much more honest about an instrumental. A good show is one that is really heartfelt, like the music was painful for the band to express and painful for you to hear, you feel it like an epiphany—you feel like you are there too. (R.W.)

The audience wants to *believe* the musicians feel the emotion of the music, feel the performance, despite the fact that this may be the hundredth time the band has played this song in the last three months. By valuing authenticity, indie strives for verisimilitude in performance. In performance, the indie audience wants to believe that what they are seeing is *the truth in music.*

Indie's Conventions of Being in Performance

"Beingness" is the word I use to describe an emotional presence viewed by participants as authentic. It is a concept that represents the antithesis of a performance in which the performer and the part he plays are seen to be separate and distinct from one another. I invoke performance in the theatrical sense as opposed to the sociolinguistic sense. In the former, the actor plays a role in a drama; in the latter, the social actor performs himself or herself in interactions. There are several ways that beingness is conveyed in indie performance genre: (1) a lack of stress on virtuosity; (2) a visual strategy where performers do not register the visual gaze of audience members; (3) a restraint on commentary during performance, suggesting a self-awareness and an intellectual distance from the unfolding event; and (4) an avoidance of the performance postures of other genres, particularly mainstream rock.

(1) A LACK OF STRESS ON VIRTUOSITY

Indie gigs differ greatly from classical music performance. In classical performance, the composer's composition is a "sacred text," and the audience sees how well this particular realization lives up to or releases a postulated ideal existing in an original textual form (see Small 1998). This characterization is particularly apt and suggests parallels to liturgical experiences of the ideal text of the Bible. The Bible is viewed as an eternal, infallilble, and unalterable textual authority to be enlivened note for note, word for word. In classical music, the composition is the ideal template, and the live performance strives to live up to this ideal. In the philosophy of symphonic performance, the live performance cannot surpass or even contribute to the ideal text.[3] Indie is different. Although it has a musical text, indie privileges the live over the written or recorded forms. It is thus closer to jazz in its valuing of spontaneous creation than it is to classical's enlivening of an ideal text.[4] For indie, the live performance is the originary art object, and the CD is the reproduction. Recordings can be modified by all forms of technical wizardry, but it is in the live show that a band can reveal if it is a true conduit of musical revelation.

Because the live performance is the ideal, the indie show has no set template. The perfect manifestation of the music is always unknown. This creates a different attitude toward what would conventionally be considered errors. Indie music has texts, songs that the audience may have heard in another format, but because they are not posited as the ideal, deviation is not a problem. An error during a show is an error only insofar as it interrupts the flow of the event. Broken strings, broken instruments, or musicians falling over are not considered to be impediments unless they disrupt the performance. In fact, audience members often view troubles that performers need to overcome as enhancing the gig. One of the greatest differences in perceived quality of performance between musicians and audiences concerns technical difficulties. Often musicians, thinking of the minutiae of performance, feel that a show fraught with difficulty is a failure, while many audience members may consider it a triumph. What might be considered a mistake by the musician or an outsider—the wrong chord, or an instrument out of tune—are generally viewed by the audience as unique components of an original live event. Therefore, "errors" do not intrinsically result in a positive or negative assessment by the audience. In the same way that technical proficiency is not valued in indie, the slavish reproduction of a recorded version of a song is viewed as not being present in terms of emotion or an unfolding experience of music. Virtuosity is not a virtue for indie.

(2) NOT REGISTERING THE VISUAL GAZE OF AUDIENCE MEMBERS

A major convention that demonstrates that indie performers are "being" is their self-presentation as totally absorbed in music and not overtly aware of the nature of performance as spectacle. Performers use a variety of gaze strategies during performances that suggest that they do not see audience members. Generally, musicians do not make direct eye contact with audience members. Performers stare out, unfocused, into the middle ground. This same style of unfocused gaze has been reported in certain types of ceremonial greeting exchanges in Western Samoa (Duranti 1992a). Musicians are aware of different gaze techniques.

It's really weird. When someone is really staring at you and then you decide to look back at them, then they move on to look at someone else. With our singer, it is something different. He spends the show sort of looking up or looking through people. He doesn't look them in the eye. (B.B.)

I'm always watching people during the show, but I do it in a way that they don't really know I'm doing it. I could tell you everything you did during the show and you'd never know I was paying attention to what you were doing. It is only sometimes when I see someone I know or would like to have contact with that I sometimes make eye contact. (D.M.)

At another gig, one bassist mentioned how he had worn sunglasses onstage in the past. When he took them off, he noticed that people in the audience would respond to his eye gaze: "When I first stopped wearing sunglasses onstage, I would stare directly at people. I remember this one time, I looked at this one guy who was just standing there and as soon as I looked at him he started dancing. I stopped doing it 'cause I could see it made people uncomfortable. Now I just look through them, you know what I mean?" (U.O.). The unfocused gaze of the performer allows the audience to act as though their gaze is unreturned, as though the audience can see but not be seen. This visual strategy of performance is not unlike a play in which actors perform without acknowledging the audience. Even though audience members respond to direct eye contact with performers, often intensifying their expected fan behavior, most fans find the idea that the performers actually can see them during the performance highly improbable.[5] The diffuse gaze of musicians during performance supports the idea that the musician does not register the presence of the audience while playing and is therefore not performing, but—in the ultimate cliché of rock—that the band members are playing music for themselves. By using an unregistering gaze, the performer partly denies that the performance is a spectacle.

Another gaze strategy common to performers is to close their eyes, suggesting an inward concentration and a lack of orientation to the world beyond. By focusing vision inward, or on other performers and ritual implements, the musician suggests that he/she is wholly involved in the task at hand. Audience members express pleasure when watching the performers stare intently at their instruments. They enjoy seeing the performers seeming to be privately immersed in what they are doing.[6] Immersion in the performance suggests to the audience that the performer is "being," not pandering to a crowd of spectators. Performance strategies such as using a gaze that does not acknowledge the audience, closing one's eyes, or directing one's gaze toward fellow performers and instruments suggest involvement in the unfolding event and fosters the central illusion of "being," not "posing."

(3) REFRAINING FROM COMMENTARY DURING PERFORMANCE

Performance details that suggest that a musician approaches the performance analytically deny the central illusion of beingness. Audience members are usually dismayed when performers criticize the unfolding performance. Commentary or criticism, reflexive forms of speech, suggest that the performer is not in the moment but rather analyzing it. Meta-speech, complaints about equipment, or requests for the audience to move forward are problematic because they take the audience out of its reverie and instead draw attention to the staged nature of the show. Commentary suggests that the performer has a cognitive and analytic awareness of a technical project. It is similar to the reflexive moment in a film or play in which the actor turns to the camera or audience and addresses them directly. It makes the audience confront the fact that what they are seeing is a performance. The audience becomes self-conscious, aware of themselves as audience members at a staged event. Since the goal of indie is to be completely present during performance, meta-commentary that takes audience members out of the moment is antithetical to the event's goals.

(4) AVOIDANCE OF MAINSTREAM PERFORMANCE POSTURES

In an attempt to display themselves as "being" and as authentically present, indie performers actively eschew traditional generic rock and roll postures and facial expressions. The postures of the mainstream are considered empty forms that represent inauthenticity. Thus, indie actively avoids all of these clichéd forms of the mainstream (for example, the pained expression of the guitarist wheedling away at his "axe," the head flung back with jaw agape, the guitar thrust forward from the groin as a phallic extension, the drummer's crinkled face and mouth in an "Oh" sign, the singer's depiction of earnestness).[7] The mainstream cliché of the hackneyed rock performer calling out "Hello, Wembley" or "Hello, Denver" suggests to the indie crowd that values the personal and intimate that this change in nomination is perhaps the only element of this performance that is catered to this particular audience. It implies that there is a set format and the only way to reach out to the audience is in the broadest and most general terms. For indie, the conventional has questionable emotional veracity. To understand why indie conflates the conventional with the artificial, we must turn to broader cultural notions of emotional veracity. In the West, we confer emotional value on the novel and unique, and we see cliché as representing emptiness.[8] Cliché or routine is seen as the opposite of true feeling. This tendency to privilege the new and different is present in indie's self-definitions. Indie privileges itself over other genres by its purportedly original, self-made, personal unconventionality rather than by the purportedly impersonal, undifferentiated, other-made, phony, generic, empty manipulations of other musical genres. This contributes to the rapid turnover of indie's trends and formalities. When any particular trend is canonized in the press, soon after it will be flouted.[9] Thus indie has two internally conflicting drives: a drive for emotional veracity in the novel and unique, and a drive toward a purer, circumscribed code of Puritan simplicity that limits the boundaries of elaboration.

Indie utilizes performance conventions that present performers as wholly involved in a singular unfolding event. Idiosyncrasies of live performance are considered a contribution to rather than a detraction from a show. These are indie's conventions to suggest to audiences that what they are seeing is real.

Emotion and the Decay of Emotion

now I understand why words mean so much to you
they'll never be about you . . .
Idlewild

Indie's conventions bring us to what is really at stake in indie performance. Being versus acting, verisimilitude versus reflexivity, is really about
doing versus *thinking, emotion* versus *rationality*. The goal in indie performance is to be in the moment rather than to think about the moment.
To think about the moment is to fail. The goal of indie performance is to
capture the ephemerality of emotion. The revelation of indie performance
is to be in the present tense, to be emotion, to transcend distance and self-
awareness, to make one moment real. For indie, the important issue is not
the skill or mastery of the performance but the musician's ability to capture
emotion. Bands exist in a pantheon of emotional extremes, deities of particular emotions: angst, hedonistic pleasure, joy, regret, bravado, melancholy. Lyrics discuss emotional states and feelings: "how does it feel to
feel?"[10] The art form of indie music asserts feeling over thinking, being in
the moment over reflexivity, informality over formality, intimacy over distance, the decadent aesthete over the androgyne of manners. Indie valorizes emotion as the wellspring of meaning.

Audiences enjoy the destruction of instruments. It suggests that musicians are so carried away by emotion that they sacrifice their own valuable ritual implements. The audience wants there to be congruence among the
sound, the emotion, and the performer. This is the sentiment that is at once
parodied and reasserted by Johnny Rotten's sneered exclamation: "We mean
it, man." The scornful utterance denies the veracity of the sentiment expressed on the surface: "We mean it." It makes fun of the earnestness of the
mainstream and the desire of audiences for verisimilitude. Indie demands
congruence between expression in performance and emotion: "My words fly
up to heaven, my thoughts remain below. Words said without feeling never
to heaven go" (the Divine Comedy).[11] The audience wants to believe that the
artists feel the music, that they have become the conduits of pure emotion.

The audience wants the performers to succeed in capturing emotions,
because if musicians can succeed, then the audience can succeed as well. A
successful gig unites audience, performer, and music. As one musician described it to me:

There is no bigger difference than being in the audience and looking up at the stage
and being on the stage looking at the audience. It's the biggest gulf in the world . . .
Sometimes, and these are the days that you realize why you're doing it, the communication is such that everyone is lost in it. Even the band doesn't know what it's

doing. It's just doing something right. The excitement is really incredible. The adrenaline is pumping like crazy and just the absolute joy of the performance is shared by everyone equally and it's really, really fucking intense. This usually only happens in small clubs. (B.H.)

All are merged when the audience believes that the musicians are experiencing real emotion and in turn the audience experiences real emotion, too.

If the audience sees the performers as being rather than performing, they no longer perceive themselves as audience members observing a performance but rather as participants. If the performer ceases to be a performer, the audience ceases to be an audience. As Stanley Walens notes: "In the act of forgetting the performers as performers, the audience must also in some way forget its existence as audience. The trick of a good performer then is to make the audience vanish, to break down the boundary between stage and outside the proscenium, to make the audience and performer act in a larger play, not the one on stage, but the play—the interplay between performance and perceivers" (Walens 1996: 375–376). The act of believing that what the performers are portraying is real is a unification of the audience's and the artists' visions. The boundary between performer and audience is effaced. If the performers are present, the audience can also be present. An essential component of successful audience participation is the inhabiting of a spectorial mode of nonselfconsciousness: *to be* rather than to have a selfconscious awareness of being. If the performer is believed to be being rather than performing, the event is transformed from impersonation to incarnation, from act to actuality. The gig is no longer a show, the audience is no longer an audience, and the musician is no longer a performer. Whether the performer can forget himself and actually emotionally experience the music is irrelevant. What matters in performance is whether or not *the audience* can forget it is a performance.

Since the illusion of performance is that the music, the musicians, and the audience are united during an event, the distances between performers and audience members change after a show. There are discrete differences between the behavior of audience members toward performers before and after a gig. Because indie performers often mingle in the crowd during supporting bands' slots, certain audience members interact with musicians at some point during the evening. The interaction with non-professional fans prior to shows will be marked by some formality—a deferential approach, handshaking, relatively short conversations, or the presentation of compliments, good luck wishes, or perhaps questions regarding the tour. After a good show, the barriers shift. Audience interaction with performers is still deferential, but instead of formal handshaking, audience members will generally touch the performers—pat them on the back, rub their arms, touch their heads, engage in physical contact that suggests intimacy. A transformation occurs during performance; the formality of strangers is exchanged for the closeness of intimates. This desire for physical contact after a performance is not a unique dimension of indie music. After particularly good lectures, students or audience members will often come up and touch a lecturer's arm or shoulder. When a performance has worked properly, when the audience feels moved, the relationship between performer and audience is altered. However, this closeness is based on an illusion, the illusion of the effacement of barriers between audience and performer. This is the trick—that the show was not a show at all.

However, given the indie gig's emphasis on novelty, experience with the conventions of indie performance eventually distances the fan from the event.[12] The first time we experience something, we are involved with the unfolding and our referents are internal and narrative. The first time you see a film, it's all about what happens next. But after some experience, we are no longer held by the unfolding of events, the what happens next, but by the nuances of the art object. Each viewing brings a different experience base, even if that experience difference is only having seen the film previously—like reading the same book at different stages in a reader's life. For the novice gig goer, it's about the unfolding of the performance: What happens next? When will the band start? What is this going to be like? What happens if I fall over? Will the band do an encore? For the experienced fan, it is different: How does this relate to other performances, to other recordings, to other pieces by the artist, or other pieces by other artists? ("Oh, now they are going to do another encore because the house lights are down," or "It was better when they played at the Town and Country last year.") For example, on one occasion a fan in zone two told me I need not clap following a performance because the band would be doing an encore. He knew that irrespective of my applause the band would do an encore, because the house lights were still down. He could not construe my applause as a response, just as I, at Jabberjaw, could not imagine walking across the stage. Experience with any genre teaches the audience member the conventions of performance, and conventions remind the viewer of the event's fictionality. Knowledge of generic conventions increases the reflexive awareness of the audience member. The experience of the performance becomes more intellectual and less immediate, and that distancing is physically enacted in the indie participant structure as older fans move back in the venue.[13] Since the goal of performance is to be totally emotionally present, reflexive selfconsciousness is irreconcilable.

The more experience and familiarity with the genre and history of indie music the audience members have, the more they recognize conventionality, and the more difficult it is for them to lose themselves in the event. A song that is new to the young fan in the front may be a remake of a Wire song to the older fan in the back; an Interpol song—just a Joy Division song. Older fans comment on how derivative new bands are of old bands, bands they saw the first time around.[14] The more the participant knows, the higher the ante is lifted. As the stakes rise, sheer power, volume, and participation are no longer enough. Release is less easy to achieve. Emotional reverie is less attainable. Those who have moved into the recesses of zone two often envy how easy it is for young fans to become overwhelmed and enthused by music. It takes so much more for older fans to feel the same way. For a culture that associates verisimilitude with the novel and the unique, the more one is exposed to a ritual, the more difficult it is to attain "beingness." While those in the back are hypercritical, however, they do not want the band to fail. Older fans hope very much to get what they want, to become present, to overcome their own resistance to the event that is the result of their own overexposure. However, for the older fan, transcending selfconsciousness and "being" becomes a much more difficult enterprise.

The more one sees the performance *as* performance, the more one questions the veracity of previously experienced emotions. Feelings experienced during performances, once taken for granted as real, are now questioned. It is not merely that this performance is not working for the older fan, but that all those young people in the front think that it is. What the older fan sees as clichéd emptiness, young fans see as authentic. Gigs begin to appear manipulative, stupid, and empty. The more the performance is viewed as artifice, the more the substance and authenticity of emotions that the audience member felt (not just at this gig but all gigs) are undermined. Emotions once believed to be true are remembered in retrospect like a play. The decay of emotional signification in the indie gig makes one question not only the veracity of emotions that are felt in the gig setting but the reliability of emotions in general. Indie, whose language is the language of emotion, offers a ritual event in which participation first validates the veracity and power of emotion but, over time, ultimately undermines this very assertion. If emotions once made you believe something was true with all your heart, then when you believe the truth to be otherwise, emotions themselves appear dubious. Emotions appear to be the empty manipulators. You've been betrayed.

Within the diachronic experience of the ritual event of the indie gig, emotions are shown to be at first transitory and ephemeral and later worthless and trivial. Were those feelings based in reality? It certainly suits contemporary notions of emotion. In the late twentieth and early twenty-first centuries, emotions are considered little more than chemical secretions that cause misplaced signification. Psychological ailments are treated chemically, with Prozac, Paxil, or Ritalin, rather than therapy. The treatment of psychology is biology. Feelings are treated as unreliable representations of reality. If emotions are false, then a life built on valuing emotional epiphany is a sham. After the magic show, mundane reality denies the validity of the world projected on the stage. For indie, that world is the world of feeling, not thinking; being, not pretending. As the audience member moves from insider to outsider, he no longer trusts indie's central tenet that to be in the moment is the most important thing in the world. Certainly it is not as important as making a living and establishing a family. After all, what difference *does* it make if your friends like different music than you do?

The ritual of the gig designates emotion as a component of youth as a liminal phase. It is a rite of passage to take audience members from adolescence to adulthood, from the point of valuing emotions to not trusting the internal world of sentiments. Emotions are left for the young and the working classes with their football allegiances. The anger of the youthful artist is viewed as beautiful, but his anger as an older man is detested; he is a pathetic old man who does not know enough to leave adolescent concerns behind. The gig is to produce a person who will leave youth culture denying the validity of emotions—been there, done that, over it. Indie asserts and later obviates the veracity of the emotional world.[15]

When the ritual is seen to be an illusion, when the emotional veracity of performance is found to be unreliable, the audience feels betrayed. They have been tricked and someone needs to be held responsible. The two most common responses to this betrayal are either to feel that the musician has misled the audience, often resulting in the feeling of anger, or to feel that one has betrayed oneself. When the audience holds the performer responsible, fan adulation turns to vilification. This is part of the backlash phenomenon of the indie community. Often backlash is attributed solely to the foibles of the British indie press, but in truth fans are just as likely to turn on performers of their own accord. The status conferred by one's participation in musical performance is fleeting for nearly all musicians. The love and adulation given by the audience can quickly turn to hostility and resentment. Because musicians are to play themselves, fans demand that the musicians live up to their fantasies. Fans turn on performers who no longer make music they like or whose offstage personae are seen to be different from their onstage personae. The performer is viewed as having misrepresented himself. As one fan put it, "I can remember when this guy lit a light in my mind, now he just seems to pour bile into it. Maybe I was just fooled" (letters page, *NME*, February 8, 2005). Even if the artist simply stops producing music the audience approves of, the audience feels betrayed. The once exalted magicians/musicians are called frauds—charlatans, tricksters, or salesmen who made you think they were wizards. Here, the audience holds the musician responsible for its own fantasies, and he is punished for the audience's belief in him.

When the audience members assume responsibility, adulation turns to disappointment and disillusionment. The audience members admit that they have invested the performance and music with its meaning. They can no longer believe in the trick. When the journalists say "never meet your idols," they are actually saying it is better to believe the trick than to know it is a trick. It is akin to Harvey Weinstein's admission that in understanding the magician's trick, "I ruined it for myself. Now I can never go to a magic show again." The phrase "never meet your idols" tells you that musical performance has something to hide, something behind the curtain that can be revealed in the mundane interactions of everyday life.

When I started writing about indie music, I was told often and at length that music was the most important thing in fans' lives. I also found this sentiment expressed in letters and articles in the press. In order to treat the subject with honesty, I knew I would need to understand why that music assumed such importance. And as I found the answer to that question, I found indie's heart. Music is the most important thing in the world to indie fans because this music is a medium of emotion. When indie fans say music is the most important thing in the world, they are saying that emotion and feelings are the most important elements of experience. When emotion is the center of your world, then the art form that conveys it is an all-consuming passion. The language of indie is the language of emotion, told in word and sound.

Indie is a performance genre with a concern for verisimilitude manifested in public discourse in the guise of authenticity and credibility. The central illusion of musical performance is that it allows the audience to believe that the performers are actually experiencing the sentiments they perform. This allows the audience to stop being an audience and become participants instead in the larger play. However, by valuing verisimilitude and novelty and adhering to a circumscribed performance code, the indie genre has a built-in obsolescence. Over time, the ritual dynamics of the gig become predictable and more apparent to participants. The encore, once a spontaneous return, is now a predictable routine. The emotional epiphanies that once seemed so evident are few and far between. The result is a questioning of the ritual's veracity. However, in questioning the importance of the ritual, one also questions what the ritual posits as important. An event that valorizes the role of emotion in life, in its decay of signification, invalidates emotion. At one point, it seems natural to think that these odes to sentiments are the most important thing in the world; later it seems like nothing more than silly, skinny young men on a stage, playing instruments, making songs of as little import as a discarded newspaper advertisement. The cigar becomes just a cigar and nothing more.

The indie gig is a ritual about producing adults who believe that being overwhelmed by emotional sentiment is a merely youthful thing, a phase that people go through. While one is involved in the event, the emotional world is given shape and encouraged by participation. At the point of exit, however, the emotional world is asserted to be unreliable and worthless. This is a ritual of transition to convey youth from adolescence to adulthood, where emotional sentiment is a misleading and empty trifle of a world best left behind. Indie's trick is to assert first that emotions are the center of the universe and then, in the decay of signification caused by the immersion in the very thing loved, it shows what was once considered truth is mere performance, spontaneous creation is cliché, and what was once considered the center of the universe is just entertainment. It becomes simply a leisure activity on par with golfing, bird-watching, trainspotting, or any other activity that outsiders might observe with incredulity and wonder why anyone would waste their time doing that.

CHAPTER 6

Sex and the Ritual Practitioners

But we know it's just a lie
scare your son, scare your daughter . . .
Arcade Fire

This final chapter is devoted to indie's ritual practitioners: the performers, the crew, the audience members who do not opt out of the community, those who seek intimate relations with performers, and the professionals who still look for meaning in music. These ritual practitioners fight against conversion to the values of their Protestant society. They devote their lives to the transitory rewards of participating in gigs.

Within this chapter's discussion of spectatorship, mainstream rock imagery is the backdrop for the distinct practices and moral distinctions made by the indie community. Gender roles and sexual expression are inscribed in the spectatorship associated with the different narrative categories of audience members and performers. Though indie espouses a pro-female agenda, an egalitarian stance, and a prohibition against sexual promiscuity, the spectorial lens of the event is presented as having two possible perspectives: either the unindividuated crowd of "kids" or a sexually out-of-control female. The image of the overzealous female spectator is rooted in the mainstream rock stereotype of the sexually rapacious groupie who pursues casual sexual contact with male performers. In addition, there is also a narrative category of the musician onto whom audience members project their own fantasies of desire and authenticity. Both the groupie and the mainstream musician are antitypes in the indie community. That is, indie musicians and sexual acolytes define themselves in opposition to these stereotypes, but they also both overlap to some degree with the behaviors associated with them. Groupies are seen as evidence of the overindulgence and the inappropriateness of mainstream rock and an illustration of how performer/audience relations can degenerate. The stereotypical main-stream "musician" is portrayed as possessing epic carnal appetites, vacillating between lofty and vulgar attributes that recall the forms of creativity found in the trickster figure of mythology. Indie's ritual practitioners attempt to distinguish themselves from the mainstream by applying their own moral principles to the practices of "sex, drugs, and rock and roll." In this, we will see the intersection of sexual politics, gendered commodity exchange, and the reciprocal nature of the interplay between two categories of ritual practitioners. By examining the perspectives and tropes that shape audience expectations and the actual behaviors of members of the community, spectatorship emerges as a fully human manifestation rather than a mere abstraction.

Gendered Spectatorship

Since the early work of Laura Mulvey (1975) on the constructions of gendered audiences in cinema, scholars in several disciplines have begun to examine the phenomenon of gendered spectatorship (Haraway 1989, Rose 1988). As I discussed in the introduction, spectatorship is different from vision; it is an implicit perspective through which an audience views an event, and it emerges from structural and narrative conventions. The gig is one of the few Western spectacles in which female (rather than male) spectatorship is fetishized—overvalued and overexpressed. This is despite the fact that females are the minority in the majority of rock music genres. In music's female spectorial subject, there are both inversions and equivalencies to standard Western spectorial modes.

The image of female spectatorship found in media representations, journalistic critiques, and audience and performers' accounts is characterized as hysterical and consumed by overwhelming sexual longing. In British and American documentary films and cinematic representations of audiences, male spectators are persistently shown en masse. Close-ups are consistently reserved for females (*Backbeat* [1993], *The Beach Boys* [1985], *Beatles: First U.S. Tour* [1964], *The Commitments* [1992], *Gimme Shelter* [1970], *Hype* [1997], *Monterey Pop* [1968]). Male spectators, on the other hand, are displayed in shots with two or more persons, distancing the viewer from their emotion.[1] Reserving the close-up for females suggests that females' spectatorship is intimate, personalized, and proximate. In the West, female spectatorship is presented as out of control and overly invested. Mary Ann Doane has suggested that this is due to Western conceptions of female naiveté in relationship to systems of signification (Doane 1982).[2] In contrast, male spectatorship is impersonal and generalized. In rock and roll, the female has been represented as overly close and out of control, and a female out of control is considered to be a sexually available one.[3]

By locating sexual desire in the female spectator, the rock performance inverts the traditional Western object of erotica from the female to the male. Here both men and women gaze upon men, and men are recognized to be the libidinal objects. Bono, the lead singer of the band U2, once said: "Being a rock 'n' roll star is like having a sex change. People treat you like a girl—they stare at you and follow you down the street. I now know what it's like to be a babe" (*Melody Maker*, September 19, 1992).[4] This comment encapsulates some specific gender inversions that occur in rock performance. It notes that in standard Western ideology, the female is the locus of beauty, the object of desire. The Western convention is for women to be the object of a male gaze (Doane 1982). This Western convention contrasts with the other cultures' notions of the subject and object of beauty and gaze. For example, both the African Wodaabe and the Kaluli of Papua New Guinea view males as the objects of sexual desire and sexual spectacle (Bovin 2001, Schieffelin 1976). Rock inverts the Western convention by making male performers the repositories of the gaze and of sexual longing.[5]

While the image of the sexually available female in the throes of sexual desire for a male libidinal object proliferates in mainstream rock, female spectatorship at the indie gig is also represented in terms of a sexualized vision. Female spectorial enjoyment of the performance is attributed in large part to sexual desire for the performers. This representation is consistent in indie media discourse:

That's why I can peer into the eyes of every woman in the room and see them mentally undressing Dulli. Dulli never looks them in the eyes. He's too busy pouting, sneering, growling fragments of Suede's "The Drowners" in the middle of "My World Is Empty Without You" and exchanging asides with colleagues, to pay attention. Which excites them more. And all the time, the taut explosive tension that lies at the heart of the songs is utterly sexual. (*Melody Maker*, March 5, 1994)

Not for him the thrust of the hips to send sticky eyed teenage girls into the throes of orgasm. (*NME*, June 14, 1994)

Two Huggy Bears and the monumentally lardy Dale playing beered-up blues to a handful of scrubbed clean, over-excited girls in tarty sixties gear. (*NME*, September 18, 1993)

What people are moved by—and they are, there's genuine wet-eyed mania *(You're sure it's their eyes that are wet?—Jealous, bitter, appalled, etc. Ed)* going on down front. (*Melody Maker*, July 8, 1995)[6]

Girls with sex-coloured eyes stand and gape in wonder as the speakers erupt their eardrums at every chorus. (*NME*, June 4, 1994)

"I'm up for it," says Damon as I leave him with three diminutive Blurettes hanging from his neck like live breathing pendants. (*Melody Maker*, May 21, 1994)

Bands are regularly assessed by both male and female journalists in terms of their perceived sexual desirability. Wetness becomes a trope for female sexual reaction to the performance. Though the journalist in the July 8, 1995, piece from *Melody Maker* did not make an explicit claim of gendered spectatorship (wet-eyed mania could be masculine or feminine), the editor's parenthetical remark implies that the fans of this band are females in the throes of sexual arousal. However, as we know from our discussion of zone one, both male and female fans *are* wet up front—wet with sweat from heat, exertion, and propinquity. Here, we see the first in a series of ways that male spectatorship is hidden behind a public façade of aggressive female sexual longing.

This version of sexualized female spectatorship is so strong that even when the performers are females, sexual desire is still located in the female: "Justine—with her hair behind her ears the spit of Cindy off Eastenders—sends the hormones of otherwise heterosexual girls into a jumble only rivaled in recent years by PJ Harvey" (*Melody Maker*, November 6, 1993). This idea of the female in a sexual frenzy permeates rock music. The stereotype of the female fan from mainstream rock that we see inserted in indie discourse is someone screaming, panting, crying, and wet.[7]

The sexually out-of-control female audience member is not the only discursively marked mode of spectatorship in indie. The other image of spectatorship that emerges in both mainstream and indie discourse is that of the undifferentiated crowd. Here, the individual audience member is subsumed in a group identity and characterized as genderless. This indie spectator is "the kids."

Goosebumps erupt, as the kids surrender themselves to the joys of mindless behavior. (*Melody Maker*, February 8, 1994)

This may be an under-18's only, alcohol-free benefit gig in a village youth club, but the kids here are working themselves up into an adrenaline-charged frenzy. Kitted out in the latest indie T-shirts, these impossibly hip teens are here to freak out to a live band. (*Melody Maker*, October 2, 1993)

I'm confronted by the amazing sight of lemming-like hordes, arms aloft, waiting for one pearl of wisdom. (*Melody Maker*, September 4, 1993)

The kids are hordes, T-shirts that announce band affiliations, lemmings, the great unwashed masses. They are not under individual control and not subject to individual will.

Thus we find two potential spectorial locations for indie audience members—genderless spectators who form a collective mass devoid of individual will and a gender-marked spectatorship that is feminine, individualized, and sexualized. The former is acceptable to indie ideology: gender-neutral, de-sexualized, egalitarian, one that effaces difference. The latter is threatening to indie: sexual, differentiating, and dangerous. By inscribing sexual difference, the marked female spectator endangers the purity of indie and inserts the threat of mainstream promiscuity and moral decay.

The fetishization of the overzealous sexualized female gaze obscures the gaze of men upon men and preserves the desexualized context of male–male interaction unquestioned.[8] The construction of a female hypersexuality obscures the homoerotic elements of the intense and intimate male-to-male body contact in the crowd. The fact that male spectators are watching male or female performers utilizing both masculine and feminine gestural styles, postures, and clothing is effectively shrouded by the image of the wet female fan overwhelmed by her sexual desire.[9] The gig is an event where the audience wants to believe that the boundaries between music, performer, audience, and emotion are effaced. However, the sexual component to this merging is constantly repressed and repudiated. The sexualized female spectator thus serves as a figurehead for all sexual desire and provides an outlet for the sexual underpinnings of the event. The spectacular nature of her image masks other sexual desires and renders them invisible.

The Groupie as Sexual Predator

go on take everything, take everything, i want you to . . .
Hole

This threatening vision of female sexuality reaches to the heart of rock. As a ritual event, rock addresses the roles of sex, sexuality, and gender in our society by exaggerating and inverting its codes. In order to understand the sexual practices within indie, we first have to understand the stereotype of groupies that comes from the popular media, because it provides the cultural context for their behaviors. It is important to remember that this is a representation of groupies and not an ethnographic depiction of the sexual practices of performers and audience members in mainstream or other rock genres of music. In both the fetishized and denigrated image of the groupie, gender roles are inverted—males are passive libidinal objects and females are active sexual subjects. This inversion undermines the Western sexual exchange system, in which women are valued material resources exchanged by men. The image of the mainstream groupie undercuts the currency value of sex by diminishing its market value. In this way, the groupie is a threatening, disruptive, and problematic figure, not just for indie, with its tenets of asceticism, but for the broader culture as well.

While the term "groupie" can apply to any number of fans and fan behaviors, its specific connotation in broad parlance is sexual. It evokes an image of a sexually promiscuous female who attends shows with the goal of having sexual relations with musicians. This category of sexual groupiedom is not the exclusive domain of musical performances. Almost every field has aficionados who pursue sexual relations with professionals of a particular vocation—"baseball Annies," political groupies, sports groupies, animation groupies, comedy groupies, intellectual groupies. The majority of these nomenclatures borrow the term "groupie" from musical performance, in part because no other field has been as strongly and publicly associated with female sexual frenzy as music. Moreover, sexual groupiedom is not an exclusive enclave for females. There are male groupies pursuing male performers; there are male groupies pursuing female performers; there are female groupies pursuing female performers. My discussion of the sexual groupie will be restricted primarily to the female who pursues a male performer (the archetypal groupie image) and its reverse, the male groupie who pursues a female performer.

Although it is a popular stereotype, the sexual groupie is frowned upon and denigrated in general representations and by the indie community in particular. A good summary of the groupie stereotype appeared in *Select* magazine in the humorous quiz section, which I excerpt below. In this quiz, readers were invited to rate their level of groupiedom by answering questions regarding their sexual behavior.[10]

Are You a Groupie?

Alarmed that you've woken up in Clint Poppie's bath, naked but for a strategically placed J-cloth? Try this month's quiz and find out if you have any self-respect left at all. . .

Which of the following most accurately describes your ideal night out?
Inveigle way backstage at Motley Crue show by any means necessary. Attempt to cop off with lead singer and demonologist. Failing that, guitarist. Or drummer. Actually, that roadie doesn't look so bad.

Do you think oral sex is:
It's more effective than the guest list.

When you wake up in the morning, do you:
Get up off floor, pick up a pair of souvenir celebrity underpants, crawl from tour bus/transit, update your *National Enquirer* League Ladder of Porking, try to establish what country you're in.

Which of the following things do you always carry with you?
Complete set of 1994–95 tour laminates . . . Novelty Saxon snowstorm presented to you as token of affection by their roadie "Mad Jock" after last year's British dates.

How many people have you had sex with?
Four or less. Oh what you mean, like, ever? It was definitely four or less last night,

but to be honest, you know, you lose track so quickly, don't you? I'd put it in the low hundreds. I guess.

How do you picture yourself in five years' time?
Inspecting the lengthy list of dates for signings and readings for my newly published book of shag-and-tell revelations, *Kissing, Dreams, Amphetamines, and Felching.*

Verdict: 91–110 points: You are the disgusting pinnacle of groupiedom. You will shag anything with a heartbeat and a record contract.
110+ points: So, is it true what they say about Jimi, or what?

The quiz reveals that the rock groupie is represented as undiscerning and sexually promiscuous, a woman who regularly has sex with multiple partners whom she knows nothing about, rarely obtains the partner she actually wants, and is more than willing to work her way down the band status hierarchy until she finds a partner.[11] She is willing to trade oral sex for access, finds herself dumped out on the street in squalor, treasures worthless trinkets, and doesn't even have the self-respect to be embarrassed about the whole thing, instead writes a tell-all book.[12] The groupie stereotype portrays a woman who is willing to do anything, no matter how debasing, to get what she wants.[13] Significantly, what she wants is represented as worthless and trivial.

In the groupie stereotype, we see one of the most important inversions that takes place in musical performance: females become the sexual predators and males the sexual prey, inverting traditional Western gender roles. The groupie is the sexual initiator, in pursuit of the passive male sex object. This image of the sexually passive performer in mainstream rock is demonstrated in the light bulb joke cycle. As Alan Dundes wrote in *Cracking Jokes*, the *screw* in the light bulb joke cycle is a commentary on sexual practices (Dundes 1987a):

How many lead singers does it take to screw in a light bulb? Just one, and the whole world to revolve around him.

How many drummers does it take to screw in a light bulb? Just one, so long as a roadie gets the ladder, sets it up, and puts the bulb in the socket for him.

How many musicians does it take to change a light bulb? Twenty. One to hold the bulb and nineteen to drink until the room spins.

These jokes characterize the musician as sexually passive, the "screwed" rather than the "screwer." Those around him do all the work.* This is part of the general representation of musicians as sexually quiescent, the object of sexual longing; the sex comes to them.

* There is also a joke for guitarists that represents them as sexually competitive: How many guitarists does it take to screw in a light bulb? One hundred. One to do it and ninety-nine to

The inversion of male and female gender roles also occurs in the representation of male groupies as coy and emasculated. Public references to male groupies are few and far between, but when they do occur, male groupies are represented as sexually passive and unappealing:

The mental image of the female groupie is that of the tart or bimbo dressed to kill. Their male counterparts tend to look poorly groomed, with bad posture, unimpressive physiques, dirty T-shirts, and bad haircuts. Persistent they are. Most are the "buzzing fly" school of courtship; that is, they dream if they stay near long enough, conquest is assured. (*L.A. Weekly,* February 1993)

More than a sprinkling of pot-bellied computer engineers wait, stoic as dairy cattle . . . all clutch a plethora of CDs, posters, drawings, poems, and in one case a toffee apple, for Tori to sign or accept. (*NME,* March 19, 1994)

Male groupies are viewed as unable to have actual sexual contact with performers; instead, they are happy to be in the proximity of a female performer. The male groupie is "a suitor trying to woo his love object with gifts and attention, but . . . seems too self-denigrating to ever cross the line" (*L.A. Weekly,* February 1993). Male groupies conform to gender norms in that the male pursues the female, and the female performer's high status accentuates their differences, making sexual contact less likely. Articles usually point out that male groupies do not have girlfriends. Rather than being seen as a sexual subject, the male groupie is seen as sexually impotent; he hovers in an irritating yet harmless way, dreaming sexual dreams that will never be fulfilled. He is the apogee of passive subservience.

By contrast, the female groupie is a disruptive figure. Basically, she is considered a specialized slut, not a slut who will sleep with anyone, but a slut who will sleep with anyone who has the right job. It is important to remember that in Western dating styles, males are expected to be the initiators of sexual contact and females the guardians, the ones who limit access to sex.[14] Sex is seen as something women *possess* that heterosexual men try to access *from* them. Within this context, sex is commodified, a resource that females are seen to trade in exchange for monetary advantage or status such as marriage. The mainstream groupie, by giving away sex (recall the "by any means necessary" in the first answer in the *Select* survey) in exchange for worthless trifles, undermines the market value of the female

(*note continued*)   say "I could do it better than that." Here, guitarists' sexual interest is oriented more toward performing better than other guitarists than toward the light bulb. It also shows how musicians' onstage togetherness is often accompanied by offstage competitiveness. In addition, there is an American variant of the light bulb joke for indie fans: How many indie fans does it take to screw in a light bulb? You mean YOU don't know? This points to the perceived elitism of the indie fan, who is always trying to one up everyone else with his esoteric knowledge of music. Its implicit subtext is that indie fans would rather make you think they have sex than actually do it.

commodity of sex: by proffering sex freely, they reduce its commodity value by increasing the availability of free or inexpensive sex in the market place. It is the hackneyed "why buy the cow when you can get the milk for free?" Here, groupies are seen as giving sex for worthless trinkets (a snow dome or a slip of paper that lets you into a grotty backstage area). By providing sex without restraint and unchecked, they are seen to diminish the exchange value of sex by introducing "cheap" sex into the marketplace.

The relationship between groupies and musicians also inverts the traditional gender roles in which men are expected to support women financially. In the realm of music, it is the female who is the financial provider and the musician, the pretty dandy, who is provided for. Again, from the musician's joke cycle: What do you call a musician without a girlfriend? Homeless. What is the difference between a musician and a savings bond? One of them eventually matures and earns money. It is well known that most musicians do not make a great deal of money. While the most successful performers are exceptions, musicians generally finish music with less money than when they started. Participants with even a very little experience know that the female provider will get very little return on any financial outlay she makes for a musician (Interpol: "I know you've supported me for a long time. Somehow I'm not impressed"; the Wonder Stuff: "It's your money I'm after baby"). In the ritual domain of music performance, the de facto roles of males and females within culture are inverted.

Yet at a more profound level, the groupie stereotype reveals that the cultural presuppositions regarding male/female sexual roles are merely an artifice of our own making. Our social system of sexual exchange is predicated on sex as a female commodity sought by men. Here, the groupie seeks sex provided by a man. If women own sex, why would they need to seek it? The groupie is actually the antithesis of the prostitute who trades sex for money, something that makes sense for a capital-based society. The groupie's goal is sex and she is willing to pay for it. However, in trading sex for trinkets or in exchange for access, she merely depreciates sex's commodity value.

Yet at another level, the groupie, unlike other audience members, successfully crosses the boundary between audience and performer and concretely enacts the desire on the part of the audience for obliterating the membrane between stage and life. As mentioned above, the sexual component of this merging is repressed and repudiated. The groupie is the symbol that renders the audience's sexual desires unacknowledged. By doing what the other audience members do not, she is seen by necessity as doing something "tricky" or wrong. Of course, what she does wrong is the misuse of what is seen as the trickiest possession that women have, that is, their sexuality. Sexuality is seen as the sole source of female power. By misappropriating her power, she becomes the ultimate image of audience "inauthenticity." In taking on the onus of the sin of the sexual desires of the audience, she becomes the sin-eater that allows the other audience members to feel morally superior and authentic in their spectatorship in relation to her. Not only is she inauthentic, but she undermines the musicians' authenticity. The temptation she provides by the misuse of her power undermines the credible musician's integrity, not just in the sense of providing the temptation for undermining moral codes but also disturbing the notion of his completeness that is portrayed on stage. Like the musician who should not be in it for anything other than artistic expression, women should not be in it for the sex (Hole: "you should learn how to say no . . ."). She becomes the first repository of audience resentment, long before the performers themselves are resented.

The images of male and female groupies invert traditional masculine and feminine roles. The female groupie is represented as sexually rapacious and indiscriminate. The male groupie is represented as someone for whom sex is more an idealized fantasy than a reality. In the rock music milieu, the male is feminized by becoming the object of the gaze and assumes a passive role while the female is masculinized by taking on the role of sexual predator.

Indie Versus Mainstream: Groupie Troublesomeness

Boo to the business world
. . . you are working for the joy of giving . . .
Belle and Sebastian

For indie, the category of groupie is a particularly troublesome one. The sexually aspiring female is a threat to indie's modest and austere ideology. Just as indie perceives mainstream rock as empty, impersonal, self-indulgent, and meaningless, groupie behaviors are considered to lie at the core of mainstream music's sloth and corruption. This is not to say that there are not females in the world of indie who pursue sexual contact with performers, but rather that the category of a sexual ritual practitioner is unacknowledged and only becomes marked when the ritual practitioner fails the norms that govern sexual contact with performers. The practices of these ritual practitioners in indie are considered different from the sexually debauched groupies of the mainstream, whose sexual contact with performers is deemed inappropriate for being easy, unemotional, and disconnected.[15] For the indie sexual ritual practitioner, sex is a recapitulation of the drama onstage, in which male and female powers combine to manifest the spirit of music and divine emotion. When it occurs, the sexual union between performer and audience member is idealized as discerning, emotional, and connected. Both sides protect against being debased by the other by letting sex become a purely physical act rather than an emotional one.

For indie, the term "groupie" is not attributed exclusively to those who wish to engage in sexual interaction. It can also be applied to a number of different fan behaviors that suggest intensive fanship. The term is used variously to describe male or female fans who travel from city to city following a band, fans who demonstrate subservient or reverential behavior, fans who try to get backstage, or fans who show a great deal of devotion to a particular band. In fact, the term applies generally to the behaviors of the inhabitants of zone one: waiting for autographs, trying to meet performers, exhibiting submissive interactive strategies and postures. The following comments by indie musicians underscore the considerable ambiguity around the term "groupie" within indie parlance.

Most groupies are male. After our shows the backstage area is always filled with young guys hanging around. They want to have contact with us, whether it be talking to us, just to get us to sign something, or just stealing a beer from our rider. Most groupies I meet are guys. (C.C.)

I don't know what you mean by groupies. Do you mean girls who come on to us? Do you mean the people who follow us on tours? Guys who want to be able to hang out with us a little while and offer us stuff? What do you mean? (B.H.)

The first example suggests that the groupies' interests are asexual. The second proposes a number of meanings for the term "groupie." In the latter example, a groupie might be male or female and interested in the band sexually or non-sexually. Thus, "groupie" in indie covers a broad number of behaviors that suggest intensive fanship or a desire to have personal contact with a performer.

The sexualized image of the groupie is so potent that it can sexualize behaviors that do not necessarily have a libidinal origin, particularly for females, whose activities in music are always read in the context of potential sexual rapaciousness. Despite the flexible nature of the term "groupie," it is almost always perceived to be a sexual epithet when it is applied toward a female. When a male is called a groupie, it is assumed he demonstrates the broad fan behaviors discussed above, following a band on the road, collecting all of their recordings, and so on. When a female is called a groupie for exhibiting the same fan behaviors, the term will take on the connotation that the woman is sexually available to the band.[16] This sexualization of female fanship is the bane of females who work in the music industry.[17] As Sara Cohen points out, "Women who 'hang out' in Liverpool rehearsal or recording studios . . . are likely to attract attention and jokes about 'groupies,' the assumption being that they are there primarily for sexual reasons" (Cohen 1997: 31). Females who follow bands or have contact of any nature with a band, even female artists, must always deal with this potential stigma. When the term "groupie" is applied to a female, it has sexual implications regardless of the behavior it describes.

Indie's sexual acolytes patently distance themselves from mainstream groupie behaviors in the same way that indie musicians eschew guitar solos. There are different performance conventions for the indie sexual acolyte. Indie asserts that there are proper and improper sexual interactions. Within the mainstream stereotype, the fetishized groupie-performer transaction is fellatio. The third question of *Select*'s rock groupie survey ("What do you think oral sex is?") and its answer of carelessly distributed oral sex pointed to this stereotype. In a piece on groupies in the *Modern Review*, Fred Vermorel states: "They [groupies] worship directly at the originary shrine of celebrity: the star's body. Only instead of braving the lepers and sewers of downtown Delhi, these sisters brave other kinds of disgust and disease to snuggle up to inhale and minister to the phalluses of our favorite stars" (*Modern Review*, April–May 1994). A song lyric points to the centrality of fellatio in the stereotypical groupie-performer interaction as well. In the song "Line Up," by the band Elastica, the character of "drivel head" is presented. She is someone who spends her time hanging out with the nouveau glitterati and is described with metaphors and allusions to fellatio including sucking on guitars and being on her knees.[18]

In each of these examples, the archetype of groupie sex is fellatio.[19] The relationship between parties is represented as asymmetric. The female is the active sexual participant and the male is the passive object of her libidinal worship. The sources for each of these quotes are intriguing. The first comes from outside the indie music community, from a scholar whose work centers on mainstream fanship within the context of performers such as Barry Manilow; here he is commenting on the satirical fanzine *Slapper*, which was written by a female member of the indie community.[20] The second comes from an indie insider. It is a lyric from the band Elastica, which was led by Justine Frischmann (the same Justine who was thought to whip the hormones of otherwise heterosexual females into a frenzy).[21] Its status as a lyric underscores the prevalence of the pejorative image of the female groupie within the indie community in a way that an academic article does not: songs receive airplay and are more widely and repeatedly distributed than a quote in the weekly press or a scholarly review. One of the ways indie acolytes differentiate themselves from the rock stereotype is by initially avoiding fellatio because it evokes the passive/aggressor, worshipped/devotee relationship. For indie, asymmetry is seen as impersonal and suggests distance between partners. In the Elastica song, the female persona is criticized because she is sexually servile ("loves to suck their shining guitars," "you can't see the wood for the trees on your knees"). Indie still enacts a sexual transaction between parties, but it is idealized as mutual—copulation, not supplication; intercourse, not fellatio.

Within the indie community promiscuity is not defined by the number of sexual partners one has; rather, it is an issue of discernment. The groupie in essence lacks discrimination. In the *Select* quiz, a lack of discernment is articulated in the groupie answer to the first question: "Attempt to cop off with lead singer and demonologist. Failing that, guitarist. Or drummer. Actually, that roadie doesn't look so bad." Here the groupie is represented as not caring whom she sleeps with as long as she gets to sleep with someone, no matter how tenuous the association to the band. The groupie answer to the question about the number of sexual partners is "Four or less. Oh what you mean, like, ever? It was definitely four or less last night." Multiple sex partners in a single night whom one cannot remember suggests both that the sex act makes little connection between parties and that it is of little consequence.

This lack of discernment in the groupie persona is also evident in Elastica's song. The protagonist knows *all* the stars and any new band. Here, the groupie attempts to have relations with any well-known musician, regardless of his or her personal attributes or the music's quality. This suggests a lack of taste not only in her sexual relations but in her musical sensibilities. She does not personally constitute her own canon; she loves *whoever* is the next big thing. Thus, the groupie is seen to be the consummate "starfucker": she seeks to bask in the reflected fame of any musician. She has sexual relations with the star, not the musician. Her sexual motivation is seen to be not for the act itself but for the status it confers.

In order to acquire reflected fame/infamy, the individual needs to let other people know of her conquests. Thus, groupies are seen as boastful about their sexual contacts with performers. The appropriate indie fan *should* not care about such things. However, as our discussion of zone one fans indicates, privileged access to performers does elevate a fan's status among other fans of a particular band. To guard against the negative groupie appellation, the indie sexual acolyte therefore must not draw attention to her activities. Within indie, the label of groupie is a form of censure. It denotes a highly inappropriate form of hedonistic and excessive fanship that debases music. Therefore, those who do seek to efface the boundaries between performer and audience by sexual contact need to be invisible.

Sexual interactions between performers and audience members are governed by a specific code. The indie sexual ritual practitioner should seek parity in sexual relations and should be discerning. Her contact should not be with the public persona of a musician but with the individual himself, and above all sex itself should not be merchandise. The indie sexual acolyte must remain private, unknown. To draw attention to one's role in the event will result in being named. Being designated a groupie has the same consequences as a performer who is revealed as a poseur—loss of social standing and credibility.

Offstage Behavior Mirrors Onstage Spectacle

The sexual merging of performer and audience member offstage is an important component to the overall indie spectacle. Indeed, it is part of the symbolic structure of musical performance within rock generally. The term "rock and roll" itself derives from African American Vernacular English slang for sexual intercourse (Dawson and Propes 1992). This sexual component is unmistakable when we consider the gender-coded displays of musical personae, the gender-stylized gestures, and the sexual song content. The ways that performance eroticizes musicians is part of the mystique of rock music generally. Many audience members recounted stories of being at gigs and not finding any of the performers attractive initially, then later becoming sexually attracted to a performer.

In the pantheon of rock and roll one finds a panoply of hypersexual imagery. The imagery of performers, performance, and the music has been extensively studied by popular music scholars. Some have looked to lyrical content to examine the construction of subjectivity in audience members as specifically masculine or feminine (Greig 1997). Music performances utilize sexualized imagery, exaggeration, and the combining of gender types (Walser 1993). There are copious examples of male performers using masculine imagery, lyrical content and posturing in rock music (Frith and McRobbie 1978, Palmer 1997, Reynolds and Press 1996). Depending on the genre, one may find a bare-chested display of muscles, dedicated workmanlike posturing, or cropped hair. In fact, many scholars find the masculine context of music performance so overwhelming that there is little room for females in the domain of rock at all (Bayton 1992, Coates 2003). However, female performers also participate in exaggerated feminine gender codes— the display of cleavage or the curve of a back, a slinky walk, the use of make-up—in their performance of femininity (McClary 1991, O'Brien 2002). But the most prevalent trope is the simultaneous combination of masculine and feminine codes.[22] It is a cliché of the mainstream male rock performer to wear feminine garb and make-up, to have long hair, and to move in ways usually reserved for females. In turn, female performers also participate in masculine codes, such as cropped hair, aggressive stances, and Doc Martens boots (Ehrenreich, Hess, and Jacobs 1995, Negus 1999). These scholars correctly identify the concept of gender as masquerade at work and at play within the popular music spectacle (Butler 1990).[23] With this exaggeration and inversion of gender codes, gender is quite literally performed, put on rather than a natural extension of biological categories. Of course, anthropologists have noted the same phenomenon in their examinations of what constitutes gender-coded imagery and behaviors in other societies (Mead 1935). However, when one limits the discussion to either image or music content, the complexity of the interplay of gender signs is often reduced. Sheila Whiteley notes that while Rolling Stones' lyrics are highly masculinized, they can be heard differently within the context of performance: the singer's use of feminine imagery—his hair, lips, and style of dance, and his own references to performing like a dancing girl—counters the masculine lyrics (Whiteley 1997). Such observations demonstrate the limitations of analyses that confine themselves to a single mode of communication in the abstract rather than addressing the context for the readings of images and lyrics in relationship to other performance codes. Feminine lyrics can be transformed by a female's masculine stage persona (O'Brien 2002). The impact of a song covered by an artist of a different sex can show a blending of gender perspectives.[24] For example, the White Stripes, a band with a male singer, covered the Dolly Parton song "Jolene," in which the protagonist begs another woman not to take away her/his man. The scholarship around gendered signs in musical performance has produced a discourse of opposition between masculine and feminine codes rather than an examination of the complexity of sexuality in ritual. In the various genres of rock and pop music, gender and sexual codes are at play and comprise a spectacle of erotica (Dyer 1990, Frith 1990b, Reynolds and Press 1996).

For British indie, there are few examples of hypermasculine or hyperfeminine artists. Indie's musical terrain is composed primarily of the androgynous blending of male and female attributes. In indie, where make-up and artifice are generally eschewed, male performers nevertheless tend toward the feminine with their slender bodies, pouty lips, and fringed hair. In fact, the male performer is regularly feminized: "It becomes clear why Jon Spencer's Blues Explosion has created such hysteria. They exude femininity. Feminine as in fluid, driven, and contrary as f*** . . . It's strange that Jon Spencer—a man so beautifully overdosed in testosterone—is so adept at manifesting the feminine" (*NME*, February 26, 1994). It is not only in body and dress that we find a trend toward the femininization of male performers, but also in posture and gesture—flipping one's hair, shaking one's

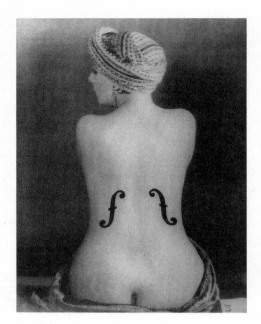

IMAGE 6.1. Man Ray. *Le Violon
D'Ingres,* 1924 *Permission to reproduce granted by ARS*

hips, and a whole slew of other behaviors and postures coded as feminine. Similarly, the female performer is also masculinized: "Kim Deal is everyone's favourite Breeder. Something about the way she swears like a truck driver, dresses like an auto mechanic, and sings like a sleepy-eyed angel. A history of bar-room brawls with sexist rednecks pretty much clinches her elevation to rock'n'roll sainthood" (*NME,* August 7 1993). The sexual imagery of indie is one of the first ways we see the combination of male and female powers that is at the heart of musical performance.

In rock generally, and in indie specifically, there is an abundance of sexual iconography. Musical instruments are often utilized to augment sexualized spectacle. It is a mistake to think of a guitar as a phallic symbol, for this reduces a complicated ritual object into a two-dimensional cipher. Certainly, the guitar can be utilized for phallic effect, especially when it is played in front of the groin and extended outward (Bayton 1997). In contrast, mariachi bands play the guitar high over the chest, where its phallic potential is not emphasized.[25] The phallic shape of the contemporary microphone, with its slender shaft and rounded top, is often utilized in performance as a sexualized prop. However, the guitar is a much more complicated object in the context of rock music.

IMAGE 6.2. Epiphone Casio guitar.
Photo by author.

The guitar is a potent image of the union of male and female forces. The prototypical guitar has archetypal feminine curves to its body. In Emily Apter's discussion of the development of Oriental fetishism in France at the turn of the twentieth century, she demonstrates the association of the serpentine curve with femaleness in Western ideology and the association of linearity with masculinity and rationality (Apter 1992). This similarity between instrument curvature and feminine body is the impulse behind Man Ray's *Le Violon D'Ingres,* in which the female torso is likened to the body of a violin (image 6.1). The violin's hourglass figure is echoed in the hourglass figure of the guitar. While the main body of the guitar suggests the feminine body, the neck and head suggest masculine-coded traits of linearity and the phallic (image 6.2). The headstock (the protruding part at the top of the guitar where the tuning pegs are) is joined to the long slender neck. The similarity between the neck and head of the guitar and the phallus is the impulse behind the guitarist's extension of the instrument from the groin during performance. The strings continue from the headstock to the bridge, the part of the guitar where the strings are held in place on the lower portion of the guitar's body. On an acoustic guitar, the bridge is located at the base of the open sound hole. This is a blatant image of combined male and female powers, the phallic neck extended by linear strings joining the curvaceous body at an open hole. It is at this location that the guitarist strums or finger picks; the locus for creativity is at the nexus of masculine and feminine elements. On electric guitars, there is no sound hole, but guitarists still strum and pick at the location immediately in front of the bridge where a sound hole would be. Hence, the guitar's imagery suggests a combination of the masculine and the feminine at the point where the guitarist's hand produces sound.[26]

Sexuality pervades not only rock and indie's imagery but their discourses as well. Indie bands' performance practices are regularly assessed in terms of the appropriateness of sexual behaviors. The guitar solo is eschewed in indie because it is likened to masturbation. Listening to records alone in one's room is referred to as wanking. Behaviors that are perceived as self-focused or self-indulgent are equated with inappropriate sexual expression; consequently they are isolating and subject to censure. If playing alone is masturbation, then what could playing as a band be but copulation—mutual sexual expression?[27] Functioning as a unit is consistently valorized. Even the term "band" itself denotes musicians who act as a single identity (Cohen 1991). Thus the indie event is one of highly sexualized imagery and sexualized posturing in which individual performers are assessed in terms of appropriate and inappropriate sexual behaviors and musicians combine with other musicians to produce music. It becomes obvious that rock music, including indie, displays symbolic sexual union in its joining of masculine and feminine, musicians and instruments, guitar and drum, audience and performer.

The symbolic blending of masculine and feminine onstage is concretely enacted offstage after the performance is over in the sexual intercourse of ritual practitioners. Sexual contact between audience members and performers as a recapitulation of the drama onstage is not novel for indie and has been recognized before in rock: "The sexual act itself was little more than symbolic. It was a demonstration that the barrier between audience and performer had come down for her, setting her above the crowd. Sex was the show carried on backstage—no longer a surrogate, but the act itself" (Herman 1970: 36). After watching the fleeting union of male and female power and emotion onstage, the ritual practitioners reenact this fleeting union in private. The sexual union contains the same illusion of temporary effacement of the boundaries between performer and audience member, male and female, sex and emotion that occurs onstage in performance. Offstage sexual expression is the pair part of the onstage sexual spectacle.

Come Together

waiting for a passing feeling . . .
Elliott Smith

Not every audience member wishes to enact this sexual drama offstage after the show is over. Individual motivations and interpersonal variation strongly determine which audience members seek additional contact. When most fans interact with performers offstage, they maintain status differentials and boundaries. Ritual practitioners seek personal contact where performer and audience member interact as peers. However, they seek this parity of contact precisely because of the disparity of their roles in this social drama. According to indie norms, one should not want to have contact with a musician simply because he or she is a musician. There is an inherent double bind for the indie sexual acolyte: she seeks personal, intimate contact with a performer but must not be seen to be seeking it.

Thus the indie ritual practitioner orchestrates events to look like happenstance. She performs in order to not reveal her intentions. For indie, individuals who plan to gain privileged contact with performers but have not yet established ties to the music industry know that during the course of the evening that they must find a person who does have privileged access. They take up positions in the venue so that they can observe access points. These access points are rarely near the stage, and thus zone one fans are generally unaware of them. For an observer, however, these access points are prominent, because there will be a few people facing toward the access point rather than the stage, in contrast to the bodily orientation of the rest of the fans in the venue. Observing these areas, fans can ascertain not only if any of the band members are milling around in the crowd but also who the other people are who have access to the band.[28] Having determined who has access, a fan can then initiate interaction with these people. Bands' crews are easy to spot, because their laminates are usually visible. At small indie shows, the T-shirt vendor is another individual connected to the tour with whom fans can try to initiate a friendly relationship in order to get privileged access.[29]

The ritual practitioner begins her performance from the moment she starts interacting with performers or those in their entourage. She generally feigns ignorance of their status or lack of recognition. Alternatively, she may admit recognition but adopt the blasé manner of the professional. In both cases, the audience member seeking contact must exert self-control in her display of communicative features so as to disguise her intentions.

The sexual ritual practitioner attempts to make the progress toward sexual contact seem natural and imperceptible. Therefore, she tries to frame sexual contact so that the performer thinks it is his idea:

Listen, I know that guys think I'm goodlooking and I'm a really great dancer. I know it turns musicians on to see me dance to their music, and they want to talk to me. After the show, I just place myself in a good location where it will be easy for them to start a conversation with me. If they are being particularly shy, I'll ask for a cigarette or trip over them, something that will start a conversation but looks totally unintentional on my part. I mean no one who knows me would ever say that my boyfriends are selected by me. I mean. they've witnessed it, and they say, how come these musician guys are always after you? (D.H.)

The ritual practitioner also tries to hide the fact that she has met the musician at a show. The indie sexual ritual practitioner knows she wants intimate contact, but by revealing that desire she also reveals that she too is playing a role in the ritual drama. If her role is foregrounded, her verisimilitude is suspect. Is this performance real or is this the same show they got at Wembley? The poor performer never lets the audience forget they are playing a role. Within indie, the groupie is a poor performer, an actress who never lets the audience forget that she is acting. The good performer plays her part so well that she is indivisible from it. The goal of the indie ritual practitioner is like that of the musician—to be in the moment, so that the line between self and role in a social drama is imperceptible.

The practitioners themselves often suggest that their contact with musicians completes a relationship that they have already entered into through their experience of music. Many fans feel that they have already entered into an exchange with performers even before they meet them personally. Many mentioned a feeling of indebtedness toward specific performers: "The reason I started talking to musicians in the first place is that I felt that I owed them something. I had gotten so much out of their music, so much feeling and it really means so much in my life, I felt an obligation to share it" (L.S.). This need to give back is also a dimension of the sacrifice fans feel they make at the front of the venue. The intense conditions of the front, the bruises and the scrapes that they receive, are badges of the offerings submitted during the experience of live music.

Most sexual ritual practitioners find their contact with musicians highly satisfying, even personally validating. Performers are at the apex of the gig's status hierarchy and are generally lavished with attention and treated with great deference by most audience members. Although it is untrue, a prevalent idea is that band members can choose to sleep with whomever they want. Therefore, if the performer chooses someone, the implication is that this individual stands out from the crowd. Selection and privileged access confer tremendous validation. Nearly all of the individuals I spoke to discussed the heady feeling of validation that they experienced when performers opted to spend time with them, become their friends, or have sex with them:

D—— can pretty much get whoever he wants, but he wants me. You know when you're at a show and a guy gives you that look. You know he wants you and everyone else wants him. For me, that look is everything. (D.H.)

Having these guys want me makes me feel powerful and good about myself. (M.K.)

Every once in a while someone asks me how come I only go out with musicians; the answer to that is in part that I want to and I can. But the real reason, I don't know the answer to that myself. Maybe it's because I like the feeling that they could choose anyone and then they pick me. It makes me feel special. And to tell you the truth most of them are really great in bed. (K.S.)

Getting affirmation, particularly sexual affirmation, from someone whom others treat with respect and reverence makes the sexual ritual practitioner feel exceptional. These unions can be empowering and elevating.

For many, the validation that one experiences becomes something the fan wants again. It can become a repetition compulsion, a desire to be validated over and over, to tell the same story with the same happy ending. Most females in this category never make a conscious decision to one day become sexually involved with performers. Rather, they happen upon it: "I remember I'd be at shows and I'd go up just to say hello and tell them how much I liked the music, and I'd be so flattered that they would want to stay and talk with me and want me to go out for drinks with them after. I'd feel great for days, you know, worthwhile, but then it was always back to normal. I'd find at the next show I'd want the same thing to happen" (N.T.). Privileged access becomes one of the goals of attending a show. The validation provided is fleeting, and therefore needs to be repeated.

While these interactions can be validating, they also present potential risk. Although being showered with attention confers validation, the withdrawal of attention or being treated with disrespect can result in a sense of rejection and potential stigmatization. The sexual acolyte feels bad about having sex if she is treated poorly afterward:

I don't talk to him anymore. Last time I saw him, he picked up on some girl in front of me and I'm sorry, but that is just not on. I mean who does he think I am? A fucking groupie? Like I think sex is so meaningless that I wouldn't mind if he slept with someone else? It's not that I don't know that he sleeps with other people, but you don't do that in my face. (M.R.)

I can only remember one time that was really bad. The week after I ran into him at a club and he acted like he didn't even know me. I felt so awful, a stupid idiot. I thought he had actually had some regard for me. What a total pig. I decided I had to be more careful. Worse than that, he slept with my sister, can you believe that? Later on he apologized and has wanted to get together with me again, but no way. (S.P.)

In both cases, it is being treated poorly afterward that makes the individual regret the interaction. Both women consciously distinguish themselves from groupies in their refusal to accept what they regard as humiliating treatment. For indie's unmarked sexual ritual practitioners, the issue isn't how many partners one has but the quality of sexual interaction—how respectful, how connected, and how intense.

Here, sex and music are conceived similarly. Both are transitory creative phenomena born of the collapse of boundaries between male and female, self and other, music and emotion. Music and sex exist in their enlivening. One person explained it to me like this: "I always felt that L [musician] has the same relationship to the music that I have, just a really intense fan. R [band] doesn't exist in him; it is just this magic thing that happens when the four of them come together onstage" (D.H.). Indie music is not something created by a single musician, but through the combination of musicians. It is not something possessed by the individual; it lives in moments of time. For these ritual practitioners, the sexual act is the complement/completion of the music experience.

Indie's sexual ritual practitioner denies sex a commodity value. Rather than treating sex as cheap (as they view the mainstream groupie doing—that girl who is willing to trade sex for trinkets, or so other people will think she is special), indie sexual acolytes treat sex as priceless. This ritual practitioner does not trade sex. Instead, she pursues a sexual contact for the experience itself. Sex is no longer a resource possessed by females and sought after by males offering financial rewards. Sex is not something one trades to get other things. It *is* the thing: an ephemeral experience, non-commodifiable, without price. Sex is shown to be created by both male and female. Viewed from this perspective, sex is a verb, not a noun. When the sexual exchange is the exchange, it requires no additional transaction. The indie sexual acolyte subverts the mainstream's commodity exchange not by flooding the market with cheap and available sex; instead she decommodifies sex by making it unavailable as property.

When sexual interaction between a musician and an audience member is accomplished appropriately, as a discerning, emotional, connected, personal union of peers, there exists the potential for sex that is elevating. In the sex that occurs after the experience of music, it is the spirit of the music that has bought them together. Just like music, sex is the medium in which divine ephemeral emotion is made manifest in the temporal union: "Come together."[30] This offstage interaction is a subversion of cultural values. In ritual, indie transforms one of the most religiously problematic and threatening of human acts into art.

Sing for the Moment

These pleasures a wayward distraction, this is my one lucky prize . . .
Joy Division

The offstage connection between the ritual practitioners is important not just in terms of the symbolic structure of the event but also for the musicians themselves, who despite popular misconceptions rarely receive material recompense for their music. Contrary to popular belief, the life of a musician is not "money for nothing and chicks for free." Sexual contacts are one of the momentary and fleeting benefits in an art form designed for youth with built-in obsolescence. The life of the touring musician is difficult. Just as audience members find it hard to achieve emotional presence over time, musicians and touring crew find it difficult to experience music directly because of the monotony of repeated performance. The audience member who interacts personally with performers or crew members translates the feelings of excitement and connection that the audience has during the performance back to the performers.

Most of the benefits conferred on artists in the music world are short lived—the status, the funds, and even the joy of performing. Most musicians, regardless of genre, end their careers with very little, and sometimes even less than they had when they started. The majority never recoup the money that record companies lend them. Record advances are loans that bands pay back with their percentage points (generally between 12 and 15 percent of the net profit of retail price) from sales. Additionally, depending on the contract, other marketing expenses are debited to the band's account to be paid back by the band. Thus, a band can sell a huge number of records and still not recoup. During my time at a major record label in the United States, one of the label's artists was given a platinum album representing a million albums shipped to stores and Soundscan sales of over 800,000 units. On the same day, they were told by the label that they had yet to recoup their debt.[31]

Because money rarely comes from the record companies, except in the form of advances to pay for the next record (which in turn increases a band's debt), musicians rarely have an income except from selling the publishing rights to their songs. Publishing money comes from the fee that a record company or advertiser has to pay the owner of music when it is used. Because most contemporary rock acts play their own music, this money goes to the band—usually shared with a publishing company who has bought the rights to the band's music.[32] The indie band Kingmaker has always seemed to me to embody the financial forfeiture of musical performance. In 1993, Kingmaker was the hot new thing. They had a Top 20 hit, played on *Top of the Pops,* and were written about in the gossip pages, and only a couple of years later they had to sell their equipment to pay outstanding band debts.

Most bands are lucky to break even on tours, even tours that are sold out. Ticket monies are shared by the venue, the booking agent, the ticketing agency, and the promoter. In addition, bands have the overhead of crews, transport, and lodging. At the end of a tour, it is common for the crew to have earned money while the band has only increased its debt to its record label.[33] Record labels generally lend money for tour support, a certain percentage of which is to be recouped from the band's points. For a period in the early 1990s, the time of the T-shirt bands, fans bought enough merchandise for bands to make a profit. Later, however, this lucrative area was targeted by corporations. Companies would buy merchandising rights for young, cash-strapped bands, and all future profits would be split. Some venues began charging exorbitant percentages to allow a band to sell its merchandise at shows. For the most part, neither touring nor merchandising provides the band with any income and often merely increases the band's debt.

Even performing live becomes difficult for professional musicians. Over time the experience of gigs changes and becomes mundane, which makes it more difficult for performers to experience the music directly. For most performers, their early live experiences are intimidating and fraught with anxiety: "When I first started playing the bad thing was, it was all about fear, fear of messing up, fear of being disliked, but now it's about not getting bored" (C.E.). Performing the same material day in and day out for months has an inevitable dulling effect on musicians. As I discussed earlier, very soon after a band has a modicum of success, band members move into zone three at other bands' gigs. But experience does not affect only musicians' spectatorship at other performances; it also affects their own experience of performing.

Performers try to retain a sense of joy in playing their own music. The goal of the performer is the same as the audience: verisimilitude, to be fully present and efface the boundaries between themselves and the audience:

"For me a good show is when I'm into it and the audience is into it—just wrapped up in the music. At a good show, I have no idea what I'm thinking, I'm just feeling good. But at a bad show, you're analyzing everything—why is it going bad, I'm out of tune, B——'s a bastard" (B.B.). Here the good performance is defined by the performer being in the moment. The bad performance is an emotionally distant one in which the performer analyzes the performance or thinks about other things. Performers have the same issues as audience members who have participated in hundreds of performances. How can they be in the moment instead of simply going through the motions? After a band has been on tour for a while, playing songs is a physical memory that requires no mental energy or thought:

I remember our worst show. We had been on tour in Europe for a month so we were really tight. It was our first show in the UK in a bit and we were opening for someone. During the show everyone was on autopilot. I mean there were no mistakes, but there was no vibe, no atmosphere. It felt really strange, like I wasn't there. I was looking at my hands playing, and I could hear myself singing, but it was as if I wasn't there. (R.G.)

The musician begins to have a performance "autopilot." At this point the performers often feel as if they are witnesses to their own shows—watching the audience react, watching their fellow musicians, and even watching themselves play the music.

In the same manner that audiences become immune to the ritual event, many performers experience the same diminishing efficacy, and in a much more tangible way. The performers and crew, having experienced hundreds of shows, recognize the formulaic elements and the same reflexive distancing that occurs for experienced audience members. It is a battle for all professionals to maintain *beingness* in the face of repetition and the specter of boredom. The indie music performer wants to experience the music, but his own exposure to it makes non-reflexive experience difficult.

While audience members want to believe that performers are filled with music and are experiencing it during performance, these performers are often feeling absolutely unmoved. There are times when, although the audience seems to get something from the performance, the performer feels nothing: "A bad show is when you can't get involved with the music. Sometimes it's funny because you are just thinking how it is not working, and the audience doesn't seem to notice or mind. But other times, it is a nightmare and you are just thinking get off the stage as quickly as possible" (N.H.). The musician who observes the emotional response of the audience and yet is unmoved himself can feel extreme frustration. Julian Cope related a well-known incident about a show with his previous band, A Teardrop Explodes. Upset that the show wasn't going well and wanting to feel anything, even pain, he cut his stomach with the microphone stand. He told of how shocked he has been over the years by people's comments that it was the best show they had ever seen, as he lacerated himself in frustration at how poorly the show was going. Thus, there is often a great disparity between the audience's and the performers' evaluation of a show. The emotion of the audience can alienate the performer in the same manner as an audience member standing in the front of a gig when it appears to be working for everyone else around him, but him. The audience member who is utterly unmoved can leave. But unlike an audience member, the performer cannot just opt out. After significant touring, musicians' experience of their own music is often through the responses of the audience. Sexual acolytes are one of the means to access this.

The Tricksters

I want a range life,
If I could settle down,
then I would settle down . . .
Pavement

Having examined the actual practices of sexual acolytes and their role in the indie music spectacle, I will now address the ritual persona of the musician in this event. The mythic image of the "musician" is a trickster figure. Just as the groupie stereotype presents unique challenges to indie's Puritan ideology, so does the image of the libidinous and amoral musician of rock mythology.

With tricking such a central theme in the performance of music, it should come as no surprise that musicians express and exhibit so many characteristics of the trickster.[34] This interconnection between tricksterism and musicians is ripe for analysis, and a full examination is beyond the scope of my project here. In his wonderful book *Trickster Makes This World*, Lewis Hyde examines the trickster-like qualities of several public figures, including Frederick Douglass, Alan Ginsberg, Marcel Duchamp, Maxine Hong Kingston, and John Cage (Hyde 1998). His superb argument demonstrates that the simultaneously creative and destructive veins of trickster are prevalent in the myriad forms of Western artistic communication—oratory, poetry, painting, writing, and music. Hyde's thesis examines how social life depends on treating antisocial characters as part of the sacred and how art can function as the lie that tells the truth.

Trickster is a figure of creativity that alternately amuses, disgusts, scandalizes, awes, humiliates, and is humiliated by others. Fueled by his instinctive energies and cunning, he represents the most basic instincts.[35] He is at the mercy of his carnal passions and appetites. He will use any means necessary, the conceived and the inconceivable, to meet his own self-ish ends. However, trickster rarely gets to enjoy the long-term fruits of his trickery and is often tricked himself. Trickster is a "creator, but at the same time he remains a clown, a buffoon not to be taken seriously" (Hynes 1993: 34).[36] He is the fool who makes us laugh, the thief who may or may not enjoy his ill-gotten gains, the cross-dresser, the braggart, the animal ruled by brutish drives, the child who plays with his own mess, the pirate looking for swag on the open sea, and the man in black at the crossroads—all at the same time. He is eternally on the road, moving between fixed locales, scavenging for food and sex, stepping in dirt all along the way. Despite trickster's scandalous behaviors, it is often through his actions that cultural values come into being. Yet his contributions come from his desire to satisfy his own selfish needs.

Trickster's creativity lies in defying the expectations of others. He is a transgressor, a rebel, and a violator. In various cultures, the trickster, often in the guise of Coyote, Raven, Rabbit, or Monkey, reveals the creative and destructive powers that lie outside cultural conventions and cultural categories. His behavior is often bizarre and outrageous. Trickster may eat from a tree, produce mountains of feces, and blind himself in his own filth; he may juggle his eyeballs to get a different point of view; he may bury himself underground to fool women into playing with his genitals. He is always unpredictable, defying cultural expectations that result from our socially sanctioned actions and bounded categories. Vainglorious trickster does not act as society says one ought to; trickster acts "bad." However, trickster is not immoral but amoral. The immoral defy morality, while the amoral act without regard to morality. Trickster does not think of the consequences of his actions. He has no shame or moral compass. The power of trickster comes from his violations of social norms and expectations.

Trickster's unpredictability lies in forces outside of society. He is motivated by feral instinct rather than by thought and reason. He is governed by his insatiable appetites. His hunger for food cannot be filled. He is oversexed. Yet trickster's sexuality is not procreative. As Robert Pelton points out, trickster has sex for his own pleasure (Pelton 1993). His sexual energies are not directed toward morally justified and socially acceptable forms of sex for reproduction. Rather, his sexual energies are directed toward the erotic for its own sake.[37] Sex is to satisfy trickster's lust alone. His creativity is not the family's creativity.

Trickster is "on the road." His insatiable lusts motivate his incessant wandering. Perpetually between destinations, trickster is a liminal entity. His sojourns in situated locales are only temporary. Trickster inhabits the byways of transit and the transitional. For the Navajo, trickster stories begin and end with "Coyote walking." As Lewis Hyde puts it, "Coyote, Hermes, Mercury . . . all tricksters are 'on the road.' They are the lords of in-between . . . He [trickster] is the spirit of the road at dusk, the one that runs from one town to another and belongs to neither. That road is inhabited by strangers and thieves, a realm of transitivity" (Hyde 1998: 3).

Trickster's in-betweenness is also the wellspring of his unpredictability. His crossings also include transgressing the borders of our cultural categories. He blurs the line between male and female, between cunning and stupidity, between animal and human, between fooler and fooled, between divine and lewd. He may turn himself into a pine needle or use the skin of a seal to masquerade as seal's wife. He may get his head caught in a trap but then use that trap to trap another. "His lying, cheating, tricking, and deceiving may derive from the trickster being simply an unconscious numbskull, or, at other times, from being a malicious spoiler" (Hynes 1993: 35). Trickster moves between creation and destruction (Street 1972). One of the reasons that trickster often occurs in animal form is that he blurs the lines between the cultural world of man and the natural world of instinct. When trickster occurs in the form of a human, he is associated with animals. Legba/Eshu, the trickster figure of West Africa and of particular interest here because of the West African influence on rock music, wears animal skins. This puts an entirely different spin on the association of rock musicians with leather jackets and trousers. This symbol of rebellion so often referred to in the literature on rock gets its power not merely through the historic associations with particular social classes, but also its cultural association with the animal world and boundary violation.[38] Trickster is an embodiment of the creative tensions that exist between opposites.

Since trickster acts outside of society, he is associated with the taboo.[39] He has a shameless attraction to dirt and is often associated with the scatological. For example, in Winnebago mythology, trickster scatters human beings around the globe by the power of a massive flatulent outburst. As Laura Makarius characterizes it: "Since immoderation is the lot of the being who knows neither laws nor checks nor limits, certain qualities are attributed to the violator: unbridled sexuality, a pronounced phallic character and an insatiable greediness and hunger. . . . All that is impure is his. . . . Hence, we should not be astonished when his behavior is dirty, obscene, and gross" (Makarius 1993: 85). Trickster is often found in the midst of refuse and the dross of human society.

In classic trickster narratives, trickster is often a thief. Raven may steal the sun, which is why we have daylight. Prometheus steals fire and gives it to humans. Coyote may try to steal his wife from the land of the dead, but his failure means that for us death is final. The transgression of boundaries requires a master of deceit. He must fool us; he needs to blag his way in. And like a thief, the outcome of his actions is never assured. Trickster often loses, destroys, or is himself tricked out of his own prize, making us laugh at his follies. Trickster often dies in the midst of his exploits, but he always comes back to life. Sometimes it is because his nose has not been destroyed or because someone steps over him four times. Trickster's death is not an end, merely a punishment along the way. For trickster, death is just another boundary to transgress. He always comes back in another narrative or guise.

These thwartings and punishments are society's revenge on the trickster for his crimes against its laws. Trickster needs to be punished for his violations. The outsider eventually needs to pay the price of betraying society's values. Society needs its redress and so do we. Coyote fools us. We enjoy trickster's follies and are appalled at his gall. We are disgusted, incredulous, admiring, and envious, and yet we really do not want him to get away with his crimes for long. The audience laughs at trickster, but the story itself is serious. He cannot always be victorious. Breaking cultural taboos that we need to abide by requires recompense, and because trickster refuses to be ashamed, we take it out on his hide.

The figure of trickster has consistently lain just beneath the surface of rock lore and the stereotype of the popular music performer, from the legend of musicians selling their souls to the devil at the crossroads to the innumerable narratives of colossal consumption and destruction attributed to musicians on tour.[40] With some regularity, magazines print out epic narratives of musicians' debauchery, dissipation, and folly. A cursory review of rock's infamous exploits reads like trickster's: musician picks up what looks like a woman but turns out to be a man and doesn't care; guitarist fakes his own death and loses his record contract; producer trashes his own studio; musician is sent to a hospital for the criminally insane; singer sniffs dead crow and vomits into crowd; guitarist hides drugs under a barn and the barn disappears; band's bassist kills his guitarist; drummer drives a Rolls Royce into a swimming pool; guitarist bites journalist on the leg; musician brought back to life by CPR after an overdose demands another line of cocaine in order to go to the party.[41]

This image of the mainstream musician is not an ethnographic account but rather a representation created and circulated in popular discourse. This is not to say that all musicians act the same or conform to this stereotype, but rather that the mythic representation distilled from countless stories and incidences exists in the popular imagination and resembles the trickster figure. While the representations of the "musician" are gathered from the media and urban lore, the specifics regarding indie practices come from interviews with professionals and first-hand observations of bands while on tour. The representation of the debauched "musician" provides the stereotype that indie performers define themselves alongside. This relationship is more fraught with ambiguity than the sexual acolyte. In some cases, the representation provides a straw man that musicians can reject. In others, they embrace it, along with the generative mythology of how a musician ought to act. In still others, they participate in "musician" activities but keep them hidden from their audiences.

Like trickster, the stereotype of the rock musician is that he is governed by insatiable, wanton appetites. The mantra of rock music, "sex, drugs and rock 'n' roll," explicitly communicates the embrace of carnality. The "musician's" purported exploits are based on hedonistic excess. "Musicians" are often portrayed as spending their time on the road, drunk, on drugs, and having sex with strange women in corridors. Unlike the trickster of myth, rock's gluttony is not directed toward food. While trickster is constantly seeking to satiate his hunger, the "musician" is on the hunt for illicit drugs. In the stereotypical renderings, the musician is a drug fiend surrounded by lines of cocaine or a sot whose consumption of gallons of alcohol results in a state in which he may soil himself.[42] Or he is the heroin junkie whose need for drugs eclipses all else.[43] Like trickster, rock's stereotypical renderings are voluptuous gluttony.

The tales of excessive consumption of mind-altering substances are only surpassed by the narratives of immodest sexual exploits.[44] Classic rock books on touring are peppered with stories of the lengths to which women will go in order to get access to the rock musician. Their attempts are met with playful perversions on the parts of musicians. Stories of mainstream and hard rock include throwing raw meat at naked girls, having multiple sexual partners, and sexual penetration with a fish (*L.A. Weekly,* March 2003; Davis 2001). How can the ends be far, unless the musician sets the bar so low? Stories of perverted, insatiable sexuality permeate rock and roll lore. For example, there is the urban legend of the musical performer who collapsed onstage, only to have his stomach pumped by doctors, who found quarts of semen. This urban legend has circulated in many guises with a variety of musicians in the role of its subject.[45] The repetitive casting of real performers as protagonists in this legend demonstrates that the sexually licentious principle character must be a musician. The musician's sex drive is reputedly so great that he is willing to have sex with anyone. The protagonist may or may not be thought to be homosexual; in some variants, the protagonist is a female. The perversity of the musician here is not so much in same-sex preference as in the fantasy of insatiability—they found QUARTS! The "musician" is cast as a sexual libertine.

Even the very reasonable requirements of the rider in a band's touring contract are framed as perversions.[46] They want five bottles of Evian water, not any old water. They want only green M&Ms in their dressing room.[47] They must be perverted.

The trickster can also be seen in the destructive, thieving, and sordid behaviors attributed to "musicians." "Musicians" on tour are seen as a threat to anything that is not tied down and sometimes even things that are. They constantly test the fixity of fixtures.[48] What the "musician" doesn't steal, he may render useless by destroying it. "Musicians" make "trash" a verb. They trash hotel rooms or throw television sets out of windows.[49] Optimally, if you destroy something in your own room, you should steal the same thing from a bandmate's room so he or she will have to pay for it, an artful combination of prankishness and destruction. Many of the circulated narratives of rock musicians have a scatological element. A wonderful combination of wit and vileness can be found in the urban legend that Frank Zappa ate excrement on stage. In his autobiography *The Real Frank Zappa Book,* he refutes this narrative: "For the record, folks: I never took a shit on stage, and the closest I ever came to eating shit anywhere was at a Holiday Inn buffet in Fayetteville, North Carolina, in 1973" (Zappa 1989: 14). In one case, a rock musician publicly reported that he put his own excrement in a hotel hairdryer and replaced the cover. The attribution of disgusting behavior to the rock musician is part and parcel of the mainstream stereotype.

Indie musicians differentiate their behaviors from those of the mainstream rock musician stereotype, particularly those discussed thus far. However, some of the indie musicians' behaviors and practices are consistent with mainstream musician narratives, specifically in the area of thievery and the challenges of being on the road. The means of the stereotypical musician are deceit and larceny. This trickster-like thieving is part of rock mythology (consider the account of Steve Jones, formerly of the Sex Pistols, in which he stole a guitar from David Bowie). Indie musicians do participate in playful pilfering in some cases, more so, because they often have little money and few possessions. At shows, bands help themselves to equipment, gaffer tape, bottle openers, posters, and signs such as "NO STAGE DIVING" or "DANGER HIGH VOLTAGE."* As one musician told me, "At a venue in Italy, they left the kitchen open. So we nicked joints of meat

---

* The taking of warning signs is a wonderful trickster gesture where musicians remove the signal that warns others that they are in violation of rules or at risk. Trickster often lures others into misfortune. One other theme in the signage that musicians carry away with them is awkward English translations such as "Please be drinkable: or "In case of fire, burn." These unexpected commands and requests are ideal for a life of travel filled with unexpected contingencies.

and hid them on the tour bus. We always tried to get away with taking everything that we could" (P.C.). At hotels, indie musicians often stuff towels, pillows, linen, bottles, glasses, and ashtrays into their bags. On some occasions, they may take furniture or a hairdryer. At in-stores (live performances at record stores), they commonly make away with CDs and records.[50] Even if the store gifts them with merchandise, they want more. I was told that if the record store is foolish enough to let them in back and trust them, what do they expect?

Many bands get particular pleasure in stealing from each other. Bands make a habit of trying to nick each other's riders.[51] When one band is on-stage, another band may sneak into the other's dressing room and drink all its beer or load the other band's spirits onto its own bus. In one infamous Mancunian case, the opening band had taken all of the alcoholic beverages from the headliner's room and secreted them on its own bus. The headliners sent the band's manager, who was a rather hard sort, to get the liquor back. As the alcohol was being unloaded and returned, the singer of the opening band, in a fit of pique, booted out the tour bus window, which fell out and smashed. The opening band had to make the journey all the way back to Manchester in the dead of winter with no front windscreen. If musicians and crew are not misappropriating things from another band, they may just steal things from each other—clothes, the use of a mobile phone, the contents of a bandmate's mini-bar, or perhaps each others' girl-friends.[52] One label boss pointed out that "even their riffs are lifted from blues musicians. They all steal parts from other people's songs" (L.B.).

Regardless of genre, the musician on tour is a figure of transitivity, persistently "on the road," a wandering troubadour. Simon Reynolds and Joy Press devote an entire chapter, "Born to Run," on the longing in rock music for speed and movement between fixed locales, in order to be on a permanent "road to nowhere" (Reynolds and Press 1996). However, while the trickster of myth may wander because of his lusts and appetites, musicians often are the inverse: they lust and have appetites *because* they are wandering. Musicians and crew attribute the characteristics and temptations of excess to the freedom that comes from being on the road: "It's different on the road than at home. You don't act that way at home because on the road you've got the freedom to do so. Freedom to be a child, to be spoilt, to do what you want, take what you want and move on" (P.H.). Home is rule governed, whereas life on the road is shaped by contingencies. The question of what to do with this freedom is an ethical one within the indie community.

Scholars such as Abrahams have noted an infantile aspect to the trickster figure. Musicians too are infantilized by their touring experience: previously competent individuals suddenly cannot call a cab to get themselves to the venue for a soundcheck. As one successful musician wrote on his Friendster Web page near the end of a year of touring, "Over the last year, I have regressed in maturity significantly. I am incapable of doing anything for myself anymore and I am not expected to" (B.H.). As mentioned in an earlier chapter, when musicians have problems getting into a gig, they stand there and wait for someone else to fix it.*

This "money for nothing and chicks for free" vocation, rock and roll, is portrayed in wider public discourse as a swindle. Since the "musician's" trade is viewed as illegitimate, his gains appear ill-gotten. Like trickster, our musician is often tricked out of his prizes—he is constantly pick-pocketed by an army of industry insiders. He returns backstage to find all his beer has been drunk, or his wallet and video camera have been taken from his bag. He wakes up to find that the van has been broken into and all his equipment is gone, or at the pool party he throws at the studio house, his iPod with the only copies of the new songs for the album has been lifted. He, too, has the feeling that he's been cheated.

In the general depiction of the musician, we see the unconscious numbskull and the malicious spoiler, the pirate, the mad egotist, the poet, the genius, the fool, and the stranger in a strange town.[53] Rather than watching TVs, he destroys them. The stereotypical musician is perverted, weird, amoral, disgusting, silly, brilliant, and playful, on the road, looking for sex, drugs, and teenage kicks. He moves between art and farce, masculine and feminine, predator and prey, exalter and debaser, pretensions and filth, beauty and ugliness.[54] Musicians are on the road tricking us, creating moving emotions and destroying our property, powerful gods of libido one moment, pathetic monkeys the next.

This vast body of rock music lore—some real, some magnified, some patently false—produces contradictory responses of awe, disgust, admiration, envy, shock, and amusement in audiences.[55] These stories of misbehavior give us a sense of awesome foolishness. How could Coyote allow a chipmunk to damage his penis because of his insatiable lust for women? How could a musician forget his flight departure time, take two Viagra before leaving his Japanese hotel, and spend fifteen hours in abject pain? We laugh at his magnificently foolish behavior and wonder how someone could be so governed by lust that he no longer has the faculties of good reason. We envy him for his unwarranted plunder, are scandalized by his violations of

---

* The musician joke cycle speaks to the infantilized aspects of the musician stereotype: Mother, I want to grow up and be a musician. Now son, you know you have to pick one or the other. Why is psychoanalysis a lot quicker for a musician? When it's time to go back to his childhood, he's already there.

our most sacrosanct rules, are disgusted by the humiliations he visits on others, and see him punished by crashing to his death or witness his resurrection from a drug overdose.[56] In music, immortality is conferred upon those who live fast and die young (Neil Young: "It's better to burn out than to fade away . . ."). Like the trickster, the musician must pay the price for breaking cultural rules.

The stereotypical musician is a problem for indie musicians, just as the notion of a groupie is a problem for indie's female fans and sexual acolytes. However, indie musicians have a much more complicated relationship to the rock musician stereotype. While the groupie appellation is uniformly viewed as negative within the indie community, the indie musician exhibits greater ambivalence toward the rock musician stereotype. As mentioned before, indie musicians often reject the behaviors associated with the stereotype, at times embrace them, but very unlike trickster, they may feel guilty about having done so. The stereotype is frowned upon but it doesn't stop indie musicians from participating in its behaviors to various degrees. At times there is a difference between what indie musicians do and what they are willing to have publicly attributed to them. They may avoid wearing leather trousers or ridicule the sexual excesses of the mainstream, yet they indulge in some of the same traditions of "sex, drugs, and rock and roll" and its accompanying self-destructive behaviors. However, they do it according to indie's notions of permissible excess.[57]

The major areas in which indie musicians place moral limitations on their behavior are primarily around rock's hedonism, egotism, and destructiveness. The sex and drugs clichés are generally viewed as "that lame, old-school rock and roll stuff" (L.B.). Nevertheless, a significant number of indie musicians participate in alcohol, drugs, and sex while on the road. Excessive drinking is seen as acceptable, and alcohol is the substance of choice for the community. Colossal alcohol consumption is bragged about and highly covered in the music press. Drugs, however, are a more complicated matter. Drug use is generally seen as self-indulgent and part of the corpulent excesses of the mainstream; it is therefore viewed negatively. However, many lauded and credible musicians from the past are associated with drug use. Sometimes, drugs are seen as a tour necessity; when a musician is "tired and bored, uppers keep you going" (N.H.). When indie bands consume class A drugs, they generally don't talk about it, and the journalists who may take drugs with them generally don't write about it. Thus, in using illicit drugs indie musicians walk a fine line between acceptable recreational use and gluttonous indulgence.

The rules of the sexual acolyte also hold for the indie musicians. Within indie, the groupie interaction is seen as degrading not only to the audience member but to the performer as well. Musicians who pick up girls regularly are viewed as sleazy, even more so if they have a girlfriend at home. Without a doubt, one finds less sexual activity in indie circles than in other genres that do not place prohibitions on sexual excess.[58] One musician characterized picking up on girls at shows as "taking advantage of the power you have" (A.K.). Violations of sexual behavioral norms can also impact the indie musician's credibility, not only with audiences but with fellow musicians and professionals, who are more likely to witness transgressions. The sexually profligate musician is viewed as playing music to get girls rather than for music's sake. This undermines both the musician's and the band's credibility. Just as the sexual acolyte may regret a sexual encounter, so, too, may the indie musician: "You wake up the next day and say, what have I done? It didn't feel fulfilling. So I guess it depends on if I felt a real connection with the person" (N.H.); "If you feel it was sex and nothing else then you feel bad about it" (M.G.). This is the Puritan vein manifesting itself again. The mainstream rock musician is viewed as participating in indiscriminate sex. The indie musician's sexual relations need to be discerning, discreet, but, most importantly, meaningful. In a parallel to groupies, those musicians who are witnessed participating in indiscriminant sexual encounters become the subject of simultaneous ridicule and envy.

Indie also places limits on trickster-like destruction. Indie musicians may destroy their own equipment, kicking in amplifiers, throwing themselves headfirst into drum kits, or smashing their guitars into fragments. They may also mildly trash their hotel rooms. The remains of the rider are strewn about. Because every night is spent in a different place, musicians and crew sometimes have trouble finding a toilet in the middle of the night. They have on occasion urinated into closets, on walls, and in that wonderful trickster combination, into their own suitcases. This effectively soils their home for the duration of the tour. However, while it is fine to wreck one's own or another band's equipment, to defile a suitcase, or to urinate on a wall, extensive destruction is not accepted. In one telling narrative, an opening band trashed headliner Radiohead's dressing room. Apparently embarrassed by the state of the place, Radiohead cleaned it up. Both the attribution of shame and the undoing of damage significantly express indie's ambivalence toward destructiveness. Indie is also less involved in revolting behaviors than the stereotype of mainstream musicians. One musician felt this indicated that "in some ways, indie is repressed. There is politeness in it" (L.B.). Another musician characterized indie's paltry indulgence in disgusting and destructive activities as counter to the sensibilities of the community: "Indie music is more studied. They don't have it in them to be that uninhibited" (N.H.). The mainstream's lore of reveling in refuse transgresses indie's norms of morality.

Indie musicians often conceive of touring as a temptation to potential corruption. Not only are sex and drugs seen as potential corruptors, but also the adulation from fans. Fans regard performers as having an exalted status, and musicians are generally treated with deference by everyone around them (except their fellow bandmates). This adulation confers power. In popular lore and media representations such as the film *Rock Star*, the musician who accepts this approbation as his due becomes an egomaniac, a paradigmatic form of decadence for the indie community. The foundational premises of indie in the ordinary and the lack of distance between performers and audience members mean that the bloated ego and expectations of special treatment are antithetical to indie ideology. Indie musicians are expected to be approachable. Once a band achieves success, the audience vigilantly looks for signs that the musicians have changed and are no longer down to earth.[59] Ironically, they do so while proffering the exact behaviors that they consider to be corrupting. Indie musicians also are sensitive to how they respond to veneration and deferential behaviors from audience members. They feel a great obligation to show respect and not to violate the expectations of fans. Of course, this is a no-win situation, as artists are often held responsible for the illusion of verisimilitude and the fantasies of audience members. Indie musicians know that their actions are closely monitored for any of the clichéd behaviors associated with self-absorption or pretense. Often indie musicians feel estranged or guilty about their valorized status when interacting with fans:

When fans come up to you like that it's nice and embarrassing at the same time. You just know that you are not as good as they think you are. They've got a different idea of you than you actually are. I feel I have to be nice to them, but I want to get out of the situation as soon as possible. (B.A.)

It makes me so uncomfortable. You are expected to behave in a certain way and you know that you can't possibly live up to their expectations, whatever they are. I feel when they offer me stuff that it is so misplaced. I just start drinking loads so I don't even have to think about it. (N.H.)

People around you have an inflated idea of who you are and you could make the most of that. You are living in a bubble. You're living in a new place every night. We all have a version of ourselves, who we think we are. And if you believe all that adulation, that is a form of self-corruption. (M.G.)

Here, in addition to the potential for engaging in deleterious excess, the musician experiences himself as someone who tricks his fans by allowing them to believe he is something special when he feels he is not. Others merely wonder how long they can keep getting away with fooling them.

One of indie's tricks is to convince itself that its artists are different from "musicians." Just as with the sexual acolytes, when indie musicians engage in stereotypical behaviors, they try and hide them. Indie's trickster is diminutive. His sexual expressions are muted, and discussion of sexual exploits in the press is taboo. His pranks are mild and his destructions harmless. He doesn't make holes in walls or throw televisions out the window (well, sometimes he does, but he doesn't want it published in the press).[60] He may toss a plastic chair out a venue window, but unlike Coyote, he will check to see that no one is standing underneath. He hides his drinking and shagging behind higher thoughts. Indie hides its tricksterism behind an earnest Puritan façade.

Effectively, the trickster/musician scenario has three outcomes/options—apotheosis, destruction, or to just keep going. As Lewis Hyde points out for trickster: "There are only a few ways to deal with [trickster] . . . only a limited number of plots. From the edge of the group or the threshold of the house there are only a few ways a trickster can move: he can come inside, he can leave entirely, or he can stay exactly where he started, resisting all attempts to civilize or exile" (Hyde 1998: 220). In the second scenario, the musician is destroyed or exiled. Like Loki, he is pushed out beyond the threshold and made to pay for his crimes. He falls out the window. He chokes on his vomit. He goes to jail. He is killed by his father. He is electrocuted. He swims too far and drowns. He overdoses. He commits suicide. Her plane crashes.[61] Perhaps, he just becomes too old to participate. In the first scenario, apotheosis, he is like Hermes, upgraded to the status of a deity, and he becomes a sterile part of the established order, perhaps being given an O.B.E. by the Queen.[62] He is domesticated, like the drug addict Renton at the end of the film *Trainspotting*. After Renton's trickster journey, governed by insatiable pleasure seeking and debasement, he chooses the social order. He chooses life:

I'm moving on, going straight and choosing life. I'm looking forward to it already. I'm going to be just like you: the job, the family, the fucking big television, the washing machine, the car, the compact disc and electrical tin opener, good health, low cholesterol, dental insurance, mortgage, starter home, leisurewear, luggage, three-piece suite, DIY, game shows, junk food, children, walks in the park, nine to five, good at golf, washing the car, choice of sweaters, family Christmas, indexed pension, tax exemption, clearing the gutters, getting by, looking ahead, to the day you die. (*Trainspotting* 1996)

In the third scenario, Coyote walks. He holds onto the rising balloon and sees how long he can hang onto the rope.

Indie Coyotes and Foxes

we can live our misbehavior . . .
Arcade Fire

In the trickster cycles, there is a Fox for every Coyote. Fox is a minor trickster. Coyote creates by fooling us, but he too must be tricked. The Fox fools the one who fools us. The sexual acolyte is also a trickster—the trickster's trickster. She plays Fox to the indie musician's Coyote.[63] The sexual acolyte knows she is attracted to the performer primarily because of the role he plays in a spectacle, in which ordinary blokes are transformed into highly validated, sexually desirable idols. In the interaction that leads up to sexual contact, the sexual acolyte tricks the performer into thinking she is oblivious or indifferent to the role he plays in the event. Acolytes also perform, but their audience is the artist.

In the acolyte's successful performance, the musician feels desired for himself. The relationship between the sexual acolyte and the performer is symbiotic: she gets validation and completes her experience of music by connecting with the musician, and the performer feels the intensity of his own performance reflected back to him in a mutual sexual exchange. For the ritual practitioners, sex is an exaltation to divinity, a sacred communion. Indie's tricksters demonstrate that the sexual relations between male and female are animal, human, and transcendent.

Rather than being tricked by the illusion of performance, the ritual practitioners know even better than outsiders the illusion of performance, that it valorizes ordinary people with a specific talent and transforms them into libidinal idols. Sexual acolytes interact with performers in mundane interactions. Both performers and sexual acolytes learn that musicians are just like everybody else, with no greater or lesser insight. Ritual practitioners know the trick of performance. They see the artifice and play their roles nonetheless. They make sacrifices to ephemeral experience by forgoing a life of permanent bonds and social stability to transiently defy separation and the decay of signification. They don't choose life; they choose art.

In the lives of the ritual practitioners, we see a ritual drama enfold. For the majority, success and beauty are short lived. The life of a decadent aesthete takes a physical toll. Ritual practitioners are lauded and exalted, then tossed aside when the next musician with a new trick up his sleeve or the next pretty young thing comes along. But trickster is eternal. Not everyone can get away with trickster's game, only the ones with the skills to trick us, to make us believe that the trick is real. Then the rewards of the kingdom are theirs, only to be lost when artifice is revealed again.

It would be an oversight not to mention that our musicians and sexual acolytes are not the only ritual practitioners of indie music.[64] There are also industry personnel who look to their occupation to maintain the values with which they entered the community; those professionals who still want to find meaning in music. They face a constant battle when making their decisions based on aesthetic and moral concerns rather than on perceived profitability. They fear selling out, giving their art over to commerce. They fight for their theocratic capitalism, a system of exchange that is true to indie's values, while maintaining their jobs. Amidst the men in suits, they exert constant vigilance lest they become one of them. These record company owners, booking agents, managers, A&R reps, store owners, journalists, distributors, office managers, publicists, and promoters have not given up their metaphysical quest. The professional's potential outcomes are like those of the other ritual practitioners — incorporation into the musical order of commerce, where their previous values come to seem like the follies of youth; exile from the music industry; or continuing to walk the tightrope, fight the good fight, and look for interstitial spaces that allow them to exist in the threshold between worlds. For all of indie's ritual practitioners, music is a true vocation, a calling to a certain kind of work of divine significance. Unlike other audience members, the ritual practitioners do not move gradually to the back of the venue, allowing music to become an amusement, a footnote in one's life. They hold on to music tenaciously as a source of meaning. They remain in a state of arrested youth, assiduously asserting the value of emotional experience and ephemerally defying a social order that posits emotions as a phase of development and money as the final arbiter of value. As long as they perform as ritual practitioners, they remain outsiders, defying the values of Western society.

What is sacrifice? It is the offering up of oneself, one's future, one's body to the altar of a cosmological system, despite the fact that to an outsider that altar may seem base or meaningless. The emotional intensity of music and sexual interaction is the recompense that ritual practitioners get for their sacrifice to this ritual drama, for devoting their lives to a liminal performance that functions to teach youth that, when they become adults, music and emotion say nothing to them about their lives.

Afterword
My Music Is Your Dirt

I always cry at endings
Oh that wasn't what I meant to say at all . . .
Belle and Sebastian

Musical performances are ritual events—they invert, obviate, and reinforce our cultural values. Throughout this study, I have been untying the knots of the significance of the gig to reveal the wealth of constructed meaning that lies beneath the surface of this beautiful spectacle. This book is about how a group of people feel when they listen to a particular type of music and use their bodies to experience it. Bodies in action evoke sensations, and meanings are generated within a cultural context. Rituals are about trying to make people feel the culturally desired emotions at the appropriate time. Actions are good to feel. How does it feel to sit, stand, dance, read a book, eat peppers, or eat sweets? In ritual, cultural ideas intersect with physical experience to engage the social subject. Rituals are the interpenetration of sensation and sentiment.

Meaning is produced in ritual as it is produced in everyday life. Culture is performed artifice. Cultural behaviors from brushing one's teeth to saying hello can be understood as rituals, a sequenced series of repetitive actions that are meaningful within a cultural context. All culture is convention—conventions built on material reality, but conventions nonetheless. There is a reality outside of culture, but our perceptions and interactions with it are shaped by socialization within a specific cultural system. Thus, our culture is art, an art we perceive as reality. Culture's symbols are arbitrary representations. The process of naturalization makes us think they are not. By having everyone around us collude with our representations, we believe the world we make is the world as it is. We believe in our symbols because we participate in the cultural sentiments they represent. We struggle through an artificial world, a world that everyone around us treats as real. Culture is art that denies its status as art.

Culture divides and organizes our social structure and perceived world into discrete categories that we accept as transparently natural (for example, male and female, reason and emotion, mind and body, commerce and art). Social structure is what organizes our social relationships and our social distances. It keeps the categories and socioeconomic classes separate. It separates teacher from student, neighbor from neighbor, man from woman, performer from audience, author from reader.

In cultural action, we try to keep proving to ourselves that the cultural world is the natural world. We create the same stories over and over because we prefer the devil we know to the angel we do not. We prefer the stories we know regardless of their outcomes, because no matter whether the story's outcome is good or bad, at least we know it and the world appears predictable: meaning appears fixed. Things happen, but through our cultural veil we make them meaningful. The world of culture is the world of meaning. This is culture's ritual process. New ideas, new social actors, new technologies are introduced, but they are interpreted through an existing cultural repertoire. In our stories, our rituals, our daily conventions, we assert that meaning is out there or in objects themselves. The world appears organized. The universe makes sense. There is a plan. By repeating the same stories over and over, by producing the same types of social actors with similar subjectivities, culture is projected both back into a mythical past and forward into an unending future. The world is made to appear eternal and culture, its immutable nature.

While we want to think meaning is out there, meaning is provisional; it is something we make. It is as ephemeral as the vibrations of a stick on drum or an imprint in snow. Behind our webs of signification is emptiness. We fight against this unbearable truth. Outside of culture lies chaos, where things merely happen and we don't even rate as bit players. Culture is the lie that tries to hide a truth: that nothing is fixed, that our categories and rituals are of our own devising. The empire is always built on sand, because culture is built on sand.

Yet culture reserves a special code in which we show how the social world we inhabit could be different, illustrating that our world is not the only way. The world of ritual and art is that other code; they are the Other to our everyday reality. Rituals and art show us the things we need to ignore in our everyday lives in order to make our lives clean and manageable. Ritual and art are the times and spaces of anti-structure where the rules that govern our social relationships differ from those we follow everyday. In ritual and artistic anti-structure, our categories are blurred and the barriers that organize us and keep us apart are temporarily altered.

Specific rituals address specific categories of relationships. In the festival of fools, masters served servants, parishioners acted as bishops, and one could insult the king with impunity, as the relationships between the powerful and the plebeians were inverted and engaged. The Ndembu milk tree ritual addresses the relationship between mothers and daughters in a matrilineal society. Daughters leave to go live with their husbands. Daughters and mothers must separate, yet this relationship that must break is the one that holds the family together. It is in ritual that women put asunder by cultural practice are temporarily reunited (Turner 1968). Our music ritual addresses an array of social relationships—adult and child, male and female, sex and commerce, art and money, secular and sacred, onstage and offstage. During your time in the indie community, it is more consequential what sort of music you like than if you are a member of the same social class. It matters more if you are a punter or a ligger. Masculine and feminine are turned on their heads. Men are the objects of beauty and women are the sexual pursuers playing the role of breadwinning suitors. In indie, your value is not what you are paid or how large the diamond is in your ring. What matters is what music you like. Of course, it is all under the guise of plausible deniability. The artificiality of ritual and artistic construction means we can always deny that they hold value or truth. After all, isn't a guitar just wood and string? Only a fool would think beyond its face value.

Art and ritual are the manmade, the constructed, the patently not real, and yet we look for the real in paint on paper, actors on stage, sounds in air. Is this not like trying to find the real in culture, trying to perceive the natural world through our cultural eyes? Art and ritual are the lies that try to tell a truth. How do we find the real in the unreal world of culture? Ritual is a "falseness" that undermines the current fiction of our cultural "reality."

All spectacles of beauty have something to hide—they hide the things we want to ignore. The beautiful, lithe creatures and the clothes they model on the catwalk hide the sweatshops of the third world and the need to constantly create new desires and new fashions to feed an economic system based on the ever-expanding consumption of consumer goods. The zoos and public aquariums with their brightly colored fish in pseudo-ecological environments hide the destruction of animals in our oceans and on our planet. Beautiful displays of athletic prowess or the fleeting images on celluloid of the action hero who will run, jump, and kill for us hide the marginalization of our bodies into cubby holes in front of television sets. Our daily lives are filled with papers and electronic blips, sitting in chairs with bodies we ignore. "Things go better with a little razzamatazz" (Pulp).

At the end of his insightful book on classical music, Christopher Small comes to the conclusion that he dislikes the values and relationships expressed in classical music—the masculine thematic elements vanquishing the feminine motifs and the hierarchy of social stratification and controlled, isolated contemplation—yet he is still amazed at the pleasurable beauty he finds in this music. Similar sentiments are expressed at the end of the film *Another Country*, a fictionalized account of an English upper-class man who becomes a communist spy. Guy Burgess, living in exile in the Soviet Union, is asked if there is anything he misses about England, and his answer is "The cricket." He defected because of the hypocrisy he found in the repressive English class system and yet the game that so expresses Englishness and colonialist values (manners, orderliness, nobility, clean white uniforms) he still finds irresistibly compelling. He still sees the spectacular façade veiling those values he disdains. Those hot, bright lights focused on our beautiful spectacles make us look away from those social details in the shadows we don't want to know about. Aesthetics are in the service of the status quo, our metaphysical system, our culture's way of doing things. How could we tolerate it, if it wasn't so beautiful?

Gigs, too, have something to hide. Gigs, as part of the youth phenomenon, perform youth as unconverted others who ultimately are transformed into respectable moral adults. Youth is produced as liminal, a time of physical and emotional expressiveness succeeded by a temperate, reserved, sedentary adulthood. The beautiful sounds of indie's hopeful melancholia hide the vanquishing of romanticism, as our emotional lives and sentient bodies acquiesce into a Protestant cultural system. "Birth, school, work, death" (The Godfathers). In indie, we can temporarily ignore the limits of our gender roles, the sublimation of our bodies, the religious assumptions pervading our lives, our persistent demands that other cultures conform to a Protestant domination and that emotions are deceptive illusions produced by a defective, irrational body.

Yet indie is a particular ritual of youth—those sad songs of longing and wanting to belong, those songs of love, of a return to childhood, of temporary relief. "Still I send all the time / My request for relief / Down those dead power lines" (Elliott Smith). Why this need for communion and search for something lost? Because youth has lost something. Youth stands between the world of childhood and adulthood, between two families. All societies have some form of kinship and marriage pattern. In every society, someone must leave in order to form a new family—daughters, or sons, or sons and daughters. In English and American industrial society, family is viewed as the nuclear family, parents and children, small mobile units that can move to wherever the best-paying job is relative to the cost of living. If the nuclear family is the primary family unit, both daughters and sons must leave the home of origin to create a new home and a new family, to be the parents in a new family drama. The family of origin must break apart. In nuclear family societies, youths must leave their family of childhood.

Culture works by making the obligatory desirable; it makes you want to do what you have to do. In the nuclear family society, youth must want to leave their family of origin. Young children fit within their nuclear family of origin, but as they become older, this family no longer meets their needs. The individual must look beyond this family to have his or her needs met elsewhere, to form a new nuclear family unit of his or her own. The family we say we cherish must fall apart. The only way to embrace nuclear family values is to produce adolescents who desire to leave their families. Youth is the in-between time—the time between the family of childhood and the family of adulthood. Youth is the time when you have no family.

Indie longs for the past, some Puritan return, some distant period of connectedness. It is a longing for the distant ideal of unity felt in the family of childhood, the only period of stability in the nuclear family. It is the time when we ate our meals together. It is the time when there was a home you belonged to. The adolescent is stranded between two families. He is alienated from them both and he looks for a way back to that feeling. Indie wants to return to a time when things felt different, a time when one felt connected. The home you've left behind doesn't fit anymore, anymore than those oversized or undersized clothes. Youth seeks a place that fits again, where you can recapture that feeling in a new landscape with new people who feel the same, who dream the same dreams. This is why most leave the community when they enter into committed "adult" relationships.

In those musical moments in the space of ritual, it feels like we are together. For a moment you are not alone in your room listening to the other isolated souls singing of not belonging. In those temporary ritual moments we feel united—an abolition of finitude. While you are still inside the indie community, you are still wrestling with the contradictions, still hoping to find a place between childhood and adulthood that feels right. If you work hard, if you wait, if you practice asceticism, if you suffer enough, maybe one day it can be that way again. Somewhere in the future, you can return to the murky recesses of time and find what was left behind. We can be together at the table again, even if you can't remember if you ever were there before. "Home, home is where I wanted to go" (Coldplay).

Most youth move successfully through this liminal period. Eventually, this ritual process no longer works. While inside the community, in the ritual moments, boundaries disappear—performer, music, and audience are all present in the temporary experience of transitory sentiment. With experience and "maturity" audience members come to view gigs as mere artifice—"just 20,000 people standing in a field . . . and this hollow feeling grows . . . and you want to phone your mother and say Mother, I can never come home again" (Pulp). Youth decamps to the world of adulthood, of commerce, of their new families. "It's a bittersweet symphony this life . . . trying to make ends meet, you're a slave to money then you die" (The Verve). When youth become "rational," they know that music, art, and poetry are valuable only in terms of dollars and cents, pounds and pence. As the audience member moves from insider to outsider, he no longer trusts music. When this inverted world is rejected, the social order is revalidated. It confirms to us that the world *is* the way we *think* it is. Women are the ones to be sought and men are the seekers. Money is more important than emotion. Work takes precedence over relationships. Art is a superfluous vanity. Music is frivolous, disposable, and immaterial. What was once the most important thing in the world—indie music and its values—becomes irrelevant. It was just a phase you went through. To the outsider, indie music is dirt.

Every culture has a rubbish heap for those messy things that don't fit into its nice, neat categories. Dirt threatens our ordered world of masculine and feminine, children and adults, black and white, mind and body, emotion and reason, man and divinity, animal and human, you and me. Dirt is the union of culturally produced opposites. Dirt is miscegenation, the taboo. Dirt is what is left over after we've picked sides.

Dirt is the domain of the trickster. He is the son of an incestuous union of our cultural categories. The musician is a wizard who makes us take a journey that has no purpose in mind and no power to return us home. Music is polytheistic; each band has its own emotional province. In polytheism, tricksters are at play. Trickster blurs the boundaries of the gods and goddesses—their provinces of domesticity, warfare, hunting, commerce, and the underworld. The gods pretend that their domains are discrete, but trickster knows they are just towns with unclear borders. Musicians are gods to insiders and false idols to outsiders. In the realm of music ritual, the world is upside down, making ugly boys beautiful, play more important than work. This music ritual blends the cultural categories that organize and constrain—our racial divisions, our gender divisions, our religious divisions, the categories that were made by our forefathers and remade again by us. It celebrates all those vile taboo things, uncontrollable emotions, sex, drugs, and music itself. The insider's beauty is the outsider's discord. Dirt is noise, the sounds that don't make sense to us. But if you listen, you can hear it pulling you toward the chaos of possibility of the world outside our own. The creative and destructive possibilities of dirt are endless.

Humans find it hard to live with the chaos that trickster reveals to us: better to destroy him, to prove him wrong. He'll get it in the end. Trickster's musical domain has built-in obsolescence. Indie music is the province of youth, which means that even those tricksters who hold onto the rope will eventually be cut off, and the longer they held on, the farther their fall. If you can't destroy him, just get him to conform to our ideals and act like a proper human being. Make your artists suffer until they revoke their sin and declare that being good is more important than feeling happy, until they admit that being in the moment is a temporary pleasure while working for money is deferring to some greater form of gratification to be experienced in some golden time in the future. If not in this life, then in the next. If not your life, then in your kids' lives. But in the meantime, buy some stuff to fill the empty hole.

Anything is better than to think our rules are arbitrary—why then would people obey? Better to give it a momentary articulation and then deny it. Tricksters are the violators, and while we enjoy brief glimpses into their world and their possibilities, we don't want to live there. Those who like the world as it is fear trickster: "the well-fed take the artifice of their situations and pass it off as an eternal verity" (Hyde 1998: 6). But those who do not like the world as it is—the disenfranchised—hope that trickster's pecking at the edges will make a world where there is space for them just the way they are. "I just wasn't made for these times" (The Beach Boys).

For most, the gig is a passing sojourn between their two families. The adults will find a destination to lay their heads. But for those of the in-between, the gig is the place that fits. The beer-drenched carpeting of the venue, the dirty backstage corridors, the graffitied and stickered dressing rooms, the door next to the garbage dump at night, and the gutter cluttered with crumpled tickets and flyers for other shows feel like home. For those who live for music, missing a show is worthy of tears, akin to someone stealing the key to the only place you belong and telling you to go live somewhere else. Tricksters' in-between territory is littered with other restless souls—thieves, foreigners, and shadowy figures—but also the merchants traveling home to their fixed destinations, where their families await their arrival after a day at the market.

Our trickster goes walking, defacing our sacred categories, and, like the deconstructionist, he leaves no primary signifier in his wake, only music that floats outside the venue and dissipates into nothingness. Musicians blur the line between life and performance, between good and bad, between adulation and disgust, between carnality and temperance, between selfishness and unintended gifts, between what is within culture and what lies beyond our perceptions. Trickster juggles his eyeballs so he can get a peek at the world just over the trees. If culture is our illusion, why not choose the illusion that you like. Choose life? Our tricksters choose something else. They choose music.

My trick has been indie's trick—that music and emotional epiphanies matter. If popular music is not worthy of study, then it's because it is not worthy. It's not worthy because it is ephemeral. It doesn't last. It is our trash. You can't see it in a museum in two thousand years. It is dirt. Do we not live in a world where it does not matter what sort of music you like? Does it matter if artists make music independently or under corporate auspices, extravagantly or modestly? Will it help you get a job? Will it feed your family? To the outsider, the emotional epiphanies of the indie community are as insignificant as documenting fleeting trains as they speed by your platform.

Yet this book is also the story of people who refuse to leave, who want a world that is different from the one we are given, who want to find out what lies outside our limited view. They find beauty in the dirt we tread on and ignore. They turn our trash upside down and use it for something else. They live for the refuse that we throw into our societies' garbage dumps. They show that there is another way, a different narrative to live. This book is the story of those who perceive morality in what is posited as vulgarity. It is the story of those who keep looking, keep moving, making mountains of dirt to be washed away in the rain. It is the story of a woman who looks under the asphalt and sees the sea. Your dirt is my music.

NME's Top 100 Albums of All Time

1.	*Pet Sounds*	The Beach Boys	Capital 1966
2.	*Revolver*	The Beatles	Parlophone 1966
3.	*Never Mind the Bollocks, Here's the Sex Pistols*	The Sex Pistols	Virgin 1977
4.	*What's Going On*	Marvin Gaye	Tamla Motown 1971
5.	*The Stone Roses*	The Stone Roses	Silvertone 1989
6.	*The Velvet Underground & Nico*	The Velvet Underground	Verve 1967
7.	*London Calling*	The Clash	CBS 1979
8.	*The Beatles*	The Beatles	Apple 1968
9.	*It Takes a Nation of Millions to Hold Us Back*	Public Enemy	Def Jam 1988
10.	*The Queen Is Dead*	The Smiths	Rough Trade 1986
11.	*Exile on Main Street*	The Rolling Stones	Virgin 1972
12.	*Nevermind*	Nirvana	Geffen 1991
13.	*The Clash*	The Clash	CBS 1977
14.	*Highway 61 Revisited*	Bob Dylan	Columbia 1965
15.	*Astral Weeks*	Van Morrison	Warners 1968
16.	*Sign 'O' the Times*	Prince	Paisley Park 1987
17.	*Blonde On Blonde*	Bob Dylan	Columbia 1966
18.	*Forever Changes*	Love	Elektra 1966
19.	*Three Feet High and Rising*	De La Soul	Big Life 1989
20.	*Closer*	Joy Division	Factory 1980
21.	*Screamadelica*	Primal Scream	Creation 1991
22.	*Let It Bleed*	The Rolling Stones	Decca 1969
23.	*Automatic for the People*	REM	WEA 1992
24.	*The Elvis Presley Sun Collection*	Elvis Presley	RCA 1975
25.	*The Doors*	The Doors	Elektra 1967
26.	*Marquee Moon*	Television	Elektra 1977
27.	*Psychocandy*	Jesus and Mary Chain	blanco y negro 1985
28.	*Blue*	Joni Mitchell	Reprise 1972
29.	*Are You Experienced?*	The Jimi Hendrix Experience	Track 1967
30.	*Live at the Apollo*	James Brown	London 1963
31.	*Horses*	Patti Smith	Arista 1975
32.	*Innervisions*	Stevie Wonder	Tamla Motown 1973
33.	*Sgt. Pepper's Lonely Hearts Club Band*	The Beatles	Parlophone 1967

34.	*Songs for Swingin' Lovers!*	Frank Sinatra	Capital 1958
35.	*Otis Blue*	Otis Redding	Atco 1966
36.	*A Love Supreme*	John Coltrane	Impulse 1967
37.	*Fear of a Black Planet*	Public Enemy	Def Jam 1990
38.	*Hunky Dory*	David Bowie	RCA 1971
39.	*Blood & Chocolate*	Elvis Costello and the Attractions	Impulse 1986
40.	*The Rise and Fall of Ziggy Stardust and the Spiders from Mars*	David Bowie	RCA 1972
41.	*Hatful of Hollow*	The Smiths	Rough Trade 1984
42.	*Technique*	New Order	Factory 1989
43.	*Unknown Pleasures*	Joy Division	Factory 1979
44.	*Surfer Rosa*	The Pixies	4AD 1988
45.	*Adventures Beyond the Ultraworld*	The Orb	Wau Mr Modo 1991
46.	*Surf's Up*	Beach Boys	Stateside 1971
47.	*Lust for Life*	Iggy Pop	RCA 1977
48.	*Bringing It All Back Home*	Bob Dylan	CBS 1965
49.	*Warehouse: Songs and Stories*	Hüsker Dü	Warners 1987
50.	*Low Life*	New Order	Factory 1985
51.	*Heaven Up Here*	Echo and the Bunnymen	Korova 1981
52.	*Parallel Lines*	Blondie	Chrysalis 1978
53.	*Grievous Angel*	Gram Parsons	Reprise 1974
54.	*Dusty in Memphis*	Dusty Springfield	Philips 1969
55.	*Transformer*	Lou Reed	RCA 1973
56.	*Led Zeppelin IV*	Led Zeppelin	Atlantic 1971
57.	*All Mod Cons*	The Jam	Polydor 1978
58.	*The Velvet Underground*	The Velvet Underground	MGM 1969
59.	*We're Only in It for the Money*	Mothers of Invention	MGM 1967
60.	*Harvest*	Neil Young	Reprise 1972
61.	*Scott*	Scott Walker	Philips 1967
62.	*The Stooges*	The Stooges	Elektra 1969
63.	*Everybody Knows This Is Nowhere*	Neil Young	Reprise 1969
64.	*Rubber Soul*	The Beatles	Parlophone 1967
65.	*Greatest Hits*	Aretha Franklin	Atlantic 1971
66.	*After the Goldrush*	Neil Young	Reprise 1970
67.	*Low*	David Bowie	RCA 1977
68.	*Remain in Light*	Talking Heads	Sire 1980
69.	*Marcus Garvey*	Burning Spear	Island 1975
70.	*Raindogs*	Tom Waits	Island 1985
71.	*Dry*	PJ Harvey	Too Pure 1992
72.	*The Smiths*	The Smiths	Rough Trade 1984
73.	*Lazer Guided Melodies*	Spiritualized	Dedicated 1992
74.	*Five Leaves Left*	Nick Drake	Island 1969
75.	*Clear Spot*	Captain Beefheart	Reprise 1972
76.	*16 Lovers Lane*	The Go-Betweens	Beggars 1988
77.	*Pink Flag*	Wire	Harvest 1977
78.	*Natty Dread*	Bob Marley	Island 1975
79.	*Sound Effects*	The Jam	Polydor 1980
80.	*Sister*	Sonic Youth	Blast First 1987
81.	*The White Room*	KLF	KLF Communications 1991
82.	*Junkyard*	The Birthday Party	4AD 1982
83.	*The Kick Inside*	Kate Bush	EMI 1978

84.	*Searching for the Young Soul Rebels*	Dexys Midnight Runners	Parlophone 1980
85.	*Blood on the Tracks*	Bob Dylan	CBS 1975
86.	*Rum, Sodomy & The Lash*	The Pogues	Stiff 1985
87.	*Give 'em Enough Rope*	The Clash	CBS 1978
88.	*King of America*	Elvis Costello	F-Beat 1986
89.	*Talking with the Taxman About Poetry*	Billy Bragg	Go! Discs 1986
90.	*Third/Sisters Lovers*	Big Star	Ardent 1978
91.	*Like a Prayer*	Madonna	Sire 1989
92.	*Reading, Writing and Arithmetic*	The Sundays	Rough Trade 1990
93.	*Off the Wall*	Michael Jackson	Epic 1979
94.	*Tonight's the Night*	Neil Young	Reprise 1975
95.	*This Nation's Saving Grace*	The Fall	Beggars 1985
96.	*Metal Box*	PIL	Virgin 1979
97.	*Blue Lines*	Massive Attack	Wild Bunch 1991
98.	*Younger Than Yesterday*	The Byrds	CBS 1967
99.	*Who's Next*	The Who	Track 1971
100.	To be announced	—	—

NME's Top 50 Albums of the 1980s

1.	*The Stone Roses*	The Stone Roses	Silvertone 1989
2.	*The Queen is Dead*	The Smiths	Rough Trade 1985
3.	*Three Feet High and Rising*	De La Soul	Big Life 1989
4.	*Sign 'O' the Times*	Prince	Paisley Park 1987
5.	*It Takes a Nation of Millions to Hold Us Back*	Public Enemy	Def Jam 1988
6.	*Psychocandy*	Jesus and Mary Chain	blanco y negro 1985
7.	*Hatful of Hollow*	The Smiths	Rough Trade 1984
8.	*Closer*	Joy Division	Factory 1980
9.	*Sound Effects*	The Jam	Polydor 1980
10.	*Low Life*	New Order	Factory 1985
11.	*Remain in Light*	Talking Heads	Sire 1980
12.	*Searching for the Young Soul Rebels*	Dexys Midnight Runners	Parlophone 1980
13.	*Bummed*	Happy Mondays	Factory 1989
14.	*Surfer Rosa*	The Pixies	4AD 1988
15.	*The Lexicon of Love*	ABC	Neutron 1982
16.	*Swordfishtrombones*	Tom Waits	Island 1983
17.	*Kilimanjaro*	A Teardrop Explodes	Mercury 1980
18.	*Dare*	The Human League	Virgin 1981
19.	*Parade*	Prince	Paisley Park 1986
20.	*16 Lover's Lane*	The Go-Betweens	Beggars Banquet 1988
21.	*Rain Dogs*	Tom Waits	Island 1985
22.	*This Nation's Saving Grace*	The Fall	Beggars Banquet 1985
23.	*Rum, Sodomy & the Lash*	The Pogues	Stiff 1985
24.	*The Smiths*	The Smiths	Rough Trade 1984
25.	*Blood & Chocolate*	Elvis Costello and the Attractions	Impulse 1986
26.	*Don't Stand Me Down*	Dexys Midnight Runners	Mercury 1985
27.	*The Eight Legged Groove Machine*	The Wonder Stuff	Polydor 1988
28.	*Crocodiles*	Echo and the Bunnymen	Korova 1980
29.	*Nebraska*	Bruce Springsteen	CBS 1982
30.	*The Nightfly*	Donald Fagen	Warners 1982
31.	*Talking with the Taxman About Poetry*	Billy Bragg	Go! Discs 1986
32.	*Miss America*	Mary Margaret O'Hara	Virgin 1988

33.	*Rattlesnakes*	Lloyd Cole and the Commotions	Polydor 1984
34.	*George Best*	The Wedding Present	Reception 1987
35.	*Atomizer*	Big Black	Blast First 1987
36.	*My Life in the Bush of Ghosts*	David Byrne and Brian Eno	Polydor 1981
37.	*Sister*	Sonic Youth	Blast First 1987
38.	*Straight Out of the Jungle*	The Jungle Brothers	Gee Street 1988
39.	*Heaven Up Here*	Echo and the Bunnymen	Korova 1981
40.	*Green*	REM	Warners 1988
41.	*Imperial Bedroom*	Elvis Costello and the Attractions	F-Beat 1982
42.	*You Can't Hide Your Love Forever*	Orange Juice	Polydor 1982
43.	*Midnight Love*	Marvin Gaye	CBS 1982
44.	*Like a Prayer*	Madonna	Sire 1989
45.	*Beautiful Vision*	Van Morrison	Mercury 1982
46.	*Infected*	The The	Some Bizarre 1986
47.	*Meat Is Murder*	The Smiths	Rough Trade 1985
48.	*New York*	Lou Reed	Sire 1989
49.	*Yo! Bum Rush the Show*	Public Enemy	Def Jam 1987
50.	*Warehouse: Songs and Stories*	Hüsker Dü	Warners 1987

Select Magazine Survey, 1994

Are You A Groupie?

Alarmed that you've woken up in Clint Poppie's bath, naked but for a strategically-placed J-cloth? Try this month's quiz and find out if you have any self-respect left at all. . .

1. Which of the following most accurately describes your ideal night out?
   a. Nice bath, visit to Options wine bar, and then a meal in a local trattoria.
   b. Inveigle way backstage at Motley Crue show by any means necessary. Attempt to cop off with lead singer and demonologist. Failing that, guitarist. Or drummer. Actually, that roadie doesn't look so bad.
   c. Video of last week's Chelsea match, Sham 69's *That's Life,* a wrap of speed, down to the pub for 15 pints of lager export, a frenzied snog in the car park with someone you've never met before and/or brutal beating administered to his/her girlfriend/boyfriend.
   d. Emerge from hole, take in a couple more small fish, hang out with Jacques Cousteau or film crew from Supersense for a few hours.

2. Do you think oral sex is:
   a. Fellatio, cunnilingus, etc. An act indulged in as normal and reasonable sexual optional extra by free-thinking consenting adults everywhere.
   b. It's more effective than the guest list.
   c. Not as good as a wank.
   d. Don't know.

3. When you wake up in the morning, do you:
   a. Rise early, shower, dress, watch GMTV, read *Daily Mail* over healthy muesli-oriented repast, brace yourself to meet the new day.
   b. Get up off floor, pick up a pair of souvenir celebrity underpants, crawl from tour bus/transit, update your *National Enquirer* League Ladder of Porking, try to establish what country you're in.

c. Regain consciousness, scrape powdery residue from around nostrils, finish off remainder of last night's red wine, desperately try to establish where the bathroom is.

d. Get up, have a quick swim. Have a few initial nibbles of small fish.

4. **Which of the following things do you always carry with you?**

a. Three-pack of Caramac-flavored condoms.

b. Autographed 8 × 10 glossy photo of Richey Manic.

c. Complete set of 1994–95 tour laminates.

d. Box of Mars Bars.

e. Full-size plaster cast of Jimi Hendrix's knob.

f. Novelty Saxon snowstorm presented to you as token of affection by their roadie "Mad Jock" after last year's British dates.

g. Handcuffs, truncheon, notebook, whistle, walkie-talkie.

h. Wrap of speed, switchblade.

i. Tangerine, stockings, four–foot length of electrical flex, plastic bag.

j. Have no material possessions whatsoever.

5. **How many people have you had sex with?**

a. Four or less (not including myself). Ha ha.

b. Four or less. Oh what you mean, like, ever? It was definitely four or less last night, but to be honest, you know, you lose track so quickly, don't you? I'd put it in the low hundreds. I guess.

c. 50–100.

d. Can't remember. Only have four-second memory.

6. **What is the predominant fabric or material in your wardrobe?**

a. Denim and leather.

b. Fake fur and Spandex.

c. Nylon and terylene.

d. Wet-look lycra and fishnet.

e. Latex and PVC.

f. Scales.

7. **How do you picture yourself in five years' time?**

a. Well, pretty much the same as now, but if I'm totally honest, I'd hope to be branch manager.

b. Inspecting the lengthy list of dates for signings and readings for my newly published book of shag-and-tell revelations, *Kissing, Dreams, Amphetamines, and Felching.*

c. I'll be dead, right (sniff). Someone like me ain't 'ere for the long haul, if you know what I mean . . . Jimmie Dean, Marilyn, Malcolm Owen.

d. Don't know, have no concept of time.

ANSWERS

1. a. 1; b. 15, yes he does; c. 5; d. 0
2. a. 3, steady on; b. 10; c. 5; d. –1
3. a. 1; b. 10; c. 5; d. 0
4. a. 5, you saucy devil; b. 10; c. 250; d. 50; e. 90; f. 250; g. 0, get back to doctoring arrest reports; h. 10; i. 0. seek professional help; j. –5
5. a. 1; b. 50; c. 2; d. 0
6. a. 10; b. 15; c. 1; d. 60; e. 40; f. 0
7. a. 1; b. 60; c. 30; d. 0

VERDICT

Less than zero points: You are not in fact a groupie but a grouper—a spectacularly coloured tropical fish not renowned for your involvement with the music industry or indeed for your ability to breathe outside water. So how you came to be doing this quiz at all is a complete mystery to us.

0–30 points: Your name is Dennis. You are a counter clerk at the TSB in Well, Somerset. Rock on, Dennis!

30–60 points: You are either a member of Primal Scream, These Animal Men, or a pathological liar.

61–90 points: You are Caitlin Moran.

91–110 points: You are the disgusting pinnacle of groupiedom. You will shag anything with a heartbeat and a record contract.

110+ points: So is it true what they say about Jimi, or what?

Notes

Introduction (pp. 1–24)

1. Cohen, Finnegan, and Frith all suggest that live music performances should be examined as ritual events (Cohen 1991, Finnegan 1989, Frith 1991).

2. Following Susan Philips, I use a slightly modified version of Goffman's participant framework called participant structure (Philips 1983).

3. By the 1980s, many anthropologists were calling for a reassertion of the body in ethnography (Clifford 1988, Fabian 1983, Jackson 1989, Turner 1986, Tyler 1987). Contemporary anthropologists have noted that published ethnography and analysis "typically have repressed bodily experience in favor of abstracted theory and analysis" (Conquergood 1991: 181). Bodies in their physical presence assert a cotemporality of parties. This undermines anthropology's historic "temporal setup," which locates anthropology's "others" as outside of time (Clifford 1988, Fabian 1983). Thus, attending to the body asserts the subjective, interactive, and contemporary sharing of space that is fundamental to ethnographic research.

4. Max Weber, in his influential sociological text *The Protestant Ethic and the Spirit of Capitalism* posits a causal relationship between Calvinist Protestantism and the economic and social domains of the modern capitalist culture (Weber 1958).

5. Talking back to the screen and other audience members has also been noted in African American audiences.

6. *Turn on the Bright Lights* is the title of the band Interpol's debut album.

7. The analysis of music forms has been the traditional province of ethnomusicology and is beyond the scope of this project.

8. Traditional concerts have tickets with specific seating locations. There are numerous factors that affect what tickets a patron purchases for a performance, including variable prices for seats that are considered better quality, the practices of ticketing, the involvement of ticket brokers, and the number of tickets set aside by the performer or the record company. There are other types of venues with seats—supper clubs, for example, which have seats and tables around an open dance floor—and they all have different limitations and potentials for interaction.

9. Small makes a similar argument regarding audience comportment for orchestral music by looking at the varied settings and audience behaviors for the experience of classical music in different historic periods as well as comparing them to different performance events in a variety of cultures from around the world (Small 1998).

10. The American artist Beck, who is very popular in the indie scene, utilized many of the conventions of hip-hop performance during his 1996 *Odelay* tour. During shows he did "call outs" to various segments of the audience for them to respond to. This required substantial goading, because indie audiences do not usually participate in call outs. In contrast, call outs are an expected component of audience behavior at hip-hop shows.

11. The gender ratio of readers for the indie weekly music press is 66 percent male and 34 percent female (IPC Music Press 1993). This is consistent with the gender ratios I found at gigs. At four various-sized gigs, I tabulated male and female attendance ratios that ranged from 25 to 37 percent female. At thirteen other performances, I did random twenty-person samples of audience members entering the venue. Females ranged between 30 and 40 percent in the random samples.

12. At four various-sized gigs, I tabulated minority attendance ratios that ranged between 1 and 3 percent. At fifteen other performances I did random forty-person samples of audience members entering the venue and found approximately 1 to 2 percent. Even at a benefit show for the anti-fascist league by the indie-supported, ethnically diverse band Rage Against the Machine there was only a very slight increase in ethnic minorities.

13. However, the American indie audience is far more physically circumspect than the British indie audience. It is a repeated joke among British and American musicians and audience members that American indie fans do not dance.

14. In 2001 *Melody Maker* and *New Musical Express* were collapsed into a single entity, the *New Musical Express,* by IPC Press, their publisher. *NME* currently touts itself as the most successful music website in Europe.

15. By 2004, the indie movement in the United States had taken on a greater role with the recognition that it was distinct from Alternative music, a genre seen as opposed to the mainstream during the 1990s. American indie even gained a radio station with the premiere of "indie 103.1" in Los Angeles. While indie has become an important genre in the United States, American CD classifications (the Gracenote CDDB music recognition database, etc.) and ringtone notations still refer to bands from this community as "Alternative." In the United Kingdom, internet and ringtone sites classify this music as indie.

16. *Gig* is also used to refer to performances of other genres of music. According to the *Oxford English Dictionary,* gig originally denoted a vocational engagement. The audience members' use of the term gig may suggest some identification with performers.

17. This is the number of gigs attended during the initial fieldwork period, but I have now attended well over one thousand performances, at least half of which were in the United Kingdom.

18. The following venues were included in this study: Bath Moles Club, Blackpool Tower Ballroom, Brighton Concorde, Brighton Zap Club, Bristol Fleece and Firkin, Brixton Academy, Brixton Ivy, Cambridge Corn Exchange, Camden Dublin Castle, Camden Electric Ballroom, Camden Falcon, Camden Laurel Tree, Camden Lock HQ Club, Camden Palais, Camden Underworld, Cardiff Sam's Bar, Chelmsford Army and Navy, Clapham Grand, Colchester Oliver Twist, Covent Garden Rock Garden, Edinburgh Jaffe Cake, Edinburgh Queen's Hall, Euston Russell Arms, Finsbury George Robey, Finsbury Park Fleadh Festival, Glasgow Cat House, Glasgow Garage, Glasgow Nice'n'Sleazy, Glasgow 13th Note, Glasgow King Tut's Wah Wah Hut, Harlesden Mean Fiddler, Islington Garage, Islington Hope and Anchor, Islington Powerhaus, Kentish Town Bull and Gate, Kentish Town Forum, Kings Cross Water Rats, Kingston Baccus Wine Bar, Leeds Duchess of York, Leeds Festival, Leicester University, Liverpool Olympia, London Astoria, London Astoria Two, London Borderline, London Marquee, London 100 Club, London Subterrania, Manchester Academy, Manchester Apollo, Manchester Night and Day, Manchester Roadhouse, New Cross Venue, Norwich UEA, Oxford Jerico Tavern, Oxford Zodiac, Pilton Glastonbury, Reading Festival, Reading Youth Center, Sheffield Leadmill, Sheffield Octagon, Shepherd's Bush Empire, Stratford-upon-Avon Phoenix Festival, Tunbridge Wells Forum, Uxbridge University.

19. Formats are the different types of record products available for purchase—compact disc, twelve-inch vinyl, seven-inch vinyl, cassette, DVD, mp3, and so on. Formatting rules govern formats for inclusion in the music charts.

Chapter 1: What is Indie? (pp. 25–78)

1. This difficulty was highlighted in 1992 when the British music industry contemplated changing criteria for inclusion in the Independent chart, the eligibility for which constitutes the industrial definition of the genre. At that time, the industry could not form a consensus and let the previous criteria stand, with the caveat that the most obvious forms of dance music would be excluded.

2. The weekly newspapers were called "inkies" because they were printed with ink on low-grade newspaper rather than the offset ink used for glossy paper of the magazines. As mentioned previously, *Melody Maker* was folded into *NME* in 2001, due to declining readership and problems in the British publishing industry that were attributed to challenges from the internet. *Sounds* folded during the 1980s. *NME* can be purchased at most large newsstands, by subscription or online. In 1998, the *NME* changed format and now uses a higher grade ink.

3. *NME* generally comes out on Wednesdays. At a few key vendors in London, *NME* is available on Tuesday afternoons.

4. The motto "Tomorrow's Music, Today" was the *Melody Maker* slogan for most of the 1990s, until it was replaced after their seventieth anniversary issue in 1996.

5. With the dissolving of *Melody Maker,* this option no longer presented itself. In truth, there *was* a rivalry between staff members of the two papers. Each staff saw itself as having a writing style distinct from the other. This tension between the papers created opportunities for bands, as a rejection by one paper could mean an open door at the other.

6. Protestantism is the broad term used to characterize Christian religious traditions that are not part of the Catholic or Greek Orthodox churches. Almost immediately following the Reformation, various sects of Protestantism emerged. For the most part, Protestants do not recognize papal authority, put their faith in God alone, and believe in the Bible as infallible truth.

7. This is a rather compelling contradiction, a secular entertainment espousing a Puritan ideology. The contradiction is even more startling in that rock music's origins lie in part in West African possession rites, where the body plays a very different role in religious experience. The contradiction of the values of asceticism within a ritual of physical pleasure will be discussed in a later chapter.

8. Barry Shank documents a similar narrative framework for the punk scene in Austin, Texas: "Punks and postpunk musicians struggled to recuperate sincerity through a purification of the expressive impulse. The lessons of punk in Austin reinforced a utopian romantic urge for a cultural marketplace free of deceit, where sincere expression, a pure representation, could arise from some essence of the performer untainted by the polluting structures of capitalism and then could be distributed through direct channels to a populace longing for it" (Shank 1994: 147–148). These themes of local control, authenticity, and unmediated artistic expression are persistently noted: "The hope was that by developing and implementing a locally controlled industrial strategy, the necessary commodification of Austin music could avoid inauthenticity. No outside interests would interfere in the cycle of production and consumption. This concept of an industrial production purified of outside interests continues to be the dream of those involved in the music business in Austin" (Shank 1994: 89).

9. In 1996 there were five major corporations. Their main distribution companies in the United Kingdom were:

Corporation	Distribution Company
Bertelsmann (A&M, RCA, Arista)	BMG
Seagram's (MCA, Geffen, PolyGram, Polydor, Island)	PolyGram
Sony (Columbia, Epic)	Sony
Thorne-EMI (Capital, Virgin)	EMI
Time Warner (Elektra, Atlantic, Reprise)	WEA

As of 2005 there were four majors:

Vivendi (MCA, Interscope, PolyGram, Island)	Universal
Sony (Columbia, Epic)	Sony
Thorne-EMI (Capital, Virgin)	EMI
Time Warner (Elektra, Atlantic, Reprise)	WEA

10. The fact that this is perception rather than fact is demonstrated by some Bhangra (uptempo music from the Punjab region of India and Pakistan) acts that do not get national airplay and lack chart placement yet have immense sales.

11. Radios One, Two, Three, and Four were inaugurated in 1967 as a result of the Marine Offences Bill, which was designed to end the era of pirate radio stations. These unlicensed stations broadcasted primarily pop and rock records from ships anchored off the British shoreline (Hunter 1977).

12. In 1952 the first chart debuted in *NME* as a Top 12. It became a Top 20 in 1954 and a Top 30 in 1956. In 1966 *Record Retailer,* an industry trade paper later renamed *Music Week,* developed a Top 40. In 1969, the first true "industry chart" was published by the British Market Research Bureau. This chart eventually stabilized as a Top 50. In 1978, the "industry" chart was increased to a Top 100. In 1971, Radio One commenced a weekly Top 40 show, playing a weekly countdown of the top-selling singles. The resulting air play of singles in the Top 40, along with the publication and marketing of charts, means that artists with chart placement get crucial additional publicity and radio airplay.

13. The reason for bulk deals rather than lowered unit prices is that industry rules govern minimum prices. In 1996, the lowest prices for the sale of a single to a retail outlet was 55p for a seven-inch single, £2.39 for a twelve-inch single, and £2.43 for a CD single. Additionally, there are lower limits on retail prices as well: 99p for a seven-inch single, £1.99 for a twelve-inch single, and £1.99 for a CD single. The majority of labels do not have to pay royalties on free products. By offering a "buy one, get one free" deal, the label does not have to pay the artist royalties for the free single. The majors are not required to pay mechanical royalties on promotional materials. Independents, on the other hand, are required to pay mechanical royalties on all CDs manufactured irregardless of their promotional use, unless they can get an AP2 (audio product) agreement that allows them to pay royalties on sales rather than pressings. These agreements are difficult to obtain. The Association for Independent Music (AIM), a trade body, is working to relax the rules for obtaining AP2 agreements. Retail limits were changed again in 1998, reducing the lowest dealer price on a CD single to £1.98 and instituting a rule of no more than one free for two singles purchased. At first glance the new rules appeared to benefit artists, but since royalties are tied to dealer price, the reduction in price effectively paid artists less money than the previous agreement.

14. National charts are counted using Epson scanners that register sales by barcode. There are more than 1,800 Epson scanners in Britain for 3,200 shops eligible to have their sales included in the national charts. Shops that record their sales for the national charts are called chart return shops. For a shop to be eligible for chart return, it needs to sell more than one hundred units (records) per week. In 1995, the company that held exclusive license to the independent as well as the mainstream

national charts was the Chart Information Network (CIN). However, they do not compile the charts themselves. CIN hires the marketing company Millward Brown to monitor chart scanners and compile a variety of weekly music charts. CIN licenses these charts to *Music Week*, the industry publication, as well as other national media.

15. As some chart return shops were in rather obscure locations, some bands would purposely play shows on the "chart return circuit" as another means to strengthen their chart position.

16. Capital Radio is one of London's radio stations.

17. The first UK national charts were initiated by *NME* by polling selected retail outlets.

18. An independent chart appeared in *Melody Maker* for the first time on October 25, 1980. This chart included many of the artists and labels who formed the core of the early indie music scene.

Song	Band	Label
"Blue Boy"	Orange Juice	Postcard
"Totally Wired"	The Fall	Rough Trade
"Radio Drill Time"	Joseph K	Postcard
"Requiem"	Killing Joke	Malicious Damage
"Shack Up"	A Certain Ratio	Factory
"I Need Two Heads"	The Go-Betweens	Postcard
"Atmosphere"	Joy Division	Factory
"Big City-Bright Lights"	Missing Scientists	Rough Trade
"Fireside Favourites"	Fad Gadget	Mute
"Leisure Time"	Methodishca Tune	Eusture

19. EP stands for "extended player." which is a release that is longer than a single but shorter than an album.

20. Rough Trade began in the 1970s as a London record store. A year later it began releasing records, and gradually it developed a distribution company. In 1980 the label and distribution companies split. Rough Trade eventually went bankrupt, and Geoff Travis lost the name Rough Trade in receivership. However, in 1999 he bought back the name and reopened Rough Trade Records. Its first new release was the band Terrix in 1999.

21. The new opportunities for direct distribution by labels via the internet has been pointed to as a further democratizing and empowering venue for artists to put out records themselves—true DIY.

22. One-off projects are deals to press and distribute a single release by an artist.

23. Rough Trade Distribution collapsed in 1991 with the demise of the Rough Trade label. It was considered a severe blow to the independent sector, and many independent labels lost money. There is much dispute about the events that led to the end of Rough Trade, but many felt that Rough Trade had not been able to maintain their values and organizational structure as the company grew and became successful. The wage structure changed and became tiered; company meetings became hierarchical. A gap grew between those who worked in the warehouses and those in the offices. The regional and local distribution offices were closed, and the company was centralized in London. Poor management decisions led to eventual bankruptcy.

By 1991, there were other, less ideological alternatives for independent distribution: Pinnacle, SRD, and Vital. Many labels had lost money on the Rough Trade collapse, but they still wanted to work with its staff. Former Rough Trade staffers formed Rough Trade Management (RTM) and continued to provide independent distribution. The Merger of RTM with Vital in 1997 was in many ways another reformation of the Cartel. Vital was formed from the merger of ATP (which was owned by PIAS and Pete Thompson of Red Rhino in York) and Revolver (which was established by Mike Chadwick of Revolver in Bristol). Hence the merger of Vital and RTM reunited key descendants of the Cartel.

24. Special formats are specific versions of a release, such as a single made of white vinyl issued in limited quantities. Often, special formats are offered exclusively to a particular retail chain.

25. When Vital and RTM merged in 1997, Vital took over the name Chain with No Name for their affiliated stores.

26. Many of the early punk bands' one-offs would catapult the band to a record contract with a major label. For many bands, signing with a major label and receiving a large advance is a matter of survival. Just as for the broader culture, the bohemian ethic demands the divorce of money from art, thus fetishizing poverty for musicians. Of course, it is easy for one who is being paid for his or her own job to insist that someone else work for free.

27. This relationship was established when PolyGram was trying to sign Chapterhouse, a band that insisted on being on the independent chart. Dedicated charged much of the institutionalization costs to the band's recoupable expenses. Chapterhouse thus paid for the system that subsequent bands at the label would use.

28. In 1992, Clive Selwood's independent record company changed from an independent distributor to Rio, which was affiliated with PolyGram, and was thereby excluded from the independent chart, which resulted in an industry-wide debate about the criteria for the independent chart.

29. In 2004, a new editorial decision by *NME* to distance itself from its perceived niche has resulted in *NME*'s termination of publication of the independent and national charts. This greatly reduced the profile of the independent chart and its role in the British music industry.

30. Interestingly, one of the roots of the term "romantic" is *enromancier*, which means to translate texts in the local vernacular.

31. The distinction between British and American indie and Alternative musical styles is also recognized in Holland, Finland, and Australia (1995 IASPM conference discussion).

32. Madchester was a music scene focused in Manchester, England, during the mid- to late 1980s. Madchester's music combined influences from indie and dance, and it was strongly associated with Ecstasy use.

33. In 1997, Creation started a dance imprint, Infonet, in an attempt to diversify the label.

34. On its ten-year anniversary, *NME* put out a C96 compilation tape. It included tracks by Mogwai, Tiger, Dweeb, Magoo, Urusei Yatsura, and Babybird.

35. For example, Kim Deal of the internationally successful Breeders and the Pixies put out a four-track recording on the British 4AD label under the name the Amps. Furthermore, there is a scene under the patronage of indie called lo-fi (short for "low-fidelity") that takes the anti-production bias of indie to an extreme, releasing highly underproduced music often done in home settings with four- or eight-track recording devices.

36. The middle-eight is a section of a song usually eight bars long that provides a contrast to the rest of the song. The bridge is a transition passage connecting two movements. In this case, it usually connects the middle-eight to the chorus.

37. Some of the more successful indie bands have branched out from indie's generic format. Radiohead is one of the best examples of a band that exemplified many of the conventions of indie and then expanded upon them in production and in song length while maintaining ties to the indie community.

38. Intriguingly, this hairstyle is reminiscent of the Roundheads, the Puritan supporters of Parliament who opposed the Cavaliers, the Church of England Royalist supporters of Charles I of England.

39. Though not shoe-gazers, Oasis, one of the most successful indie genre bands, also exhibited a paradigmatic indie performance style. The band remained relatively static during shows, wore plain clothes, and relied heavily on guitars. However, Oasis, while emerging from the indie community and exhibiting many indie generic qualities in both their music and their visual style, actively distanced themselves from indie's other behavioral imperatives. In interviews, they discussed drug use, advocated conspicuous consumption, and had no problem playing large venues traditionally associated with mainstream bands.

40. Start-Rite is a brand of children's shoes.

41. The diminutive in grammar indicates smallness, familiarity, youth, affection, or contempt (*American Heritage Dictionary*). The diminutive was part of the dual expressive nature of Nabokov's *Lolita*—the creature between adulthood and childhood. Nabokov explicitly set out to select a diminutive for the name of his heroine. "For my nymphet I needed a diminutive with a lyrical lilt to it. One of the most limpid and luminous letters is 'L.' The suffix '-ita' has a lot of Latin tenderness, and this I required too. Hence: Lolita. . . . . . Another consideration was the welcome murmur of its source name, the fountain name: those roses and tears in 'Dolores.' My little girl's heart-rending fate had to be taken into account together with the cuteness and limpidity. Dolores also provided her with another, plainer, more familiar and infantile diminutive: Dolly, which went nicely with the surname 'Haze,' where Irish mists blend with a German bunny—I mean a small German hare [hase]" (Nabokov, 1990: 25).

42. The Luddites were a group of English artisans in the early 1800s who destroyed new machinery they thought took away their livelihoods. The term Luddite since has become synonymous with technophobia.

43. The bands on Chemikal Underground Records of Glasgow are good examples, such as bis and Arab Strap.

44. CD1 and CD2 are two different releases of the same single that have different B-sides. This is to encourage fans to buy two versions of the same single and thus boost its position in the charts.

45. The scratches and crackles of vinyl are even at times sampled and then digitized onto CDs.

46. Vinyl junkies also feel that CDs are a record company scam with artificially high prices. Since CDs cost much less to produce than vinyl, there is much speculation regarding the higher costs of CDs. A feeling that major recording companies are a syndicate controlling the music business is part of the formative ideology of the independent sector.

47. In the early journalistic pieces introducing electronic band the Prodigy to the indie audience, the weekly press represented the band as legitimate because members could perform their music in a convincing way in a live setting.

48. Starting a band on an independent label has been considered such an effective way to introduce a band into the marketplace that many majors who have signed bands in the United States offer their acts to unaffiliated independent companies in the United Kingdom. Cibo Matto and Scarce are two bands initially signed to a major in the United States and then offered to independents in the United Kingdom. Additionally, many bands that are signed to independents in Britain will maintain the status after signing to a major corporation worldwide. Elastica, a London indie band signed to independent Deceptive in Britain, was on DGC (Geffen) worldwide. The band Ash signed to independent Infectious in Britain and Warner's Reprise outside of Europe.

49. Many date the inception of the modern era of independent labels at the release of the Buzzcocks' *Spiral Scratch* EP on their own New Hormones label in January 1977.

50. While this is the expectation, it is not always the case.

51. This data comes from research by IPC Music Press for use by advertisers. IPC Press is the publisher of *New Musical Express* and the now-defunct *Melody Maker*. These two weekly publications were widely recognized as catering to the indie fan base. The age breakdown of readers for those weeklies was: 45 percent, 15–19; 35 percent, 20–24; 15 percent, 25–29; 5 percent, 30 and up (IPC Music Press 1993).

52. However, many independent labels and indie bands eschew multi-formatting, seeing it as exploiting their fan base.

53. The initial limitation on formats was placed at five in 1990 and then four in 1991. Before rules limiting formats, it was not uncommon for a single to be released in seven different formats, with different versions of singles and an assortment of B-sides. Even after the four-format rule was institutionalized, some acts continued to put out more than four formats. This created a rather strange situation for the band Erasure, whose various formats of its single "Am I Right?" sold so prodigiously that in January 1991 the single charted simultaneously at numbers 22 and 73. In 1995, the number of formats was reduced from four to three, a decision that had a negative impact on the availability of vinyl releases, as the standard formats became two versions of a CD, and cassette. In 1998, formatting rules again changed the permitted number of B-sides and additional tracks on a single from three to two.

54. "Wanking" is a slang term for masturbation.

55. Significantly, the indie fan is seen as wanking in private, while the mainstream rock performer is seen as wanking in public due to his excessive soloing.

56. Bands' videos often picture them in natural environments, walking on the beach or playing in the forest, for example, reflecting the Romantic interest in nature.

57. The Reading festival has been in existence as a rock festival for more than twenty years. In 1989, the Mean Fiddler organization took over the promotion of the event and began to book indie bands. Since then the Reading festival has been one of the premier events for indie bands, consistently voted by *NME* readers as the "event of the year." The originators of the American mobile festival Lollapalooza attended the Reading festival in 1990 and decided to create a similar event for the United States.

By 1997, Reading's role as the premier indie event had begun to wane. Their success in the early 1990s with the indie format meant a proliferation of summer festivals. V Festival, T in the Park, and several other corporate-sponsored festivals all book indie bands. Additionally, festivals in other countries have taken on greater precedence in the annual festival calendar. With more festivals, there has been greater competition for bands and therefore fewer exclusive contracts for bands playing a particular festival.

58. Indie's self-proclaimed ability to see true merit in music was reiterated in its press releases for its 2004 awards ceremony, when the editor of *NME* proclaimed that the BRATs were "the only award for real music lovers."

59. Ironically, in 1999 indie favorites Belle and Sebastian won the BRIT award for "best newcomer," and mainstream industry stalwart Pete Waterman claimed vote rigging because Steps, the pop dance quintet he fabricated from applications sent in response to a magazine advertisement, had lost.

60. Subsequent Mercury award winners were bestowed on various genres. These winners included Roni Size (1997), Gomez (1998), Talvin Singh (1999), Badly Drawn Boy (2000), PJ Harvey (2001), Ms. Dynamite (2002), Dizzee Rascal

(2003), and Franz Ferdinand (2004). Four of the eight clearly emerged from the indie community (Gomez, Badly Drawn Boy, PJ Harvey, and Franz Ferdinand).

61. As of 1995, *Vox* had been taken over by *NME* staff members. In 1998, IPC closed *Vox*.

62. Many of these writers began their careers by putting out their own fanzines. They were later hired by the national music press.

63. At the 1994 Reading festival, Lou Barlow became upset during his band's set, broke his guitar, then hit himself in the head with it.

64. A "studio" album uses production techniques to create sounds in the studio that are difficult, if not impossible, to replicate live.

65. Interestingly, it is the images of rebellion and the counter-cultural in pop music that are embraced and fetishized in cultural studies. The potential social and political changes that can result from popular aesthetic productions is the primary means for making them potential objects of inquiry. As Simon Frith points out in a discussion of cultural studies, anthropologists tend to look at popular social phenomena as ordered and controlled. Cultural studies, on the other hand, tends to examine popular phenomena through the veil of "resistance through rituals" and concludes that these youth phenomena are attempts to subvert the dominant hegemony (Frith 1993). The apotheosis of this perspective is Susan McClary's description of the beat in Wilson Pickett's "In the Midnight Hour" as the harbinger of the sexual and political upheavals of the 1960s (McClary 1994). Her underlying association of musical phenomena with the counter-cultural and the consistent valuing of the position of rebellion is clear. However, this idea of resistance is not merely an external representation grafted onto music by academics, but an important generative narrative for the music communities themselves.

66. There is in fact an avoidance of too much focus on the self or anything else that can be construed as narcissistic. Indie has a tendency to play down performers as individuals. The solo displays a musician as a singular identity within the band ensemble. Therefore, it is very uncommon for indie bands to have performers play one at a time. Additionally, indie solo artists often take "band" names rather than perform as solo acts. Thus, when Leslie Rankin, a member of the indie band Silverfish, later went on to do her solo work, she released it under the band name Ruby. Will Oldham has performed under the names Palace Brothers, Palace Music, and Palace. Conor Oberst performs as Bright Eyes.

67. This issue of thinness plays out differently in the United States. The Alternative bands with ties to skateboarding and punk are often multiethnic and feature physically large performers. One Norwegian band characterized these American bands as "pizza bands" because they appeared to have eaten too much fattening food. However, the American scene that calls itself indie or underground more often has bands that physically resemble their British counterparts.

68. Dance music that is appreciated by indie is usually performed by the composers themselves, who have band names rather than DJ names, such as the Chemical Brothers, though this is changing as dance has become more accepted by the indie community.

69. For a history of the discourse on the value of live performance, see Thornton 1995. Sarah Thornton argues that the notion of "live performance" arose from the advent of disc culture and the proliferation of venues that played records. Previously, of course, all music was performed by live musicians.

70. Deejaying is extremely lucrative, much more so than playing gigs, because there is virtually no overhead and almost everything a DJ is paid is profit. Fatboy Slim, who was once in the indie band the Housemartins, commented that he made much more money as a DJ than as a band member. For the dance community, it is very important that the mix be created live. However, it is not uncommon for a DJ

to make up his set in advance, put it on DAT (digital audio tape), and then just drink, dance, and mime a live mix.

71. When the weekly press promotes dance acts, they often do so by emphasizing the acts' personalities, or their exhibition of clichéd rock and roll characteristics. For example, in a piece on the Prodigy *NME* included a list of ten reasons why the Prodigy is in fact a rock-and-roll band. This list included audience behavior that made the band into personalities because fans wanted to touch the performers as well as obtain autographs. Dance magazines are not averse to creating "star" personalities for DJs by using the same rock-and-roll prosaisms. Often lurid titles are used, such as "DJs and their groupies."

72. E is the abbreviation of ecstasy, the name applied to the drugs MDMA and MDA, which have the pharmacological effect of inducing dopamine secretion, thereby producing a euphoric sensation. Wizz is slang for speed or methamphetamine, a stimulant used for maintaining wakefulness and at times a sense of intense self-confidence.

73. In the film *Live Forever* (2003), a review of the heyday of Britpop with interviews with some of the indie community's leading lights, Damon Albarn of Blur and Gorillaz calls Ecstasy "synthetic rubbish." He linked dance's drug of choice to an overall modern attraction to artificiality, ripping "everything out and replacing it with plastic."

74. Interestingly, a segment of the dance community expresses similar Romantic values. For example, Dave Haslam, DJ at the Haçienda, makes a strong argument for dance music's immediacy, originality, organic connection to local community, and unmediated artistic vision (Haslam 2000). Haslam's DJ career at the Haçienda began with his indie night, called "Temperance." Temperance was aptly titled for its original context of indie, mutating into playful irony as house music, a sub-genre of dance, and ecstasy took over the Manchester music scene.

75. Indie recordings are often treated as precious commodities and released in numbered limited editions, in the same way that limited edition lithographs are created by artists.

76. The alternative K may be suggestive of ketamine, also known as Special K, a drug that is associated with rave culture. Others have suggested that the K is a reference to the Germanic origins of electronic music in bands such as Kraftwerk, spelled with a K.

77. Creation Records also used what appeared to be a handwritten style of font on their website.

78. This is a play on the title of the Smashing Pumpkins album named *Mellon Collie and the Infinite Sadness* (1995).

Chapter 2. The Zones of Participation (pp. 79–121)

1. As I mentioned in chapter 1, generally when bands change from non-seated to seated venues, they have generally attained mainstream success. This is a critical period during which indie fans watch to see if a band, under the temptations of the mainstream "church," can nevertheless adhere to their independent principles. While a dislike of large size is an issue for indie fans, seating is even more critical. At open-field festivals such as Reading, T in the Park, and Glastonbury, audiences swell to mammoth proportions. Playing to large audiences at a festival is not seen in any way as affecting one's membership in the indie community, but playing at a stadium such as Wembley does.

2. For the oldest participants, this is reversed. With sufficient time many Top 40 bands come back into favor as influences for contemporary indie acts. If this happens, it is no longer considered embarrassing to have seen them perform.

3. Sometimes performers do not face the audience either, as in early Jesus and Mary Chain shows.

4. In this respect, the gig event suggests Michel Foucault's discussion of the Panopticon. His notion of the relationship between the Panopticon and the arts is discussed in detail by Donald Preziosi (Preziosi 1989).

5. For example, Sid Vicious in his pre–Sex Pistols days famously whipped a chain across journalist Nick Kent's face.

6. This dancing was hypervertical and hypermasculine. As Emily Apter has pointed out, in the West the serpentine curve has been associated with femininity and the exotic other, linearity with masculine rationality (Apter 1992).

7. Many scholars locate the origins of punk in New York with music figures such as Richard Hell, although John Lydon, in his autobiography *Rotten: No Irish, No Blacks, No Dogs* (1995), vigorously disputes this claim.

8. A particularly fine demonstration of this dance style is given by a Torontonian punk in the Social Distortion tour film, *Another State of Mind* (1986).

9. For example, at the Reading festival, which is traditionally very accommodating to the activity of crowd surfing, surfers are pushed back by security into the crowd during the day, allowing individuals to stay on top for a longer time. At night, security automatically pulls out surfers who make it to the front, resulting in much shorter periods on top of the crowd. If an audience member appears to be in any distress, security personnel remove him or her. The reason for the difference between day and night practices is that at night it is more difficult to determine if a fan is distressed, and therefore all people passed to the front are removed. In the early 2000s, the Reading festival added signs prohibiting crowd surfing as a requirement for the promoters to get a city permit to hold the festival.

10. There are several possible factors that may explain why the crowd at this show was adverse to crowd surfing. While the Lemonheads were very popular with the indie press, their audience configuration was not particularly indie. The crowd was significantly younger than the average indie gig and had a significantly higher percentage of females. The combination of less experienced gig goers with audience members who did not actively participate in crowd surfing (females) made it apparent that most of the people were there to watch the performers onstage rather than participate in gig activities.

11. The set list is the listing of songs that will be performed by the band. It is written or printed on a piece of paper and taped to the stage to remind performers of the sequence of songs in the band's set. These same fans are likely to ask for the set list after the show.

12. Calling out obscure tracks can at times surprise the band and produce some response from the performers.

13. Although close to the stage and free of crowd surfers, these side periphery locations have strong drawbacks. Because audio loudspeakers most commonly sit on the sides of the stage, the side front is the loudest and most ear-damaging location in the venue. Also, the sound quality is inferior.

14. The summer indie festivals are often characterized by a higher and wider range of drug use, mainly speed and marijuana, but even in these settings alcohol is still the most prevalent substance. Illegal drug use is far more common among performers and industry professionals.

15. One major contrast between British and American pits is that location selection is more flexible at UK indie gigs. Audience members can redistribute themselves during performances with much more ease than in the United States, moving from the front to the middle and back to the front. At American gigs, audience members are more likely to stay at the front for the duration of the gig, because if they move they are considered to have lost their places.

16. For a particularly well-written fictionalized account of this, see Gwendoline Riley's *Cold Water,* where she writes of a fan's obsession with a band from Maccles-field (Riley 2003).

17. Sara Cohen discusses how the Liverpudlian rock musician's performance also allows men to "express ideas and sentiments in a manner that is discouraged in other public settings" (Cohen 1997: 31).

18. However, for some of the most significant cultural rituals, the activities required have such strong physiological components that the sentiments become extraordinarily compelling. The physical responses to pain from stinging ants or circumcision without anesthetic produce far less variation in subjects than an event such as a possession trance, which uses hypertrophic dance in which only a few subjects become possessed.

19. Altered states of consciousness are an integral part of the sacred domain in many cultures, often playing a dramatic role in ritual; 90 percent of all societies have institutionalized means of accessing altered states of consciousness (Bourguig-non 1973: 3). Mostly these experiences are considered constitutive of the sacred. In official religious contexts, ASCs are also vital for eliciting spiritual experiences.

20. On occasion, there are individuals in zone two who do dance. However, when they do, they do not touch other audience members. One's movement is confined to one's own personal space. Additionally, the movement is much less vigorous than in zone one. At gigs for bands whose music is sedate, there is far less movement in zone one as well, and the distinction between the two zones is much more subtle.

21. The three major exceptions to this are gigs at which the majority of participants are professionals (such as showcases), at the large festivals, or at a show of an unpopular band that does not have a fan base. In each of these cases, zone three has the greatest number of participants.

22. The Powerhaus is no longer a venue. In the mid-1990s, it was converted into an upscale drinking pub.

23. On one occasion when I was applauding vigorously in the back of zone two, I was told by a fellow audience member that I didn't need to applaud because the band would come back on. His assumption was that if I was applauding in this area, I must not know the norms of gigs—which are that if the house lights are kept off, then the band plans to do an encore. His comment demonstrated both his experience of gigs and his knowledge of performance conventions and their routinized nature.

24. People face toward the stage despite the fact that very often one cannot see the performers at all; people usually orient themselves to sound. Such was the case when Liz Phair played at the Camden HQ, a venue where the stage was hardly elevated and the floor was entirely flat. On the floor one could not see the stage past eight rows of bodies back. Throughout the venue, though, people gazed in the direction of the stage despite the fact they could not see Liz Phair. After a third of the performance, a female fan in the middle of the audience asked, "What does she look like?" The person in front of her replied, "She looks like the back of someone's head."

25. When a zone two fan gets really excited and wants to move up, he or she usually asks friends to come along. If the friends decline, many will stay in zone two rather than enter zone one alone, spending the rest of the performance slightly dissatisfied that they are not participating in the manner that they desired.

26. Very few individuals have stories of significant injury. For the most part, promoters in Britain devise means of managing the popular activities of audience members rather than precluding them. For example, Brixton Academy in London placed metal barricades at strategic locations on the dance floor to stop audience members in the back from pushing forward and placing too much pressure on audience members in the front. The large festivals have huge security forces to monitor

audiences. Since security generally works with audience members rather than against them, serious injury is infrequent. However, the specter of serious injury is part of the urban lore of rock concerts.

27. Individuals at the front of zone one are packed so closely that they are often unable to move. While this makes these individuals exhibit some similarity to those in zone two, their spectatorship is still very physically oriented. Some people may even dance using their heads, but they will generally use a side-to-side motion, because the vertical motion is recognized as "headbanging," part of the metal genre from which indie people distance themselves.

28. "Rave friends" are involved in dance culture rather than in gig culture.

29. This issue of spontaneous performance and conventionalized ritual will be dealt with in detail in chapter 5.

30. Those who are in romantic relationships do not usually feel a social void by leaving music and are therefore much more likely to leave the music scene than their single counterparts.

31. Many readers of the weekly press see a paper as having a single voice rather than as the hotbed of debate between journalists. Readers complain when the papers present contradictory evaluations or present reversals of previous evaluations. In a response to a letter-writer charging the paper with a "build 'em up, knock 'em down" editorial policy, NME editor Steve Sutherland characterized the process in the following manner: "(1) Writer discovers band and gets all excited. (2) Other writers, fired by that enthusiasm, champion that band. (3) Debut single and album come out and, quite naturally, those writers want to enthuse you, the readers, about them. (4) The public takes to the band. (5) In order that we don't repeat ourselves, other writers, who have different opinions, get their chance to have their say about said band. Sometimes they are critical. This is because, contrary to myth, music papers are made up of people who disagree and argue all the time" (NME, January 23, 1993). Although most bands find their indie press coverage conforming to this principle—initially positive and then later negative—this is not always the case. If a band is heavily supported by a powerful editor, he will not allocate a piece to a writer whom he knows will slate "his" band. However, a negative review in a different section of the paper may be run by a different editor. Thus, a positive review could be found in the album reviews section and negative comments in a live gig review or a feature within the same issue. Because readers perceive the papers as having a single voice rather than many different writers expressing different views on the same topic, these contradictions between different writers' opinions are often viewed as hypocritical or as a plot to take down bands that have a modicum of success.

32. Moving farther back from the stage into the very outposts of zone two may also be necessary because of hearing loss. Since the sound generally emanates from the speaker stacks at the sides of the stage, standing farther back is a means of reducing sound levels. For the older people who stand in zone two who have attended hundreds of gigs, serious ear damage may have taken place. For many, there is a choice between exacerbating a condition of tinnitus, wearing earplugs, standing as far back as possible, or no longer coming to gigs. A surprisingly small number of people select earplugs—the music does not sound as good, and people see it as a sign of age. Older fans remember when they were young and laughed at older fans at gigs whom they saw wearing earplugs.

Chapter 3. Zone Three and the Music Industry (pp. 122–153)

1. The relative number of people in zone three varies wildly, depending on the number of professionals, the number of people who are not enjoying the performance, and the size of the band's fan base.

2. These terms are not used in the United States, except by those involved in the British music scene.

3. Historically, the term "punter" was used to refer to the individuals who paid for the company of prostitutes. Punting is a form of boating that is popular at public universities, and it entails the use of long poles to push a boat down a river. The slang use of punting may have evolved from the motion of inserting and reinserting a pole into water, thereby becoming slang for sexual contact in the same way that "screwing" is in the American dialect, or "sweeping" in Italian. The use of this term for those who paid for sex with prostitutes is a provocative association when applied to the relationship between audience members and performers.

4. Liggers are people who habitually get on guest lists and are somewhat ensconced within the industry. For example, parents of band members or friends who come only to the occasional show by a particular band are not liggers.

5. According to the *Oxford English Dictionary,* the term "ligger" finds its roots in the term "lig," a cover that hung from the king's bed. Thus, ligging was identified with the process of hanging onto someone or something prominent.

6. At large gigs where zone three constitutes a large physical portion of the venue, there is usually a particular side of zone three where industry members tend to congregate. For example, at the Forum in Kentish Town, zone three was very large. Industry personnel habitually stood on the right side of the venue, next to a bar. Initially this appeared to me to be merely a matter of precedent; this is where they have found colleagues on previous occasions, and therefore they locate themselves in this region through convention. However, there are features in the venue that influenced the preference toward the right side. The access point between the arena and the backstage is on the right anterior side of the venue. Therefore, performers or professionals who are moving between the backstage, the bar, and the back of the venue pass through the right side. At large venues, there is a consistent correlation between side preference and backstage access point.

7. A bidding war is when record companies compete to sign a new artist. Different labels bid against each other with escalating offers. There is a great deal of prestige for the label and the individuals involved in winning a bidding war. Interestingly, the eventual success or failure of the band is far less significant to a professional's career advancement than the prestige that comes from winning the band to one's label in the first place.

8. Senior personnel may also attend an unsigned band's performance when the band is the focus of a bidding war. This is a power play to demonstrate to the band the label's commitment to them.

9. This is actually a rather modest approximation. Junior squad members will attend several gigs in a single night at several venues, four to six nights a week, generally for about two years. Individuals settling into more established positions attend performances between two and four nights a week and will do so for several years, with occasional vacations. When one particular industry insider calculated the number of shows she had attended in the last ten years for me, she figured it to be over ten thousand band sets.

10. Artists are paid no royalties on any of the promotional products or recordings exchanged in this manner.

11. A tight list is one with few positions available.

12. I was often asked the difference between my colleagues in the United States and the United Kingdom. For Americans, particularly West Coast professionals, the appearance of not putting in too much effort is far more important than getting in on the guest list. If one needs to make more than one or two calls, the professional usually purchases a ticket so that it will be waiting for him or her at the door. Gigs do not play as important a role in the American industry. American record in-

dustry professionals attend far fewer shows, and most shows do not have ligs associated with them. For the American industry, dining with colleagues in the correct restaurants plays a role similar to that of gigs in the United Kingdom. Even at the huge conferences, such as CMJ (*College Music Journal*'s Music Marathon) in New York or South by Southwest in Austin, Texas, a significant number of professionals do not leave the hotel bars except to go to dinner with a colleague, seeing perhaps one or two bands during a five-day event.

13. Experienced scenesters realize that at shows no one knows everyone, and that if one comports oneself with the appropriate demeanor one can walk backstage with or without a pass. The major modes of professional behavior exhibited at access points are haste, nonchalance, or abject boredom. Professional fans may show up to performances early, waltz into the soundcheck, plop down somewhere with a bored expression, and be left alone until the show begins. Only by acting excited or confused or otherwise drawing attention to themselves will their presence be questioned.

14. I showed many industry professionals the videotapes of guest list transactions, and this interaction was selected repeatedly as exemplary of good door strategy. However, on one occasion when my friends from Domino Records came to Los Angeles, we were examining the videotape when this interaction caught everyone's attention. Two people shouted out, "That's a good one," but the third said, "Wait a minute, I know Emma F——and that's not her." I later confirmed that this was indeed a blag: the interaction that seemed to display so perfectly the professional strategy of the guest list interaction was actually a performance that so perfectly embodied the ideal that it demonstrated the norms better than ordinary professional strategy.

15. Code switching is an alteration between two different styles of speech that can include switching between languages, dialects, or linguistic registers.

16. This has implications for routine 1, in which the guest does not code-switch: because she was attempting to get in using the name of another, her concern would not end with the name being found on the list but rather when the entire transaction was successfully accomplished.

17. Generally, photo passes allow access in this region for the first three songs only.

18. Guest passes are often collected and treated as valued objects—an outgrowth of saving ticket stubs and other performance mementos, a practice common among indie music fans. Many professionals keep pass collections, in shoeboxes, framed on walls, stuck on room doors, on refrigerators, and on wardrobes. After a few years of professional status, professionals acquire a huge number of passes. They become more selective in the passes they retain, keeping only key bands or high-status passes. Many professionals eventually retain laminates alone.

19. There are some notable exceptions: J.K., a well-known pop music impresario and a fixture in the backstage areas at summer festivals, brings and wears what appears to be every laminate he has ever acquired. However, most professionals find his display of passes something of a joke.

20. Sexual behavior is discussed in chapter 6.

21. Those in the industry who still look to gigs for meaning find the most conflict between the requirements of being a professional and the desire to still experience music in the live setting. These individuals will be considered in my final chapter.

Chapter 4. The Participant Structure and
the Metaphysics of Spectatorship (pp. 154–186)

1. The idea that gaze acknowledges status is very important in offstage behavior as well. Backstage ligs are often characterized by conversations in which speakers do

not make a good deal of eye contact with one another and rather converse while scanning the room and monitoring the high-status individuals present.

2. This was not a typical venue, but a pub with no cover charge. Therefore, there were fewer people there for the express purpose of watching the band, as well as a cross-section of ages not characteristic of the indie community. When I commented to my two companions about this man's behavior, they both looked at me with horror, and one said, "Don't go near him, he's looking to fight." Obviously, his antagonistic behavior was recognized as aberrant.

3. Showcases are composed primarily of professionals who actively eschew standing in the front. During the early and mid-1990s, Water Rats in Kings Cross often showcased new talent. At these performances, zone one was, for the most part, empty (with the exception of photographers), but the region in back was packed with professionals.

4. This was the case of the man in Brixton who stood adjacent to the stage and turned his back to the performers. His actions demonstrate that both comportment and location are legible communicative acts articulating the quality of affiliation.

5. The consensus-building dimension of gig participation is in line with Emile Durkheim's notion of ritual acting to reify the social group (Durkheim 1995).

6. It is interesting to note that according to Western conventions, interpersonal distance attributes greater social distance and therefore is often used to impute status differentials between social actors.

7. I specify *habitual* denizens of each zone because those in zone three who do not like the specific performance are not habitual members of this zone. Those who do not like the performance do not privilege their spectatorship as the other members of zone three do. However, these individuals, like most indie fans, will usually privilege their own discernment in assessing the quality of bands.

8. In many ways becoming a member of the industry is a way to continue to participate in gigs after an individual's "sell by" date, with people in their thirties and a few in their forties still attending gigs.

9. Friedlander also notes that American folk and country music were a "synthesis of black and white musical forms" (Friedlander 1996: 16). Barlow notes that the term "blues" has its origins in an English expression (Barlow 1989). Each has European and West African elements.

10. Jazz has also been explicitly discussed as having both European and West African antecedents: "[Jazz] is the result of a 300-year-old blending in the United States of two great musical traditions, the European and the West African . . . The call and response pattern occurs throughout jazz . . . Another characteristic of jazz that comes from West Africa may be called the falsetto break" (Stearns 1970: 3). This is not to dilute the influence of other traditions on these music forms, nor to underestimate the influence of the slave experience on the content of these music styles. My interest at this time is to show connection to a particular cultural-religious system.

11. This slippage is due in part to American ethnic identity politics, in which the devising of an African American cultural identity is linked to "Africa." Scholars recognize that the majority of African Americans are the descendents of West African slaves. This is not unlike the creation of a Latino identity, where the huge diversity of South American and Central American populations are lumped together in a single category to form a larger political ethnic base.

12. Currently, the slave trade in Africa exploits the populations of Central and East Africa, particularly in the Sudan. The travesty of slavery is not a thing of the past.

13. Scholars traditionally have characterized this interdependence of parts of a social system as "functional integration."

14. It should be evident that I find this separation equally artificial and misleading for Western societies as well. It is a Western vanity to conceive of art as having meaning in itself, devoid of its cultural context. This idea of an isolated art object, as discussed below, is the product of Western historic developments and cultural practices. For example, positing masterpiece value to work from another era suggests that it has qualities beyond its cultural context. Valuing the artistic productions of past eras is an essential practice of the concept that the meaning of art lies in the object itself. It suggests that art can transcend time and place.

15. Possession trance can be induced either by increasing or by decreasing sensory stimulation. Techniques to increase stimulation include "singing, chanting, drumming, clapping, monotonous dancing, inhaling incense or other fumes and the repetitive play of light and dark" (Crapanzano 1987: 13).

16. In a discussion of Ewe drumming, Seth Cudjoe reports that the drum master may have drum initiates lie face down while he "beats the rhythms into their body and soul," once again underscoring the importance of the physicality involved in musical and spiritual apprehension (Cudjoe 1953: 284).

17. For more on the multivocality of spirit possession, see Boddy 1989 and Stoller 1995.

18. "Lining" refers to the practice of singing a number of notes into one syllable of text.

19. The different philosophies of the Catholic and Protestant Churches in their approaches to indigenous traditions and belief systems is worthy of a separate study but beyond my discussion here. The Catholic policy of cooptation rather than outlawing has more than a little to do with New Orleans being one of the few places in the continental United States where religious drumming was not banned. The consequences of Protestant and Catholic philosophies regarding native religious practices for music in America, particularly jazz, can hardly be understated. However, the ban on drumming by Protestants in other regions did not remove the importance of percussion for African American religious expression. As Lynne Emery characterizes it, "Drums were prohibited and yet the rhythms of Africa lived on in new forms among the slaves as base feet stomped on hard earth, hands clapped and songs were sung" (Emery 1972: 80). For more on the influence of West African religions in the regions of Catholic colonialism and the African Diaspora, see Donald Cosentino's brilliant *Sacred Arts of Haitian Vodou* (1995), Migene Gonzalez-Wippler's *Santeria: African Magic in Latin America* (1973), James Houk's *Spirits, Blood, and Drums: The Orisha Religion in Trinidad* (1995), Robert Voek's *Sacred Leaves of Candomblé : African Magic, Medicine, and Religion in Brazil* (1997), and Robert Farris Thompson's *Flash of the Spirit* (1983), which includes material on both Protestant and Catholic contexts. For more on traditions in areas of Protestant slavery, see Albert Raboteau's *Slave Religion: "The Invisible Institution" in the Antebellum South* (1978), or Mechal Sobel's *Trabelin' On: The Slave Journey to an Afro-Baptist Faith* (1979).

20. The concept of intense mental focus as a form of listening is also expressed as a theme by interviewees in a 1932 English text *Music and Its Lovers*. For example, "Unless one follows every note and feels its relationship with the others, one is not listening" (Lee 1932: 35).

21. Small goes so far as to characterize the concert hall as a sacred space and aptly notes the correspondences between patterns of behavior of audience members and church congregants (Small 1998).

22. There are singular challenges in trying to characterize Western and Christian attitudes toward dance, because there are a multitude of denominations and varied Church histories with a variety of attitudes expressed over time. Many denominations are also the result of syncretism, such as Pentecostalism. Both Jewish and early

Christian traditions had dance celebrations. The negative attitude toward dance was intensified during the sixteenth century. A fear of sensuality in dance meant that there were often penalties for dancing within Christianity: "Some Christians hold any glorification of the body, including dancing, anathema; outspoken enemies of physicality with as ascetic dislike of eroticism which could undermine faith and un-settle the hierarchy of the status quo, they preach the ideal of the Virgin" (Hanna 1987: 204). The examples of preachers railing against dance are legion.

23. Drums are included only in a few scattered, atypical cases in Christianity. Interestingly, this includes the Ethiopian Coptics, where the incorporation of drums is often attributed to their central importance in the indigenous traditions of West Africa (Lévi-Strauss 1973). Drums and percussion "are so integral that even re-ligious traditions of Near Eastern origin—Falasha Jews, Coptic Christians, and Is-lamic Sufis—overcome reservations widespread among the non-African branches of their respective religious traditions to the extent of allowing some liturgical drumming by members, leaders, and priests" (Ellingson 1987: 496).

24. As my subject is music in the United Kingdom and the United States, the context for its development was broadly Protestant. The Catholic city of New Or-leans provided a very different context. As I noted, it was one of the few places in the United States where drums were not banned. Slaves and ex-slaves had the right to gather. Just five years after the Louisiana Purchase, new ordinances were put in place to curtail dancing and congregating by "people of color" in Congo Square. A quote from 1853 illustrates Catholicism's more open attitude toward indigenous practices: "Since I have seen in Cuba the negroes in their savage, original state—seen their dances, heard their songs, and am able to compare them with what they are at the best in the United States, there remains no longer a doubt in my mind as to the beneficial influence of Anglo-American culture on the negro . . . there is a vast, vast difference between the screeching improvisation of the negroes in Cuba, and the inspired and inspiring preaching of the savior which I have heard extem-porized in South Carolina, Georgia, Maryland, and Louisiana. And low and sensual is that lawless life, and intoxication of the senses in those wild negro-dancers, and those noisy festivities to the beat of the drum, compared with that life and that spir-itual intoxication in song and prayer and religious joy" (Fredrika Bremer in John-son 1999: 21).

25. For most people, habitual residency in zone three is merely a blip on one's journey to the exit. However, there are significant exceptions within the profes-sional class.

26. For example, the explicit rationale for banning African drums in the United States was the perception of their use for revolt, a perspective that has been roundly critiqued by Christopher Johnson (Johnson 1999). Drumming was military for the West and therefore viewed as a signal of revolt when used by slaves. However, an implicit rationale was to be found in the anxiety expressed over their use in rituals, which was viewed as sexual, heathen, and immoral. There are cases of drumming playing an important role in military function, such as in Haiti, where an entire class of gods, the Petro loa, are associated with military action (Cosentino 1995, Deren 1953). This has been attributed to European providence within the Vodou re-ligious system (Averill and Yuen-Ming 2003).

27. The comments that refer to paganism are particularly informative, as a pagan is differentiated from a heathen by an association with polytheism. This connection comes from the root of the word "pagan," which referred to those of the country. During Christianity's initial success, urban areas were the centers of Christian in-struction. Those people in villages and outlying areas were more likely to continue to worship the polytheistic gods. The West African religions were also polytheistic, and the rock pantheon, with its multiple idols, suggests a polytheistic character.

28. Much has been written on the connection between colonialism, missionaries, and the origins of anthropology and ethnography: see Asad 1973, Clifford 1988, Clifford and Marcus 1986, and Miller 1990. At this time I'm not concerned with the origin of this narrative imperative, but rather with the fact that this narrative continues to express itself and generate similar representations.

29. The waltz was met in Europe with a moral outrage regarding its style of dance, in which partners would touch each other.

30. Here I use "Protestant" in the broad sense of the religions that flourished in protest against the Catholic faith. The United States and the United Kingdom are broadly Protestant. However, Anglican Protestantism is more complicated in terms of the issue of centralized authority. The Church of England shares much in common with the structural organization of the Catholic faith, in that the head of the royal family serves as the head of the Church just as the pope serves as head of the Catholic Church. The English civil war was fought by the supporters of the distributed power of Parliament, who were primarily Puritans, and the Royalist supporters of the king and his centralized authority.

31. The teddy boy was a style movement of the 1950s. Young men (teds) wore clothes that were linked to the Edwardian period—long jackets with velvet collars and drain-pipe trousers. The requisite hairstyle was a greased quiff in the front, sideburns, and a ducktail in the back. "Teddy" is the diminutive of "Edward."

32. Some have criticized Weber for using the term "Protestantism" because the premises of his argument were based on Calvinism (Campbell 1987).

33. Pearson notes that the historical claims regarding the imminent moral decay of Britain are attributed repetitively to the same causes of newfound affluence and excessive freedom, foreign influence (American, Irish, or Italian), the demoralizing influences of amusements as an incitement to crime, and a hot-blooded spiritedness of the people. These are precisely the same claims levied at youth cultures today. Although the locus of the foreign keeps moving, the newfound affluence keeps rising, and the forms of the amusements keep changing.

34. This search for the enemy within society can also be seen in the American "red scare," during which communists were thought to be undermining American capitalist values.

35. The payola scandal was the government crackdown at the behest of ASCAP (American Society of Composers, Authors, and Publishers) on the practice of paying DJs cash or giving them gifts in return for airplay. ASCAP was the dominant licenser of songs and initially ignored rock and roll, allowing BMI (Broadcast Music, Inc.) to quickly embrace it and gain a major foothold in popular music. ASCAP attributed rock and roll's success to payola. "Payola" is the contraction of the words "pay" and "Victrola," reflecting money paid to play records. Payola is illegal, but most record companies have marketing specialists who travel the country taking radio station music directors out for dinners and providing any other perk they can ply legally.

36. This narrative organization within the gig's participant structure raises important questions regarding ritual. Ritual cannot transform an individual's sensibility without one's participation in that cultural system. Without an opening to spirit possession, one will not experience possession. Similarly, the person who does not believe in the power of the healer is unlikely to have a placebo effect from his participation in a ritual healing event. Without some participation in the cultural system, these different participatory modes are merely differences. Experiences are interpreted through acculturated perceptions and sensibilities (Turner 1974). The understanding of these events for a participant occurs within a situated religious and cultural context. Yet, the power of ritual stems in part from the mechanisms of transformation not being fully understood by participants.

37. This mutually produced contrast could easily be expressed as the tension between the Apollonian and Dionysian; both are recurrent conflicts for indie's brand of rock and roll.

38. Not all participants make this transformation. The majority of those who do not leave the music community choose to function in some professional capacity for the music industry, whether it is as performers, journalists, record company executives, or in some other institutional domain. These people will be discussed in the final chapter on ritual practitioners.

Chapter 5. Performance, Authenticity, and Emotion (pp. 187–202)

1. NIN is the abbreviation for Nine Inch Nails, an American band.

2. Fred Pfeil has also written that rock fans generally "expect continuity and coherence from stars between on and offstage" (Pfeil 1995: 81). This contrasts with hip-hop, in which authenticity, "keeping it real," is largely constituted by addressing the hip-hop community. Music does not need to reflect one's personal life but instead the life of community members (Morgan 1993). The same has been noted by Charles Keil with regard to blues musicians: "the bluesman's first obligation is to his public" (Keil 1966: 155).

3. One cellist remarked to me that whenever he performed, he felt that the audience was listening solely to see if he made a mistake, not for anything his rendition added. This comment shows his adherence to his music community's idea of performance as execution rather than creation.

4. This is particularly interesting given that indie does not permit soloing. Without soloing, there is little room for true improvisation—indie musicians consistently need to coordinate their music to a prewritten song. At its heart, then, indie is actually very different from jazz. In jazz, virtuosity is valued. In indie, virtuosity is seen as institutional training that removes one from the direct experience of music.

5. The supposed unreturnable gaze of the audience is a striking dimension of gig spectacle. The visual set-up for gigs is to let a viewing subject see and maintain an illusion of not being seen in return. Because the performers are brightly lit and the audience is in shadow, the audience can behave as though they are not being looked at by performers. The spectator indulges in the voyeuristic pleasure that one's looking is not returned. When an audience member does see a performer look at him, it is subject to skepticism and debate. Outside a gig, I brought up the topic of audience members' acting as if they cannot be seen to a guitarist and his girlfriend. She had been to many gigs and said there were times when she saw performers look directly at her:

> E.B.: *I've been in the audience and I think . . . No, they can't be looking at me.*
> B.B.: *Well, they are. I can see everything. I spend the whole show looking at the audience to see how it is progressing, to see how loud or how timid they are, to see if we can play the slow songs. If they are being violent and kicking each other.*

Despite an inordinate amount of evidence to the contrary, audience members act as if they cannot be seen by the band. Why, despite their inexperience of visual perceptive distances, do audience members want to indulge this illusion? Being a member of an audience removes the responsibility that comes with prolonged looking in non-spectorial contexts. In conversations, prolonged looking has different social implications. Being a member of an audience at a show, a drama, or a sporting event allows one to gaze with a voyeuristic pleasure that comes from visual apprehension without responsibility.

6. There is an obvious voyeuristic sexual component to this observation. The gendered nature of spectatorship in music performance will be dealt with in the next chapter.

7. In a *Spin* magazine article, the "Oh" facial expression was referred to as "the catfish."

8. This can be contrasted with the Japanese conventions of appropriateness, which carries the correct emotion. A good gift is the conventional gift; it demonstrates that the giver possesses the correct emotion.

9. A particularly good example of this is the naming of the shoe-gazers bands as the "Scene that Celebrates Itself." Within a week of this term being applied as a compliment, the bands included in this scene were criticized as being conformist.

10. There are several songs and numerous covers of the songs with this line in it; the Creation's "How Does It Feel to Feel" (also recorded by Ride, the Godfathers, Chopper, Halo of Flies), Swervedriver's "Sandblasted," and Adorable's "Sunshine Smile." Variants of the line are found in the Wannadies "How Does It Feel?," Oasis's "Live Forever," Puressence's "How Does It Feel?" and of course Dylan's famous call "How does it feel?" as a refrain on "Like a Rolling Stone."

11. This is the artist's modification of the famous lines from Shakespeare's *Hamlet*. In act 3, scene 3, the king reflects on the emptiness of his prayers and states "My words fly up, my thoughts remain below. Words without thoughts never to heaven go."

12. There are some individuals who are highly resistant to repetition, who do not become distanced from repeated exposure. These individuals are most likely to become ritual practitioners.

13. This is one of the reasons that musicians usually move directly from zone one to zone three. Very soon after performers have a modicum of success, they find it impossible to play the fan role they had once held. The high concentration of experience distances them very quickly from the front of the stage.

14. When older fans were novices, they did not have the background to recognize the older bands' influences or comment on their "derivativeness."

15. This is not to say that all members of the indie community eventually leave music and deny the veracity of emotion. Some individuals decide to make music their livelihood and look to it for emotional resonance. However, embedded in a culture that links authenticity with novelty, this produces skepticism toward the veracity, value, and reliability of emotions.

Chapter 6. Sex and the Ritual Practitioners (pp. 203–241)

1. While male close-ups are extremely rare, there are three general exceptions. First is the close-up of the impassive male spectator, juxtaposed with the image of a hysterical female (see the Beatles on the *Ed Sullivan Show* in *The Beatles First U.S. Tour*). Second is the male obviously under the influence of pharmacological substances (see Altamont in the Rolling Stone's *Gimme Shelter*). Third is the male who directly addresses the camera eye (the Monomen in *Hype*).

2. Interestingly, this depiction of young women as overly invested and susceptible to influence is also characteristic of the discourse for Gothic and Romantic novels (Campbell 1987).

3. The mere presence of females in a privileged area often leads to the assumption that they have been brought there for sexual purposes and that they are willing sexual partners: "Somebody in the Depeche Mode camp obviously likes young girls. After the show in Hungary, there was a whole retinue of them, fresh-faced pubescents, some unable to speak English, clad in stockings and suspenders. I mean how did these girls get there? Who rounded them up? The girls are always there for the band and crew when they need to be entertained. There is a girl from France who is following them all across Europe, she met them during the last tour in Paris and now is

provided with passage and tickets everywhere she goes" (*NME*, September 18, 1993). This description of the presence of females is enough to imply that their purpose is for the sexual satisfaction of the band. What other reason would there be for females to be around? There is no such questioning of the presence of males.

4. The de facto roles of female watcher and male watchee are well established in rock and roll. From a piece entitled "Maximum Rock and Roll": "The pub mirror catches the reflection of Keith Moon, Roger Daltry, and John Entwhistle mucking about, looning around on the way to the Goldhawk Social Club. The girls giggle and blush with embarrassment. The boys are going to work and the girls are going to watch" (*Sounds*, October 18, 1975).

5. Paul McDonald develops a discussion of this inversion by making the male body the object of the spectacle of desire in "Feeling and Fun" (McDonald 1997).

6. When indie editors wish to interject a comment into a piece written by another author, they will put their interjections in italics.

7. The film footage of the arrival of the Beatles in the United States is a particularly good example of this archetypal representation of female spectatorship.

8. This idea is also addressed by Simon Frith, who notes the contradiction of treating the context of male spectatorship as desexualized when males are viewing other males performing (Frith 1991).

9. Norma Coates asserts a similar argument about groupies in reference to an exposé in *Rolling Stone* in 1969: "The presence of groupies in their rock scene also helps to expunge the specter of homosexuality that haunts the homosociality of rock music performance and male fandom" (Coates 2003).

10. A complete version of the quiz, with point values for all answers, appears in appendix 3.

11. There is a general, but flexible, status hierarchy for bands: the singer and the guitarist (the voice and the guitar voice) hold the highest positions. Then comes the bass player (referred to in a joke as "a cross between a musician and a drummer"), the drummer (in another joke characterized as one "who hangs out with musicians"), the manager and/or tour manager, the guitar tech and sound team, and the drum tech. However, a particularly attractive or talented musician or member of the entourage may move up the hierarchy.

12. There have been several tell-all books written by women who have been serially sexually involved with musicians: see Bebe Buell, *Rebel Heart* (2002); Pamela Des Barres, *I'm with the Band: Confessions of a Groupie* (1991); Connie Hamzy, *Rock Groupie: The Intimate Adventures of "Sweet Connie" from Little Rock* (1995).

13. In an academic article, Norma Coates refers to groupies as "grotesques" (Coates 2003).

14. At the same time that young females experience sexual desire, they are given the social responsibility to learn to put limits on sexual activity (Ehrenreich, Hess, and Jacobs 1992). The young female who becomes indiscriminately sexually active is called a "slag" or a "slut" or any one of a litany of negative social epithets. As has been well documented, there is no derogatory masculine equivalent; indeed, a sexually promiscuous young male is likely to be evaluated in positive terms (White 2003). Positioning females as the regulators of sexual activity places females in the double bind of wanting to have sex but also having to control those desires. Distant and erotic, bands become an important outlet for the temporary resolution of this conflict. Sexual attraction to performers in bands allows young girls to indulge in the desire to have sex without any of the anxiety-ridden consequences of actually doing so. For more, see Cline 1992 and Ehrenreich, Hess, and Jacobs 1992.

15. In the early 2000s, there has been a sea change in the UK music scene. With the increase in drinking and the tacit acceptance of young women acting like "lads," the music scene has become much more sexually ribald. For more see note 58.

16. In one case, while I was sitting in a coffeehouse with a female informant who regularly traveled city to city following a particular band, her good friend behind the counter referred to her as a groupie to another male patron, though she had never talked to or initiated contact with any member of the band. Her friend was referring to her non-sexual fan behavior, but this male patron looked over at the woman with an expression of scorn and disgust.

17. The context of a sexualized fanship badgers female industry professionals (Cline 1992). Many professional women refuse to date performers. If they do, they try to keep it quiet so as not to affect their professional status. This ban on dating performers does not apply to male record company personnel, however, since going out with a female performer does not undermine their status as a professional. There is no assumption that one's participation in the industry is for the purpose of obtaining sexual liaisons with performers. It is female sexualized spectatorship and the mythic image of the groupie that creates the double standards. Ironically, the term "groupie" is most often used by women about other women as a form of censure.

18. John Harris notes that the chorus of this song, "Line up in line," referred to "Frischmann's wry observation that the music press was in the ongoing habit of placing groups on its conveyor belt, well knowing that all but a few would quickly topple off" (Harris 2003: 134).

19. This can also be seen in the joke about groupies from the screw in the light bulb cycle: How many groupies does it take to change a light bulb?. . .Never let a groupie change a light bulb. She'll blow the fuse. Blowing is slang for fellatio. The ingestion of semen has interesting ritual connections in other societies. Semen may be conceived as a potent source of concentrated spiritual substance. In the male initiation rites of the Eastern highland region of Papua New Guinea, male initiates ingest the semen of older males as a way of transferring masculine power from one generation to the next (Herdt 1982). Male sexual substance is there considered necessary in order for men to create men. Thus there is an interesting potential connection between ingesting semen and incorporating masculine power from the donor.

20. The term "slapper" is British slang for a sexually promiscuous woman.

21. Frischmann entered public awareness as an artist and a sexual partner to not one but two well-known and successful indie music performers—Brett Anderson and Damon Albarn. Despite her history she distances herself from the category of groupie by criticizing this stereotype in a song.

22. John Blacking also notes gender inversion among Venda musicians: "One might go so far as to say that in Venda society, outstanding musicians are often people who depart from the innate nature of their sex. The best female musicians are aggressively masculine and the best males are rather unapologetically feminine" (Blacking 1976). The androgyne is also a venerable tradition in mainstream rock (Whiteley 1997).

23. For an extended discussion of the hypermasculine, the hyperfeminine, gender inverting, and gender blending in rock music via the analysis of music, musical personae, and lyric content, see Reynolds and Press 1996.

24. A "cover" is a performance of a song originally written and performed by another. The history of this term for music is a rather interesting province of study, as many of the earliest performers did not write their own music and would select from an existent repertoire of songs they wished to perform. In other cases, songwriters would write songs for a specific artist. In other genres, it is common to perform songs made famous by other performers. For example, the performance of a classic number in jazz is called a "standard," and one's rendition is thought to reveal one's individual musical abilities.

25. Sara Cohen also notes that the high placement of the guitar conveys a different significance than its lower position at the pelvis (Cohen 1997).

26. The guitar as a symbol of sexual union goes some way toward making sense of the informal joke: "You can make any guy more sexually appealing by putting a guitar around his neck." In an article by Mavis Bayton, a female guitarist muses on the electric guitar and guitar placement: "I've always thought guitars are really sexy . . . I like the fact they're slung where they are . . . It's all about sex, really" (Bayton 1997: 45). There are other guitar designs, of course. For example, the Flying V has an entirely different body shape. Instead of a curvaceous body, the neck of the guitar extends into two geometric triangles that make the entire guitar look like a giant V. This guitar augments only masculine components, "the ultimate expression of the electric guitar's phallic imagery" (Trynka 1993: 95). Many of my female informants mentioned that they reviled this guitar. When I asked why, I was repeatedly told, "It's ugly."

27. The proliferation of slash fiction around musicians supports this assertion. Slash fiction is fan writing that imagines sexual contact between fictional or public performers and is generally characterized by same-sex liaisons between otherwise heterosexual characters.

28. As I noted in chapter 3, professionals with privileged access generally use discreet pass placement and therefore are not necessarily obvious to fans in the audience.

29. In indie, there is no sexual bartering to gain passes or access. For indie, the idea of bartering sex is considered heinous and is actually as reviled by crew as by the general community.

30. This is a very common line in lyrics and song titles. It is a song title on Primal Scream's award-winning *Screamadelica* album, Spiritualized's *Ladies and Gentlemen We Are Floating in Space,* and the Beatles' *Abbey Road.*

31. Soundscan tracks the sales of records at retail outlets throughout the United States by compiling registered sales by bar code.

32. The system of publishing rights was developed in the era of songwriting teams comprised of a musician and a lyricist. Publishing companies would sell sheet music to be used by artists and the public in their own homes. The lyricist and the musician would split royalties evenly. This tradition has generally resulted in a disparity of payments for members of the same band. Because the guitar player and singer are usually the primary songwriters, the contributions of drummer and bassist are often not listed in songwriting credits. The result is that two members of a band have income and two live in abject poverty despite their moderate success. This disparity in pay-outs from the only real source of income for most bands is one of the primary reasons that bands break up. The distribution of publishing funds and songwriting credits becomes a key point of dispute and puts pressure on each band member to have their own songwriting credit. Hence, another part of the musician joke cycle: What's the last thing a drummer says in a band? Hey guys— why don't we try one of my songs? The disparity in status and funds between members of bands manifests itself in the sexual politics of bands as well. Band members disproportionately take advantage of the sex available on the road. The members of the rhythm section, who are less likely to receive material rewards, are more likely to pursue carnal ones.

33. Often the only income band members get on tour are their PDs (per diems), the money they are given by the tour manager each day for food and expenses. These range between £5 and £50, with an average of £15.

34. Some have claimed the analytic category of trickster is over-generalized. Lewis Hyde addresses this issue by observing that "indigenous terms doubtless allow a fuller feeling for trickster's sacred complexity" (Hyde 1998: 7). He then goes

on to argue that there is no single trickster but a common mythological trope with countless culture-specific variations (Hyde 1998; see also Hynes and Doty 1993). He suggests that tricksters are treated with different degrees of seriousness in different cultures. In West African religions, the trickster plays a pivotal role. In his discussion of the emergence of the blues, William Barlow also cites West African trickster folktales as highly influential. Given its West African influences, it is not surprising that the trickster is part of rock and roll's heredity (Barlow 1989).

35. Cross-culturally, tricksters generally appear as males or are referred to as he. Yet trickster is sexually flexible. Tricksters often physically transform themselves into other guises, including females. An example of this is the Clackamas Chinook narrative "The Wife Who 'Goes Out' Like a Man" (Hymes 1981). There are also female tricksters, such as the Hopi Kokopelli Mana, who appear alongside male counterparts.

36. The term "buffoon" comes from the denigration of the Count de Buffon, who rightfully supported evolutionary theory. The buffoon, the fool, is derived from discounting a man who told a truth that society did not want to hear.

37. In some trickster narratives, trickster also violates incest taboos. Trickster's sexual impulses display a blatant disregard for social consequences. Some scholars, such as Lewis Hyde, suggest that the potential reproductive consequences of sexually profligate behavior for females may be one reason why female tricksters appear less frequently in the literature.

38. Leather trousers are quite uncommon for indie performers, as they are viewed as part of the clichéd imagery of the mainstream, and therefore as inauthentic. Within the indie community, a musician wearing leather trousers is often ridiculed even by members of his own band (B.S.).

39. Edmund Leach, Claude Lévi-Strauss, and Mary Douglas all conceive of the taboo as being that which does not fit neatly into a culture's categories. The taboo has ritual value, whether it be high or low. Dirt, by definition, is taboo because it is unclean. For example, the "unclean" aspects of the body violate the boundary between self and world: blood, mucus, hair, scabs, excrement, urine, and so on (Douglas 1966). The taboo trickster also invokes Julia Kristeva's notion of the abject, the symbolic complications between sign and signified, subject and object, and identity and other in the context of the ontogenetic development of the individual (Kristeva 1982). Her notion of the abject standing in for a terrifying nothingness is rather suggestive of the trickster figure, whose violations of cultural categories reveals culture's artifice and meaninglessness outside of its own self-proscribed system.

40. In his study of southern folklore, Harry Hyatt collected the emotionally resonant but historically inaccurate narratives of musical performers going to the crossroads to gain preternatural skills (Hyatt 1970). This legend is most famously attributed to Robert Johnson, who purportedly sold his soul to the devil in return for his musical prowess. This attribution has been extensively examined by Elijah Wald in his *Escaping the Delta: Robert Johnson and the Invention of the Blues* (Wald 2004). Wald suggests that this narrative is the romantic desire by modern white audiences to associate the blues with "mysterious demonic forces" (Wald 2004: 266). The crossroads is an important feature of this narrative, a sacred junction in Vodou and West African possession rites. The cross is the intersection of the mundane world of humans and the divine world of the gods. Gods and humans use this intersection to communicate and to become mutually energized. This narrative is a wonderful example of the way in which the venerable connection between humans and the polytheistic gods of a non-Western tradition are reframed as devilry. The soulselling narrative exhibits great similarity to the legend of Jack o' the Lantern, who tricks the devil while on a road and ends his life with no place in the afterworld. Jack wanders the earth tricking other travelers to their deaths.

41. The majority of these can be found in *Q* magazine's "50 Most Outrageous Incidents in Rock and Roll" (December 2003), which were culled from newspaper accounts, legends, and primary sources such as musician interviews and band biographies and autobiographies. The last example was an account given to me by an internationally successful musician.

42. The guitarist Slash from Guns and Roses recounted in interviews being carried to his room in an alcoholic stupor and soiling himself in the elevator.

43. Many rock musicians' biographies and autobiographies provide accounts of heroin use and descents into drug addiction: *Hammer of the Gods* (Davis 2001), *No One Here Gets Out Alive* (Sugerman and Hopkins 1995), *Walk This Way: The Autobiography of Aerosmith* (Aerosmith and Davis 1999), and *Don't Try This At Home* (Navarro 2004). For more extensive examples, see *The Rolling Stone Encyclopedia of Rock & Roll* (2001), *Rock and Roll War Stories* (Gebert and Ramage 2004), and *Take a Walk on the Dark Side: Rock and Roll's Myths, Legends, and Curses* (Patterson 2004).

44. Sexual success with women has often been represented as tricksterism. In Tirso de Molina's "The Trickster of Seville," the sexually prolific ladykiller is explicitly characterized as a trickster.

45. The protagonist has been variously cast as a member of the boy band New Kids on the Block, Rod Stewart, Marc Almond, Alanis Morrissette, and Li'l Kim. In its earliest documented guise, it was attributed to Jim Nabors, better known in the United States as Gomer Pyle. Jim Nabors was initially famous as a musician. This tale type can be classified as part of the urban legend cycle in which medical science reveals a famous sex symbol to be sexually rapacious or perverse.

46. The rider stipulates the provisions required by the band from the promoter. It often has very specific requirements that alert the touring party to whether the promoter has adhered to all of the stipulations within the contract. The touring contract specifies precise equipment and performing requirements. If a band enters its dressing room and sees that food and beverage requirements have not been followed, there may be problems in other areas as well. Specific rider requirements comprise a kind of shorthand assessment that allows bands to see if promoters have met their obligations.

47. This was attributed to the band Van Halen. In folklore, green M&M candies are said to make one sexually aroused.

48. One of trickster's most important characteristics is to show us that the world we take as given is actually the world the way we have made it. Tricksters' play with our "fixtures" shows us that they merely *appear* to be fixed.

49. The classic narrative of throwing a television out of a window has been attributed to Led Zeppelin, the Who, and the Rolling Stones.

50. With portable computers and mp3 players, musicians will open CDs, upload music to their computers, and then replace them, a slightly more subtle form of thievery.

51. There wasn't a single band in my study that did not have a story of having their rider stolen by another band.

52. For indie bands, going after the girlfriend of another band member exceeds the playful and is viewed as a moral violation.

53. Alan Merriam notes that "this pattern of low status and high importance, deviant behavior and capitalization of it" characterizes musicians in a number of societies (Merriam 1964: 140). For example, the music griots of the Wolof of West Africa are allowed to behave in ways not permissible to others. They are associated with drunkenness and licentiousness and are seen being as indisposed to Islam.

54. While I use "he" here, female musicians are not excluded from this category. They too combine gender types, violate boundaries, and experience the transitivity of being on the road. Perhaps no artist illustrates this point better than Courtney Love, who has produced legions of narratives regarding her own magnificent misbehavior (Rossi 1996).

55. Christopher Small also notes that the value of mythic lore depicting the "great composers" lies not in its degree of truthfulness but in its revelation of what the present wants to take from the past. This sentiment is also expressed in the fictionalized portrayal of Tony Wilson in Michael Winterbottom's 24 *Hour Party People,* who said, "I agree with John Ford. When you have to choose between truth and the legend, print the legend."

56. As any fan of Trivial Pursuit knows, if the question asks how a musician died, the two most likely answers are plane crash or drug overdose.

57. However, bands from Manchester are an exception. They have always played by their own rules. Oasis, despite having an indie sound, openly embraced sexual and pharmacological excess. New Order violated nearly every tacitly held rule in music and has one of the longest and most influential careers in UK music. For the mythology of Manchester, see 24 *Hour Party People* (2002).

58. In the early 2000s, there has been a major shift in sexual mores, which has corresponded with the upswing of binge drinking by women and an increase in binge drinking by men. Until 2005, licensing hours generally prohibited drinking after 11:00 P.M. However, there has been a gradual relaxation of licensing laws with twenty-four hour licensing starting in November of 2005. Binge drinking has long been a characteristic of British culture, but it reached epidemic proportions in the early 2000s, with the government regularly citing studies of the increase in sick days and costs for hospitals from alcohol-related incidents. The most salient factor in the increase in drinking has been the ready access to cash from ATM machines, many of which are located in bars and pubs, and the use of credit cards at drinking establishments. Both provide ready funds on tap. The indie scene has also been affected by excessive alcohol consumption, where far more audience members exhibit the behavioral excesses associated with binge drinking, such as relaxed sexual proscriptions.

59. "Fame, fatal fame, it plays hideous tricks on the brain"—an apt commentary from the track "Frankly Mr. Shankley" by the Smiths.

60. One indie musician told me of a time when he and his bandmates had a television in their room that wouldn't work properly. The band decided to throw it out the window, only to find it merely dangling outside because they had forgotten to unplug it. When they saw cars below, they tried to pull it back into the room, to no avail. Finally a crew member unplugged it and it plunged to the ground. The band was relieved that it didn't hit the BMW below. The band then turned out the lights and hid. The musician characterized their amateurishness as not being "rock and roll" enough: "I realized I just don't have that rock and roll sensibility. If you do, you're in Motley Crue." Here, we can see the influence of the mainstream stereotype on the actual behavior of indie performers, but also how touring can produce fits of pique that result in the destruction of property.

61. Examples: (a) falls out window—Chet Baker; (b) chokes on vomit—Jimi Hendrix, Jon Bonham, Bon Scott; (c) jail—see *The Encyclopedia of Rock and Roll* for copious examples (George-Warren 2001); (d) killed by father—Marvin Gaye; (e) electrocuted—Les Harvey, Jon Rostill; (f) drowns—Jeff Buckley, Will Sinnott; (g) overdose—Keith Moon, Tim Buckley, Frankie Lymon, Gram Parsons, Sid Vicious; (h) suicide—Ian Curtis, Nick Drake, Kurt Cobain, Chris Acland, Wendy O. Williams; (i) plane crash—Patsy Cline, Buddy Holly, Richie Valens, Otis Redding, Jim Croce, Ricky Nelson.

62. In 2002, Mick Jagger was given a knighthood by the Queen of England.

63. Female coyotes have their own tricksters to deal with as well. Female musicians tend to date those professionals of the in-between—musicians, crew personnel, or managers.

64. This is another subject well deserving of more attention and further research, but it is beyond the purview of this chapter.

References

Abrahams, Roger, and John Szwed, eds. 1983. *After Africa*. New Haven: Yale University Press.

Aerosmith and Stephen Davis. 1999. *Walk This Way: The Autobiography of Aerosmith*. New York: Avon.

Appadurai, Arjun. 1990. "Topographies of the Self: Praise and Emotion in Hindu India." In *Language and the Politics of Emotions*, ed. Charles Lutz and Lila Abu-Lughod, 92–112. Cambridge: Cambridge University Press.

Apter, Emily. 1992. "Post-Colonial Seductions and the Multicultural Fetish." Paper presented at Getty Lecture Series "Shifting Boundaries/Contested Spaces," Los Angeles.

———. 1993. *Feminizing the Fetish: Psychoanalysis and Narrative Obsession in Turn-of-the-Century France*. Ithaca: Cornell University Press.

Aquila, Richard. 1989. *That Old Time Rock and Roll: A Chronicle of an Era, 1954–1963*. New York: Scribner.

Asad, Talal. 1973. *Anthropology and the Colonial Encounter*. London: Ithaca Press.

Auer, Peter, and Aldo di Luzio. 1992. *The Contextualization of Language*. Philadelphia: J. Benjamins.

Averill, Gage, and Yuen-Ming David Yih. 2003. "Militarism in Haitian Music." In *African Diaspora: A Musical Perspective*, ed. Ingrid Monson, 23–82. New York: Garland Publishing.

Babb, Lawrence. 1981. "Glancing: Visual Interaction in Hinduism." *Journal of Anthropological Research* 37, no. 4: 387–401.

Babcock, Barbara. 1978. *The Reversible World: Symbolic Inversion in Art and Society*. Ithaca: Cornell University Press.

Bakhtin, Mikhail. 1981. *The Dialogic Imagination: Four Essays*. Austin: University of Texas Press.

———. 1986. *Speech Genres and Other Late Essays*. Austin: University of Texas Press.

Bangs, Lester. 1987. *Psychotic Reactions and Carburetor Dung*. New York: Knopf.

Barlow, William. 1989. *Looking Up at Down: The Emergence of Blues Culture*. Philadelphia: Temple University Press.

Barthes, Roland. 1977. *Image-Music-Text*. New York: Hill and Wang.

Bascom, William. 1969. *The Yoruba of Southwestern Nigeria*. New York: Holt, Rinehart & Winston.

Basso, Ellen. 1985. *A Musical View of the Universe: Kalapalo Myth and Ritual Performances*. Philadelphia: University of Pennsylvania Press.

Basso, Keith. 1979. *Portraits of "the Whiteman": Linguistic Play and Cultural Symbols among the Western Apache.* Cambridge: Cambridge University Press.

Bateson, Gregory. 1958. *Naven: A Survey of the Problem Suggested by a Composite Picture of the Culture of a New Guinea Tribe Drawn from Three Points of View.* Stanford: Stanford University Press.

———. 1972. *Steps to an Ecology of the Mind.* New York: Ballantine Books.

———. 1979. *Mind and Nature: A Necessary Unity.* New York: Bantam.

———. 1985. *Balinese Character Photographic Analysis.* New York: New York Academy of Sciences.

Bayton, Mavis. 1992. "Feminist Musical Practice: Problems and Contradictions." In *Rock and Popular Music: Politics, Policies, and Institutions,* ed. Tony Bennett, 177–192. London: Routledge.

———. 1997. "Women and the Electric Guitar." In *Sexing the Groove: Popular Music and Gender,* ed. Sheila Whiteley, 37–49. New York: Routledge.

Bebey, Francis. 1975. *African Music: A People's Art.* New York: Lawrence Hill.

Becker, Judith. 1997. "Tantrism, Rasa, and Javanese Gamelan Music." In *Enchanting Powers: Music in the World's Religions,* ed. Lawrence Sullivan, 15–60. Cambridge, Mass.: Harvard University Press.

Bellour, Raymond. 1979. "Psychosis, Neurosis, and Perversion." *Camera Obscura* 3, no. 4: 105–132.

Belz, Carl. 1969. *The Story of Rock.* Oxford: Oxford University Press.

Bennett, Andy, and Richard Peterson. 2004. *Music Scenes: Local, Translocal, and Virtual.* Nashville: Vanderbilt University Press.

Bennett, Tony. 1988. "The Exhibitionary Complex." *New Formations* 4: 73–102.

———. 1990. "The Political Rationality of the Museum." *Continuum* 3, no. 1: 35–55.

Berger, Harris. 1999. *Metal, Rock, and Jazz: Perception and the Phenomenology of Musical Experience.* Hanover, N.H.: Wesleyan University Press.

Bergstrom, Janet. 1979. "Enunciation and Sexual Difference." *Camera Obscura* 3, no. 4: 33–70.

Bireley, Robert. 1981. *Religion and Politics in the Age of the Counter-reformation and the Formation of Imperial Policy.* Chapel Hill: University of North Carolina Press.

Blacking, John. 1976. *How Musical Is Man?* London: Faber and Faber.

Blecha, Peter. 2004. *Taboo Tunes.* London: Backbeat.

Bockie, Simon. 1994. *Death and the Invisible Powers: The World of Kongo Belief.* Bloomington: Indiana University Press.

Boddy, Janice. 1989. *Wombs and Alien Spirits.* Madison: University of Wisconsin Press.

Bogdanor, Vernon, and Robert Skidelsky. 1970. *The Age of Affluence, 1951–1964.* London: Macmillan.

Born, Georgina, and David Hesmondhalgh. 2000. *Western Music and Its Others: Difference, Representation, and Appropriation in Music.* Berkeley: University of California Press.

Borneman, Ernest. 1975. "The Roots of Jazz." In *Jazz: New Perspectives on the History of Jazz by Twelve of the World's Foremost Jazz Critics and Scholars,* ed. Nat Hentoff and Albert McCarthy, 1–20. New York: Da Capo.

Bourdieu, Pierre. 1977. *Outline of a Theory of Practice.* Cambridge: Cambridge University Press.

Bourguignon, Erika. 1968. "World Distribution and Patterns of Possession States." In *Trance and Possession,* ed. Raymond Prince, 3–34. Montreal: R. M. Bucke Memorial Society.

———. 1972. "Dreams and Altered States of Consciousness in Anthropological Research." In *Psychological Anthropology,* ed. Francis Hsu, 401–434. Cambridge, Mass.: Schenkman.

———. 1973. *Religion, Altered States of Consciousness, and Social Change.* Columbus: Ohio State University Press.

Bovin, Mette. 2001. *Nomads Who Cultivate Beauty: Wodaabe Dances and Visual Arts in Niger.* Uppsala, Sweden: Nordic African Institute.

Bremer, Francis. 2005. "Puritanism." In *The Encyclopedia of Religion,* ed. Lindsay Jones, 7833–7848. New York: Macmillan.

Brooker, Will, and Deborah Jermyn. 2002. *The Audience Studies Reader.* New York: Routledge.

Buell, Bebe. 2002. *Rebel Heart.* New York: St. Martin's.

Butler, Judith. 1990. *Gender Trouble: Feminism and the Subversion of Identity.* New York: Routledge.

Campbell, Colin. 1987. *The Romantic Ethic and the Spirit of Modern Consumerism.* New York: Blackwell.

Campbell, Joseph. 1959. *The Masks of God: Primitive Mythology.* New York: Viking.

Canizares, Raul. 1999. *Cuban Santeria: Walking with the Night.* Rochester, N.Y.: Destiny Books.

Cavanagh, David. 2000. *The Creation Records Story: My Magpie Eyes Are Hungry for the Prize.* London: Virgin Publishing.

Chapple, Steve, and Reebee Garofalo. 1977. *Rock 'n' Roll Is Here to Pay: The History and Politics of the Music Industry.* Chicago: Nelson Hall.

Chart Information Network. 1993. *Chart Information Network: The Information.* London: Spotlight Publications Limited.

Chernoff, John. 1979. *African Rhythm and African Sensibility: Aesthetics and Social Action in African Musical Idioms.* Chicago: University of Chicago Press.

Cho, Minu, and Chong Heup Cho. 1990. "Women Watching Together: An Ethnographic Study of Korean Soap Opera Fans in the United States." In *Gender, Race and Class in Media: A Text-Reader,* ed. Gail Dines and Jean Humez, 355–361. Thousand Oaks, Calif.: Sage.

Clifford, James. 1988. *The Predicament of Culture: Twentieth-Century Ethnography, Literature, and Art.* Cambridge, Mass.: Harvard University Press.

Clifford, James, and George Marcus. 1986. *Writing Culture: The Poetics and Politics of Ethnography.* Berkeley: University of California Press.

Cline, Cheryl. 1992. "Essays from Bitch: The Woman's Rock Newsletter with Bite." In *The Adoring Audience,* ed. Lisa Lewis, 69–83. London: Routledge.

Coates, Norma. 2003. "Teenyboppers, Groupies and Other Grotesques." *Journal of Popular Music Studies* 15, no. 1: 65–94.

Codrington, Robert. 1891. *The Melanesians: Studies in the Anthropology and Folklore.* Oxford: Clarendon Press.

Cohen, Sara. 1991. *Rock Culture in Liverpool.* Oxford: Clarendon Press.

———. 1997. "Men Making a Scene: Rock Music and the Production of Gender." In *Sexing the Groove: Popular Music and Gender,* ed. Sheila Whiteley, 17–36. New York: Routledge.

Cohen, Stanley. 1971. *Images of Deviance.* Harmondsworth: Penguin.

———. 1980. *Folk Devils and Moral Panics: The Creation of the Mods and the Rockers.* Oxford: Basil Blackwell.

Cohen, Stanley, and Jock Young. 1973. *The Manufacture of the News: Deviance, Social Problems, and the Mass Media.* London: Constable.

Comaroff, Jean, and John Comaroff. 1992. *Ethnography and the Historical Imagination.* Boulder, Colo.: Westview Press.

Conboy, Katie. 1997. *Writing on the Body: Female Embodiment and Feminist Theory.* New York: Columbia University Press.

Conquergood, Dwight. 1991. "Rethinking Ethnography: Towards a Critical Cultural Politics." *Communication Monographs* 58, no. 2: 179–194.

Cosentino, Donald. 1995. *Sacred Arts of Haitian Vodou.* Los Angeles: UCLA Fowler Museum of Cultural History.

Courlander, Harold. 1963. *Negro Folk Music U.S.A.* New York: Columbia University Press.

———. 2002. *A Treasury of Afro-American Folklore: The Oral Literature, Traditions, Recollections, Legends, Tales, Songs, Religious Beliefs, Customs, Sayings, and Humor of Peoples of African American Descent in the Americas.* New York: Marlowe & Company.

Cox, Harvey. 2001. *Fire from Heaven: The Rise of Pentecostal Spirituality and the Reshaping of Religion in the Twenty-first Century.* New York: Da Capo.

Crapanzano, Vincent. 1987. "Spirit Possession." In *The Encyclopedia of Religion,* ed. Mircea Eliade, 12–19. New York: Macmillan.

Crapanzano, Vincent, and Vivian Garrison. 1977. *Case Studies in Spirit Possession.* New York: John Wiley and Sons.

Crary, Jonathan. 1988. *Techniques of the Observer.* Cambridge, Mass.: MIT Press.

Csordas, Thomas. 1993. "Embodiment as a Paradigm for Anthropology." *Ethos* 18: 5–47.

———. 1994. *The Sacred Self: A Cultural Phenomenology of Charismatic Healing.* Berkeley: University of California Press.

———. 1997. *Language, Charisma, and Creativity: The Ritual Life of a Religious Movement.* Berkeley: University of California Press.

Csordas, Thomas, and Alan Harwood, eds. 1994. *Embodiment and Experience: The Existential Ground of Culture and Self.* Cambridge: Cambridge University Press.

Cudjoe, Seth D. 1953. "Techniques of Ewe Drumming and the Social Importance of Music in Africa." *Phylon* 14: 280–291.

Curtis, Jim. 1987. *Rock Eras: Interpretations of Music and Society, 1954–1984.* Bowling Green: Bowling Green University Popular Press.

Davis, Stephen. 2001. *Hammer of the Gods.* New York: Berkeley Publishing Group.

Dawson, Jim, and Steve Propes. 1992. *What Was the First Rock 'n' Roll Record?* Boston: Faber & Faber.

DeCurtis, Anthony. 1992. *The Rolling Stone Album Guide.* New York: Random House.

Denisoff, R. Serge. 1975. *Solid Gold: The Popular Record Industry.* New Brunswick: Transaction Books.

Denisoff, R. Serge, and Charles McCaghy. 1973. *Deviance, Conflict, and Criminality.* Chicago: Rand McNally.

Deren, Maya. 1953. *Divine Horsemen: The Living Gods of Haiti.* New York: MacPhear and Company.

Derrida, Jacques. 1974. *Of Grammatology.* Baltimore: Johns Hopkins University Press.

———. 1987. *The Truth in Painting.* Chicago: University of Chicago Press.

Des Barres, Pamela. 1991. *I'm with the Band: Confessions of a Groupie.* New York: Jove Books.

Devereux, George. 1971. "Art and Mythology: A General Theory." In *Art and Aesthetics in Primitive Societies,* ed. Carol Jopling, 193–224. New York: E. P. Dutton.

DiStasi, Lawrence. 1981. *Mal Occhio: The Underside of Vision.* San Francisco: North Point Press.

Doane, Mary Ann. 1982. "Film and the Masquerade: Theorizing the Female Spectator." *Screen* 23, no. 3–4 (September/October): 74–87.

———. 1987. *The Desire to Desire: The Women's Film of the 1940s.* Bloomington: Indiana University Press.

Doherty, Thomas. 1988. *Teenagers and Teenpics: The Juvenilization of American Movies in the 1950s.* London: Unwin Hyman.

Douglas, Mary. 1966. *Purity and Danger: An Analysis of the Concepts of Pollution and Taboo.* New York: Praeger.

———. 1970. *Natural Symbols: Explorations in Cosmology.* New York: Pantheon Books.

Dundes, Alan. 1980. *Interpreting Folklore.* Bloomington: Indiana University Press.

———. 1987a. *Cracking Jokes: Studies of Sick Humor Cycles and Stereotypes.* Berkeley: Ten Speed Press.

———. 1987b. *Parsing Through Customs: Essays by a Freudian Folklorist.* Madison: University of Wisconsin Press.

Dunn, Leslie, Nancy Jones, Jeffrey Kallberg, Anthony Newcomb, and Ruth Solie, eds. 1996. *Embodied Voices: Representing Female Vocality in Western Culture.* Cambridge: Cambridge University Press.

Duranti, Alessandro. 1992a. "Language and Bodies in Social Space: Samoan Ceremonial Greetings." *American Anthropologist* 94: 657–691.

———. 1992b. "Oratory." In *Folklore, Cultural Performances, and Popular Entertainments,* ed. Richard Bauman, 154–158. Oxford: University of Oxford Press.

———. 1994. *From Grammar to Politics: Linguistic Anthropology in a Western Samoan Village.* Berkeley: University of California Press.

———. 1997. *Linguistic Anthropology.* Cambridge, Mass.: Cambridge University Press.

Duranti, Alessandro, and Donald Brenneis. 1986. "Audience as Co-Author." *Text* 6, no. 3: 239–347.

Duranti, Alessandro, and Charles Goodwin. 1992. *Rethinking Context: Language as Interactive Phenomenon.* Cambridge: Cambridge University Press.

Durkheim, Emile. 1995. *The Elementary Forms of Religious Life.* Trans. Karen Fields. New York: Free Press.

Dyer, Richard. 1979. *Stars.* London: British Film Institute.

———. 1990. "In Defense of Disco." In *On Record: Rock, Pop, and the Written Word,* ed. Simon Frith and Andrew Goodwin, 410–418. New York: Pantheon Books.

Ehrenreich, Barbara, Elizabeth Hess, and Gloria Jacobs. 1992. "Beatlemania: Girls Just Want to Have Fun." In *The Adoring Audience,* ed. Lisa Lewis, 84–106. London: Routledge.

———. 1995. "Beatlemania: A Sexually Defiant Consumer Subculture? In *The Subcultures Reader,* ed. Ken Gelder and Sarah Thornton, 523–536. London: Routledge.

Eibl-Eibesfeldt, Irenaus. 1972. "Similarities and Differences between Cultures in Expressive Movements." In *Non-Verbal Communication,* ed. Robert Hinde, 297–312. Cambridge: Cambridge University Press.

Eliade, Mircea. 1964. *The Sacred and the Profane: The Nature of Religion.* New York: Harper Torch Books.

———. 1967. *Myths, Dreams, and Mysteries.* New York: Harper Torch Books.

Ellingson, Ter. 1987. "Drums." In *The Encyclopedia of Religion,* ed. Mircea Eliade, 494–503. New York: Macmillan.

Emery, Lynne. 1972. *Black Dance in the United States from 1619 to 1970.* Princeton: Princeton Book Co.

Emery, Thomas. 1849. *The Causes of Crime: Its Prevention and Punishment.* Leicester: Jayer.

Emoff, Ron. 2002. *Recollecting from the Past: Musical Practice and Spirit Possession on the East Coast of Madagascar.* Hanover, N.H.: Wesleyan University Press.

Epstein, Dena. 1977. *Sinful Tunes and Spirituals: Black Folk Music to the Civil War.* Urbana: University of Illinois Press.

Erikson, Kai. 1966. *Wayward Puritans: A Study in the Sociology of Deviance*. New York: Wiley.

Evans-Pritchard, Edward E. 1968. *The Nuer: A Description of the Modes of Livelihood and Political Institutions of a Nilotic People*. New York: Oxford University Press.

Fabian, Johannes. 1983. *Time and the Other: How Anthropology Makes Its Object*. New York: Columbia University Press.

Fanon, Frantz. 1967. *Black Skin, White Mask*. New York: Grove Weidenfeld.

Feld, Steven. 1982. *Sound and Sentiment: Birds, Weeping, Poetics, and Song in Kaluli Expression*. Philadelphia: University of Pennsylvania Press.

Fernandez, James. 1986. *Persuasions and Performances: The Play of Tropes in Culture*. Bloomington: Indiana University Press.

Finnegan, Ruth. 1989. *Hidden Musicians: Music-Making in an English Town*. Cambridge: Cambridge University Press.

Firth, Raymond. 1940. "The Analysis of Mana: An Empirical Approach." *The Journal of the Polynesian Society* 49: 483–510.

———. 1957. *Man and Culture: An Evaluation of the Work of Bronislaw Malinowski*. London: Routledge and Kegan Paul.

———. 1973. *Symbols: Public and Private*. Ithaca: Cornell University Press.

———. 1978. "Postures and Gestures of Respect." In *The Body Reader: Social Aspects of the Human Body*, ed. Ted Polhemus, 88–108. New York: Pantheon.

Fischer, Roland. 1970. "Prediction and Measurement of Perceptual Behavioral Change in Drug-Induced Hallucination." In *Origin and Mechanisms of Hallucinations*, ed. Wolfram Keup, 303–332. New York: Plenum Press.

———. 1975. "Cartology of Inner Space." In *Altered States of Consciousness: Current Problems and Research*, 78–102. Washington, D.C.: The Drug Abuse Council.

Fiske, John. 1992. "The Cultural Economy of Fandom." In *The Adoring Audience*, ed. Lisa Lewis, 30–49. London: Routledge.

Fitzgerald, F. Scott. 1925. *The Great Gatsby*. New York: Scribner.

Floyd, Samuel Jr. 1995. *The Power of Black Music: Interpreting Its History from Africa to the United States*. New York: Oxford University Press.

Forman, Murray. 2002. *The 'Hood Comes First: Race, Space, and Place in Rap and Hip-Hop*. Hanover, N.H.: Wesleyan University Press.

Foster, Hal. 1985. *Recodings: Art, Spectacle, and Cultural Politics*. Seattle, Wash.: Bay Press.

Foucault, Michel. 1979. *Discipline and Punish: The Birth of the Prison*. New York: Random House.

———. 1980. *Power/Knowledge: Selected Interviews and Other Writings, 1972–1977*. New York: Pantheon Books.

———. 1986. "What Is an Author?" In *Critical Theory since 1965,* ed. Hazard Adams and Leroy Searle, 138–148. Tallahassee: University Presses of Florida.

Freud, Sigmund. 1918. *Totem and Taboo*. New York: Vintage Books.

———. 1955. "Beyond the Pleasure Principle." In *The Complete Works of Sigmund Freud, Standard Edition*, vol. 3. London: Hogarth Press.

———. 1962. *Future of an Illusion*. London: Hogarth Press.

Friedenberg, Edgar. 1963. "Image of Adolescent Minority." *Dissent* 10 (spring): 151.

———. 1964. *The Vanishing Adolescent*. New York: Beacon Press.

Friedlander, Paul. 1996. *Rock and Roll: A Social History*. Boulder, Colo.: Westland Press.

Frith, Simon. 1981. *Sound Effects: Youth, Leisure, and the Politics of Rock and Roll*. New York: Pantheon.

———. 1983. "Post-Punk Blues." *Marxism Today* 2 (March): 18–23.

———. 1987. "The Making of the British Music Industry, 1920–1964." In *Impacts and Influences: Essays on Media Power in the Twentieth Century,* ed. James Curran, Anthony Smith, and Pauline Wingate, 278–300. London: Methuen.

———. 1990a. "Groundworks." In *On Record: Rock, Pop, and the Written Word,* ed. Simon Frith and Andrew Goodwin, 1–4. New York: Pantheon Books.

———. 1990b. "Afterthoughts." In *On Record: Rock, Pop, and the Written Word,* ed. Simon Frith and Andrew Goodwin, 419–424. New York: Pantheon Books.

———. 1991. "The Cultural Study of Popular Music." In *Cultural Studies,* ed. Lawrence Grossberg, Cary Nelson, and Paula Treichler, 174–186. New York: Routledge.

Frith, Simon, Andrew Goodwin, and Lawrence Grossberg. 1993. *Sound and Vision: The Music Video Reader.* London: Routledge.

Frith, Simon, and Angela McRobbie. 1978. "Rock and Sexuality." *Screen Education* 29: 3–19.

Furst, Peter. 1972. *Flesh of the Gods: The Ritual Use of Hallucinogens.* New York: Praeger Publishers.

Gallup Poll. 1993. *The Gallup UK Music Chart Report: January.* London: Gallup Poll Limited.

Garfias, Robert. 1975. *Music of a Thousand Autumns: The Tagaku Style of Japanese Court Music.* Berkeley: University of California Press.

Gebert, Gordon, and Lynn Ramage. 2004. *Rock and Roll War Stories.* Fleetwood, N.Y.: Pitbull Publishing.

Geertz, Clifford. 1973. *The Interpretation of Cultures.* New York: Basic Books.

———. 1983. *Local Knowledge: Further Essays in Interpretive Anthropology.* New York: Basic Books.

———. 1988. *Works and Lives: The Anthropologist as Author.* Stanford: Stanford University Press.

Genovese, Eugene. 1979. *From Rebellion to Revolution: Afro-American Slave Revolts in the Making of the Modern World.* Baton Rouge: Louisiana State University Press.

George-Warren, Holly, Patricia Romanowski, and Jon Pareles. 2001. *The Rolling Stone Encyclopedia of Rock & Roll.* New York: Fireside.

Gerstin, Julian. 2000. "Musical Revivals and Social Movements in Contemporary Martinique: Ideology, Identity, and Ambivalence." In *African Diaspora: A Musical Perspective,* ed. Ingrid Monson, 295–328. New York: Garland.

Gibson, James. 1986. *The Ecological Approach to Visual Perception.* Hillsdale, N.J.: Erlbaum.

Gillett, Charlie. 1970. *The Sound of the City: The Rise of Rock and Roll.* New York: Da Capo.

Gilroy, Paul. 1991. *"There Ain't No Black in the Union Jack": The Cultural Politics of Race and Nation.* Chicago: Chicago University Press.

———. 1993. *The Black Atlantic: Modernity and the Double Consciousness.* London: Verso.

Gioia, Ted. 1997. *The History of Jazz.* New York: Oxford University Press.

Gluckman, Max. 1964. *Closed Systems and Open Minds: The Limits of Naivety in Social Anthropology.* Edinburgh: Oliver and Boyd.

Goffman, Erving. 1959. *The Presentation of Self in Everyday Life.* Woodstock: Overlook Press.

———. 1967. *Interaction Ritual: Essays on Face-to-Face Behavior.* Garden City, N.Y.: Anchor Books.

———. 1974. *Frame Analysis: An Essay on the Organization of Experience.* Cambridge, Mass.: Harvard University Press.

———. 1981. *Forms of Talk*. Philadelphia: University of Pennsylvania Press.

Gonzalez-Wippler, Migene. 1973. *Santeria: African Magic in Latin America*. New York: Julian Press.

Goodwin, Charles. 1979. "The Interactive Construction of a Sentence in Natural Conversation." In *Everyday Language: Studies in Ethnomethodology*, ed. George Psathas, 97–121. New York: Irvington Publishers.

———. 1981. *Conversational Organization: Interaction between Speakers and Hearers*. New York: Academic Press.

———. 1984. "Notes on Story Structure and the Organization of Participation." In *Structures of Social Action*, ed. Maxwell Atkinson and John Heritage, 225–246. Cambridge: Cambridge University Press.

———. 1991. "Transparent Vision." Paper presented at the American Anthropological Association, Chicago.

———. 1994. "Professional Vision." *American Anthropologist* 96, no. 3: 606–633.

Goodwin, Charles, and Marjorie Goodwin. 1987. "Concurrent Operations on Talk: Notes on the Interactive Organization of Assessments." *IPrA Papers in Pragmatics* 1, no. 1: 1–52.

———. 1992. "Context, Activity, and Participation." In *The Contextualization of Language*, ed. Peter Auer and Aida di Luzio, 77–99. Amsterdam: Benjamins.

———. 1996. "Formulating Planes: Seeing as a Situated Activity." In *Cognition and Communication at Work*, ed. David Middleton and Yrjv Engestrom, 61–95. Cambridge, Mass.: Cambridge University Press.

Goodwin, Marjorie. 1980. "Process of Mutual Monitoring Implicated in the Production of Descriptive Sequences." *Sociological Inquiry* 50: 303–317.

Greenbaum, Lenora. 1973. "Possession Trance in Sub-Saharan Africa: A Descriptive Analysis of Fourteen Societies." In *Religion, Altered States of Consciousness, and Social Change*, ed. Erika Bourguignon, 58–87. Columbus: Ohio University Press.

Greig, Charlotte. 1997. "Female Identity and the Woman Songwriter." In *Sexing the Groove: Popular Music and Gender*, ed. Sheila Whiteley, 168–177. New York: Routledge.

Grossberg, Lawrence. 1992. *We Gotta Get Out of This Place: Popular Conservatism and Postmodern Culture*. New York: Routledge.

———. 1997. *Dancing in Spite of Myself: Essays on Popular Culture*. Durham, N.C.: Duke University Press.

Gumperz, John. 1982. *Discourse Strategies*. Cambridge: Cambridge University Press.

Halberstam, David. 1993. *The Fifties*. New York: Villard Books.

Hall, Stuart. 1979. *Policing the Crisis: Mugging the State and Law and Order*. London: Macmillan.

Hall, Stuart, and Tony Jefferson. 1976. *Resistance through Rituals: Youth Subcultures in Post-War Britain*. London: Unwin Hyman.

Hall, Stuart, and Paddy Whannel. 1964. *The Young Audience: 1964*. London: Pantheon Books.

Hallowell, A. Irving. 1977. "Cultural Factors in Spatial Organization." In *Symbolic Anthropology: A Reader in the Study of Symbols and Meanings*, ed. Janet Dolgin, David Kemnitzer, and David Schneider, 131–150. New York: Columbia University Press.

Hamzy, Connie. 1995. *Rock Groupie: The Intimate Adventures of "Sweet Connie" from Little Rock*. New York: Ulverscroft.

Hanks, William. 1990. *Referential Practice: Language and Lived Space among the Maya*. Chicago: University of Chicago Press.

Hanna, Judith. 1983. *The Performer-Audience Connection: Emotion to Metaphor in Dance and Society*. Austin: University of Texas Press.

———. 1987. "Dance." In *The Encyclopedia of Religion,* ed. Mircea Eliade, 203–212. New York: Macmillan.

———. 1988. *Dance, Sex, and Gender: Signs of Identity, Dominance, Defiance, and Desire.* Chicago: University of Chicago Press.

Haraway, Donna. 1989. *Primate Visions.* New York: Routledge.

Harris, John. 2003. *The Last Party: Britpop, Blair, and the Demise of English Rock.* London: Fourth Estate.

Hart, Mickey, and Fredric Lieberman. 1991. *Planet Drum.* San Francisco: Harper Collins.

Haslam, Dave. 2000. *Manchester, England: The Story of the Pop Cult City.* London: Fourth Estate.

Heath, Christian. 1986. *Body Movement and Speech in Medical Interaction.* Cambridge: Cambridge University Press.

Heath, Shirley Brice. 1987. "What No Bedtime Story Means." In *Language Socialization across Cultures.* Ed. Bambi Schieffelin and Elinor Ochs, 97–126. Cambridge: Cambridge University Press.

Hebdige, Dick. 1979. *Subculture: The Meaning of Style.* London: Methuen.

Hendler, Herb. 1983. *Year by Year in the Rock Era: Events and Conditions Shaping the Rock Generations that Reshaped America.* Westport, Conn.: Greenwood Press.

Hentoff, Nat, and Albert McCarthy. 1975. *Jazz: New Perspectives on the History of Jazz by Twelve of the World's Foremost Jazz Critics and Scholars.* New York: Da Capo.

Herdt, Gilbert. 1982. *Rituals of Manhood: Male Initiation in Papua New Guinea.* Berkeley: University of California Press.

Herman, Gary. 1970. *Rock 'n' Roll Babylon.* New York: G. P. Putnam's Sons.

Herskovits, Melville. 1938. *Dahomey, an Ancient West African Kingdom.* New York, J. J. Augustin.

———. 1941. *The Myth of the Negro Past.* New York: Harper & Row.

Hesmondhalgh, David. 1997. "Post-Punk's Attempt to Democratize the Music Industry: The Success and Failure of Rough Trade." *Popular Music* 16, no. 3: 255–274.

Hibbard, Don, and Carol Kaleialoha. 1983. *The Role of Rock.* Englewood Cliffs, N.J.: Prentice-Hall.

Hillerbrand, Hans. 2005. "The Reformation." In *The Encyclopedia of Religion,* ed. Lindsay Jones, 7656–7665. New York: Macmillan.

Hills, Matthew. 2002. *Fan Cultures.* New York: Routledge.

Hollan, Douglas. 1994. *Contentment and Suffering: Culture and Experience in Toraja.* New York: Columbia University Press.

Honko, Lauri. 1984. *Sacred Narrative.* Berkeley: University of California Press.

Hornby, Nick. 1992. *Fever Pitch.* London: Victor Gollancz.

Houk, James. 1995. *Spirits, Blood, and Drums: The Orisha Religion in Trinidad.* Philadelphia: Temple University Press.

Hughes, Dureen, and Norbert Melville. 1990. "Changes in Brain Wave Activity during Trance Channeling: A Pilot Study." *Journal of Transpersonal Psychology* 22, no. 10: 78–97.

Hughes, Helen. 1972. *Crowd and Mass Behavior.* Boston: Allyn and Bacon Press.

Hunter, Nigel. 1977. *The BPI Yearbook 1977.* London: British Phonographic Industry Limited.

Hyatt, Harry Middleton. 1970. *Hoodoo—Conjuration—Witchcraft—Rootwork: Beliefs Accepted by Many Negroes and White Persons, These Being Orally Recorded between Blacks and Whites.* Hannibal, Missouri: Western Publishing.

Hyde, Lewis. 1998. *Trickster Makes This World.* New York: North Point Press.

Hymes, Dell. 1972. "On Communicative Competence." In *Sociolinguistics,* ed. J. B. Pride and Janet Holmes, 269–285. Harmondsworth: Penguin.

———. 1974. "Ways of Speaking." In *Explorations in the Ethnography of Speaking,* ed. Richard Bauman and Joel Sherzer, 433–451. Cambridge: Cambridge University Press.

———. 1974. *Foundations of Sociolinguistics: An Ethnographic Approach.* Philadelphia: University of Pennsylvania Press.

———. 1975. "Breakthrough into Performance." In *Folklore, Performance, and Communication,* ed. Dan Ben-Amos and K. Goldstein, 11–74. The Hague: Mouton.

———. 1981. "The Wife who 'Goes Out' Like a Man." In *In Vain I Tried to Tell You: Essays in Native American Ethnopoetics,* 271–299. Philadelphia: Philadelphia University Press.

Hynes, William. 1993. "Mapping the Characteristics of Mythic Tricksters: A Heuristic Guide." In *Mythical Trickster Figures: Contours, Contexts, and Criticisms,* ed. William Hynes and William Doty, 33–45. Tuscaloosa: University of Alabama Press.

Hynes, William, and William Doty. 1993. *Mythical Trickster Figures: Contours, Contexts, and Criticisms.* Tuscaloosa: University of Alabama Press.

IPC Music Press. 1993. *A Guide to Music Purchase: Attitude and Lifestyle Readership Survey 1993.* London: IPC Music Press.

Iser, Wolfgang. 1980. *Act of Reading: A Theory of Aesthetic Response.* Baltimore: Johns Hopkins University Press.

Jackson, Michael. 1989. *Paths toward a Clearing: Radical Empiricism and Ethnographic Inquiry.* Bloomington: Indiana University Press.

Jackson, Travis. 2003. "Jazz Performance as Ritual: The Blues Aesthetic and the African Diaspora." In *African Diaspora: A Musical Perspective,* ed. Ingrid Monson, 23–82. New York: Routledge.

James, William. 1961. *The Varieties of Religious Experience: A Study in Human Nature.* New York: Penguin Books.

Jenson, Joli. 1992. "Fandom as Pathology: The Consequences of a Characterization." In *The Adoring Audience,* ed. Lisa Lewis, 9–29. London: Routledge.

Johnson, Christopher. 1999. A Social History of the Drum. Ph.D. dissertation, New York University.

Jones, Stephen. 1990. "Black Music and Young People in Birmingham." *Studies of Cultural Sociology* 28: 126–135.

Kapferer, Bruce. 1983. *A Celebration of Demons: Exorcism and the Aesthetics of Healing in Sri Lanka.* Bloomington: Indiana University Press.

Keesing, Roger. 1984. "Rethinking Mana." *Journal of Anthropological Research* 40, no. 1: 137–156.

Keil, Charles. 1966. *Urban Blues.* Chicago: University of Chicago Press.

Keil, Charles, and Steven Feld. 1994. *Music Grooves: Essays and Dialogues.* Chicago: University of Chicago Press.

Kendon, Adam. 1985. "The Behavioral Foundations for the Process of Frame Attunement in Face-to-Face Interaction." In *Discovery Strategies in the Psychology of Action,* ed. G. Ginsburg, M. Brenner, and M. Von Cranach, 229–253. London: Academic Press.

———. 1990. *Conducting Interaction: Patterns of Behavior in Focused Encounters.* Cambridge: Cambridge University Press.

———. 1992. "The Negotiation of Context in Face-to-Face Interaction." In *Rethinking Context: Language as an Interactive Phenomenon,* ed. Alessandro Duranti and Charles Goodwin, 323–334. Cambridge: Cambridge University Press.

Kendon, Adam, and Abby Ferber. 1973. "A Description of Some Human Greet-ings." In *Comparative Ecology and Behavior of Primates,* ed. R. Michaels and J. Cook, 591–668. London: Academic Press.

Kerman, Joseph. 1985. *Contemplating Music: Challenges to Musicology.* Cambridge, Mass.: Harvard University Press.

Kiev, Ari. 1961. "Spirit Possession in Haiti." *American Journal of Psychiatry* 188, 133–138.

King, Erika. 1991. *Crowd Theory: As a Psychology of the Leader and the Led.* Lewis-ton, N.Y.: Edwin Mellen Press.

Knappen, Marshall. 1965. *Tudor Puritanism.* Chicago: University of Chicago Press.

———. 2005. "Puritanism." In *The Encyclopedia of Religion,* ed. Lindsay Jones, 5718–5721. New York: Macmillan.

Kotarbo, Joseph, and Laura Wells. 1987. "Styles of Adolescent Participation in an All-Ages Rock 'n' Roll Nightclub: An Ethnographic Analysis." *Youth and Society* 18, no. 4 (June): 398–417.

Kristeva, Julia. 1982. *Powers of Horror: An Essay on Abjection.* Trans. Leon S. Rou-diez. New York: Columbia University Press.

Kruse, Holly. 1993. "Subcultural Identity in Alternative Music Culture." *Popular Music* 7, no 1, 33–41.

LaBarre, Weston. 1970. "Old and New World Narcotics: A Statistical Question and an Ethnological Reply." *Economic Botany* 24: 73–80.

Labov, William. 1972. *Language in the Inner City: Studies in Black English Ver-nacular.* Philadelphia: University of Philadelphia Press.

Lacan, Jacques. 1981. *The Four Fundamental Concepts of Psycho-Analysis.* New York: W. W. Norton & Company.

———. 1986. "The Mirror Stage." In *Critical Theory since 1965,* ed. Hazard Adams and Leroy Searle, 734–737. Tallahassee: University of Florida Press.

Laderman, Carol. 1995. *The Performance of Healing.* New York: Routledge.

Laing, Dave. 1969. *Sound of Our Time.* London: Sheed & Ward.

———. 1985. *One Chord Wonders: Power and Meaning in Punk Rock.* Milton Keynes: Open University Press.

Lambek, Michael. 1989. "From Disease to Discourse: Remarks on the Conceptual-ization of Trance and Spirit Possession." In *Altered States of Consciousness and Mental Health: A Cross-Cultural Perspective,* ed. Colleen Ward, 36–61. New-bury Park, Cal.: Sage.

Larkin, Colin. 1992. *The Guinness Who's Who of Indie and New Wave Music.* Lon-don: Guinness Publishing.

Lave, Jean. 1991. *Situated Learning: Legitimate Peripheral Participation.* Cam-bridge: Cambridge University Press.

Leach, Edmund. 1976. *Culture and Communication: The Logic By Which Symbols Are Connected: An Introduction to the Use of Structural Analysis in Social Anthropology.* Cambridge: Cambridge University Press.

Lee, Stephen. 1995. "Re-examining the Concept of the 'Independent' Record Com-pany: The Case of Wax Trax! Records." *Popular Music* 14, no. 1: 13–31.

Lee, Vernon. 1932. *Music and Its Lovers: An Empirical Study of Emotion and Imag-inative Responses to Music.* London: Allen & Unwin.

Leisure Consultants. 1990. *Leisure Trends: The Thatcher Years.* London: Leisure Consultants.

Lévi-Strauss, Claude. 1961. "The Many Faces of Man." *World Theatre* 10: 3–61.

———. 1969. *The Raw and the Cooked.* Chicago: Chicago University Press.

———. 1973. *From Honey to Ashes.* London: Cape.

———. 1978. *Myth and Meaning.* New York: Schocken Books.

Levine, Lawrence. 1978. *Black Culture and Black Consciousness: Afro-American Folk Thought from Slavery to Freedom.* New York: Oxford University Press.

Lewis, Donald. 1986. *Lighten Their Darkness: The Evangelical Mission to Working-Class London, 1828–1860.* New York: Greenwood Press.

Lewis, Ioan M. 1966. "Spirit Possession and Depravation Cults." *Man* 1: 307–329.

———. 1971. *Ecstatic Religion: An Anthropological Study of Spirit Possession and Shamanism.* Harmondworth, Middlesex: Penguin Books.

Lewis, Lisa. 1992. *The Adoring Audience: Fan Culture and Popular Media.* New York: Routledge.

Lipsitz, George. 1994. *Dangerous Crossroads: Popular Music, Postmodernism, and the Poetics of Place.* New York: Verso.

Live Forever. 2003. Director: John Dower. First Look Studios.

Locke, Ralph, and Edward Kelly. 1985. "A Preliminary Model for the Cross-Cultural Analysis of Altered States of Consciousness." *Ethos* 13, no. 1 (spring): 193–255.

Lomax, Alan. 1973. *Mister Jelly Roll.* Berkeley: University of California Press.

———. 1993. *The Land Where Blues Began.* New York: New Press.

Ludwig, Arnold. 1969. "Altered States of Consciousness." In *Altered States of Consciousness,* ed. Charles Tart, 9–22. New York: Wiley.

Lydon, John. 1995. *Rotten: No Irish, No Blacks, No Dogs.* New York: Picador.

Lynch, Michael. 1988. "The Externalized Retina: Selection and Mathematization in the Visual Documentation of Object in the Life Sciences." In *Representation in Scientific Practice,* ed. Michael Lynch and Steve Woolgar, 201–234. Cambridge, Mass.: MIT Press.

Makarius, Laura. 1993. "The Myth of the Trickster: The Necessary Breaker of Taboos." In *Mythical Trickster Figures: Contours, Contexts, and Criticisms,* ed. William Hynes and William Doty, 66–86. Tuscaloosa: University of Alabama Press.

Malinowski, Bronislaw. 1961. *Argonauts of the Western Pacific.* New York: E. P. Dutton.

Maquet, Jacques. 1972. *Africanity: The Cultural Unity of Black Africa.* New York: Oxford University Press.

———. 1979. *Introduction to Aesthetic Anthropology.* Malibu: Undena Publications.

———. 1986. *The Aesthetic Experience.* New Haven: Yale University Press.

Marcus, George. 1998. *Corporate Futures: The Diffusion of the Culturally Sensitive Corporate Form.* Chicago: University of Chicago Press.

Marcus, George, and Michael Fischer. 1986. *Anthropology as Cultural Critique: An Experimental Moment in the Human Sciences.* Chicago: University of Chicago Press.

Marcus, Greil. 1975. *Mystery Train: Images of America in Rock'n'Roll.* New York: Dutton.

———. 1990. *Lipstick Traces: A Secret History of the Twentieth Century.* Cambridge, Mass.: Harvard University Press.

Marett, Robert. 1909. *The Threshold of Religion.* London: Methuen.

Martin, Linda, and Kerry Segrave. 1988. *Anti-Rock: The Opposition to Rock and Roll.* Hamden, Conn.: Archon Books.

Marty, Martin. 2005. "Protestantism." In *The Encyclopedia of Religion,* ed. Lindsay Jones, 7447–7459. New York: Macmillan.

Masai Women. 1975. Director: Chris Carling. Anthropologist: Melissa Llewelyn-Davies. London: Granada.

Mauss, Marcel. 1967. *The Gift.* New York: Norton Library.

May, Lary. 1980. *Screening Out the Past: The Birth of Mass Culture and the Motion Picture Industry.* New York: Oxford University Press.

McClary, Susan. 1991. *Feminine Endings: Music, Gender, and Sexuality.* Duluth: University of Minnesota Press.

———. 1994. "Same as It Ever Was: Youth Culture and Music." In *Microphone Fiends: Youth Music and Youth Culture,* ed. Andrew Ross and Tricia Rose, 20–40. New York: Routledge.

McDonald, Paul. 1997. "Feeling and Fun: Romance, Dance, and the Performing of the Body in Take That Videos." In *Sexing the Groove,* ed. Sheila Whiteley, 277–294. London: Routledge.

McRobbie, Angela, ed. 1989. *Zoot Suits and Second-Hand Dresses: An Anthology of Fashion and Music.* Basingstoke: Macmillan.

McRobbie, Angela, and Sarah Thornton. 1995. "Rethinking 'Moral Panic' for Multi-Mediated Social Worlds." *British Journal of Society* 46, no. 4: 559–574.

Mead, Margaret. 1935. *Sex and Temperament in Three Primitive Societies.* New York: W. Morrow & Company.

———. 1973. *Coming of Age in Samoa.* New York: Morrow Quill Paperbacks.

Meltzer, Richard. 1970. *The Aesthetics of Rock.* New York: Da Capo.

Merriam, Alan. 1964. *The Anthropology of Music.* Evanston, Ill.: Northwestern University Press.

Metraux, Alfred. 1972. *Voodoo in Haiti.* New York: Schocken.

Metz, Christian. 1986. "The Imaginary Signifier." In *Narrative, Apparatus, Ideology: A Film Theory Reader,* ed. Philip Rosen, 245–278. New York: Columbia University Press.

Miller, Christopher. 1990. *Theories of Africans: Francophone Literature and Anthropology in Africa.* Chicago: Chicago University Press.

Mitchell, John. 1805. *An Essay on the Best Means of Civilizing the Subjects of the British Empire in India and of Diffusing the Light of the Christian Religion through the Eastern World.* Edinburgh: W. Blackwood.

Modleski, Tania. 1986. "Femininity as Mas(s)querade: A Feminist Approach to Mass Culture." In *High Theory/Low Culture,* ed. Colin MacCabe, 37–52. Manchester: Manchester University Press.

Monson, Ingrid. 2003. *African Diaspora: A Musical Perspective.* New York: Garland Publishing.

Morgan, Marcyliena. 1993. "Hip-Hop Style." Lecture presented at UCLA as part of the course entitled "Urban Speech Communities."

Moscovici, Serge. 1985. *The Age of the Crowd: A Historical Treatise on Mass Psychology.* Cambridge: Cambridge University Press.

Mulvey, Laura. 1975. "Visual Pleasure and Narrative Cinema." *Screen* 16, no. 3, 6–18.

———. 1989. *Visual and Other Pleasures.* Bloomington: Indiana University Press.

Murray, Albert. 1989. *Stomping the Blues.* New York: Da Capo.

Nabokov, Vladimir. 1990. *Strong Opinions.* New York: Vintage.

Navarro, Dave, and Neil Strauss. 2004. *Don't Try This At Home.* New York: Regan Books.

Needham, Rodney. 1979. "Percussion and Transition." In *Reader in Comparative Religion,* ed. William Lessa and Evon Vogt, 313–318. Boston: Allyn & Bacon.

Needleman, Jacob. 1982. *Consciousness and Tradition.* New York: Cross Road.

Negus, Keith. 1999. *Music Genres and Corporate Cultures.* New York: Routledge.

Neher, Andrew. 1962. "The Physiological Results of Patterned Auditory Stimuli." *Human Behavior* 34: 151–160.

Nicholls, Geoff. 1997. *The Drum Book.* San Francisco: Miller Freeman Books.

Nutall, Jeff. 1968. *Bomb Culture.* London: MacGibbon and Kee.

Obeyesekere, Gananath. 1981. *Medusa's Hair: An Essay on Personal Symbols and Religious Experience.* Chicago: University of Chicago Press.

O'Brien, Lucy. 2002. *She Bop Two: The Definitive History of Women in Rock, Pop, and Soul*. London: Continuum.

Ochs, Elinor. 1988. *Culture and Language Development: Language Acquisition in a Samoan Village*. Cambridge: Cambridge University Press.

Ochs, Elinor, and Bambi Schieffelin. 1984. "Language Acquisition and Socialization: Three Developmental Stories and Their Implications." In *Culture Theory*, ed. Richard Shweder and Robert LeVine, 276–320. Cambridge: Cambridge University Press.

Oliver, Paul. 1970. *Savannah Syncopators: African Retentions in the Blues*. New York: Collier Books.

———. 1995. "Greasy Greens: A Slippery Problem in Popular Music History." Lecture at ISPMA conference, Glasgow.

———. 2001. *Yonder Comes the Blues: The Evolution of a Genre*. Cambridge: Cambridge University Press.

Our Time. 2004. Director Piper Ferguson. Los Angeles: Piper Ferguson Films.

Pader, Ellen. 1988. "Inside Spatial Relations." *Architecture and Comport/Architectural Behavior* 4: 251–267.

Paglia, Camille. 1990. *Sexual Personae: Art and Decadence from Nefertiti to Emily Dickinson*. New York: Vintage Books.

Palmer, Gareth. 1997. "Bruce Springsteen and Masculinity." In *Sexing the Groove: Popular Music and Gender*, ed. Sheila Whiteley, 100–117. New York: Routledge.

Palmer, Gary, and William Jankowiak. 1996. "Performance and Imagination: Toward an Anthropology of the Spectacular and the Mundane." *Cultural Anthropology* 11, no. 2: 225–258.

Parsons, Talcott. 1964. *Social Structure and Personality*. New York: Free Press.

Patterson, R. Gary. 2004. *Take a Walk on the Dark Side: Rock and Roll Myths, Legends, and Curses*. New York: Fireside.

Pearson, Geoffrey. 1983. *Hooligans: A History of Respectable Fears*. London: Macmillan.

Pelton, Robert. 1993. "West African Tricksters: Web of Purpose, Dance of Delight." In *Mythical Trickster Figures: Contours, Contexts, and Criticisms*, ed. William Hynes and William Doty, 122–140. Tuscaloosa: University of Alabama Press.

Pemberton, John. 1987. "Yoruba." In *The Encyclopedia of Religion*, ed. Mircea Eliade, 535–538. New York: Macmillan.

Peterson, Richard. 1990. "Why 1955? Explaining the Advent of Rock Music." *Popular Music* 9, no. 1: 97–104.

Pfeil, Fred. 1995. *White Guys: Studies in Postmodern Domination and Difference*. New York: Verso.

Philips, Susan. 1983. *The Invisible Culture: Communication in Classroom and Community on the Warm Springs Indian Reservation*. New York: Longmans.

Polhemus, Ted. 1994. *Street Style*. London: Victoria and Albert Museum.

Pressel, Esther. 1973. "Umbanda in Sao Paulo: Religious Innovations in a Developing Society." In *Religion, Altered States of Consciousness, and Social Change*, ed. Erika Bourguignon. Columbus: Ohio State University Press.

Preziosi, Donald. 1989. *Rethinking Art History: Meditations on a Coy Science*. New Haven: Yale University Press.

Price, Janet. 1999. *Feminist Theory and the Body: A Reader*. New York: Routledge.

Prince, Raymond. 1966. *Trance and Possession States*. Montreal: R. M. Burke Memorial Society.

Raboteau, Albert. 1978. *Slave Religion: The "Invisible Institution" in the Antebellum South*. New York : Oxford University Press.

Radin, Paul. 1955. *The Trickster: A Study in American Indian Mythology*. New York: Schocken.

Radway, Janice. 1984. *Reading the Romance: Women, Patriarchy, and Popular Literature*. Durham: University of North Carolina Press.

Redhead, Steve. 1990. *The End-of-the-Century Party: Youth and Pop towards 2000*. Manchester: Manchester University Press.

Reynolds, Simon. 1989. "Against Health and Efficiency: Independent Music in the 1980s." In *Zoot Suits and Second-Hand Dresses: An Anthology of Fashion and Music,* ed. Angela McRobbie, 245–255. Basingstoke: Macmillan.

———. 1990. *Blissed Out: The Raptures of Rock*. London: Serpent's Tail.

Reynolds, Simon, and Joy Press. 1996. *The Sex Revolts: Gender, Rebellion, and Rock 'n' Roll*. Cambridge, Mass.: Harvard University Press.

Riley, Gwendoline. 2003. *Cold Water*. London: Vintage.

Rosaldo, Renato. 1989. *Culture and Truth: The Remaking of Social Analysis*. Boston: Beacon.

Rose, Jacqueline. 1988. "Sexuality and Vision: Some Questions." In *Vision and Visuality,* ed. Hal Foster, 115–127. Seattle: Bay Press.

Rose, Tricia. 1994. *Black Noise: Rap Music and Black Culture in Contemporary America*. Hanover, N.H.: Wesleyan University Press.

Rossi, Melissa. 1996. *Courtney Love: The Queen of Noise*. New York: Pocket.

Rouget, Gilbert. 1985. *Music and Trance: A Theory of the Relations between Music and Possession*. Chicago: University of Chicago Press.

Rublowsky, John. 1967. *Popular Music*. New York: Basic Books.

Rutter, Derek. 1984. *Looking and Seeing: The Role of Visual Communication in Social Interaction*. Chichester: Wiley.

Said, Edward. 1994. *Orientalism*. New York: Vintage Books.

Sargant, William. 1974. *The Mind Possessed: A Physiology of Possession, Mysticism, and Faith Healing*. New York: Penguin.

Schechner, Richard. 1985. *Between Theater and Anthropology*. Philadelphia: University of Pennsylvania Press.

———. 1988. *Performance Theory*. London: Methuen Drama.

Schegloff, Emanuel. 1986. "The Routine as Achievement." *Human Studies* 9: 111–151.

Schieffelin, Bambi, and Elinor Ochs. 1987. *Language Socialization across Cultures*. Cambridge: Cambridge University Press.

Schieffelin, Edward. 1976. *The Sorrow of the Lonely and the Burning of the Dancers*. New York: St. Martin's Press.

Scott, David. 1991. "The Cultural Poetics of Eyesight in Sri Lanka: Composure, Vulnerability, and the Sinhala Concept of Distiya." *Dialectical Anthropology* 16: 85–102.

Shaara, Lila, and Andrew Strathern. 1992. "A Preliminary Analysis of the Relationship between Altered States of Consciousness, Healing, and Social Structure." *American Anthropologist* 94 (March): 145–160.

Shank, Barry. 1994. *Dissonant Identities: The Rock'n'Roll Scene in Austin, Texas*. Hanover, N.H.: University Press of New England; Wesleyan University Press.

———. 2003. "Embodied Aesthetics and the Future of the Humanities." Paper presented at IASPM-US conference, Los Angeles.

Shaw, Arnold. 1974. *The Rockin' Fifties: The Decade That Transformed the Pop Music Scene*. New York: Hawthorn Books.

———. 1986. *Black Popular Music in America: From the Spirituals, Minstrels, and Ragtime to Soul, Disco, and Hip Hop*. New York: Schirmer Books.

Shweder, Richard. 1984. "Anthropology's Romantic Rebellion Against the Enlightenment, or There's More to Thinking than Reason and Evidence." In *Culture Theory,* ed. Richard Shweder and Robert LeVine. Cambridge: Cambridge University Press.

Silverman, Kaja. 1993. "Political Cinema." Lecture in Critical Studies at the University of California, Los Angeles.

Slobin, Mark. 1993. *Subcultural Sounds: Micromusics of the West.* Hanover, N.H.: University Press of New England; Wesleyan University Press.

Small, Christopher. 1987. *Music of the Common Tongue: Survival and Celebration in African American Music.* Reprint with new preface, 1998. Hanover, N.H.: University Press of New England; Wesleyan University Press.

————. 1998. *Musicking: The Meanings of Performing and Listening.* Hanover, N.H.: University Press of New England; Wesleyan University Press.

Sobel, Mechal. 1979. *Trabelin' On: The Slave Journey to an Afro-Baptist Faith.* Princeton: Princeton University Press.

Stearns, Marshall. 1970. *The Story of Jazz.* New York: Oxford University Press.

Stewart, Sue, and Sheryl Garratt. 1984. *Signed, Sealed, and Delivered: True Stories of Women in Pop Music.* Cambridge, Mass.: South End Press.

Stoller, Paul. 1995. *Embodying Colonial Memories: Spirit Possession, Power, and the Hauka in West Africa.* New York: Routledge.

Strathern, Andrew. 1996. *Body Thoughts.* Ann Arbor: University of Michigan Press.

Strathern, Andrew, and Pamela Stewart. 1999. *Curing and Healing: Medical Anthropology in Global Perspective.* Durham: University of North Carolina Press.

————. 2000. *Humors and Substances: Ideas of the Body in New Guinea.* Westport, Conn.: Bergin & Garvey.

Street, Brian. 1972. "The Trickster Theme: Winnebago and Azande." In *Zande Themes: Essays Presented to Sir Edward Evans Pritchard,* ed. Andre Singer and Brian Street, 82–104. Totowa, N.J.: Rowman and Littlefield.

Stringer, Julian. 1992. "The Smiths: Repressed (but Remarkably Dressed)." *Popular Music* 11, no. 1: 15–26.

Stuart, Johnny. 1987. *Rockers.* London: Plexus Publishing Limited.

Sugerman, Danny, and Jerry Hopkins. 1995. *No One Here Gets Out Alive.* New York: Warner Books.

Sullivan, Harry. 1988. *The Psychiatric Interview.* New York: W. W. Norton.

Sullivan, Lawrence. 1987. "Trickster." In *The Encyclopedia of Religion,* ed. Mircea Eliade, 45–46. New York: Macmillan.

————. 1997. *Enchanting Powers: Music in the World's Religions.* Cambridge, Mass.: Harvard University Press.

Swift, Jonathan. 1967. *Gulliver's Travels.* London: Penguin.

Szatmary, David. 2000. *Rockin' in Time: A Social History of Rock and Roll.* Englewood Cliffs, N.J.: Prentice-Hall.

Szwed, John. 1978. *Afro-American Folk Culture: An Annotated Bibliography of Materials from North, Central, and South America and the West Indies.* Philadelphia: Institute for the Study of Human Issues.

Tart, Charles. 1969. *Altered States of Consciousness.* New York: Wiley.

Taylor, Timothy. 1997. *Global Pop: World Music, World Markets.* New York: Routledge.

Theunissen, Michael. 1984. *The Other: Studies in the Social Ontology of Husserl, Heidegger, Sartre, and Buber.* Cambridge, Mass.: MIT Press.

Thompson, Robert Farris. 1966. "An Aesthetic of the Cool: West African Dance." *African Forum* 2, part 2: 85–102.

————. 1983. *Flash of the Spirit: African and Afro-American Art and Philosophy.* New York: Random House.

Thorne, Tony. 1993. *Dictionary of Popular Culture: Fads, Fashions, and Cults.* London: Bloomsbury.

Thornton, Sarah. 1994. "Moral Panic, the Media, and British Rave Culture." In *Microphone Fiends: Youth Music and Youth Culture,* ed. Andrew Ross and Tricia Rose, 176–192. New York: Routledge.

———. 1995. *Club Cultures: Music, Media, and Subcultural Capital.* London: Polity Press.

Trinh, T. Min-Ha. 1989. *Woman, Native, Other: Writing Postcoloniality and Feminism.* Bloomington: Indiana University Press.

Trynka, Paul. 1993. *The Electric Guitar: An Illustrated History.* San Francisco: Chronicle.

Turner, Ralph and Lewis Killian. 1957. *Collective Behavior.* Englewood Cliffs, N.J.: Prentice-Hall.

Turner, Ralph, and Samuel Surace. 1956. "Zoot Suiters and Mexicans: Symbols in Crowd Behavior." *American Journal of Sociology* 62: 14–20.

Turner, Victor. 1968. *The Drums of Affliction: A Study of Religious Processes among the Ndembu of Zambia.* Oxford: Clarendon Publishing.

———. 1969. *The Ritual Process: Structure and Anti-Structure.* Ithaca: Cornell University Press.

———. 1974. *Dramas, Fields, and Metaphors: Symbolic Action in Human Society.* Ithaca: Cornell University Press.

———. 1976. "Rituals." In *The Encyclopedia of Anthropology,* ed. David Hunter, 336–337. New York: Harper & Row.

———. 1982. *From Ritual to Theater: The Seriousness of Play.* Richmond, Va.: Performing Arts Journal Publications.

———. 1986. *The Anthropology of Experience.* Champaign: University of Illinois Press.

———. 1988. *The Anthropology of Performance.* New York: PAJ Publications.

Turner, Victor, ed. 1982. *Celebration: Studies in Festivity and Ritual.* Washington D.C.: Smithsonian Institution Press.

24 Hour Party People. 2002. Director: Michael Winterbottom. Metro-Goldwyn-Mayer.

Tyler, Stephen. 1987. *The Unspeakable: Discourse, Dialogue, and Rhetoric in the Postmodern World.* Madison: University of Wisconsin Press.

Urquia, Norman. 2004. "'Doin' It Right': Contested Authenticity in London's Salsa Scene." In *Music Scenes: Local, Translocal, and Virtual,* ed. Andy Bennett and Richard A. Peterson, 136–160. Nashville: Vanderbilt University Press.

Valeri, Valerio. 1985. *Kingship and Sacrifice: Ritual and Society in Ancient Hawaii.* Chicago: University of Chicago Press.

Van Gennep, Arnold. 1960. *Rites of Passage.* Chicago: University of Chicago Press.

Ventura, Michael. 1985. *Shadow Dancing in the U.S.A.* New York: St. Martins Press.

Verger, Pierre. 1969. "Trance and Convention in Nago-Yoruba Spirit Mediumship." In *Spirit Mediumship and Society in Africa,* ed. John Beattie, 50–60. London: Routledge and Kegan Paul.

Vermorel, Fred, and Judy Vermorel. 1985. *Starlust: The Secret Fantasies of Fans.* London: W. H. Allen.

———. 1994. "Groupies." *Modern Review* 34 (April–May).

Voeks, Robert. 1997. *Sacred Leaves of Candomblé : African Magic, Medicine, and Religion in Brazil.* Austin: University of Texas Press.

Wagner, Roy. 1978. *Lethal Speech: Daribi Myth as Symbolic Obviation.* Ithaca: Cornell University Press.

———. 1980. *The Invention of Culture.* Chicago: University of Chicago Press.

Wald, Elijah. 2004. *Escaping the Delta: Robert Johnson and the Invention of the Blues.* New York: Amistad.

Walens, Stanley. 1981. *Feasting with Cannibals: An Essay on Kwakiutl Cosmology.* Princeton: Princeton University Press.

———. 1983. "The Weight of My Name Is a Mountain of Blankets." In *Celebrations: Studies in Festivity and Ritual,* ed. Victor Turner, 178–189. Washington, D.C.: Smithsonian Institution Press.

———. 1996. "Smoke and Mirrors: New Perspectives on the Critical Discourse of Northwest Coast Indian History and Art." Unpublished manuscript.

Walser, Robert. 1993. *Running with the Devil: Power, Gender, and Madness in Heavy Metal Music.* Hanover, N.H.: University Press of New England; Wesleyan University Press.

Ward, Ed, Geoffrey Stokes, and Ken Tucker. 1986. *Rock of Ages: The Rolling Stone History of Rock & Roll.* New York: Summit Books.

Wasson, Robert. 1971. *Soma: Divine Mushroom of Immortality.* New York: Harcourt, Brace.

Waterman, Christopher. 1990. *Juju: A Social History and Ethnography of an African Popular Music.* Chicago: University of Chicago Press.

Waterman, Richard Alan. 1952. *African Influence on the Music of the Americas.* Chicago: University of Chicago Press.

Watney, Simon. 1987. *Policing Desire: Pornography, AIDS, and the Media.* London: Methuen.

Weber, Max. 1958. *The Protestant Ethic and the Spirit of Capitalism.* New York: Charles Scribner's Sons.

———. 1993. *The Sociology of Religion.* New York: Beacon Press.

Weiss, Gail, and Honi Fern Haber. 1999. *Perspectives on Embodiment: The Intersections of Nature and Culture.* New York: Routledge.

Welton, Donn. 1998. *Body and Flesh: A Philosophical Reader.* Malden, Mass.: Blackwell Publishers.

Wilson, Diana Drake. 1993. "When Worlds Collide and You Can't Go Home Again: Field Work in the Wild West of Los Angeles." *UCLA Anthropology Journal* 20, no. 1: 51–57.

———. 1994. "Understanding Misunderstanding: American Indians in Euro American Museums." Dissertation, University of California, Los Angeles.

White, Emily. 2003. *Fast Girls: Teenage Tribes and the Myth of the Slut.* New York: Berkley Publishing Group.

Whiteley, Sheila. 1997. "Introduction." In *Sexing the Groove: Popular Music and Gender,* ed. Sheila Whiteley, xiii–xxxvi. New York: Routledge.

Yorke, Ritchie. 1976. *History of Rock and Roll.* Toronto: Methuen.

Young, Jock. 1971. *The Drugtakers: The Social Meaning of Drug Use.* London: MacGibbon & Kee.

Young, Michael. 1983. *Magicians of Manumanua.* Berkeley: University of California Press.

Zahan, Dominique. 1987. "West African Religions." In *The Encyclopedia of Religion,* ed. Mircea Eliade, 371–377. New York: Macmillan.

Zappa, Frank. 1989. *Real Frank Zappa Book.* New York: Touchstone.

Zuesse, Evan. 2005. "Ritual." In *The Encyclopedia of Religion,* ed. Lindsay Jones, 7833–7848. New York: Macmillan.

Index

Page numbers in **bold** indicate illustrations.

gigs, 14–15, 23, 79–166, 222, 272n21; definition of, 14, 81–82, 262n16; dissatisfaction with, 117–120; as opposed to concerts, 11, 80–81; as ritual, 200, 248; role
in industry, 126–128, 274n12; as youth
events, 2, 245
Gioia, Ted, 167
Godfathers, 245, 281n10
Goffman, Erving, 4, 122, 156, 261n2
Goodwin, Charles, 8
gothic music, 46, 84
groping, 90–91, 94, 104. *See also under*
audiences
Grossberg, Lawrence, 11
groupie stereotype, 22, 203, 257–259,
270n71, 282nn12–13; male groupies,
210; referring to fan behavior, 213, 281–
282n3; as sexual predator, 207–212,
283n19; stigmatizing to women, 213–
214, 281–282n3, 283nn16–17
guest list, 20, 125, 128–137, 274n12; personable strategy, 133–136; professional
strategy, 132–133, 135–136, 275n14
guest passes, 20, 128, 138–150, **139, 143,**
275n18; covert placement 139–141, **141,**
148, **149, 150;** laminates, 138, 144–147,
145, 146, 275n19; overt placement, 138–
141, **140, 144**
guitars, 39, 46, 70–71; imagery, 218–220,
219, 284nn25–26; soloing, 42, 66–67,
78, 86, 219, 268n55

Haçienda, the, 71, 270n74
Happy Mondays, 41, 71
Haraway, Donna, 7, 204
Harris, John, 14, 40, 64, 70
Harvey, PJ, 206, 268–269n60
Haslam, Dave, 14, 70, 270n74
heat, 20, 99, 115, 176
Heavenly, 75
Hebdige, Dick, 60
Hesmondhalgh, David, 11, 33–34
hip hop, 51, 57, 261n10, 280n2
Hives, the, 41, 45
Hole. *See* Courtney Love
homoeroticism, 103–104, **105,** 207, 272n17,
282nn8–9, 284n27
Hook, Peter, 43. *See also* Joy Division;
New Order
hooliganism, 179
Hyde, Lewis, 228–230, 239, 248, 284–
285n34, 285n37
Hynes, William, 229, 285n34

hyping, 32

improvisation, 2, 9, 162–163, 280n4
independence, 51–52, 56, 64, 263n8,
267n46
independent charts, 30, 32–33, 36, 38,
265n18, 266n29
independent distribution, 30, 33–39, 51, 77,
266n21; values of, 38–39. *See also* Pinnacle; Rough Trade; Spartan; 3MV; Vital
independent labels, 12, 17, 51, 77, 267n48,
268n49; label names 74–75; as opposed
to majors (radio station), 36–37; values
of, 35–36
indie 103.1, 262n15
injuries, 99, 112, 272–273n26
innovation, 21, 195, 198
Interpol, 199, 211, 261n6
introspection, 44, 54–55
inverted distribution, 156–160, 276n3
IPC Press, 26–27, 68
irony, 54–55, 60, 78
Islam, 2, 172, 184, 278n23

Jabberjaw, 1, 198
Jackson, Travis, 11, 170
jazz, 11, 72, 166–168, 170, 192, 276n10,
277n19, 280n4
Jesus and Mary Chain, 41, 271n3
Johnson, Christopher, 171, 278n26
Johnson, Robert, 285n40
Jon Spencer's Blues Explosion, 217
journalists, 14, 17, 125, 269n62, 273n31;
association with indie community, 60–
61, 128
Joy Division, 4, 109, 199, 225
Judaism, 172, 184, 277n22, 278n23
junior squad, 127–128, 130, 269n62, 274n9

k, 75, 270n76
Kaito, 40
Keil, Charles, 11, 280n2
Kingmaker, 226
KLF, the, 70
Kristeva, Julia, 6, 285n39

La's, the, 41
label names, 74–75
Lacan, Jacques, 6
Laing, Dave, 42, 45, 49, 68
Lamacq, Steve, 55, 98
leather, 230, 285n38
Lemonheads, 90, 271n10

Mute, 33, 35, 47, 75, 265n18
My Bloody Valentine, 40, 41, 54, 65

Nabokov, Vladimir. See *Lolita*
Navajo, 229
Ned's Atomic Dustbin, 55
New Music Express. See *NME*
New Order, 46, 184, 287n57
9 Mile, 34, **35**
Nirvana, 54, 287n61
NME (music paper), 27, 61, 119, 164,
    263nn2–3, 268n58; best albums in, 58,
    251–253, 255–256; charts in, 32, 264n12,
    265n17, 266n29. *See also* weekly press
No Doubt, 125
nostalgia, 29, 39, 44–46, 48–50, 75–77, **75**
novelty. *See* innovation

Oasis, 41, 128, 137, 187, 267n39, 280n10,
    287n57
Oberst, Conor. *See* Bright Eyes
O'Brien, Lucy, 216–217
obsessiveness. *See* trainspotting
Oliver, Paul, 11, 12, 167
One Little Indian, 75
orientation, 155, 272n24, 276n4
Other Protestant Ethic. *See* romanticism
Our Time (film), 29
Outkast, 57
ownership. *See* distribution; independ-
    ence; major music corporations

Palace Brothers, 190, 269n66
Parks, Simon, 93
Parsons, Talcott, 7
participant observation. *See* methodology
participant structure, 4, 8, 261n2, 279n36;
    of indie gigs, 11–12, 19–21, 80–82, 154–
    163; ritual, 98–99, 184–185; transforma-
    tion in, 20–21. *See also* audiences; par-
    ticipatory spectatorship; zones
participatory spectatorship, 8–10, 19–22,
    120–121, 166
Pastels, the, 41, 44
pathos, 19, 49–50, 53–57, 73, 245–246; in
    lyrics, 54; and puritanism, 55–56, 76–78
Pavement, 41
payola, 181, 279n35
Peel, John, 98
Pelton, Robert, 229
percussion, 100–101, 167–172, 174, 176,
    277nn15–16
performance, 21, 187–202, 271n3, 272n23;

audience transformed by, 197–198; as
    co-constructed, 6, 9–10; illusion of,
    196–198; performance, 21, 187–202,
    271n3, 272n23; as ritual, 5, 242, 273n29;
    value on intimacy, 64, 73, 79; value on
    live within indie, 42–43, 49, 69, 195,
    267n4, 269nn64 and 69. *See also* ritual
performance theory, 3–4, 60
Pfeil, Fred, 280n2
Phair, Liz, 272n24
phenomenology, 5–6
Phillips, Susan, 4, 261n2
Pinnacle, 30, 34, 265n23
Pintupi, 2
pit, the, 82, 84, 86–91, **92, 93,** 113, 271n15
Pixies, the, 40. *See also* Kim Deal
plus one, 16, 132, 136
Poe, Edgar Allen, 53
points. *See* royalties
polytheism, 168, 176–178, 182, 184, 247–
    248, 278n27, 285n40
Pop Will Eat Itself, 55, 208
popular culture studies, 17, 269n65
popular music studies, 11, 269n65
Portishead, 60
possession, 5, 169–171, 263n7, 277n15,
    279n36, 285n40
Postal Service, the, 188
Postcard, 33, 36, 265n18
Primal Scream, 41, 59, 61, 284n30
Primitives, the, 40
Probe, 32, 34, **35**
Prodigy, the, 267n47, 270n74
professional fans, 125
professionals. *See* music industry
*Protestant Ethic and the Spirit of Capital-
    ism, The,* 179, 261n4
Protestantism, 21, 67–68, 180, 182–186,
    245, 263n6, 279n30; and colonialism,
    174, 177, 277n19, 278n24; relationship
    to divinity, 27–28, 173; West African
    influences on southern forms, 170–171.
    See also Puritanism; West European
Public Enemy, 57
Pulp, 46, 60, 64, 128, 191; lyrics of, 71, 74,
    103, 245, 247
punk, 32, 49, 180, 266n26, 271n7; audi-
    ence behavior, 83–84, 86; DYI, philoso-
    phy of, 29, 33, 63; forerunner to indie,
    33, 57; label names, 74; as musical re-
    formers, 28, 68, 77; style of, 41, 40, 44,
    45, 60, 63, 65
punters, 125–126, 152–153, 162, 244, 274n3

Puritanism, 50, 55–56, 183–184, 246, 267n38, 279n30; critique of Catholicism, 28–29; in distribution philosophy, 38–39; metaphysics, 50, 54, 77–78, 195, 263n195; unmediated relationship to the divine, 38–39, 50
purito-romantic personality system, 62, 183

Q (magazine), 60
Quasi, 40

Raboteau, Albert, 169, 277n19
racism, 174, 176, 278n24
Radcliffe-Brown, Alfred, 7
Radiohead, 41, 54, 76, 237, 266n37
Radway, Janice, 8
Razorlight, 14, 138, 182
Reading festival, 13, 18, 61, 101, 147, 268n57, 271n9. See also festivals
rebellion, 65, 72–73, 178, 269n65
reciprocity, 129–130
Record Business. See Music Week
Red Kross, 2
Red Rhino, 34, 35
reflexivity, 118, 194–195, 202
Reformation, the, 28, 67, 263n6
Reprise Records, 18
Revolver, 34, 35, 266n23
Reynolds, Simon, 39, 44–45, 216–217
Ride, 59, 93, 280n10
ritual, 21, 98, 174–175, 184, 200–202, 220–221; addressing cultural conflicts and values, 2, 183, 242–245; failure to produce desired sentiment, 103, 279n36; rites of intensification, 2, 240–241, 247–249; rites of passage, 23, 98, 169; use of the body in, 5, 98–104, 242, 272n18. See also performance
ritual practitioners. See music industry; musicians; sexual acolytes
rock and roll, 166–167, 170, 175, 177, 180
Rolling Stones, 204, 217, 239, 281n1, 287n62
Romantic Ethic and the Spirit of Modern Consumerism, The, 29, 183
romanticism, 23, 29, 73, 183–184, 268n56; in distribution philosophy, 39; and indie, 19, 29, 77–78; and pathos, 55–56; preference toward the vernacular, 43, 50, 266n30
Rough Trade, 33–36, 265n20; distribution company, 34–36, 35, 265n23; record label, 33–34, 74, 265nn18 and 23; record

shop, 32, 34
royalties, 37, 225–226, 264n13, 274n10, 284n32
RTM, 36, 38, 265n23, 266n25. See also Rough Trade

saddo, 49, 53, 55
Said, Edward, 175
Sarah Records, 40, 75
seating, 11, 80, 120 165, 261n8, 270n1
Sebadoh, 41, 61, 75, 269n63
Select (magazine), 60, 207, 210, 214, 257–259
self-consciousness, 157–160, 198
Selwood, Clive, 266n28
sensibility. See taste
Sensless Things, the, 102
seven-inch single. See vinyl
sex, 176–177, 212–213, 216, 219–221, 282n14, 285n37; as art, 224, 240; as commodity, 24, 207, 209–211, 224; in indie, 214, 224, 236–237, 282n15, 284n29, 287n58. See also sexual acolytes; tricksters
Sex Pistols, 196, 233, 271n5, 287n61
sexual acolytes, 21–23, 221–225; as cultural critique, 241; and discernment, 215–216; and tricking, 222, 240
Shank, Barry, 5, 11, 263n8
shoe-gazing, 18, 44, 267n39, 281n9
Shop Assistants, the, 41
simplicity, 19, 39, 41–43, 50, 66, 77, 195
sin-eater, 211–212
SJM Concerts, 138
slam-dancing. See moshing
slavery, 166, 175, 276nn10 and 12, 277n19
Sleeper, 40
Slowdive, 44
Small, Christopher, 8–9, 167–168, 170; on classical music, 11, 173, 192, 245, 261n9, 277n21, 287n55
smallness, 12, 52, 63–64; distrust of popularity, 64–65, 270n1. See also elitism
Smashing Pumpkins, the, 270n78
Smith, Elliott, 69, 105, 221, 245
Smiths, the, 40, 41, 46, 54, 60, 71, 117; lyrics, 287n59
social class, 16, 29, 62, 97, 183, 243, 295; and affluence, 179; and authenticity, 52, 65, 76, 188, 200; of indie, 12, 60
Some Bizzare, 33
song requests, 92, 271n12
Sonic Youth, 40, 41
Sounds (magazine), 32, 263n2
Soup Dragons, the, 41

285n34; metaphysics, 2, 21, 23, 166, 168–171, 175; value on improvisation, 9. *See also* zone one

Western European, 23, 167, 172–174; attitudes toward the body, 179, 182, 278n22; denigration of West African music forms, 175–177; metaphysics, 21, 166, 175; produced dichotomy with non-western cultures, 175–176, 182, 183; value on rationality, 172–173, 182–186, 196, 247

Whiley, Jo, 98

White Stripes, the, 40, 41, 45, 217

Whiteout, 137

Whiteley, Sheila, 158, 217

Wild One, The (film), 65

Wilson, Tony, 51, 287n55

Wolfhounds, the, 41

working class. *See* social class

x, 75

Yazoo, 46

Yoruba, 168

youth, 23, 200; comprising indie audience, 163–165, 248; as corrupt "other,"

177–183, 185–186; as liminal, 2, 165, 185–186, 245–247

Zahan, Dominique, 168, 170

Zappa, Frank, 233

zone one, 20–21, 82–105, **84;** comportment, 82, 88–95, 156; fans, 95–98, 215, 271n11, 272n16; metaphysics of, 104, 162, 171, 182; psychosomatics, 98–104, 120; and sexuality, 95, 104, **105;** waiting in line, 96–97

zone three, 122–153, 273n1, 274n6, 276n3; activities, 123; ethic of cool, 123, 133, 142, 148, 151, 153, 165, 275n13. *See also* guest lists; guest passes; liggers

zone two, 20–21, 105–120, 272n20; change from zone one, 110–116, 272n25; comportment of, 106–108, 156; and connoisseurship, 110–113; fans, 109–114; liminality of, 166, 174; metaphysics of, 171–172, 174, 182, 185; phenomenology, 115–116, 120, 277n20

zones, 79–186, **83;** privileging of spectatorship, 95, 113–115, 119, 151–152, 161–162

Zoo, 33, 35

MUSIC/CULTURE

A series from Wesleyan University Press

Edited by Harris M. Berger

Originating editors, George Lipsitz, Susan McClary, and Robert Walser

About the author: Wendy Fonarow is a lecturer in the Department of Anthropology at the University of California, Los Angeles. She has worked for music labels including MCA, Reprise, and the UK's Domino Records.